Microsoft® Internet Information Server 4.0 Sourcebook

Michele Petrovsky

WILEY COMPUTER PUBLISHING

John Wiley & Sons, Inc.
New York • Chichester • Weinheim • Brisbane • Singapore • Toronto

Publisher: Robert Ipsen
Editor: Carol Long
Assistant Editor: Kathryn A. Malm
Managing Editor: Marnie Shotsky
Text Design & Composition: Benchmark Productions, Boston, MA

Designations used by companies to distinguish their products are often claimed as trademarks. In all instances where John Wiley & Sons, Inc., is aware of a claim, the product names appear in initial capital or ALL CAPITAL LETTERS. Readers, however, should contact the appropriate companies for more complete information regarding trademarks and registration.

This book is printed on acid-free paper. ☉

This publication is designed to provide accurate and authoritative information in regard to the subject matter covered. It is sold with the understanding that the publisher is not engaged in rendering legal, accounting, or other professional services. If legal advice or other expert assistance is required, the services of a competent professional person should be sought.

The content of this book is based on Release Candidate 2 of Microsoft Internet Information Server 4.0. There may have been changes made to the product since this release. Therefore, screen shots and examples may not be identical to the final product.

For current information about Microsoft Internet Information Server 4.0, you should visit http://www.microsoft.com/

Library of Congress Cataloging-in-Publication Data:

Petrovsky, Michele, 1949–
    Internet information server sourcebook/ Michele Petrovsky.
       p. cm.
    Includes bibliographical references and index.
    ISBN 0-471-17805-5 (pbk. : alk. paper)
    1. Internet (Computer network)—Computer programs. 2. Microsoft Internet information server. 3. Microsoft Windows NT. I. Title.
TK5105.875.I57P474   1997
005.7' 13769—dc21
                                  97-13143
                                      CIP

Printed in the United States of America.
10 9 8 7 6 5 4 3 2 1

Contents

Acknowledgments

I'd like to thank some of the people who helped, directly or indirectly, to make this book possible:

My students, for all they taught me

8000 Software Engineering, for their responses to all those e-mail questions

The people at Waterside and Wiley, for being willing to take a chance

And Tommy, without whom none of this would have happened

What Is Internet Information Server and How Can I Use It?

Microsoft's Internet Information Server (IIS) is both an element of its BackOffice suite of software and an appendage to Windows NT Server, Microsoft's network operating system (NOS). Therefore, it has some of the characteristics of an application, and some of the qualities of an operating system. For example, on the application side, Internet Information Server offers World Wide Web, FTP, gopher, security, and distributed database capabilities. Yet it maintains its operating system flavor by being configured and managed largely through tools presented by Windows NT Server 4.0.

What this means to you, the user, is that gaining a true facility with Internet Information Server requires at least a nodding acquaintance with NT Server 4.0. This book provides you with a grounding in Windows NT Server 4.0, from features and constraints to a guide to installing and configuring the NOS. It offers a step-by-step presentation of Internet Information Server, including a look at its components and their relationships as well as those of its management and administrative tools that can be found in NT Server. It also covers tools contained within IIS itself and information on Internet Information Server's WWW, FTP, and gopher capabilities.

Who Should Read This Book?

Anyone who must implement or oversee the implementation of World Wide Web, FTP, or gopher services in an environment that relies on or even includes Windows NT 4.0 can benefit from this book.

What You Need to Know Ahead of Time

The *Microsoft Internet Information Sourcebook* assumes that you have basic PC literacy, as well as a grasp of the concepts that underlie the Internet. We've included an extensive glossary that reviews terms used for both Windows NT Server and Internet Information Server installations, such as:

- 10Base2 and 10BaseT
- Domains, groups, and users
- Ethernet
- Firewalls
- The differences between (and similarities of) intranets and the Internet
- OSI
- Rights and privileges
- Routing
- Servers and clients
- TCP/IP
- Topologies

Even with only a basic working knowledge of PCs and networking, you'll be able to successfully install, configure, manage, and use Internet Information Server.

Conventions Used in This Book

We've adopted a few simple conventions for *Microsoft Internet Information Sourcebook*.

Important terms are shown in boldface the first time they're used. Acronyms for them appear immediately afterwards, in bold. For example: **Domain Host Control Protocol,** or **DHCP**

Once a term has been defined in this way, it will appear in normal type from that point on.

Names of Windows NT 4.0 or Internet Information Server commands, buttons, and icons are always presented in boldface. Any responses or entries you must supply to NT or IIS also are indicated in boldface.

Part One
The Internet Information Server Platform

Windows NT
Server 4.0

This chapter presents an overview of Windows NT Server 4.0, beginning with a look at the differences between this version of the network operating system (NOS) and its earlier incarnations as well as a brief review of the features that distinguish NT Server 4.0 from Windows 95.

Finally, a recap of NT's most significant features and capabilities, emphasizing those that bear the most weight in Internet Information Server, is provided.

Differences between NT 3.51 and NT 4.0

The differences between NT 3.51 and NT 4.0 can be summed up in a single word—speed. Windows NT has been reengineered to maintain, in this new release, the operating system's renowned reliability, at the same time improving its performance.

All versions of NT use a **modified microkernel architecture**. This means that the various levels of software services—from applications down to subsystems that interact with other operating systems (OSs), down further through such low-level services as virtual memory management and the synchronization of multiple processes, and down yet again to hardware-level services such as timers and interrupt management—are isolated from one another to ensure the integrity of each level (see Figure 1.1). For instance, NT strives to make certain that a clumsily designed application can't overwrite areas of memory that are being used by the process manager.

The most significant difference between NT 3.51 and NT 4.0 is that some processes such as graphics handling, which in the earlier release ran at the application level, now are part of the kernel. This change in status gives such processes a significantly higher priority of execution. That is, they'll run faster.

Other, more directly user-oriented differences between 3.51 and 4.0 include the following:

- NT 4.0 has built-in support for a number of multimedia tools such as ActiveMovie and DirectSound.

- NT 4.0 offers a slew of Internet services that 3.51 lacks: Internet Explorer 2.0, Gopher and Web services, and Point-to-Point Protocol (PPP).

Figure 1.1 NT 4.0's architecture differs significantly from those of other Oss and NOSs.

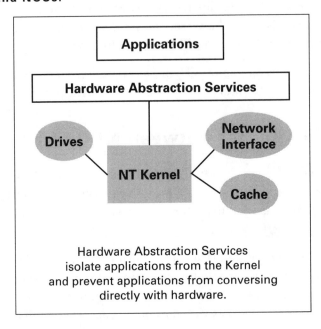

Applications

Hardware Abstraction Services

Drives

Network Interface

NT Kernel

Cache

Hardware Abstraction Services
isolate applications from the Kernel
and prevent applications from conversing
directly with hardware.

- NT 4.0 offers more remote computing possibilities than 3.51; 4.0 includes Peer Web Services in addition to the Remote Access Services made available by 3.51.

- NT's most recent incarnation includes support for the Telephony Application Program Interface (API).

- NT 4.0 is a little more greedy in asking for room on the hard drive. NT 3.51 asked for only 75–95MB. Microsoft *says* 4.0 wants 90–120MB, but be prepared to provide even more than that. During the installation of the NOS as preparation for this book, it turned out NT 4.0 needed over 127MB of free disk. Of course, the install in question loaded absolutely everything the NOS offered. But even if it hadn't, 90MB would have been cutting things too close.

TIP Don't take everything you read in Microsoft's NT documentation as gospel.

According to information on Microsoft's Web site, there's at least one instance in which NT 4.0 offers *fewer* options than its immediate predecessor. This documentation states that 4.0 can be installed only from a CD-ROM or across a network; 3.51 also makes diskettes available as its distribution medium.

However, the copy of NT 4.0 sitting underneath and controlling everything on the author's PC was loaded from a combination of three diskettes and a CD.

NT 4.0 and Windows 95

Probably the most significant aspect of NT's latest release from an end user's point of view is that the 4.0 version relies on the Windows 95 user interface. Those who are used to icons like Start, My Computer, and Explorer will feel right at home.

If, on the other hand, you're unfamiliar with Windows 95 or simply still think in terms of File Manager, Program Manager, and so on, Table 1.1 can serve as a translator to take Windows 3.x terminology and icons to Windows NT Server 4.0 (or Windows 95, for that matter) language. But be aware that this table includes only the most frequently used functions; many others have also taken on a new look in Windows NT 4.0.

Table 1.1 Going from Windows 3.x to Windows NT Server 4.0

In Windows 3.x, the Task or Icons Program Called	Uses the Icon	But in NT 4.0, It's Called	And Uses the Icon or Icons
Program Manager	(Program Manager window with icons: Accessories, Betty Crocker Cookbook, Cheyenne BitWare, Collage Complete, Games, Winkit 3.0, Main, STARTUP, Removelt, Rand McNally, Norton AntiVirus, Microsoft Tools, Microsoft Office, Paint Shop)	Start *and* Programs	Start / Programs
File Manager	File Manager	Start *and* Programs *and* Windows NT Explorer	Start / Programs / xplorer
Control Panel	Control Panel	Start *and* Settings *and* Control Panel	Start / Settings / Control Panel

Continued

Table 1.1 Continued

In Windows 3.x, the Task or Icons Program Called	Uses the Icon	But in NT 4.0, It's Called	And Uses the Icon or Icons
Print Manager	Print Manager	Start *and* Settings *and* Printers	Start / Settings / Printers
The Run Command	Run dialog (Command Line:, Run Minimized, OK, Cancel, Browse..., Help)	Start *and* Run	Start / Run...
The MS/DOS Prompt	MS-DOS Prompt	Start *and* Programs *and* Console	Start / Programs / MS-DOS Console
Task Switching (ALT *and* TAB)		ALT *and* TAB (That's right; this one still holds.)	

7

Figure 1.2 Can you tell whether this screen originated in NT or 95?

The More Things Change ... (Common Ground Between NT 3.51 and NT 4.0)

Those accustomed to Windows NT 3.51 will recognize plenty in the new release. NT 4.0 shares the following with its forerunner:

- NT 4.0, like NT 3.51, supports Application Programming Interfaces (APIs) or other means of interaction with Object Linking and Embedding (OLE), Open Graphics Interface (OpenGL), and 32-bit based Windows (Win32) applications.

- Like NT 3.51, 4.0 can handle multiple processors.

- NT 4.0 can connect to the same set of networks as can 3.51:
  - Banyan
  - Digital
  - IBM
  - Microsoft
  - Novell
  - SNA
  - TCP/IP

- NT 4.0, like 3.51, offers built-in database connectivity through its adherence to the Open DataBase Connectivity (ODBC) model.

- Both 4.0 and 3.51 retail for about $320 for a first-time purchase or $150 for an upgrade.

- According to the official documentation, both Windows NT 4.0 and Windows NT 3.51 *require a minimum* of 12MB of RAM, but Microsoft "recommends" 16MB.

TIP The recommended 16MB of RAM might not be enough, given that you're asking your NT 4.0 server to manage a LAN as well as provide Internet services—and to do both of these efficiently and securely.

The installation of NT upon which this book is based operated adequately with 16MB of memory, until we began to add a number of users, increase the size of the databases underlying our Web services, and allow wider access to some of the "lesser" Internet services such as FTP and telnet.

With 32MB of EDO RAM, however, our server was back in the fast lane.

System Requirements for NT 4.0

Many of NT 4.0's requirements have already been touched on, but the most important of them are discussed in the following sections.

Processor

Microsoft tells us that the newest version of NT Server will run on any processor from a 486/25MHz on up. The "on up" is the catch—4.0, because of the changes to its software architecture, will best show its strengths on a Pentium processor running at a minimum of 100MHz.

Microsoft also tells us, in another area of NT documentation, that 4.0 will run on any *32-bit processor* that is a 486/25 or better. *This difference is very significant.* For instance, the first few attempts to install NT Server as preparation for this book failed because, although the motherboard involved did have a "486/25 or better" processor (a 486/33, to be specific) it was an SX, rather than a DX, processor. Therefore, it was most emphatically not full 32-bit.

Your best bet is probably to read between the lines of not only the Microsoft NT documentation, but also any other sources of information you might consult regarding the NOS. For instance, the above claims by its parent notwithstanding, NT seems out-and-out to need, not just best show its strengths with, a Pentium-based machine. Scan through the lengthy outline (in the Hardware Compatibility List) of Microsoft-approved PC-based NT platforms, and we think you'll agree. There aren't too many low-end machines among them.

Remedying NT Hardware Problems

After almost a dozen failed attempts at installing NT Server 4.0, we consulted a group of engineers with whom we had worked in the past. We told them the problems we'd been having and took their advice:

- Don't even think of trying to install or run NT on anything less than a Pentium 133.

- Make sure the machine in question has a translating BIOS; NT can be picky about disk address manipulation.

- Make sure the motherboard you use has a fully Intel chip set.

- It doesn't hurt to have 32MB of RAM.

We concur, except that building a machine with these characteristics put us over the top as far as installing, booting, and running with ease were concerned. NT Server 4.0 is *very, very picky* about the hardware with which it will agree to work.

More strictly mechanical constraints also played a part. For instance, in installing, we found we couldn't install the new motherboard just outlined. That was because the drive coupling in which our hard drive sat was just bulky enough to graze one of the components of the motherboard. So we had to file away at the drive coupling until it cleared the board.

For reasons beyond time, money, and the headaches associated with acquiring new hardware piecemeal, building an NT 4.0 server may not be your best bet. Seriously consider simply buying a new box that has the NOS already loaded.

Memory

To be realistic, NT 4.0 should have *at least* 16MB of RAM with which to work. It's an indication of the operating system's power that it can support up to 4GB of memory.

Microsoft's HCL and Memory

The copy of Microsoft's Hardware Compatibility List for NT with which we worked made no statement of any kind regarding memory. So consider this the one hardware area in which 4.0's vaunted pickiness does not come into play.

Hard Drive

Although it "requires" only 90–120MB of free disk space, NT 4.0's file system (NTFS)—which supports, among other things, long file names à la Windows 95 and OS/2—can easily handle hard drives larger than 2GB (the limit for DOS and versions of Windows up to and including 3.11). Needless to say, unless your intranet or Internet site is to be an extraordinarily tightly knit environment, your NT 4.0 server would be happier and healthier with at least 1GB of hard disk storage, under whatever file system you run.

The Choice: NTFS or FAT?

NT Server 4.0 does not require you to migrate to the NTFS. If you care to, you can retain the FAT system that your PCs cut their teeth on.

Redundant Disks

Unless yours is a network with little possibility of downtime and little in the way of critical data (do any such exist, really?), should seriously consider implementing a **Redundant Array of Inexpensive Disks,** or **RAID,** scheme of some sort.

Several such methods, and their accompanying technologies, are available. Unfortunately, very few of these live up to the *inexpensive* part of the name. Each does offer a slightly-to-significantly different way of duplicating your data as a form of disaster insurance.

Peculiarities Regarding NT's Preferred Hard Drives

You're sure to run into some peculiarities, as we did, as you peruse the Hardware Compatibility List for hard drives that NT Server 4.0 likes.

For instance, in preparing for this book, we had to replace a Western Digital 1.2GB drive with a slightly older, slightly smaller model from the same manufacturer—an 850MB drive, to be specific. NT would not install on the newer, higher-capacity drive.

The Hardware Compatibility List seems sparse as far as hard drives are concerned. The copy of the List with which we worked presents only 46 models of drives that have been tested and approved as NT Server 4.0-compatible. These drives can be grouped as follows:

- 13 SCSI drives

- 22 IDE drives

- 11 PCMCIA drives

Across these three categories, a surprisingly small number of vendors—only 14—are represented:

Box Hill

Connor

Fujitsu

Hewlett-Packard

IBM

Integral Peripherals

Kingston

Maxtor

MiniStore

Noteworthy

Quantum

Seagate

Simple Technology

Western Digital

What's more, some industry leaders are, in our opinion, nearly overlooked in this group. For example, Western Digital, hardly a lightweight as far as hard drives go, has only three of its models in the HCL.

> **TIP** We can't say it too often: check the HCL!
>
> Given this relatively limited group of hard drives, we can only reiterate that you must check the Hardware Compatability List!

Multiple Processors

NT 4.0 can, with the addition of Microsoft's **Hardware Abstraction Layers** (**HAL**s—software that allows the operating system kernel and higher-level services to, effectively, ignore hardware-level services such as interrupt management), support up to 32 CPUs.

CD-ROM Drives

NT 4.0 Server can work with CD drives as basic as 2x or as fast as 8x. In addition, the OS supports such high-end devices as smart CD towers.

NT 4.0 is far more generous in the selection of CD-ROM drives it offers than it was in its available hard drive types. NT will accept any one of a rather grand total of 144 different CD drives. Of these, 86 are IDE or EIDE devices, which the Hardware Compatibility List groups as "non-SCSI" (tech-speak, but descriptive). That leaves 58 SCSI CDs.

CD Towers

A CD tower is in effect a series of CD-ROM drives housed in a single cabinet. A tower differs from a CD changer or jukebox in allowing the *simultaneous* loading and spinning of several CDs. The number of drives available in CD towers ranged, at the time this chapter was being written, from 7 to 28.

Smart Towers

A smart CD tower differs still further from any other CD-ROM drive in having its own CPU and memory. In the context of a Web server, such bells and whistles might be vital; they could permit the smart tower to remain up and running even if the network server itself has crashed.

Figures 1.3 through 1.5 illustrate the differences between jukebox, tower, and smart tower.

Of the more than 100 CD-ROM drives with which NT Server 4.0 has been successfully tested, 34 qualify as jukeboxes, 74 as towers, and 36 as smart towers. Whatever the group into which it fits, at least one model of CD drive from each of the following manufacturers has been successfully tested with NT Server 4.0:

Acer

Aztech

CD Technology

Chinon

Compaq

Creative Labs (maker of Sound Blaster)

Figure 1.3 A CD jukebox.

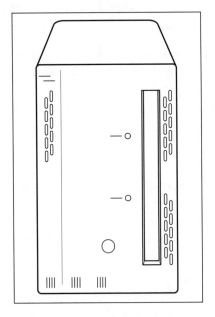

Figure 1.4 A CD tower.

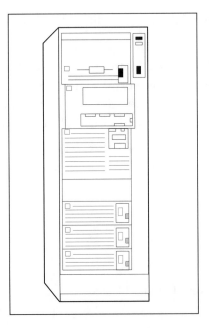

Figure 1.5 A smart CD tower.

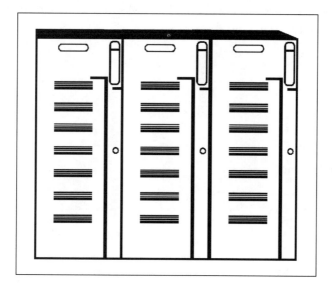

Delta Electronics

Digital Equipment Corporation

Funai Electric

Hitachi

LG Electronics

Hewlett-Packard

Lion Optics

Matsushita

Mitsumi (the manufacturer of the 8x CD drive that helped our install attempts finally succeed)

NEC

Panasonic

Philips LMS (the manufacturer of the original CD drive in our PC, which definitely did not help our install efforts, not because of any problem with the drive—it had performed quite capably till that point—but because NT Server 4.0 had no drivers for it, nor did Philips LMS have available any updated drivers with which NT would cooperate)

Pioneer

Plextor

Procom

Sanyo

Smart and Friendly

Sony

Teac

Texel

Torisan

Toshiba

Remember that some of these are SCSI drives and that Windows NT Server runs on other than PC platforms. It'll do just fine, for instance, on a DEC Alpha or a MIPS RISC machine such as a NEC RISCstation. The presence of such drive vendors as Hewlett-Packard and Digital Equipment in the list above must be understood in this context, which is to say that, as with all hardware, you must be sure that the server hardware platform you're considering will accept the drive you have in mind.

Review before Installation

This section examines some of the characteristics of Windows NT Server 4.0 for you to review before you even consider installing the operating system.

Hardware Compatibility

Think of the Hardware Compatibility List (HCL) as the Ten-Plus Commandments for hardware components to be used with NT. If a device (storage, controller, or input/output) isn't on this list, it isn't necessarily a candidate for the Rube Goldberg award. At the same time, if a device is absent from the HCL, the chances that it will be incompatible with this finicky NOS are much greater. If at all possible, don't take the chance.

The most recently updated version of the HCL is available from Microsoft's Web site; the complete URL is http://www.microsoft.com/.

Table 1.2 presents a thumbnail sketch of the HCL.

Table 1.2 The Hardware Compatability List in a Nutshell

Hardware Category	HCL-Recommended Minimums
CPU	Intel 80486 33MHz or higher/faster RISC (e.g., PowerPC or DEC Alpha).
Memory	12MB RAM on an Intel platform 16MB on a RISC platform.
Video Adapter	VGA or higher; dozens upon dozens from which to choose, many of them certified for use with more than one processor. For instance, the S3-801 from Diamond can be plugged into either an x86- or a DEC Alpha-based system.
Storage Controllers	SCSI preferred; several dozen Adaptec, as well as large handfuls of BusLogic, DPT, and other manufacturers' controllers.
	If IDE or EIDE, the manufacturer should be an "industry standard" such as Adaptec. Note that the HCL has no individual listing for IDE or EIDE controllers like that for SCSI cards.
CD Drives	One CD-ROM drive, 4x or higher, unless you plan to install and manage NT Server strictly across a net.
	For Intel platforms only, one 3.5-inch diskette drive.
SCSI Hard Drives	For Intel platforms only, models from Box Hill, Quantum, or Seagate.
IDE Hard Drives	For Intel platforms only, models from Conner, Fujitsu, Hewlett-Packard, IBM, Maxtor, Seagate, or Western Digital.
Network Interface Cards	Choose from 20 3Com, 2 Acton, 4 Advanced Micro Devices, 4 Allied Telesys, 7 Cabletron, 15 Compaq, and 17 Standard Microsystems cards, among many others.

File System Constraints

NT Server 4.0 uses the NT File System (NTFS), which provides support for case-sensitive and/or long file names, as well as added file and directory security measures. That's the upside; the downside is that NT file names, despite being structured in the same way as OS/2, UNIX, or Windows 95 file names, are not interchangeable with them. A corollary of this, and another thing to bear in mind about NTFS, is that, if you boot from a DOS diskette or DOS partition on the hard drive, you'll be unable to access your NTFS file system.

In this context, don't be misled into thinking that third-party packages such as System Commander by V Communications Inc. offer a way around this problem. Although such packages do allow you to specify to which of any number of operating systems you wish to boot, they do nothing about resolving conflicts like those just described between file systems. They may even complicate your efforts to install NT Server 4.0, as they did ours. System Commander, the package we used, operates by altering a PC's boot record. Although it thereby allows more than one operating system to reside in a single drive partition, it also annoys NT 4, which wants a partition of its own and wants its partition to be the primary one on a physical drive.

> **T I P** NTFS does have its advantages. Many features of NT Server, such as the ability to assign individual permissions to or ownership of individual files for individual users, are not available to FAT files. Keep this in mind while mulling over whether or not to adopt NTFS on your 4.0 server.

Backup Constraints

A related constraint that NTFS imposes upon your efforts to build an Internet or intranet server is that, just as NT and DOS (or any other of the operating systems mentioned above, for that matter) cannot access one another's files, they can't make use of one another's backups, regardless of the medium upon which those backups reside. More specifically, DOS cannot read, let alone restore, backups created under NT Server. Nor can NT Server run either the DOS **BACKUP** or the DOS **RESTORE** program. (Remember the discussion earlier in this chapter about NT's segregation of software levels?) It's this separation of function that is the source of NT's inability to use those old standbys BACKUP and RESTORE. DOS programs, even the seemingly innocuous, *can* manipulate hardware directly. NT won't allow

19

Windows NT Server 4.0

programs it runs to do so. Therefore, you must give some thought to how you'll back up any **File Allocation Table-** (FAT) based volumes that exist and whose files you wish to preserve on your intended server.

> **TIP** You don't have to give up FAT. NT Server 4.0 can function quite nicely with an old-fashioned, case-insensitive, short-name FAT file system. The use of NTFS only to provide longer file names might be excessive. And because a well-configured, -monitored, and -managed network is a secure network, it is possible to forgo even those security measures that NTFS provides above and beyond the familiar **RWASH** (Read, Write, Archive, System, or Hidden categories of files) scheme of a FAT system.
>
> Also be aware that a decision to implement your NT server with a FAT file system is not irrevocable. The file system can be converted to NTFS at any time you choose, with the utility FSCONVERT, which NT provides. Once converted in this way, though, an NTFS file system cannot be "uncoverted" and returned to its original FAT nature.

Applications Constraints

The good news is twofold. First, most applications that run under Windows 95 will run just as well under Windows NT 4.0, and second, 16- and 32-bit Windows applications will run under NT too, *as long as they don't attempt direct access of hardware.*

The slightly less-good news is that, if there's one category of software you'll have to be careful of in the NT 4.0 world, it's device drivers. Because of the reengineering of the operating system's software architecture, not all drivers that run under versions of Windows, or under Windows 95, will coexist peacefully with NT 4.0; in particular, keep a wary eye on graphics drivers. Microsoft tests all device drivers (its own or those written by third-party firms) and certifies only those that can work in harmony with NT's architecture. Check the Hardware Compatibility List, and then pick one of these.

IIS: Now or Later?

The September 24, 1996 issue of *PC Magazine* refers to Internet Information Server (IIS) as "one of the biggest additions to Windows NT Server" and "a snap to install and even easier to use." All true. But take a deep breath and give the matter some thought before clicking **Continue**.

As we hinted during the discussion of backup, file system, and hardware constraints, installing NT 4.0 can have its twists and turns. Add to those already mentioned the concepts of domain and user setup, which we cover thoroughly in Chapter 2, and you might be putting more on your plate than you'll be able to digest easily.

In other words, if this is your first go-round with loading and configuring an operating system as sophisticated as Windows NT Server 4.0, you might want to carry out the process in stages. Install, configure, and fine-tune NT itself. Only when you're comfortable with its form and functioning should you move on to adding IIS.

On the other hand, if you're familiar with NT and you have to get your server up and running as quickly as possible, as long as you envision no unusual requirements for your Internet Information Server, you can set up IIS as part of the overall task of installing NT Server 4.0.

BIOS Compatibility

Reports, both word-of-mouth and published in a number of forums, have circulated that very old or nonstandard BIOS versions might cause the installation of NT Server (3.x as well as 4.0) to fail. Although Microsoft's HCL did not include any information on BIOS compatibility as this book was being written, for BIOS questions and as a rule of thumb for PC hardware in general, remember the following: *If it predates 1994, you may experience incompatibility problems.*

You're almost ready to load your new operating system, but before you crack the seal on the CD case, consider the next two topics.

Planning Your Intranet or Internet Site

Intranet would surely make a good showing in any "Buzzword of the Year" contest. But just what does it mean?

An intranet is a system of information management that makes use of Web and Internet technologies and methods *within an organization*.

You can therefore plan your intranet (or Internet site) in the same way you planned your systems and your LAN(s). In other words, rely on common sense and take an orderly approach, documenting your results at each step along the way. Also, refer to the following checklist:

- *Define the information you wish to deploy.* It might be as simple as a single page, a kind of "Quick Reference" to the services your organization makes available to its employees. Or it might include a complete index of organizational information (employee names, titles, department affiliations, and on-the-job locations and phone numbers; branch locations and phone numbers; the location of such facilities as the cafeteria and first aid station; and so on).

- *For each category of information you've identified, decide how you wish to present it.* Some things, like the Quick Reference just mentioned, might be most effectively introduced as a Web page consisting primarily of bulleted text. Others, like an in-house phone directory, could be stored as an ASCII file and accessed by means of an FTP operation. Still others (a library's "card" catalog comes to mind) might be most efficiently presented by allowing those who need it to telnet to a dedicated server.

- *Sketch the server file system and user access to it.* Whether you will modify the configuration of an existing machine or build your NT server from scratch, this next task in planning your intranet is important. User access to any site running Windows NT Server 4.0 will include the concepts of domain and group membership, which we discuss in Chapter 2. For now, just decide who should get to see and/or use what and from what points of access.

- *Lay out a scheme for administering your server and the information it presents.* Some of the questions you need to ask include the following:

  - Do I want to be able to monitor the site remotely?

  - Do I want to be able to monitor the site from a number of points?

  - Do I want to assign any administrative tasks (such as printer management) to users or groups of users?

  - At what rate can I reasonably expect usage of and information deployed by site to increase? How will I handle this increase?

  - What provisions can I make to minimize downtime of the server and of networked tools such as printers? (We've not included workstations in this "preventive maintenance" list because we assume you, as system administrator, have already taken steps to keep them healthy.)

- What provisions need I make, now and as my intranet or Internet presence grows, for redundancy of data storage?

- What tools—hardware *and* software—do I have in hand? (Be exhaustive; list all operating systems, network operating systems, protocols, application packages, CPUs, memory, and adapters. In the case of hardware, specify how much/what each node or potential node offers. It's time consuming, but it's also the only way to know what you have got to work with and what more you'll need to get your intranet up and running.)

- What if anything about building my server will I have to outsource? One thing's certain—if you plan to connect to the Internet rather than simply establishing an in-house intranet, you'll have to farm out providing Internet service by obtaining an Internet service provider (ISP).

Your plans for your server now fill many pages. And that's just Volume 1. To complete your plans, look at what you'll do to connect to the Internet.

A Closer Look at RAID

RAID, mentioned briefly in the early part of this chapter, is the most common means by which preventive redundancy in data storage is accomplished.

Although there are several ways of providing RAID capabilities, none of them can truly be termed inexpensive. Whether or not you need to incorporate RAID into your NT server depends on the degree to which the information it presents can be called critical and the amount of time your users can be without it. A strong "Yes, it's critical!" coupled with a resounding "Not for long!" means you should at least begin to investigate RAID for your server. Table 1.3 outlines the characteristics of the most common RAID methods.

Table 1.3 A Summary of RAID

This RAID Level	Requires This Hardware	And Duplicates Your Data by
0	Multiple drives	Doesn't really duplicate data, but rather merely distributes your files across multiple drives in an effort to improve throughput. What's more, if any one of the drives in a RAID 0 array fails, none of the drives in that array can be accessed.

Table 1.3 *Continued*

This RAID Level	Requires This Hardware	And Duplicates Your Data by
1	A pair of drives for every original drive	Making two complete copies of everything—data, header information—on the original drive. Within RAID 1, there are two subsidiary methods: • Disk mirroring, which involves the complete duplication of all information on a drive to another drive, but the use of only one controller to access the two drives • Disk duplexing, which fully duplicates, but uses an individual controller for each member of each drive pair
2	Multiple drives (usually a fairly large number)	Writing it across these drives at the bit level, therefore requiring that a large percentage of the array of disks be used for error detection and correction.
3	Multiple drives	Writing across these drives at the byte level. Uses only one drive in an array for parity information. Therefore, unlike with RAID 0, if a RAID 3 drive other than the parity drive fails, data is not lost but rather can be reconstructed from the information contained on the parity drive.
4	Multiple drives	Writing across these drives at the sector level. Otherwise, like RAID 3.
5	Multiple drives	Writing both data and parity information across all drives. The best RAID scheme for environments in which there are frequent read and write operations. The numbers of these two types of operations are about equal, and the amount of data an individual read or write involves is relatively small.

> **TIP** In most PC-based LANs, RAID 1 or RAID 5 would be the most appropriate, because these levels offer the best combinations of data redundancy and efficiency of throughput.

Planning Your Connection to the Internet

Don't be intimidated by recommendations to "manage bandwidth distribution" or "choose a compatible protocol stack." Rather, draw upon the statistics and characteristics that form so much of your server planning documentation. Make those numbers and descriptions your Internet "must have" list, as in "must have support for/compatibility with these." Then go shopping for an ISP.

For example, if you're running Windows NT Workstation 3.51 at your user end, it's unlikely that you'll have any compatibility problems with your TCP/IP stack. NT Workstation's implementation of this protocol suite is more than able to handle any application you're likely to run under it. Furthermore, Windows for Workgroups (3.11), Windows 95, and OS/2 offer this same built-in protocol compatibility "insurance." Very few applications written for any of the operating systems just mentioned require specific protocol stacks to operate, but check yours to be sure.

One point you need to consider in connecting your site to the Internet, however, is the physical connection. Given the nature of a LAN and the information it provides, and that you consider these important enough to offer to the world at large via the Internet, you must have a means of connecting to it that is reliable and always available. The following sections evaluate three basic connectivity methods in that light.

Dial-Up

Dial-up connections (AKA **switched circuits** or **POTS**, for plain old telephone system) offer the advantage of free local calling, but the *disadvantage* of a relatively low rate of data throughput—a maximum possible 38.4 Kilobits per second (Kbps), given the state of modem technology at this writing. (See Figure 1.6.)

A reasonable solution is ISDN.

ISDN

ISDN uses a single, already-installed dedicated digital line in combination with special hardware to provide data transfer as fast as 128Kbps. The cost of ISDN has

> **TIP** That 38,400-bits-per-second rate, given 7 data bits per byte and one byte per usable character of text or pixel of graphic, works out to a little less than 5500 characters per second transferred. This might at first seem like a decent-sized handful, but keep in mind that graphics in particular are hogs. Even a simple image on your Web page might consist of a file of a meg or two, and therefore the equivalent of 20, 30, 40, or more times our 5500-character rate. So the maximum available transfer rate of a dial-up connection may not be adequate to your intranet as accessed from the Internet.

dropped significantly and should continue to do so, while its availability improves. However, the downside is that configuring and managing an ISDN-based Internet link is no small challenge. For example, something as basic to TCP/IP, Ethernet, and the Internet as routing table updates can cause ISDN connections any number of headaches. So if the prospect of certainly fast, relatively cheap throughput is appealing but the prospective headaches aren't, consider farming out the implementation of an ISDN-based Internet connection. (See Figure 1.7.)

(Routing tables are internal lists maintained by routers of not only all other routers on a network, but also, in many cases, optimum transmission paths.)

Shell Accounts
Most commonly used with dial-up links, shell accounts allow the use of a workstation as a *terminal for Internet-based programs that execute on a remote host.* Be

Figure 1.6 Connecting your NT 4.0 Server to the Internet via dial-up.

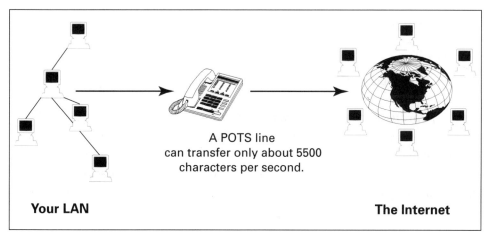

Figure 1.7 Here's how your LAN would look after being connected to the Internet via ISDN.

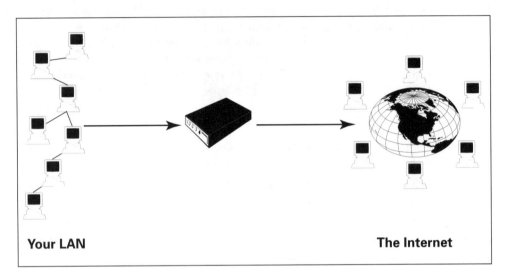

Your LAN   **The Internet**

aware that shell accounts support only text interfaces. Unless your intranet is so small and its server so maxed out that this is a reasonable solution, or unless your Web-based applications are of a very specialized nature, it's unlikely that a shell account will be a good choice for connecting your intranet to the Internet.

Deciding Which NT Services to Install

Windows NT Server 4.0 offers three types of setup:

- Typical

- Custom/Complete

- Compact

Table 1.4 compares what these three options will install to your NT server.

Typical Versus Custom/Complete Setup

Wanting to have all of NT's options and services available and to be able to tweak everything that could be tweaked, we opted for custom/complete and then selected everything there was to select. A typical setup would install the same features; that is, all available services. We describe them in the following sections in case you wish to customize or choose among them during a custom setup.

Table 1.4 Distinguishing NT Setup Types

Setup Type	Install	Allows You to Fine-Tune	And Has This Additional Feature
Typical	Installs all NT Server optional components	Only to a small degree; this setup category offers the least opportunity for user interaction	Automatically configures hardware. Asks the fewest questions. Is ordinarily the quickest.
Custom/Complete	Installs only those NT Server components you indicate	Allows you to fine-tune the greatest number of NT's characteristics	Offers the most control over the nature of your server. Requires the most knowledge on the part of the user.
Compact	Installs none of NT's optional components	Permits no fine-tuning (because no options are present)	The only choice when disk space is at a premium, but if you're this tight on free disk, you may not have the horse power needed to run IIS in any case.

TIP While installing NT Server 4.0, we ran into another interesting example of software and documentation being at odds. Table 1.4 is taken from what we saw on the monitor as we configured NT. The documentation that accompanied our software gives a different group of setup types, though. In the *Start Here—Basics and Installation Guide* that accompanied NT 4.0's distribution media, we were told that there are four setup types available:

- Typical

- Portable

- Compact

- Custom

Where the portable category has gone, we can't say. But the other three types of setup did operate as described in *Start Here*.

ClipBook Server Installing the ClipBook service will allow you to fine-tune the behavior of the ClipBook, NT's answer to Windows 3.x's Clipboard. Among the things you can define if you install this option is the size of blocks of data that can be left in the ClipBook.

Computer Browser Computer Browser isn't an option; it's what's behind all those browse buttons we've become so familiar with. But during a custom setup, or afterward if you've chosen typical or complete, accessing this feature will allow you to tailor its operations. For example, you can prevent portions of your file system from being browsed.

DHCP Client **Dynamic Host Configuration Protocol**, or **DHCP**, clients would be able, in effect, to grab an Internet address on the fly if that address is not in use. Sounds like a real time-saver, right? Does it allow you to avoid manually assigning IP addresses?

Yes to both, but there are drawbacks. If you use this service to create a pool of Internet addresses that are then allocated dynamically, you cannot guarantee that conflicts for those addresses won't arise. And when they do, you'll be faced with at least one or two very unhappy users asking, "Why can't I connect to the server all of a sudden?"

This is one service you can safely forgo, unless yours is an environment in which there is little simultaneous use of the Internet connection.

Directory Replicator The Directory Replicator allows you to copy a directory (or folder, as the 1995-ish NT documentation most frequently refers to it) to another domain or even to another computer altogether.

It may not sound like that big a deal, but surprisingly, it is. Even after this service has been installed, you'll still have a fair amount of configuring to do. What's more, NT Server places significant constraints on how you can carry out that configuring. Among these are the following:

- You must create a user whose sole reason for being is to carry out directory replication.

- The user you create must be made a member of a specific group.

- The login password for your user must never be allowed to expire.

- Your user must be allowed access to your server at all times that it is up.

If yours is not an environment in which regular transfers of significant portions of the server file system will be needed, forgo this service.

Event Viewer Windows NT Server 4.0 considers an event to be one of the following:

- Some user-initiated action (such as pressing the **ENTER** key) that is handed by the operating system to the appropriate application or utility

- A system-initiated action such as an error message

Although events like those just noted are automatically logged by NT, many others are not. In order to tailor security and performance monitoring, you must tailor the logs in which that monitoring is reflected. So, although the Event Viewer is not an optional component, the way in which it ultimately functions is largely at your discretion.

FTP Publishing Service If you install Internet Information Server at all, you'll get the FTP Publishing service, unless you specifically exclude it.

Don't be misled by the service's title. This software does not allow you to create documents, but rather to make a number of types of documents, including:

- Binary

- Common word processor formats

These are available via a number of means:

- From within a Web browser

- Through a command-line FTP utility

- Through a Windows-based FTP utility

Gopher Publishing Service As was the case with FTP Publishing, you must tell NT *not* to install its Gopher Publishing Service if you install IIS.

Gophers, like ftp agents, are not creators but rather dispensers of information. More specifically, gophers are text-based interfaces to the location and retrieval of text-based documents.

License Logging Service License logging is not an optional NT component, but your use of it can be configured in a number of ways. The most basic of the choices you will have to make in this area is that between:

What *FTP* Means

FTP—or more correctly in both the UNIX universe in which it originated and the NTFS universe where we now find it, FTP—stands for file transfer protocol. This software excels at its job because it is relatively insensitive to things like:

- Differences in transmission speeds between sender and receiver

- Variations in network traffic along the route of the transfer

- Differences in capabilities between the sender's and receiver's hardware platforms

- Per-server license distribution and management, in which enough Client Access Licenses must have been purchased to cover every anticipated *concurrent user connection* to the server

- Per-seat license distribution and management, which requires a separate Client Access License for *every computer* from which the server will be accessed

Messenger An optional component, but a very useful one, Messenger allows you to implement and fine-tune any or all of the following:

- Microsoft Exchange (in effect an enhancement to Microsoft Mail, which allows, among many other things, multiple connections to external mail handling systems)

- Microsoft Mail

- Internet Mail

Net Logon Net Logon should be self-explanatory. You need it; it's not an option.

Network DDE Network DDE or **Dynamic Data Exchange** is another term for InterProcess Communication. It is the means by which processes, whether system or application generated, pass data back and forth.

The existence of such services clearly cannot be optional, so they will be installed. What you can specify, however, are some of the characteristics of these exchanges.

Network DDE DDSM In essence, Network DDE DDSM is another management tool for interprocess communications on your NT 4.0 Server.

NT LM Security Support NT LM Security Support provides additional security measures for NT's hooks into NetWare.

Plug and Play Plug and Play allows you to incorporate such applications, originally intended for Windows 95, into NT Server 4.0.

Remote Access Autodial Manager Installing Remote Access Autodial Manager is optional, but with great potential impact on the security of your NT 4.0 server. It is through this manager that you define the characteristics of any automated dial-up access to your network.

Remote Access Connection Manager A more generalized version of the Remote Access Autodial Manager, the Remote Access Connection Manager allows you to tailor the characteristics of all forms of remote access to your net.

Remote Access Server All Remote Access utilities run under the control of the Remote Access server.

Remote Procedure Call Service and Locator A Remote Procedure Call (RPC) is an extension of the idea of interprocess communications, with a very interesting twist. RPCs allow an application to be run in parts, with those parts spread across a number of computers.

Except in very large or very busy networks, such an ability isn't critical. But it, and the corollary ability to track the sources of such calls to routines running remotely, is automatically installed by NT 4.0.

SAP Agent SAP, or the Service Advertising Protocol, is the means by which a NetWare server makes its client stations aware of the availability of certain network services. If you anticipate connecting your NT-based net to a Novell LAN, you'll need this service.

Schedule Installed but not set up automatically, the Schedule service allows you to specify when certain operations such as reindexing a database will be carried out. You'll be able to choose from:

- Immediately

- One time only

- Recurrently

You may specify a date and time as well if you select all the options the Schedule service makes available.

Server See *Network Logon* above.

Spooler Installed automatically, Spooler can nonetheless be tweaked a bit. For instance, you can choose between two options:

- Start printing after last page is spooled.

- Start printing immediately.

> **TIP** *Spooling* is the name given to the creation of temporary print files. NT 4.0 is somewhat unusual in allowing a print job to begin before the spool file is completely written out.

TCP/IP NetBios Helper Installed automatically, the TCP/IP NetBios Helper service in effect facilitates conversations between the TCP/IP and Net BIOS families of protocols. Don't tweak this one unless you're a data communications engineer.

NetBIOS or NetBEUI?

In the strictest sense, NetBIOS is not a protocol at all. Rather, it is an Application Program Interface, or **API**, and the means by which DOS programs originally talked to networks. (NetBIOS stands for Network basic input/output services.) NetBIOS evolved to become **NetBEUI**, or NetBIOS extended user interface, a true transport-level protocol.

However, even NetBEUI is not a routable protocol. You can't, for instance, tell it to go around the block, so to speak, if it encounters a traffic jam along its path. TCP/IP, on the other hand, is (eminently) routable and has therefore come to be more widely used than NetBEUI.

This Helper pitches in when data must be exchanged between these two protocols of differing capabilities.

Telephony Remote access relies on telephones, and the Telephony service allows you to configure some of those phones' characteristics, such as whether a separate digit must be entered to access a dialout line. Telephony is automatically installed but must be configured by you before it can be used.

UPS An option only, UPS service allows you to define the characteristics of Uninterruptable Power Supply devices you might wish to include in your network.

Workstation Windows NT Workstation 4.0 service is, as you would expect, installed automatically. Through it, you can set up workstation characteristics.

World Wide Web Publishing Service As was the case with the FTP and Gopher services, the World Wide Web Publishing service is automatically loaded as part of the installation of Internet Information server, unless you explicitly exclude it.

The Results of a Complete Setup

As mentioned earlier, we chose a complete setup when installing NT Server 4.0 in preparation for this book. Then, we simply selected everything that was available. This low-discernment load resulted in the display illustrated in Figure 1.8.

The following sections provide detail on the meanings behind each of these icons.

Figure 1.8 NT 4.0 looked like this after a complete setup.

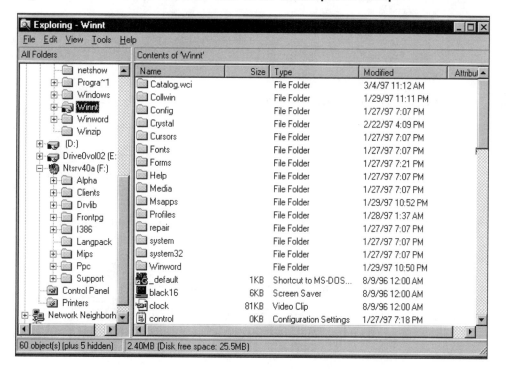

My Computer Clicking the My Computer icon brings up a window from which information about the contents and characteristics of all drives present on the server can be accessed. The Control Panel—in NT as in Windows 3.x, the entry point to modifying many system parameters—can also be reached from this window.

NT's Control Panel Windows NT Server 4.0 presents you with a Control Panel that is much more extensive than that for 3.x and allows you to modify the way the following system characteristics operate (see Figure 1.9).

- *Accessibility options.* These are for access by handicapped users.

- *Add/remove programs.* Use this where you'll need to go to install applications.

- *Console.* This is NT's name for the ability to escape to the DOS prompt.

- *Date/time.* Change the date and time using this Control Panel tool.

- *Devices.* These refer to hardware; view or change characteristics with this tool.

- *Display.* Colors, degree of definition, and so on can be viewed or changed here.

- *Fonts.* If you need to know which ones NT uses, look here.

- *Internet.* This is the icon of choice for defining Internet access parameters.

- *Keyboard.* Go here to change the language in which your keyboard operates, among other things.

- *Licensing.* This icon is one entry point to viewing and setting license management conditions.

- *Mail.* Click here to tweak the Messaging service.

- *Microsoft Mail Post Office.* Click here if you need only to modify the characteristics of MS Mail.

- *Modems.* This icon presents information about and allows you to modify the working characteristics of any modems on your network.

- *Mouse.* If you're quick on the trigger, this icon will, among other things, allow you to tell your mouse to keep up with your flying fingers.

- *Multimedia.* This is the place to go to view or modify the way NT Server 4.0 handles video, CD music, and similar tasks.

- *Network*. Clicking this icon is the first step in configuring such network characteristics as network ID, protocols used, adapters used, and bindings.

> ## Binding Definition
> A binding is one of the least self-explanatory networking terms. It is nothing more than the association of a specific protocol or protocols with a particular network adapter. You might use the Network icon to bind TCP/IP to the new 3Com NIC you just installed in workstation #17.

- *ODBC*. From this icon, you can define which DataBase Management Systems your NT server will use.

- *PCMCIA*. Click here if your network will talk to or contain any devices intended for laptop PCs.

- *Server*. This icon lets you look at the general characteristics of your server.

- *Services*. This tells you what services you've installed, whether they are running at the moment or not, and whether they are started automatically when the server boots or must be manually configured and enabled.

- *Sounds*. At this icon you get answers to "Shall I use the PC speakers, or is there a sound card available to me?" and similar server questions.

- *System*. A more general version of the Server tool, this icon accesses and allows you to modify system properties in the areas of performance, user profiles, hardware profiles, and the conditions applied at startup or shutdown.

- *Tape Devices*. If you have one, configure or view its parameters here.

- *Telephony*. This icon sets up the most basic telephone-related aspects of Remote Access.

- *UPS*. This icon defines how Uninterruptable Power Supply devices function.

Network Neighborhood In our NT Server 4.0 installation, all users were given access to all devices on the network. Therefore, when we click on the **Network Neighborhood** icon, we see a small window that contains only one icon of its own—**Entire Network**. Depending upon how you define user access, your Network Neighborhood may appear different from this one.

Figure 1.9 NT's Control Panel allows you to modify system parameters.

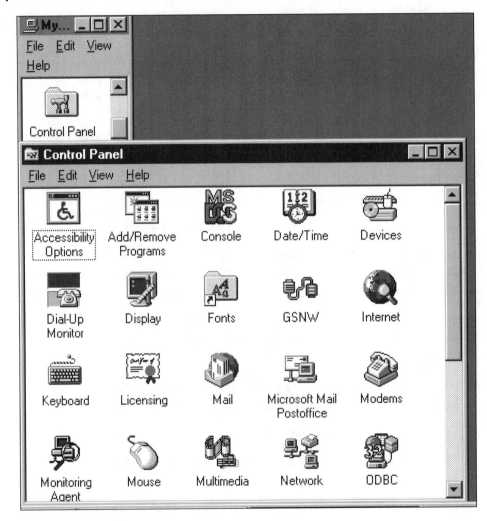

Inbox Clicking on the **Inbox** presents a window from which both Microsoft Mail and Internet Mail can be accessed (see Figure 1.10).

Figure 1.10 Accessing your mail through the NT Inbox icon.

Figure 1.11 The Recycle Bin allows you to retrieve deleted material.

Internet Explorer Microsoft's answer to Netscape, Internet Explorer is bundled with NT Server 4.0.

Recycle Bin Like DOS and Windows 3.x, NT Server 4.0 does not physically remove deleted files, but rather marks the space they occupy as available for write operations. So, putting something in the trash, to use the GUI parlance for deleting, is not irrevocable. The **Recycle Bin** is the point from which you may be able to recover "deleted" material (see Figure 1.11).

My Briefcase **My Briefcase** allows you to configure and use the Briefcase utility, which is in effect a means of exchanging files between desktop and laptop computers.

From Here

Now that you have a good grasp of the nature, structure, likes, dislikes, and capabilities of Windows NT Server 4.0, we'll proceed to learning, in Chapter 2, how to install, configure, and manage it with a minimum of tooth gnashing. Then, in Chapter 3, we'll do the same with Internet Information Server.

Installing and Configuring Windows NT Server 4.0 and Internet Information Server

Chapter 1 provided a look at the nature and features of NT Server 4.0. In this second chapter, we'll walk through everything involved in loading and configuring both NT and Internet Information Server.

This chapter assumes that you've taken to heart the cautions presented in the first chapter and therefore have at hand:

- A hardware platform that is fully in agreement with Microsoft's Hardware Compatibility List for NT Server 4.0

- An outline, verbal or graphical, of your file system

- A complete backup of that file system

- A DOS boot diskette

- The NT 4.0 distribution media

> **TIP** If you plan to install NT to your intended server from another machine across a LAN or have backed up the server-to-be file system in the same way, be sure that the machine from which you will be working is secure, trouble-free, and available for the day. Although loading and configuring NT Server 4.0 is not by definition laborious, it can sometimes turn out that way.

Installing NT Server 4.0

Depending upon the speed of your server's CPU, the amount and speed of its memory, the speed of its CD-ROM drive, and the complexity of your LAN environment (file system, number and types of users, number and types of workstations and other network devices, number and types of connectivity options your LAN requires), installing and configuring NT Server 4 can require anywhere from one to several hours.

Our First Installation Attempt

Being new to the wiles of NT, we initially tried to load it to a system with:

- A 486/33 CPU

- A single-speed CD-ROM drive

- 16MB RAM

This naivete cost us about *11 hours*. And keep in mind, this was just the installation; we never made it to configuration on this go-around. Of the components above, the CD drive was no doubt the major culprit.

On our Pentium 133, with 32MB EDO RAM and an 8-speed CD drive, installing and *fully configuring* both NT 4.0 and Internet Information Server took about two hours.

Beginning the Installation

The instructions that follow assume that you're loading the full release of NT 4.0, rather than the upgrade version, and that you're working with the most common distribution media, the combination of three 3.5-inch/1.44MB diskettes, and one CD-ROM.

> **TIP** Some of the earliest releases of NT 4.0, and many of its beta versions, did not provide the diskettes just mentioned. Rather, the installer was required to create these disks.

Power down your PC, and insert the diskette labeled *Windows NT Server 4.0 Setup Disk 1* into the appropriate drive. Powering up your machine will boot it from this diskette and begin the installation process.

> ## Documentation Discrepancies in *Start Here*
> The copy of Microsoft's *Start Here* guide that accompanied our distribution media states that the first of the three setup diskettes is labeled *Windows NT Setup Boot Disk*. Ours wasn't; yours may be.

Installation proper begins with a welcome message. It asks if you wish to proceed with the install and, if you press **ENTER** in response, moves to its first real task—identifying your machine's mass storage devices (see Figure 2.1).

At this point, press **ENTER** once again. Pressing **S** to specify additional mass storage devices will only lengthen the install unnecessarily. Additional CD or other such drives can be configured into NT Server 4.0 after it's loaded and set up.

> **TIP** *Start Here* explains how to deal with NT installation peculiarities:
>
> • Installing solely by means of a bootable CD-ROM
>
> • Installing to RISC-based platforms
>
> • Installing across a network
>
> If your server involves any of these, loading NT 4.0 will include a few extra steps, but these are simple and take place very early in the installation process. Once they're done, the install proceeds as it would for an "ordinary" server platform.

Confirming Hardware and Creating Partitions

NT's installation routine should now give you a rundown of your server hardware (Figure 2.2). This outline is terse and not fully descriptive, but if it accurately—

> **TIP** The first two or three times we tried to install NT 4.0, we didn't
> realize that it was as finicky as it later proved to be. Therefore, despite
> the tortoiselike throughput of our single-speed CD and the fact that it
> wasn't listed in the HCL, we reasoned that, because it was an IDE, ATAPI
> device, NT 4.0 should like it. So we pressed **S**, because NT had not iden-
> tified the drive. Doing so presented us with a lengthy list of mass stor-
> age device types, from which a driver could be selected, and from which
> we chose the generic ATAPI driver Setup offered.
>
> If you simply cannot, for whatever reason, bring your server hardware
> into complete agreement with the Hardware Compatibility List, you may
> have to take these same two steps:
>
> • pressing **S** to indicate that you want to define the drive yourself
>
> • selecting an appropriate driver from the NT-supplied list

albeit generally—describes your system, press **ENTER** to move to the next installation task. (In our experience, this screen never presented inaccurate information.)

**Figure 2.1 When it has detected storage devices, NT responds with
this screen.**

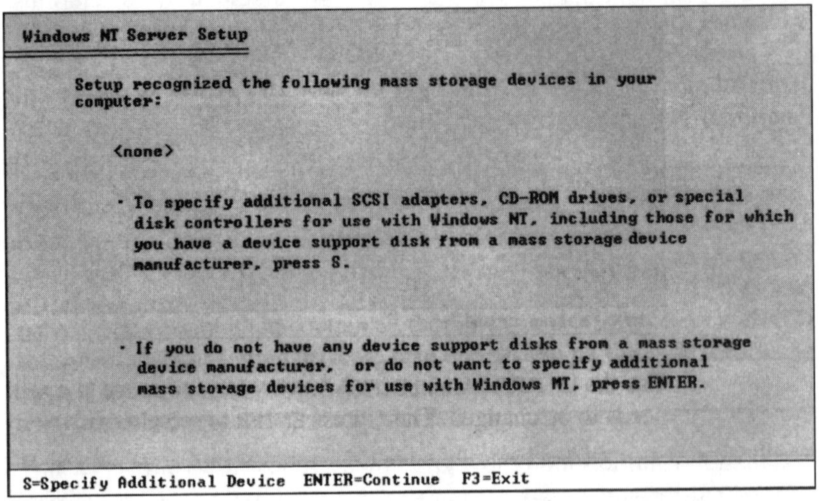

```
Windows NT Server Setup

     Setup recognized the following mass storage devices in your
     computer:

        <none>

          · To specify additional SCSI adapters, CD-ROM drives, or special
            disk controllers for use with Windows NT, including those for which
            you have a device support disk from a mass storage device
            manufacturer, press S.


          · If you do not have any device support disks from a mass storage
            device manufacturer, or do not want to specify additional
            mass storage devices for use with Windows NT, press ENTER.




   S=Specify Additional Device   ENTER=Continue   F3=Exit
```

Figure 2.2 Here's how our PC's hardware was summarized.

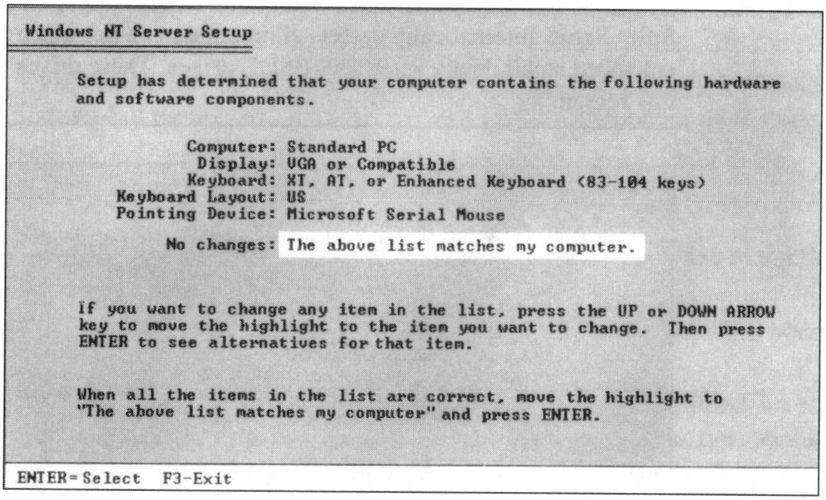

```
 Windows NT Server Setup

    Setup has determined that your computer contains the following hardware
    and software components.

              Computer: Standard PC
               Display: UGA or Compatible
              Keyboard: XT, AT, or Enhanced Keyboard (83-104 keys)
       Keyboard Layout: US
       Pointing Device: Microsoft Serial Mouse

            No changes: The above list matches my computer.


    If you want to change any item in the list, press the UP or DOWN ARROW
    key to move the highlight to the item you want to change.  Then press
    ENTER to see alternatives for that item.


    When all the items in the list are correct, move the highlight to
    "The above list matches my computer" and press ENTER.


 ENTER=Select   F3-Exit
```

Documentation's Inconsistent Use of Terms

Start Here and other MS documentations don't use terms completely
consistently. For instance, the process of loading NT Server 4.0 is called
Setup, but parts of this process are referred to variously as *configuring*
or *installing*. Admittedly, this inconsistentcy is minor, but it can cause at
least momentary confusion. Take your time and read the on-screen
instructions carefully. The gist of what they're saying will come through.

Once you've let NT know that its picture of your server hardware is correct,
you'll be asked to define the hard disk partition in which NT will live. A screen like
the one shown in Figure 2.3 will be displayed.

A number of our install attempts failed at this point in the process, for no apparent reason, even though by this time we were fully HCL compliant. Despite what
the illustration in Figure 2.4 and Microsoft's documentation seem to suggest—that
NT will load to any compatible drive with enough free space—we found that NT
would not load to a partition created by the install routine itself implicitly rather
than explicitly. Nor would it load to a secondary partition.

As Figure 2.4 shows, NT finds not only existing hard drive partitions, but also
any unpartitioned space on the same device. When, on more than one occasion, we

Figure 2.3 Defining NT's partition can be one of the trickier aspects of installing it.

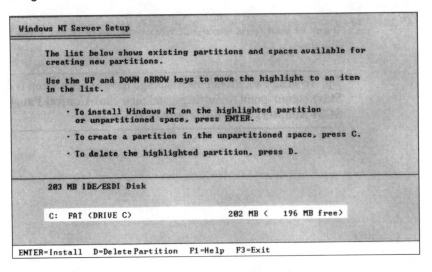

```
Windows NT Server Setup

        The list below shows existing partitions and spaces available for
        creating new partitions.

        Use the UP and DOWN ARROW keys to move the highlight to an item
        in the list.

            · To install Windows NT on the highlighted partition
              or unpartitioned space, press ENTER.
            · To create a partition in the unpartitioned space, press C.
            · To delete the highlighted partition, press D.


        203 MB IDE/ESDI Disk

          C:  FAT (DRIVE C)                   202 MB (   196 MB free)



ENTER=Install   D=Delete Partition   F1=Help   F3=Exit
```

asked NT to load itself into the highlighted unpartitioned space by simply pressing **ENTER**, it created the partition and tried to transfer itself there, but failed. However, pressing **C** at this stage to create a partition allowed the install to

Figure 2.4 Choosing a file system will cause the partition you've selected to be formatted in that system.

```
Windows NT Server Setup

        Setup will install Windows NT on partition

        C:  FAT                    325 MB (   196 MB free)

        on 326 MB IDE/ESDI Disk.

        Select the type of file system you want on this partition
        from the list below. Use the UP and DOWN ARROW keys to move the highlight
        to the selection you want.  Then press ENTER.

        If you want to select a different partition for Windows NT, press ESC.

        Convert the partition to NTFS

          Leave the current file system intact (no changes)


ENTER=Continue   ESC=Cancel
```

progress smoothly, *as long as the partition created in this way was the first one on the drive.*

Start Here and Installation Quirks

Start Here covers a number of the quirks of the installation process. Most of what it offers on the subject is helpful. However, one or two points—such as its statement "You can install the Windows NT Server files on any partition with sufficient free space"—weren't borne out in our install efforts.

Choosing a File System and Home Directory

The next step in the installation process is selecting a file system for NT Server (Figure 2.4). There's only one option at this point, in our opinion. You can convert to NTFS at any time, so there's no need to complicate your installation efforts. Stick with a FAT file system for the time being.

Once the indicated partition has been formatted, NT's installation software will ask you to specify the system's home base. It suggests the default **\WINNT.**

Unless you have a pressing reason not to do so, take this default. Doing otherwise might cause NT to fail to boot, even after a successful install, because the NOS expects to find its kernel at the root of the C drive.

You've now arrived at the coffee-break stage of the installation. You'll be prompted to insert the remaining diskettes, and finally told to clear all diskettes and CDs from the appropriate drives.

Initial Configuration

Don't worry if, after you carry out these instructions, your almost-server seems to freeze about midway through the boot. NT is, to say the least, nontrivial; it takes more than the few seconds DOS or Windows 3.x needed to load into memory.

After NT boots and you're asked if you want to continue the setup, click **Next**, and you'll be able to choose one of the Setup types discussed in Chapter 1. We'd recommend you do what we did at this point:

1. Select Custom/Complete.

2. Select all the components you're offered as a result.

Documentation Inconsistencies, Again

Start Here proved incorrect again in its mention of license management.

Once again, we found a discrepancy between *Start Here* and what we saw on our screen at this point. According to the documentation, we should have been asked to select a form of license management after entering our user and organization names. We weren't.

Before you can do the latter, though, you must tell NT the following:

- Your name

- The name of your organization

- The product or CD key number (the first located on the inside back cover of *Start Here* as well as on the registration card that accompanies the software; the latter on the CD case)

- The name by which you wish your server to be known across the network

TIP NT is fussy about the name for your computer.

One of the thorniest problems we ran into in installing NT Server 4.0 was this choice of computer name. According to *Start Here* and many non-Microsoft-generated sources of information we consulted, the only constraints on a computer (read "server") name are that it must be 15 characters or less and cannot be the same as the name of any other computer on the network, any domain on the network, or any work-group associated with the network.

Start Here states further that you can "invent a computer name" and "change the computer name after Setup is complete." So, we created the name HEART_OF_GOLD and the name HEART-OF-GOLD, neither of which NT liked. Unfortunately, it waited until we had completed the install and were trying to work with domain-related administrative tools to tell us so. Nor would NT allow us to change either name, *Start Here*'s claim notwithstanding. Our only alternative was to reinstall *from scratch*. Not add or remove. Not even upgrade. We had to do the whole thing over again from the beginning.

The only conclusion that we could come to was that "15 characters or less" must not include any underscores, hyphens, and so on.

What finally worked? The innocuous name **SERVER1**.

Defining the Server Type

Windows NT Server 4.0 recognizes three basic categories of server:

- A primary domain controller

- A backup or secondary domain controller

- A standalone server

Figure 2.5 and Table 2.1 illustrate this part of the configuration process and give you the means to decide which type of server you should select at this point.

Setting the Password for the Server Administrator

Any password of 14 characters or less will do. But whatever you do, write it down and squirrel it away with your most valued possessions. Once this password has

Table 2.1 Deciding on a Server Type

If the Machine You're Setting Up	Choose This Server Type	Because
Is the only server network	Primary Domain Controller	A Primary Domain for a Controller is the only machine on an NT LAN to house information on all computers and all users and to receive that information immediately and directly.
Is to be the major repository for network administration information	Primary Domain Controller	(See above.)
Is intended as a backup to the primary server	Backup Domain Controller	A Backup Domain Controller stores the same information as a Primary Domain Controller. However, this information is updated only periodically.
Is an application or resource server only	Standalone Server	Standalone Servers contain no network administration information.

Figure 2.5 The choice of server type is one of the most important you'll make while setting up NT Server 4.0.

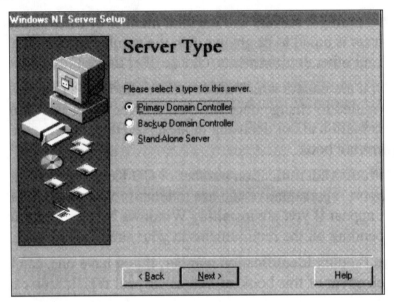

been set, your NT Server 4.0 will not boot until the password is entered correctly. If you forget it, you'll be unable to boot the server. Your only alternative at this point is to reinstall from scratch.

The nature of your file system needn't bear on the Server Administrator password you choose. If, as suggested, you've stayed with FAT for the time being, you don't have to make your password a string that DOS would recognize. We retained this file system, but were still able to use a password that consisted of 10 characters and included both upper- and lower-case letters.

NT has a legitimate reason for being so protective of the Administrator password. The only user account created automatically by NT is that of Administrator. This account is the equivalent of the Superuser in UNIX. That is, this person can do anything and everything on the server.

The next thing that Setup suggests you do is create an Emergency Repair Disk to be used if this or any subsequent configuration of NT 4.0 bombs. We didn't bother with this step, because once we got the hang of what NT expected, the complete install and setup only took about an hour. But if you have not even this much time to spare, have installed atypically, or simply want to feel more comfortable, go ahead and create the emergency disk. Know, though, that this disk will hold only server parameters and not portions of the NOS proper.

Choosing Optional Components

As you can see from Figures 2.6 and 2.7, even if you did not select a Typical or Complete setup, NT will still allow you to pick up some of its optional features. Among those you might want to consider are:

- Exchange Server (to provide your intranet or Internet site with centrally managed mail capabilities)

- DHCP Client (if you think the ability to assign IP addresses on the fly would be useful)

- Messenger (as a means of obtaining a single tool with which you can tweak not only Exchange but also Microsoft Mail)

- Schedule (to give yourself the ability to schedule execution times for database-related operations such as indexing)

Refer to the subsection "Typical Versus Custom/Complete Setup" in Chapter 1 for a complete list of NT services.

Figure 2.6 NT asks if you'd like to see a list of all its features.

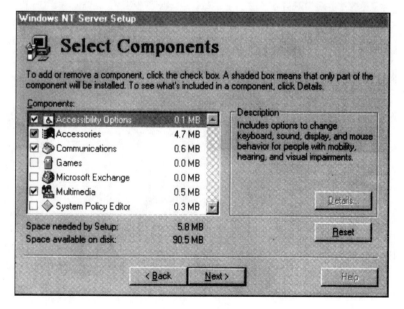

Keep in mind that the more you ask NT to do for you, the more of your server platform's hardware resources it will demand in return. In particular, if disk space is at a premium on your server, be deliberate in choosing components.

Setting Up NT Networking and Internet Information Server

The first significant decision to be made in setting up NT networking and Internet Information Server is the choice of connection method. The installation software presents you with two alternatives in this regard:

- Wired to the network

- Remote access to the network

As Figure 2.8 demonstrates, this is in fact a choice between a LAN in the most traditional sense—that is, one in which stations and resources communicate with

Figure 2.7 Choosing all available components pumps up the amount of disk space you'll need to have free.

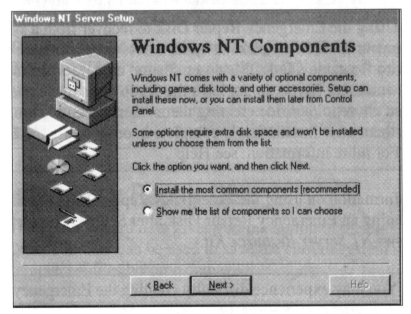

Figure 2.8 The installation software provides two types of connection methods.

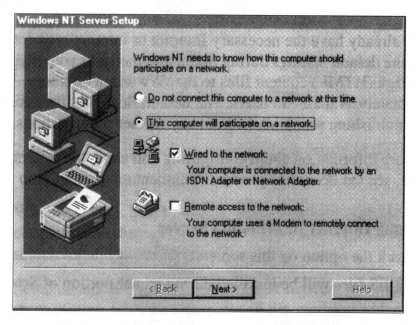

the network transmission medium by means of **Network Interface Cards (NICs)**— and LANs that may be accessed via a modem.

In most environments, dial-up access to any server is, if not a current, certainly an anticipated fact of life. So you'd be wise to check both network types. Doing so automatically alerts NT to the fact that it will have to deal with modems, remote access, and so on.

> **TIP** Choosing both network types does have some drawbacks. When you choose both network types, you lengthen and complicate the install process because you must choose and define remote access services and devices such as modems. If your NT network will not be connecting to an external LAN or other network immediately, you can forgo this option during installation. It will always be available to you through NT 4.0's **Control Panel**.

Installing Internet Information Server

As mentioned earlier, you need not install Internet Information Server at this time. The utility **Inetstp.exe**, in the **\Inetsrv** subdirectory of the directory on the CD-

ROM that matches your hardware platform, is the piece of software that actually loads IIS. Inetstp.exe can be run at any time.

If you do choose to load IIS during the overall installation of NT Server 4.0, indicate this choice by simply clicking a single box (see Figure 2.9).

The CD that is the heart of installing Windows NT Server 4.0 is set up with separate directories for each of the hardware platforms capable of supporting the NOS. So, if you look at the contents of this CD with Windows 3.x **File Manager** or the DOS **dir** command, you'll see something like what's illustrated in Figure 2.10.

In other words, the CD contains suites of software specific to:

- DEC Alphas
- MIPS-based machines
- the PowerPCs
- Intel-based PCs

Figure 2.9 Installing Internet Information Server along with NT Server requires only a single check at this point in the process.

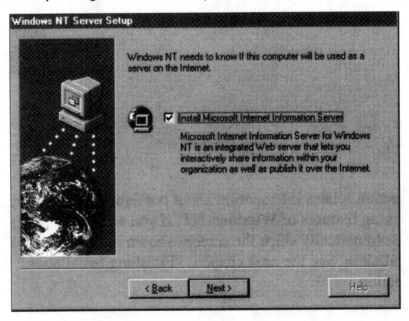

Figure 2.10 Running File Manager on our distribution CD resulted in this display.

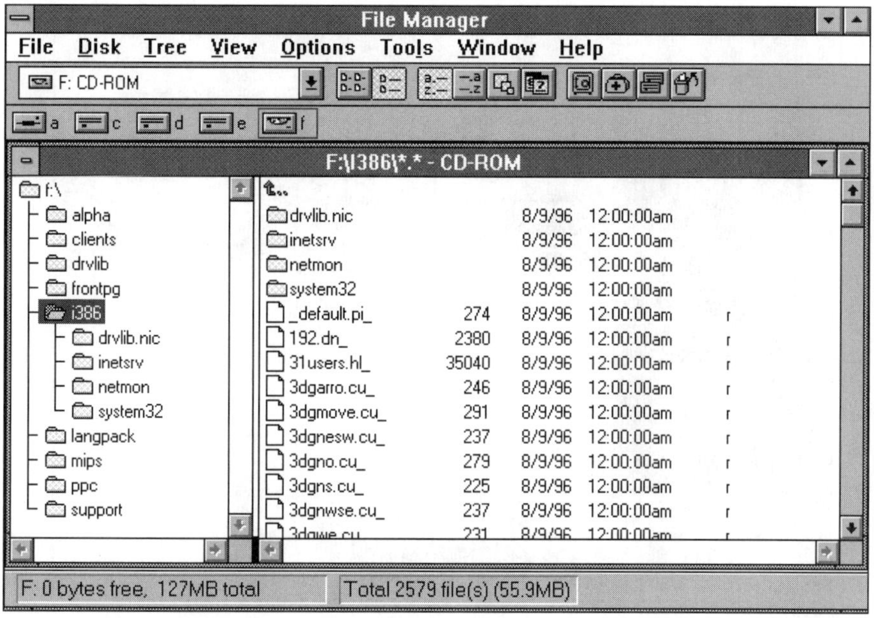

Selecting Network Adapters

You must identify network adapters that are in use on your LAN. If NT has not already automatically detected and identified your NIC, you may browse the list of Hardware Compatibility Listed cards and select the appropriate type or types from that list. However, if you follow this latter path, be sure to have handy a diskette that contains the corresponding drivers; NT may not have a driver compatible with the card you've chosen.

Figure 2.11 takes a glimpse at the NICs this browser makes available.

TIP If yours is a nonstandard NIC, you may see an additional installation window.

NT Setup's Adapter Card Setup dialog is displayed in those cases in which such parameters as IRQ, base memory address, and port aren't available in NT's database for the NIC in question. If you run into this dialog, use the manufacturer's suggested settings. If those settings conflict with those already being used by other hardware components, NT will let you know and give you the opportunity to select other settings.

Figure 2.11 We chose NE2000-compatible from the list this window provided.

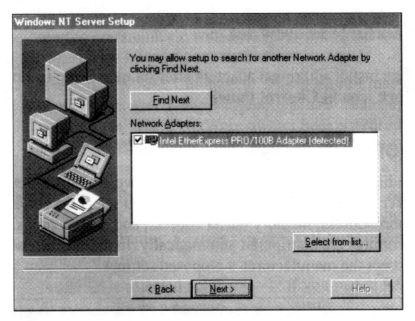

Choosing Protocols

Because they live so far down on the metal, protocols make many of us uneasy. Names like **TCP/IP** and **NetBEUI,** not exactly self-explanatory to say the least, don't ease our discomfort. If, at this point, you'd like to dispel a bit of the mystique surrounding protocols, turn to the Glossary or Appendix D at the end of the book. If, on the other hand, you want to finish setting up NT as quickly as you can, consult Table 2.2.

Table 2.2 Choosing Protocols for an NT Network

If Your Network Transmission Medium Is	And You Must Connect to	Select the Protocol
Thin Ethernet (coaxial) cable, or unshielded twisted pair	UNIX	TCP/IP
	NetWare running TCP/IP	TCP/IP
	NetWare running IPX/SPX	NWLink (an IPX/SPX compatible protocol) NetBEUI

Table 2.2 *Continued*

If Your Network Transmission Medium Is	And You Must Connect to	Select the Protocol
	Any Microsoft network running NetBEUI Macintosh machines	TCP/IP AppleTalk

Choosing Network Services

The next thing you'll see is a window that will allow you to choose from a wide variety of offerings those network services you'd like your NT server to run.

By default, Setup offers five network services (see Figure 2.12), from which you may choose any or all:

- Remote Access Service

- RPC Configuration

- NetBIOS Interface

Figure 2.12 Be sure to scan the Network Services list.

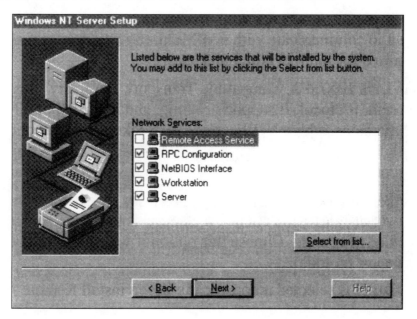

- Workstation

- Server

Click **Select from List** for the following additional choices:

- DHCP Relay Agent

- Gateway and Client Services for NetWare

- Microsoft DHCP Server

- Microsoft DNS Server

- Microsoft TCP/IP Printing

- Network Monitor Agent

- Network Monitor Tools and Agent

- Remoteboot Service

- Remote Access Service

- RIP for Internet Protocol

- RIP for NwLink (IPX/SPX-compatible transport)

- RPC support for Banyan

- SAP agent

Two Small Points about the Network Services List

We've not defined these services here, because Setup describes them to you as you select each, in the Details section of the dialog box in which they're presented. We've covered them all in the Glossary.

Be aware that you cannot **SHIFT**- or **CTRL**-click this list. You must select items from it one at a time, reclicking **Select From List** at the end of each iteration. In addition to the defaults, we picked several other network services. Among them were Gateway and Client Services for NetWare (thereby allowing stations on a Novell LAN to access our NT server) and Services for the Macintosh.

- Services for Macintosh

- Simple TCP/IP Services

- SNMP Service

- Windows Internet Name Service

Additional Dialogs Regarding Network Components

Depending upon which network adapters, protocols, and services you've identified to NT, you may, at this point in the setup process, see further dialog boxes. These windows will show you what NT considers to be the best settings for the component in question. Check the parameters you're presented with. In almost every case, they will agree with the values recommended by the item's manufacturer or by your Internet service provider (ISP). If they don't, correct them before moving on.

If You've Chosen to Install Internet Information Server

If, a couple of setup screens ago, you accepted the installation of Internet Information Server along with NT's more general networking components, you'll be presented a dialog at this point that will ask you to define an IP address for IIS. Enter the address provided to you by your ISP in this box.

DHCP for Addresses on the Fly
Your ISP may provide Internet addresses "on the fly" by means of software called **Dynamic Host Configuration Protocol**, or **DHCP**, which creates a fixed pool of IP addresses and allows these to be reused, in effect doling them out on a first-come, first-served basis. If your ISP uses DHCP, you need make no entry in this dialog box.

Dealing with Bindings

A binding is the association of a particular protocol with a particular network adapter. In relatively straightforward environments, such relationships are many-to-one. For example, the screen via which NT presents the bindings it intends to use should look like Figure 2.13 if you've told Setup that your NT server will communicate through its single NIC, with one of the following:

- Workstations on a Novell LAN

- Workstations on an older Microsoft network such as PC-LAN

- Workstations within its own NT domain

Figure 2.13 All services on this network have been told the server's adapter will "talk to them" in the NetBIOS "language."

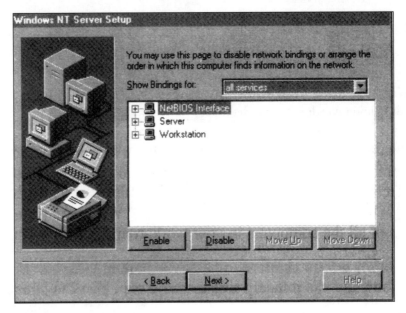

Your best bet, however, is not to deal with bindings, but to accept the defaults NT offers.

Start Here has some sage advice to offer on this topic: "Do not attempt to change bindings . . . unless you are an experienced network administrator . . ."

Dealing with the Default Domain

A domain is analogous to but not exactly equivalent to a workgroup. A domain, in the NT universe, is analogous to a workgroup in the 3.11 dimension. That is, a domain is a virtual or logical, as opposed to a physical group of devices, defined as best fits your environment's needs. So, Company X might have separate domains for its Accounting, Personnel, Research and Development, and Marketing departments but implement these separate *logical* collections of information on the same *physical* groups of devices.

The following summarizes what's important regarding domains in the context of setting up Windows NT Server 4.0:

- Users will log in to domains rather than to particular machines. This fact, coupled with the further tidbit that a domain name cannot be changed without a fair amount of difficulty, should cause you to give significant thought to the name you'll assign to each domain.

- In a domain, computers other than workstations fall into two categories:

  - **Domain controllers,** the first servers defined on an NT network and those housing all security information, in addition to applications

  - **Domain servers** or application servers

The most important function of the Domain Settings dialog, shown in Figure 2.14, is to allow you to provide a name for your Primary Domain Controller and, if you care to, for the domain it manages. These can't be just any names, though.

Although you won't be forced to reinstall the entire operating system if you need to change a controller or server name, you should still choose such names carefully.

Figure 2.14 The Domain Settings dialog is deceptive—it looks quite simple, but the information you enter here is quite important.

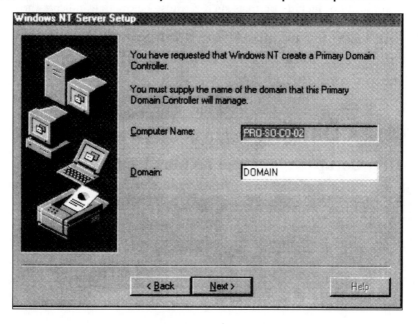

Make them mnemonic. Your users are much less likely to be confused about which machine they're on if you've named the server or controller *Personnel1* rather than *sq19723* or even *emplmnt.*

Server names under NT Server 4.0, like its file names, can include embedded spaces. But if you intend to have DOS-based machines as part of your Intranet, forgo this capability—DOS won't be able to handle it.

Names for the domain itself must be in agreement with the Internet's scheme for host name construction. In essence, this means that domain names you use in your NT server must reflect the nature of your site. So, the fictitious company Desktop Data might use the domain name *desktopd.* You need not include any of the suffixes, such as the following, that indicate the type of organization:

- .com

- .org

- .gov

These will automatically be attached at the ISP level.

You also need not include prefixes such as those below that indicate the type of service being offered:

- ftp

- www

These will be prepended by NT Server 4.0 after you configure Internet Information Server.

Finishing Setup

Only three more steps now stand between you and booting a full-blown Windows NT Server 4.0 for the first time.

Configuring Internet Information Server

The screen Microsoft Internet Information Server Setup, and the dialog and informational boxes it in turn pops up, are the means by which you do the initial configuration of Internet Information Server.

> **TIP** The tip regarding computer name applies to domain name as well.
>
> And there's more. Don't be fooled, as we were the first install attempt or two, into thinking that the name **DOMAIN**, displayed by **Setup** when the screen shown in Figure 2.18 is presented, will suffice. If you simply click **Next** with the field **Domain** containing this value, you'll get no errors, and NT will load and boot, but you'll not have a valid domain and therefore will not be able to use many domain-related tools. That means reinstalling.
>
> (We ended up with the domain name **DOMAIN1**, by the way.)

Setting Date and Time

The next thing NT shows you is a map with two tabs that together allow you to adjust the system clock on your new server. The pull-down list of time zones the map offers is quite extensive; it includes entries for Casablanca, Cairo, Berlin, Athens, Prague, Moscow, Tehran, and a few dozen more.

> **TIP** You can defer even this initial configuring of Internet Information Server until later. By starting NT's Control Panel, choosing Add/Remove Programs, and then selecting the Add/Remove Components tab, you'll be able to pick these items up.

Confirming Display Characteristics

Figure 2.15 is a representation of NT Setup's final dialog, through which you can adjust the color palette, desktop size, font size, and refresh rate of your server's display. Some of the choices we made are shown in the figure.

Starting NT Server

You'd think that this last step in Setup (as opposed to configuration, which is still to come) would be as easy as "take out any diskettes or CDs and press reset." Unfortunately, in addition to clearing all diskette and CD drives, you must respond to a text-only boot loader message and respond to the Begin Logon message with what is surely the most unexpected rejoinder possible: CTRL ALT DEL. The quintessential fallback tactic, surprisingly, is the *only* set of keystrokes that will cause NT to present you with the Login Information dialog, into which you type and confirm your password.

Figure 2.15 We selected a 256-color palette and the standard desktop and font sizes in this last NT setup step.

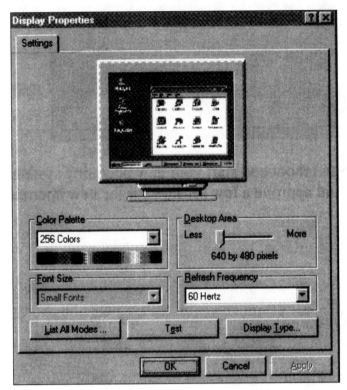

Configuring NT and IIS

Now that you've completely installed and set up the basic operating characteristics of Windows NT Server 4.0 and Internet Information Server, you're ready to define: users, the domains and groups to which they will belong, and the information and network resources users, groups, and domains will be able to access.

Setting Up Users

NT Server 4.0's scheme for controlling user access to files and directories is a fairly complicated one that combines controlling access to directories, subdirectories, and files with defining who may share those entities across the network. For now, we provide only an overview of what's involved in setting up NT users and their access abilities. In succeeding chapters, we deal with this area in much more detail.

Domain Membership

Every user for whom you establish an account must be a member of at least one domain (because he or she will log into it rather than into a machine). You can also establish accounts on several domains for a given user.

The how-tos of establishing accounts on domains are covered in Chapter 5.

Group Membership

With group membership, the specifics of NT Server's user access get a little nebulous. Domain membership does not imply, let alone equate to, group membership. User groups, however, are frequently analogous to domains.

If, for instance, you've set up a single domain called *Academia* on the machine to which you're installing 4.0, you might decide upon several areas or levels of user access within that domain: faculty, graduate students, undergraduate students, and support staff, for example.

You might decide further that all such categories of users should, through your nascent intranet, be able to access the schedule of classes being offered during the upcoming semester; the groups faculty, graduate students, and undergraduate students should have access to the library's online catalog of holdings; and the group support staff should be the only type of users with access to payroll records for faculty and transcript records for students.

As you create each user account, NT will allow you to define:

- A logon name

- The user's full name

- A brief description of the user and the nature of what he or she may access

- A password, which can be up to 15 characters long and can also be case-sensitive

- Group membership or memberships

- A user profile (in essence the name and location of a login script for this user)

- Hours during which the user may access NT Server

- Locations from which the user may connect

- Characteristics of her or his password, such as whether or not the user may change it, and if so, how frequently

> **TIP** Be careful in assigning user passwords.
>
> If your network includes DOS, vanilla Windows, or Windows 95 workstations, don't use case-sensitivity in passwords; these OSs won't recognize the difference between capital and small letters.

By default, brand-new users are automatically given membership in the group called Domain Users. This default membership will allow them to do most things that network users need to do. But if you'd like to allow a user to do something a little more racy (like managing a printer), you must either explicitly assign membership to the group (in the case of our fictitious domain Academia, the group support staff) that has that ability or give the user in question tailor-made rights and privileges that will confer the desired function.

You don't have to explicitly define groups if you don't want to, because NT offers quite a few canned groups, with preset characteristics. You can take a look at these and at User Manager for Domains proper by selecting the following from the Start button (Figure 2.16):

Programs ---> Administrative Tools ---> User Manager for Domains

Figure 2.16 User Manager is your most important tool for managing every aspect of user accounts.

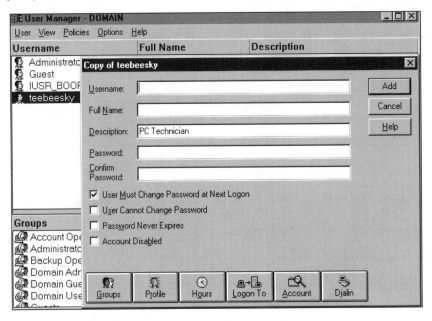

Starting the User Manager As with almost all of NT Server 4.0's administrative tools, you start the **User Manager** by clicking the **Start** button on the taskbar at the bottom of your screen. Then proceed by clicking:

- **Programs**

- **Administrative Tools** from the resulting pop-up

- **User Manager for Domains**

Built-in User Accounts Successfully installing Windows NT Server 4.0 means automatically creating two user accounts. The first, Administrator, can do everything, including the following:

- Create, modify, or delete users

- Cause network directories or printers to be shared

- Install or modify the configuration of hardware

- Install or modify the configuration of NT itself

The other account, Guest, can do almost nothing. This account is intended for occasional use only, and although automatically installed, it must be manually enabled by the Administrator.

Creating New Users Having opened the **User Manager**, you can create a new user account according to the criteria discussed in the section **Group Membership** by:

1. Pulling down the **User Manager**'s **User** menu

2. Choosing **New User**

3. Responding appropriately to the resulting dialog box, illustrated in Figure 2.17

Any user account created with this dialog box can also be deleted—or more correctly, disabled.

Manipulating User Accounts Figure 2.18 is an example of the **User Properties** dialog. To access this screen double-click a user account in the list of users presented by the **User Manager** and select a user account from that list. Then do the following:

1. Pull down the **User** menu.

2. Click **Properties** from that menu.

3. Select a user account and press **ENTER**.

Figure 2.17 You'll probably see the New User dialog box often.

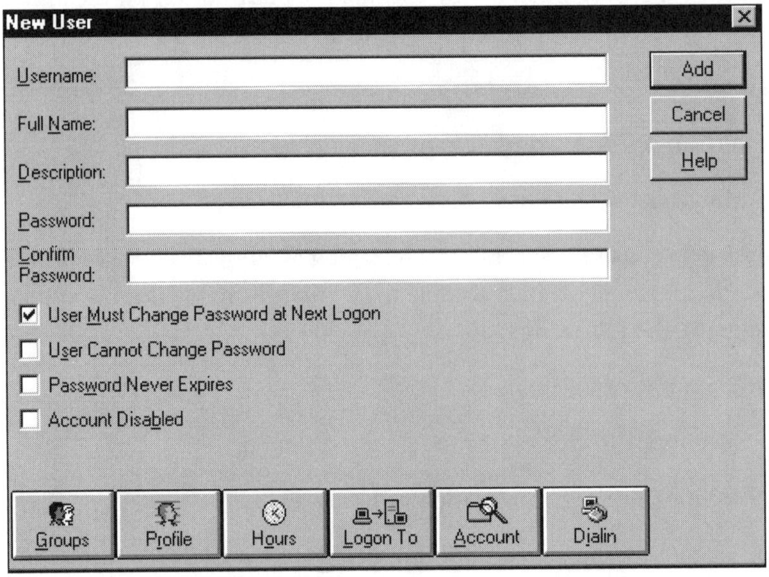

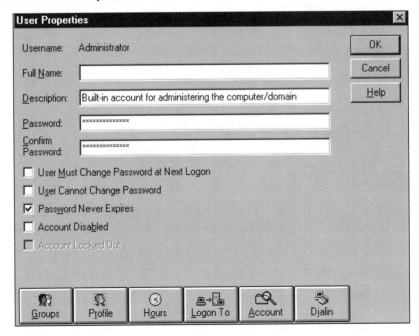

Figure 2.18 The User Properties dialog lets you change many of an account's most important characteristics.

Copying User Accounts NT makes available the Copy User dialog as a shortcut in establishing new accounts that will share characteristics with existing ones. To copy a user account as a means of creating a new user, follow these steps:

1. Open the User Manager.

2. Select the user to copy.

3. Pull down the User menu.

4. Choose Copy from that menu, which will open the Copy [Username] dialog shown in Figure 2.19.

5. Click **Add**.

> **T I P** Whether a given group is local or global, its function remains the same. That is, local administrators can do as much network management as global administrators. Similarly, local backup operators can run a tape as readily as can global backup operators.
>
> The wrinkle lies in the fact that local groups can be made up of either users or global groups, but global groups can include only users. What's important about this in the context of configuring NT 4.0 is that in assigning group membership to a user account, you *must* make the user in question a member of at least one global group (such as the default Domain Users).
>
> The only global groups that NT Server offers in its prefab set are **Domain Users** and **Domain Administrators**.

Rights and Permissions

Anyone familiar with Novell environments probably recognizes the idea of rights to a file or file subsystem, as opposed to permissions further affecting access to that data.

NT Server uses a similar system of tailoring user access. But with NT, a *right* is something a user can *do*—log on from a workstation, log on remotely, run a backup, change printer characteristics, and so on. Rights may involve but are not the same as access to files. That access is controlled through **permissions**, which include such categories of access as the ability to **read** a file, the ability to modify (**change**) it, and so on.

Figure 2.19 The Add button on the Copy user dialog creates a new user account with the characteristics you've indicated.

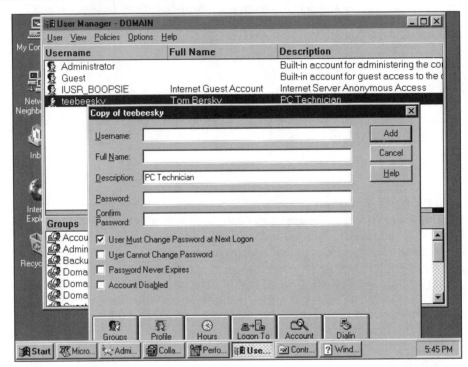

The same means of deciding which preset user group membership you might want to assign to a given user applies to deciding about rights and permissions too. Just choose the following: **Start** ---> **Programs** ---> **Administrative Tools** ---> **User Manager for Domains**. Then choose: **Policies** ---> **User Rights**.

Doing so will allow you to select a group by name and then to drop down a list detailing all rights available to that group.

Setting Up Network Monitoring and Resources

You cannot monitor who's using what files how frequently under NT Server 4.0 unless you have configured and enabled auditing. To do so, select the file, files, directories, or drives whose access you wish to view by clicking **My Computer** ---> C. Then proceed as follows:

1. Click the **File** menu.

2. Click **Properties**.

3. Click the **Security** tab.

4. Click **Auditing.**

5. Set the level to which auditing will apply:

   - Only the selected directory or directories and component files, by choosing **Replace Auditing on Existing Files**

   - Not only the selected area of your drive, but also all its subdirectories and their files, by indicating *not only* **Replace Auditing on Existing Files** *but also* **Replace Auditing on Subdirectories**

Performance Monitoring

NT Server 4.0 has two tools you can use to observe your server's performance: the Event Viewer and the Performance Monitor. Both can be accessed and configured from the **Administrative Tools** program group.

Event Viewer As its name implies, the **Event Viewer,** shown in Figure 2.20, lets you track individual occurrences (as opposed to monitoring network usage or trends over a period of time).

Figure 2.20 This look at the Event Viewer allowed us to correct a poorly configured NIC.

Date	Time	Source	Category	Event
3/6/97	10:03:41 AM	Srv	None	2013
3/6/97	10:00:26 AM	BROWSER	None	8015
3/6/97	10:00:26 AM	BROWSER	None	8015
3/6/97	10:00:26 AM	BROWSER	None	8015
3/6/97	10:00:26 AM	BROWSER	None	8015
3/6/97	9:59:33 AM	W3SVC	None	101
3/6/97	9:58:30 AM	EventLog	None	6005
3/6/97	9:59:27 AM	Nwlnklpx	None	9502
3/4/97	5:14:07 PM	BROWSER	None	8033
3/4/97	5:14:05 PM	BROWSER	None	8033
3/4/97	5:14:05 PM	BROWSER	None	8033
3/4/97	5:14:05 PM	BROWSER	None	8033
3/4/97	5:02:14 PM	Srv	None	2013
3/4/97	4:59:00 PM	BROWSER	None	8015
3/4/97	4:59:00 PM	BROWSER	None	8015
3/4/97	4:59:00 PM	BROWSER	None	8015

Event Viewer - System Log on \\BOOPSIE

Log View Options Help

Event Viewer is by default always available to the Administrator, and it maintains three logs:

- The Application Log records events generated by applications (such as a printer's being accessed in response to a user request).

- The Security Log tracks such things as logon attempts.

- The System Log monitors system-related events such as the inability to access a port.

Table 2.3 summarizes NT Server 4.0's Event Viewer.

Performance Monitor Unlike Event Viewer, Performance Monitor, as shown in Figure 2.21, is *not* fully enabled by default. To bring it to life, you must create a chart, log, alert, or report. These are basically formats NT Server 4.0 makes available for monitoring performance. See Table 2.4 for an explanation.

To make Performance Monitor's tools available, click **Start** ---> **Programs** ---> **Administrative Tools** ---> **Performance Monitor** from the Performance Monitor's menu bar. Then pull down the View menu.

To create a chart, log, alert, or report, select **Chart, Log, Alert,** or **Report** as appropriate. Pull down Performance Monitor's **File** menu and select **New Chart/Log/Alert/Report.**

Table 2.3 Event Viewer at a Glance

The Log	Allows You to Eyeball Events Like
Application	Requests for network services such as printing Requests for database access Requests for CPU time
Security	Logon attempts Changes to the Registry Changes to group or user privileges
System	Failure of an NIC Incorrectly configured modem Inability to access a network device

Figure 2.21 The Performance Monitor before it's been configured.

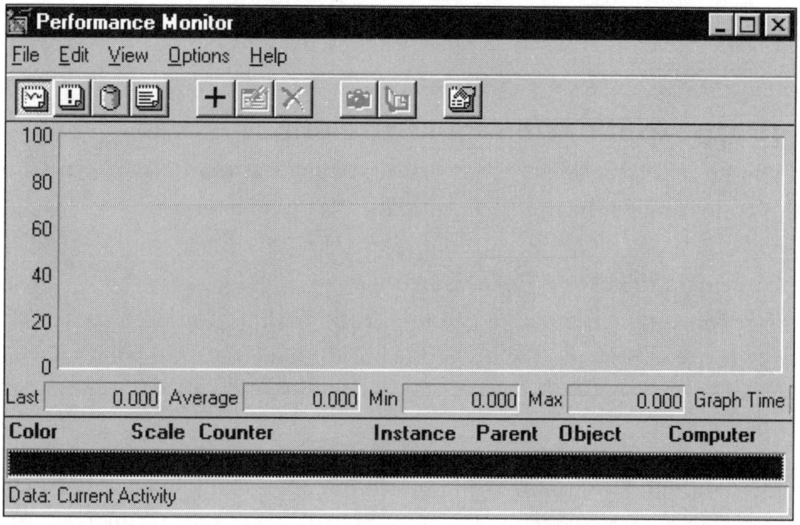

Setting Up a Printer

Under NT Server 4.0, setting up a printer is easy. Everything you need is presented in a single dialog box.

Table 2.4 Four Ways to View NT Server with Performance Monitor

This Monitoring Format	Produces (by default, on the monitor)
Chart	Line charts that represent the performance over a defined period of time of one or more system parameters such as CPU usage.
Log	Columnar (usually) presentations of previously defined (usually) system activities such as printer usage or backups.
Alert	An audible notification of the reaching or exceeding of some threshold value for a given parameter (e.g., the PC bleeps when traffic on the network goes above a certain limit).
Report	A more flexible and fuller version of Log.

From **My Computer,** click the **Control Panel,** and then choose **Printers.** Or simply click **Printers** directly from **My Computer.** In either case, the next thing you'll see is the **Printers** dialog box. From here you need only carry out the steps sketched in Table 2.5.

Setting Up Applications and the File System

Even if you thought setting up users was something less than a snap, you'll breeze through configuring applications to run under NT Server 4.0.

Basic File and Directory Permissions

Permissions control what a user or group can do with a file. As suggested in Chapter 1, the time to make the decision regarding who can do what to which files is when you're planning your Internet Information Server. But in case you missed it then, we'll repeat it here.

Whether you will modify the configuration of an existing machine or build your NT server from scratch, your most important task in planning your Internet Information Server is to sketch the server file system and user access to it.

Having this sketch in hand allows you to piggyback defining basic file and directory access permissions onto defining group membership. For instance, you could assign read and change permissions to the subdirectory theses of the directory gradstudents to the group graduatestudents (not a preset group, of course). You'd do this through NT Server's File Manager.

Table 2.5 Installing a Printer to NT Server

Carry Out the Sequence	To Accomplish	Which in Turn Allows You to
Printer ---> Add Printer	Starting the Add Printer Wizard	Define a name for the printer, assign a driver to that name, assign this combo to a printer port, and define a Share Name for the new printer.
Printer ---> File ---> Properties	Making the Printer Setup dialog available	Modify printer characteristics (e.g. change the driver associated with a printer).

Shared Files and Directories

Shared files and directories are different from basic access. If you are familiar with any version of Windows, you have probably encountered the selection path **Disk --->Share As**. The following provides a little background.

To assign sharing of a disk, file system, or file subsystem, follow these steps:

1. Select Administrative Tools from the Programs area of the Start button's display.

2. Select Administrative Wizards.

3. Click on Managing File and Folder Access.

4. Highlight the relevant storage area.

5. Navigate through and respond appropriately to the resulting dialogs.

For instance, in our hypothetical domain Academia, the path **c:\academy\ gradstu\theses** might be assigned the Share Name *Masters*. Then access to Masters could be given to any desired group or user, whatever other permissions they might have.

Backups

To back up all or any portion of NT's file system, you'll need to run a tape. To do that, you'll need to have first physically installed a tape drive. But that installation, unlike the others we've already discussed, cannot take place when you're installing NT proper. Instead, it is considered a server administration task.

To install a tape drive, do the following.

1. Connect the device to your (powered-down) server.

2. Put NT's distribution CD in the appropriate drive.

3. Open the **Control Panel**.

4. Click **Tape Devices**.

5. Click the **Drivers** tab.

6. Select a combination of drive manufacturer and drive type from the resulting dialog that matches the tape drive you've already physically installed.

After you click **OK**, NT will momentarily bounce back to the CD to load the proper driver before returning to the preceding dialog. Once it's back there, just close that box. You're done installing your tape drive.

Choosing a Tape Drive Manufacturer

Tape drive manufacturers, as well as drive types, are few and far between. In the first category, NT offered us only Archive, Digital, Exabyte, Hewlett-Packard, Quantum, Tandberg, and Wangtek.

As for drive types, we could select only from 4 mm DAT drive, floppy [QIC-117] tape drive, IDE [QIC-157] tape drive, and SCSI mini cartridge drive.

Disk Management

NT Server's **Disk Administrator** allows you to organize or reorganize the distribution of disk space on your server. You access Disk Administrator from **Administrative Tools**; the tasks you can perform once there include:

- *Create an extended partition.* Select an area of free space on the active disk and select **Partition** ---> **Create Extended.**

- *Create a logical drive.* Select an Extended partition, and select unused space within that partition. Select **Partition** ---> **Create**, then respond to the **Create Logical Drive** dialog by specifying the size the drive will occupy.

- *Create a volume set.* Select all the areas of free disk space you wish to include in the new volume set. Choose **Partition** ---> **Create Volume Set**, then pick an overall size for the set (large enough, of course, to handle the free areas you'd previously highlighted).

- *Format new disk areas.* You can format logical drives, volume set, and so forth by selecting the unformatted slice and then selecting **Tools** ---> **Format.** Pick the file system to be used for the format.

From Here

Chapter 2 provides everything you need to install and configure a basic NT network.

In Chapter 3, we turn to a discussion of the basics of Internet Information Server. Then, in Chapter 4, we look at the relationships of its most important services.

Part Two
IIS Basics and IIS Tools

3

The Basics of Internet
Information Server

In this chapter, we take a closer look at Internet Information Server (IIS), examining the features it offers, its applicability to both intranets and Internet sites, and its reliance on NT Server 4.0 for many of its tools. We also look at Internet Service Manager, the IIS management tool that's built into Internet Information Server, as well as the standard form of Internet Service Manager and the HTML-based version of Internet Service Manager.

Basic Services

Depending upon how you installed and configured Internet Information Server, you now have any or all of the following available:

- Web publishing services
- Gopher services
- FTP services
- Internet Service Manager
- The HTML-based version of Internet Service Manager

As background to a discussion of these topics, the following sections review the two types of environments in which Microsoft foresees these services running: on an Internet site and within an intranet.

IIS and an Internet Site

Microsoft's online Help for Internet Information Server defines the Internet as a "global network of computers that communicate using a common language . . . similar to the international telephone system—no one owns or controls the whole thing, but it is connected in a way that makes it work like one big network."

Even the least computer-literate of us can recognize the eminently perfunctory nature of this definition. The generality seems even more piquant when you consider what has to be done to successfully install and configure NT Server and IIS. However, the latter part of the definition is apt—"connected in a way that makes it work like one big network"—and is indeed the salient point.

All of Internet Information Server's features coexist comfortably with this one big network. That is, all FTP, gopher, and Web services can be accessed and managed from somewhere out on the Internet. Internet Information Server can exist as a single, dedicated FTP, Gopher, or Web server on the Internet. It can also provide access from an internal network to the Internet.

Through its integration with Windows NT, Internet Information Server allows you to provide and manage:

• Multiple servers, each with a specific function

• A server or servers with multiple functions

Finally, when used in combination with **Remote Access Service** (**RAS**), IIS offers dial-up access to an intranet or the Internet.

IIS: Heavily Web Oriented, But ...

There is no question that Internet Information Server is heavily slanted toward the World Wide Web, much as the Internet itself has become. Once again, let's look at some of what IIS's online Help has to say in this regard:

> *In addition to the WWW service, Microsoft Internet Information Server provides two additional services: File Transfer Protocol (FTP) and gopher. These services are "legacy" services on the Internet, meaning that they are older protocols.*

In another area of its online Help (regarding Internet publishing), IIS makes no reference at all to FTP, and only a single, coincidental mention of gopher services. But both FTP and gopher services can play an important role in your NT-based Internet presence.

The Critical Role of FTP Services The original role of FTP—transferring files *in either direction* between a client and server—remains the most important reason for including it among Internet-based IIS services. Indeed, such transfers constitute the critical need for FTP. Without it, no client will be able to transfer files to your NT server.

Gopher Services: Not Web, But More Than FTP Internet Information Server's gopher services, like its FTP services, allow you to make archives of files accessible. Further, implementing an IIS gopher lets you at least begin to approach the nonlinear, user-defines-the-order-and-logic-of-using-them nature of Web services, because the IIS gopher service, like gophers in general, can do the following:

- Create links to other computers and the archives of information they store

- Annotate files and directories as a means of summarizing the information they contain

- Create menus through which archives can be accessed, regardless of the server upon which those archives reside

The World Wide Web Under IIS

Internet Information Server can publish either information or applications. Further, an NT-/IIS-based Web site can provide information ranging in form from simple pages of text, through icons and dialog boxes, all the way up to and including animation, video, and other multimedia information.

Publish on the Internet

Internet-related subjects, like everything else about data processing, have developed their own slang and colloquialisms. *Internet Publishing* ranks high among these.

Publishing anything across the Internet or within an Intranet means, in essence, that you've made a body of information available there. That's it. Considerations such as Web page creation and manipulation, security for FTP and gopher sites, or any other such are more correctly corollaries of the underlying data communication.

So if you've correctly installed and configured NT Server and IIS, your Internet publishing is all but ready to roll.

Finally, Internet Information Server allows your users to find and extract information from, and insert information into, databases managed by its **SQL Server** and accessed by means of the **Open DataBase Connectivity (ODBC)** feature.

What Is ODBC? The Open Database Connectivity application, or more correctly the ODBC set of APIs, has been defined by Microsoft to allow applications to be database independent, in a way not made available by older schemes for database access. That is, applications that employ ODBC are not limited by the nature or structure of a database's schema—its internal blueprint—or built-in query language. In a nutshell, ODBC is more flexible than traditional DBMS/SQL schemes in that the same application programs can be used to access different DBMSs.

ODBC relies on a set of drivers and a driver manager, which create and pass, respectively, calls for database access or manipulation from the application program through underlying data communications and database access software to the particular database manager. The ODBC library contains function calls that allow an

Figure 3.1 ODBC earns its own icon and window after a successful installation.

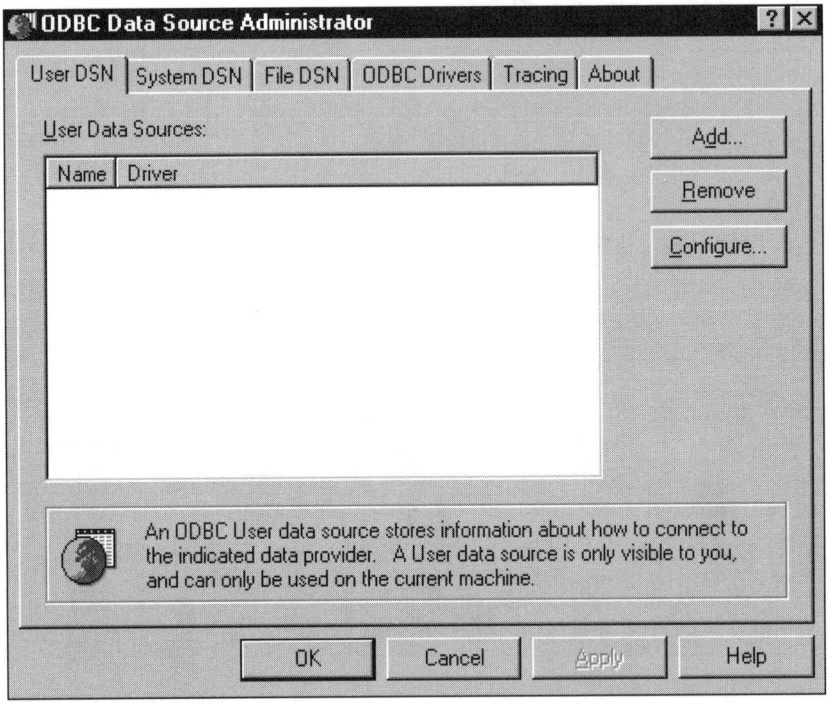

application to connect to a DBMS, execute SQL statements, and retrieve results. Further, the library defines standard error codes and standard data types. Figure 3.1 gives us a glimpse of the ODBC Manager.

In contrast, proprietary or embedded SQL/DBMS services present the following drawbacks:

- Even if available, source code must be recompiled for each new environment in which it is to function.

- Any such program strongly reflects the characteristics of the database for which it was created.

- Among the drivers that ODBC offers are hooks into dBASE, FoxPro, Paradox, and SQL Server itself.

What Is SQL Server? Microsoft SQL Server is the IIS feature through which distributed databases can be created, modified, and accessed. SQL Server can handle files ranging in size and complexity from small, one-megabyte user text files to giant, hundred-gigabyte databases used by thousands of people. SQL Server can even use Windows NT Server 4.0's ability to support multiple processors to accomplish the **symmetric multiprocessing**, or **SMP**, manipulation of data. It can also split up a very large database across a cluster of servers, each of which stores only a part of the whole and each of which can be configured to do only some of the work of manipulating the database.

What Is SMP?

Symmetric multiprocessing, as implemented under Windows NT Server 4.0, distributes tasks among CPUs, allowing those tasks to run somewhat independently of one another.

This clustering approach, as mentioned, dovetails with the ability of Windows NT Server to support as many as 32 CPUs. Furthermore, it is the direction in which Microsoft plans to move SQL Server, as well as NT Server as a whole. Microsoft intends to extend this reliance on a clustering methodology to automate the configuration, maintenance, and programming of databases. According to one of its recent white papers, Microsoft "plans to evolve Windows NT Server to support large processor and disk clusters."

What Is IDC? The **Internet Data Connector** (IDC) is another NT-based and IIS-related tool from Microsoft. Think of it as an HTML front end to ODBC. IDC, by means of an HTML file, directs SQL statements from remote clients to ODBC, which then passes them along to the appropriate DBMS.

IIS and an Intranet

Microsoft, in its Internet Information Server documentation, considers an intranet to be "any TCP/IP network that is not connected to the Internet but uses Internet communication standards and tools to provide information to users who can then . . . access information by using Web browsers." As already noted, intranets have a strong Web orientation, but one that nonetheless makes it clear that anything your NT/IIS server can do on the Internet, it can do on an internal network.

In the documentation, "any TCP/IP network that is not connected to the Internet" means that if your not-connected-to-the-Internet LAN relies on Ethernet cabling of whatever sort, and NICs of any variety, as its transmission media, it qualifies as an Intranet. It doesn't imply that TCP/IP is the only protocol suite your LAN may or does use.

In the phrase "uses Internet communications standards and tools" (also known as the above-mentioned Ethernet) Microsoft refers not only to hardware, but also to communications concepts such as packets, frames, routing, and so on.

See Appendix D for an overview of TCP/IP networking.

Internal FTP and Gopher

Although nothing in these technologies precludes their being used in an intranet, the nature of the services they provide (file transfer between client and server and file indexing and transfer offered by a server to its clients) is such that most intranets would not include them. Organizations most frequently use intranets as a means of distributing and gathering information that is meant to be accessible only within the organization. Such material can include company newsletters, sales figures, and benefits information.

Under such a scheme, people within the organization ordinarily access such items by means of a Web browser. It is unlikely that they would, therefore, need or want FTP or gopher services as well, at least for internal use alone.

Internal Webs

The purpose of an intranet is reflected not only in its being devoted almost exclusively to Webs but also in the formats in which those Webs deliver data to the user.

A Web server responds to a request for information submitted by a Web browser by returning an HTML page to the browser. Under IIS, the returned page can be one of three types:

- Static

- Dynamic

- Directory listing

Static Pages Static pages are HTML pages that are prepared in advance of the request for the information they contain. A Web server returns such pages to the user, but takes no further action of any kind.

Dynamic Pages Dynamic pages are created in response to a user's request and as the result of his or her having filled in a form of some kind. When the user clicks the appropriate button on the form, the data that had been entered there is sent to a Web server. This server either passes the data to a program to be processed or inquires of or manipulates a database, based upon the information provided through the form.

Whichever of these actions it takes, the presentation of dynamic Web information finishes with the results of the action being displayed to the user in an HTML page.

Directory-Listing Pages When no HTML document has been created as the default file presented by a given directory on a Web server, and directory browsing is configured for that server, a directory listing is returned to the user, who can then jump to the appropriate file by clicking its name in this listing. Under Internet Information Server, a directory listing consists of a hypertext version of a file listing such as might be produced by **My Computer**.

Internet Information Server and NT Server Tools

Access to Internet Information Server, like access to everything else under Windows NT Server 4.0, originates with the characteristics of user accounts as defined by **User Manager for Domains**. The distribution of material across a server's storage media must be done through **Server Manager**. To look at details of particular network events, such as, the failure of a driver to load, **Event Viewer** must be run. And to determine patterns and levels of usage of network components like the IIS services, **Performance Monitor** is called for.

The following sections examine these four NT Server tools in more detail.

User Manager

Chapter 1 presented the concepts under which User Manager functions, so we won't review those here. But we will make use of some examples from Chapter 1 in this exercise in working with User Manager by doing the following:

- Setting up the groups (Faculty, Gradstudents, Undergrads, and Support)

- Defining the areas of your NT Server 4.0's file system that each of these groups may use

- Defining any additional functions, such as printer management, that will be carried out by members of these groups

> **TIP** Only the Administrator can perform the User Manager functions unless you set up another user who has administrative privileges that allow him or her to do them.

Establishing a Domain

We defined a domain and its primary and backup controllers in the section on installation of NT Server. Making that domain a real-world, working realm within your network means adding workstation clients to it.

Workstations that can be part of an NT 4.0 domain and access any of its servers include those running Windows NT Workstation (4.0 and earlier versions), Windows 95, and Windows 3.x.

> **TIP** A workstation must of course be physically attached to the network before it can be made a member of a domain. The rest of this discussion assumes that you've attached the workstation to the network after installing and configuring the workstation-related software on the PC in question.

From the workstation, complete the following steps to add it to a domain:

1. Start Windows NT Workstation.

2. Click the Control Panel.

3. Start the Network tool (see Figure 3.2).

4. Select the **Identification** tab if it is not automatically displayed (it's the default; see Figure 3.3).

Figure 3.2 The Network Tool is your first stop on the way to assigning a workstation to a domain.

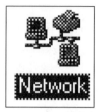

Figure 3.3 Clicking the Identification tab opens the dialog that you must use to assign a workstation to a domain.

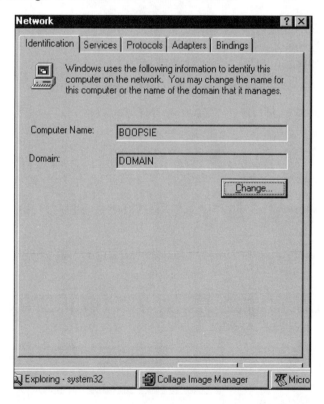

5. Open the Identification Changes dialog box and enter the name of the domain of which you wish to make the workstation a member.

6. In the same dialog box, select Create a Computer Account, enter your Administrator logon name and password, and click **OK**. Clicking OK sends the parameters you've specified to NT, as shown in Figure 3.4.

At this point, you should see a message welcoming you to the domain your workstation has just joined. You'll be instructed to restart the workstation. Once you do so, it will be ready to log into the domain with which you just associated it. In fact, the logon box for the workstation will show you the domain the workstation now belongs to and the workstation name as illustrated in Figure 3.5.

Nuances of NT Networking
The installation you just completed introduces some nuances of networking under NT.

We'll discuss these potentially thorny topics in more detail in Chapter 5 and simply identify them here: adding atypical network services, working with Server Manager, sharing network resources, and establishing trusts between domains.

Identifying a Windows 95 Client to NT Server
As was the case with an NT client, the work of making a Windows 95 client known to NT Server is done from the workstation. To do this:

1. Open the **Network** tool.

2. Click **Add**, which will open the **Select Network Component** dialog shown in Figure 3.6.

3. Select **Client** in this window.

Figure 3.4 After filling out all areas of the Identification Changes dialog, you're ready to submit the new information.

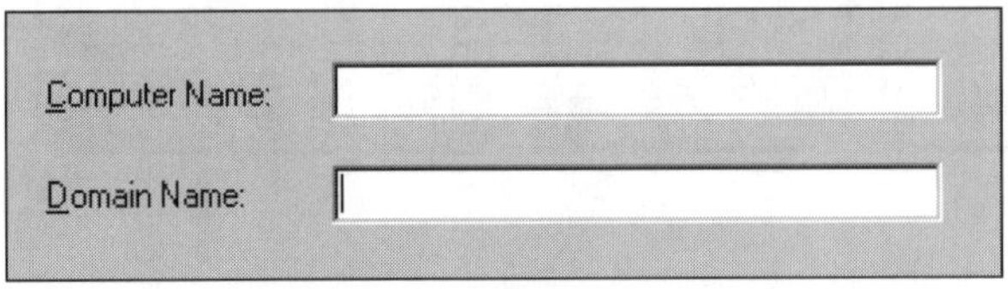

Computer Name:

Domain Name:

Figure 3.5 This Windows NT workstation is now ready to log on to the indicated domain.

Computer Name:	BOOPSIE
Domain Name:	DOMAIN

4. Click **Add**, which in turn produces the **Select Network Client** dialog box.

5. Select the appropriate client type, as well as the appellation **Client for Microsoft Networks,** the latter of which of course puts you in the NT ball-park.

6. Click **OK,** and you return to the **Network** page. From this window, you must select the **Identification** tab to continue the installation of this Windows 95 client on your NT network (see Figure 3.7).

7. In the **Computer Name** field of the **Identification** window, enter the name by which you wish this new station to be known on the network. Now, return to the **Network** window, select the **Configuration** tab, and then select **Properties.** Doing so will display the **Client for Microsoft Networks: Properties** dialog box shown in Figure 3.8.

Figure 3.6 Select Network Component allows you to specify the role a workstation will play.

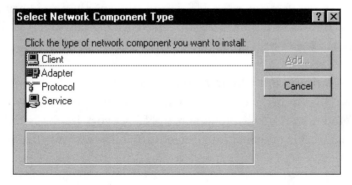

Figure 3.7 The Identification window assigns a name to the new workstation.

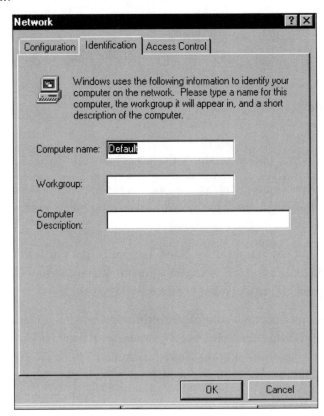

8. From the **Logon Validation** section of this new dialog, you can establish the workstation's ability to log on to an NT domain and specify that domain. After doing so, restarting the PC is the only step left in making the NT network accessible to this Windows 95 client.

Identifying a Windows 3.x Client to NT Server

Because Windows 3.1 was designed as a standalone operating system, making a client running Windows 3.1 a workstation on an NT network is a bit laborious. And despite the networking capabilities inherent in Windows for Workgroups,

Figure 3.8 This dialog is the core of the link between a Windows 95 workstation and an NT domain.

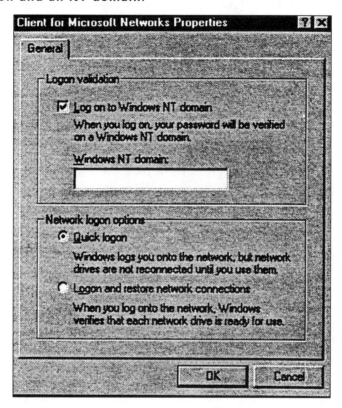

> **TIP** Save the client's current autoexec.bat, config.sys, protocol.ini, and system.ini files. These will be changed during the setting up of an NT client, whatever the *x* in that client's Windows 3.x.

associating a PC running this OS with an NT network is only slightly less so. We'll therefore look at these processes separately.

Putting a 3.1 Client on the Net This discussion assumes that, as part of your overall installation of Windows NT Server 4.0, you loaded workstation and client files. If you did not, use the tools made available by **Control Panel** (**Add/Remove Programs, Network,** and so on) to do so now.

To begin the installation of a Windows 3.1 client to your NT network, take the following path:

Start ---> Programs ---> **Administrative Tools** ---> Network Client Administrator

This series of selections will open the **Network Client Administrator** dialog, shown in Figure 3.9.

In this new box, select **Make Installation Disk Set** and click **Continue**. After that, you'll see the dialog Share Network **Client Installation Files**, as shown in Figure 3.10. From this box, you move to the dialog Network Client or Service, where you can select the client drivers that will be copied onto the diskettes you're preparing and loaded into the client-in-the-making.

Once the client installation disks are ready, move to the PC in question and put the machine in DOS mode. Insert the first of your install disks in an appropriate drive and start the setup program on that disk. Let this setup lead you through the configuration of the client. It'll seem like a snap after loading NT, and by and large it will be. But pay particular attention to:

- The name you assign to this station; it will be the PC's name on the NT network.

- Selecting the appropriate protocol to be used with this station; for some reason, the setup routine offers you the default protocol **IPX/SPX**, which doesn't make sense in the context of installing a Windows workstation. Deselect this default and highlight **NetBEUI** instead.

Figure 3.9 This NT Server dialog allows you to create installation disks, through which you transfer needed software to the 3.1-client-to-be.

Figure 3.10 Choose Network Client for DOS and Windows in the dialog that follows this one.

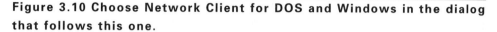

- The selection path **Change Logon Validation ---> Logon to Domain**; this set of choices is needed if you are to specify the domain to which this new station will connect.

Now go back to Windows, and navigate to the **Windows Setup** dialog. From there, take the selection path **Options ---> Change System Settings**. It will open the **Change Network Settings** dialog, shown in Figure 3.11.

Restarting Windows will make the changes you've just completed effective. To allow this client to connect to its new NT server, follow the selection path **File Manager ---> Disk ---> Network Connections**.

Putting a Workgroups (3.11) Client on the Net The process for putting a workgroups client on the Net is similar enough to that just outlined for Windows 3.1 clients that we need only note exceptions to it here:

1. When creating installation diskettes, choose TCP/IP 32 for Windows for Workgroups 3.11 (rather than Network Client for DOS).

Figure 3.11 Complete this dialog and you're nearly done setting up this client.

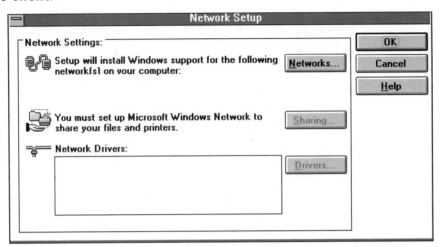

2. On the second install diskette, make the directories **\WIN** and **\SYSTEM.**

3. Copy **NET.EXE** and **NET.MSG** from the **\Clients\Update.WfW** folder of your NT server to the **\WIN** directory above.

4. Copy all other files in the client update path on your server to the **\SYSTEM** directory just mentioned.

5. Start Windows for Workgroups on the intended client and follow these selection paths:

   Network Setup ---> Networks ---> Install Microsoft Windows Network --->OK

   Network Setup ---> Drivers ---> Network Drivers ---> Add Adapter

6. Select the adapter installed in the client, and click **OK** to return to the **Network Drivers** box.

7. Select **Add Protocol** and double-click **Unlisted or Updated Protocol**. This last action will install the updated version of TCP/IP from the diskette.

Other than these, follow the prompts and use common sense to complete the installation of your Windows for Workgroups client.

Defining a Group

You have finished the grunt work of creating users under NT—configuring the clients from which those users will connect to your server. From here on, you'll use only NT tools, chiefly User Manager.

The first thing we'll do in User Manager is take a look at the built-in groups created automatically when NT Server 4.0 was loaded. To do that, take the path **Start ---> Programs ---> Administrative Tools ---> User Manager for Domains.**

Table 3.1 NT Groups and Their Characteristics

The Group	Is of the Category	And Can
Account Operators	Local	Use User Manager to create new groups and user accounts.
Administrators	Local	Carry out all domain management tasks.
Backup Operators	Local	Back up or restore on the domain's primary or backup controller.
Domain Administrators	Global, and a member, as a group, of the Administrators group	Carry out all domain management tasks, whatever the domain.
Domain Guests	Global, and a member, as a group, of the Guests group	Be used for accounts whose guest rights must be limited in some way.
Domain Users	Global, and a member, as a group, of the Users group	Log on, run applications, and use network services such as printing.
Guests	Local	Do not much more than log on and run specific applications.
Print Operators	Local	Create and manage printer sharing and log onto a server for the purpose of shutting it down.

Continued

Table 3.1 *Continued*

The Group	Is of the Category	And Can
Replicator	Local	Carry out folder replication.
Server Operators	Local	Manage a domain's controllers, whether primary or backup, as well as its standalone servers, if any.
Users	Local	Log on, run applications, and use network services such as printing.

> **TIP** Trying to decide between global and local? Simply make any group whose users must be able to access resources in more than one domain global groups. Groups that need use only their default domain's resources can be local.

At the bottom of the User Manager window, scroll through the list of groups User Manager offers. Doing so will present a display like that shown in Figure 3.12.

Table 3.1 outlines the characteristics of these built-in groups.

Adding Local Groups If, for whatever reason, these built-in NT groups don't meet your needs, you can create new local groups by doing the following:

1. Start the User Manager.

2. Pull down its User menu.

3. Select New Local Group.

4. In the resulting dialog box, type the required parameter Group Name. Any entry here can be no more than 20 characters.

5. If you care to, type a description for this group in the corresponding field.

Figure 3.12 Windows NT Server 4.0 has quite a few built-in user groups.

Domain Admins	Designated administrators of the domain
Domain Guests	All domain guests
Domain Users	All domain users
Guests	Users granted guest access to the computer/doma
Print Operators	Members can administer domain printers
PRNTR_TECH	Printer Technicians

Adding Global Groups To add a global group, do everything just discussed under "Adding Local Groups," except one. Rather than selecting **New Local Group** from the User menu, choose **New Global Group**.

> **TIP** Global groups and local groups have one very significant difference beyond the whereabouts of what they access: global groups can contain only users, but local groups can be made up of users and global groups.
>
> If this sounds confusing, consider that you may have a local group, such as the default **Print Operators**, whose members can do their group-related jobs only on the default domain. By first making such users members of a global group and then making that group a member of the local one, you enable these folks to configure and manage printers on any domain in your NT network.

Copying Groups A quick way to create new user groups is to copy the parameters that define an existing one, edit those parameters as needed to meet the new group, and create a new group name and description. Do all this through User Manager as follows:

1. Select the existing group, whether local or global, whose characteristics you wish to reproduce.

2. Select the path **User ---> Copy**.

3. Fill in the new group name and description in the **Add New ... Group** dialog, which is the next window to be displayed. (The exact title of this dialog will depend on whether the group whose attributes you're about to reproduce was local or global.)

> **POP QUIZ** At this point, you know enough about NT's methods of user and group management to deduce how to delete groups. So how do you do it? Answer at the end of this chapter; don't peek!

Deleting Groups Deleting groups is easy because no user, not even the Administrator, can delete NT Server 4.0's built-in user groups. Therefore, only groups you've created can be removed.

The Group Management Wizard For the fainthearted, NT Server 4.0 includes a **Wizard**, or **HTML-based tool**, that automates group management even beyond the degree we've already seen.

If you're at all conversant with any Windows applications, you've probably already played with other such tools, so we will say no more on this topic. But Figures 3.13 through 3.16 show you what the **Group Management Wizard** looks like.

Setting Up User Accounts

As was the case with groups, NT Server 4.0, during its installation, creates default user accounts. This time it creates only two, rather than the near-dozen default groups it set up. NT's default user accounts are **Administrator** and **Guest**.

Unless your network has a serious user deficiency, you'll probably have to establish more than these, as follows:

1. Take the path Start ---> **Programs** ---> **Administrative Tools** ---> **User Manager for Domains**.

2. Pull down the User menu.

3. Double-click (or otherwise activate) New User.

4. Respond to the resulting dialog box, illustrated in Figure 3.17, with information on:

   - User name; that is, the name by which the account you're establishing will access the NT server

   - Full name, the individual's real name

   - Description, an optional field that allows the user account to be further annotated

   - Password, for assigning a logon password to this new account

> **TIP** Don't leave these fields empty.
>
> NT Server 4.0 doesn't require you, as Administrator, to supply or confirm passwords for new users. Those users can create their own passwords during their first network session. However, such unshielded accounts are security problems begging to happen. Don't place your network in so vulnerable a position.

- Confirm password, to confirm the password just created

- User must change password at next logon, a checkbox that allows you to enforce the user's having to create his or her own password the first time the NT server is accessed

- User cannot change password, another checkbox; this one's self-explanatory

- Password never expires, the third checkbox in this dialog; also self-evident

- Account disabled, the dialog's final checkbox, which temporarily disables, but does not delete from the network, any user account for which it's been checked

> **TIP** Selecting the *user must change password* option has its own constraints. If you check this box, be sure to let the new user know immediately what his or her password has been set to.
>
> Also make sure he or she logs in and changes the password as soon as possible, in order to make that password meaningful to the user alone and to preclude the types of security problems hinted at already. This checkbox is checked by default when you enter User Manager.

Modifying User Accounts To change any of the characteristics of user accounts, including NT Server 4.0's default accounts, you need only take the following steps:

1. Start User Manager.

2. Pull down the list of users it offers.

3. Double-click, or simply highlight, and follow by pressing **Enter** or clicking **OK**, a specific user in that list.

4. Respond as desired to the User Properties dialog that is then displayed (see Figure 3.18).

Figure 3.13 The Group Management Wizard welcomes you ...

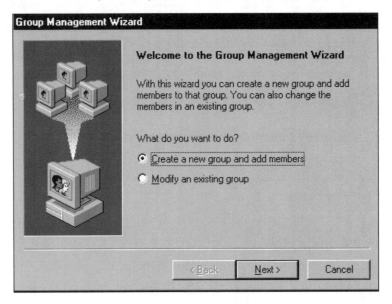

Figure 3.14 allows you, after the display of a few more dialogs, to decide between global and local groups ...

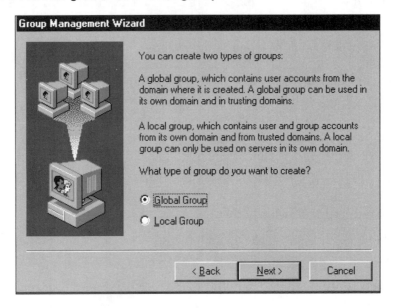

Figure 3.15 helps you to assign users to the group being created ...

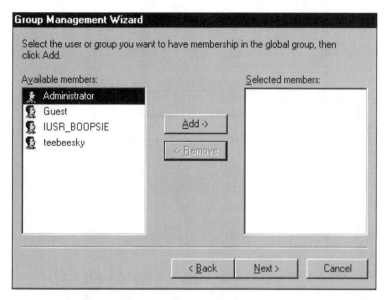

Figure 3.16 and confirms the new group you've set up.

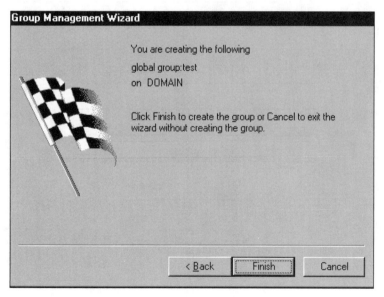

Figure 3.17 Here's a glance at a completed New User dialog box.

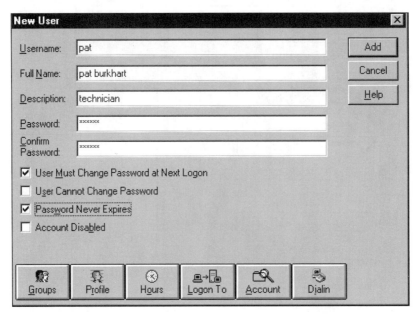

Figure 3.18 User Properties is the place to go to modify user accounts.

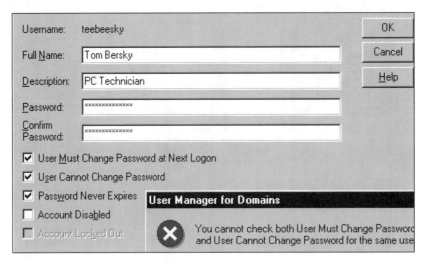

> ## Fooling NT Server
> If you examine Figure 3.18 closely, you'll see that we tried to fool NT.
>
> You'll also see that it didn't work. User manager would not allow us to execute, even though it did allow us to select, conflicting account options.

As was the case for modifying the characteristics of user accounts, associating those accounts with groups is a simple process. Just do the following:

1. Start User Manager.

2. Select a user account as previously described in **Modifying User Accounts**.

3. On the **User Properties** page for the selected account, click the **Groups** button at the lower left.

4. In the **Group Membership** dialog, the next window you see, you can add the account in question to a group, by highlighting the desired group in the list **Not Member Of** and clicking **Add.** To remove the account from a group, highlight the desired group in the list **Member Of** and click **Remove.**

Server Manager

The Server Manager administrative tool, new to the 4.0 release of Windows NT Server, allows you to view and modify a number of network parameters, including user connections to the network (that is, active user sessions); network resources in use, such as active printers; the replication of areas of the file system; and more.

Starting **Server Manager** by following the path **Start ---> Programs ---> Administrative Tools ---> Server Manager** displays the Server Manager window, shown in Figure 3.19.

Event Viewer

Atypical network happenings, such as unauthorized logon attempts, can be monitored through the **Event Viewer**, shown in Figure 3.20.

Figure 3.19 This window is your entry point into monitoring many of your server's resources.

Figure 3.20 Keep an eye on Event Viewer; it can alert you to problems in the making.

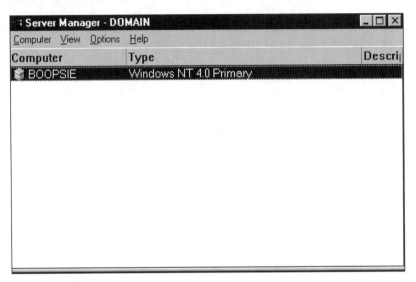

Server Manager - DOMAIN

Computer	Type	Descri
BOOPSIE	Windows NT 4.0 Primary	

Event Viewer - System Log on \\BOOPSIE

Date	Time	Source	Category	Event	User	Co
1/29/97	7:12:28 PM	BROWSER	None	8033	N/A	
1/29/97	7:12:28 PM	BROWSER	None	8033	N/A	
1/29/97	7:12:28 PM	BROWSER	None	8033	N/A	
1/29/97	7:02:14 PM	BROWSER	None	8015	N/A	
1/29/97	7:02:14 PM	BROWSER	None	8015	N/A	
1/29/97	7:02:14 PM	BROWSER	None	8015	N/A	
1/29/97	7:02:14 PM	BROWSER	None	8015	N/A	
1/29/97	7:00:18 PM	EventLog	None	6005	N/A	
1/29/97	7:01:15 PM	Nwlnklpx	None	9502	N/A	
1/28/97	1:54:46 AM	BROWSER	None	8033	N/A	
1/28/97	1:54:44 AM	BROWSER	None	8033	N/A	
1/28/97	1:54:44 AM	BROWSER	None	8033	N/A	
1/28/97	1:54:44 AM	BROWSER	None	8033	N/A	
1/28/97	1:52:54 AM	BROWSER	None	8015	N/A	
1/28/97	1:52:54 AM	BROWSER	None	8015	N/A	
1/28/97	1:52:54 AM	BROWSER	None	8015	N/A	
1/28/97	1:52:54 AM	BROWSER	None	8015	N/A	
1/28/97	1:50:59 AM	EventLog	None	6005	N/A	
1/28/97	1:52:04 AM	Nwlnklpx	None	9502	N/A	

Table 3.2 Event Viewer Parameters and What They Represent

The Event Parameter	Equates to
Source	The name of the piece of software that caused the event. Such names can include those of entire applications, or single drivers.
User	The user account active when the event occurred.
Category	A classification of the nature of the event. Can include Login and Logoff, Privilege Use, Object Access, and more.
Computer	The computer name, as defined to NT, of the station where the event took place.
Event	A number that uniquely identifies the event.
Type	Another classification of the event, which includes: Error Warning Success Audit Failure Audit

With **Event Viewer,** you can monitor many of the parameters of automatically recorded events. These parameters include the factors described in Table 3.2.

Event Viewer makes three default logs available: system, security, and applications. Each tracks events of the named category. For example, the applications log monitors requests by applications for the use of network resources such as printers. Under Event Viewer, you can tailor the way each of these logs operates. We'll learn more about that in Chapter 5.

Performance Monitor

The Performance Monitor NT administrative tool is particularly valuable in tracking and enhancing the performance of Internet Information Server. For instance, you might use Performance Monitor to automatically generate logs of usage of your IIS Web services.

Figure 3.21 Performance Monitor logs use of any NT services, including, in this example, Web services.

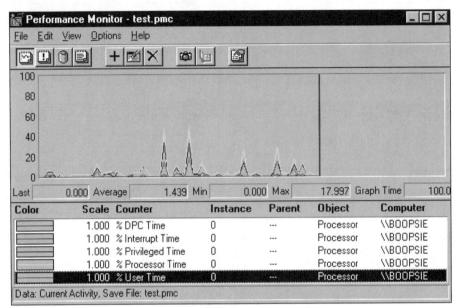

Such a log is illustrated in Figure 3.21. We'll discuss how this log was created in Chapter 5.

Internet Service Manager

From the simple window depicted in Figure 3.22, **Internet Service Manager**, the only significant management tool built into Internet Information Server, allows you to:

- Connect to a server

- Locate all servers on an NT network

- Start, stop, or pause a service

- Look at all installed Internet services, according to server, service, comment, and state

- Control access to your Internet services and log activity on those services

Figure 3.22 The default format for Internet Service Manager.

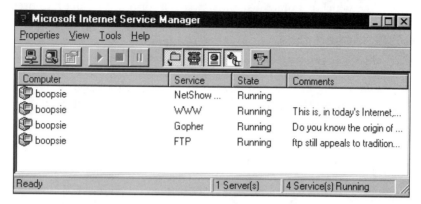

The Default ISM

Figure 3.22 is the form in which Internet Service Manager is ordinarily presented.

This default version of the tool cannot as easily view or manipulate Internet Information Server components that exist outside the default domain or somewhere

Figure 3.23 An Explorer becomes a Manager.

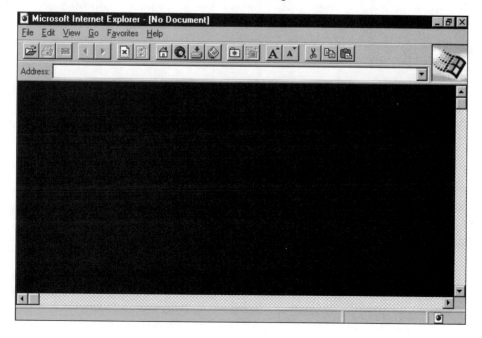

across the Internet. For that, you might want to use the HTML-based Internet Service Manager, which is in fact a slightly tweaked form of Internet Explorer.

The HTML-Based ISM

Figure 3.23 illustrates Internet Explorer in its reincarnation as Internet Service Manager.

You'll probably most frequently use this form of Internet Service Manager by pulling down the File menu, selecting Open, and filling into the resulting dialog box the **Uniform Resource Locator,** or **URL,** of the NT host to which you wish to connect and whose services you wish to manage or manipulate.

Services Under IIS

Whichever form of **Internet Service Manager** you come to rely upon, you'll use it to monitor and manage the features discussed in the remainder of this section.

> ## The Intricacies of HTML
>
> Most Web pages exist as **Hypertext Markup Language** (**HTML**) files—ASCII text files with codes that indicate formatting and hypertext links embedded in them. HTML specifications, like everything about the Web, change only slightly more slowly than the speed of light. This book doesn't address HTML questions, but if you'd like one that does, consider *HTML Sourcebook, Third Edition,* by Ian S. Graham, also published by Wiley.
>
> Any text editor can be used to create and edit HTML files, if you know the language well enough. But if the difference between **<input type=reset>** and **<onClick='JavScript1'>** is a mystery to you, you'll probably end up using one of the many HTML editors currently on the market.

Managing Web Services

When Internet Information Server is installed, NT places its World Wide Web services, installed unless you explicitly tell NT otherwise, into the default path under NT called **\Inetpub\WWWroot.**

Internet Information Server's Web services can distribute either information or applications, so your IIS Web site can include everything from strictly ASCII-text files to interactive documents. In addition, your users can, through these services, find, extract, or add information in databases.

Once you've HTMLed that part of your information base that you wish to present in linkable form, the initial configuration of your IIS Web site involves transferring its information base to the root Web directory or changing the default Web root directory to the one that already holds your Web-proffered information.

The Meaning of MIME

MIME, the standard for the format and naming of files that will be transferred across the Internet, was introduced in 1991, with the express purpose of being able to handle a wide variety of material.

More sophisticated Web-site configuration tasks include configuring **Multipurpose Internet Mail Extensions (MIME)** types. Among the many, many file types MIME makes provision for are those in Table 3.3. Another task is providing for adding information into HTML files before sending them to users (a process known as *includes*).

These Web service management jobs and more will be discussed in detail in Chapter 6.

Table 3.3 A MIME Sampler

MIME Recognizes the File Type	By the Extension
Plain text	.txt
HTML text	.htm *or* .html
GIF-format images	.gif
MPEG-format video	.mpeg *or* .mpg *or* .mpe
UNIX archives created with the *tar* command	.tar
Executable binary files	.exe *or* .bin
Macintosh archive files	.sit (which stands, so help us, for the word *stuffit*)

Managing FTP Services

FTP is the only Internet service by means of which files from a client computer can be copied to a server. Any remote users of your NT/IIS network who upload files to your server must use FTP to do so.

Because FTP has such a narrowly defined function, installing and maintaining it is similarly straightforward. Once it's been installed, you need only point the FTP service to the files you wish it to manage; no other setup is needed.

FTP can serve up files in any format, so you can use it to transfer to or receive document files, multimedia files, and even entire applications from remote clients.

What's more, any of your remote clients who use Internet Explorer can tell that application whether to download a file located for them by your FTP service or to start a helper application to view the file on the spot.

Setting up and administering FTP services under IIS 2.0 includes the following, all of which we'll cover in detail in Chapter 6:

- Configuring and viewing session activity

- Setting up and monitoring logons, including anonymous logons

- Configuring the FTP file subsystem

  - User directories

  - Anonymous directories

  - File permissions

- Using annotation files

- Setting up Wide Area Information System (WAIS) access

For now, just keep in mind that by default, all subdirectories under the root FTP directory are available to FTP users. So, in planning the distribution of files in that directory, take into account the types of information the files hold and any relationships among those types. For instance, in designing our fictitious domain **Academia**, we found that some material would need to be available to all users, while other information had relevance only to specific user groups. An FTP file subsystem for this domain might therefore look something like the one shown in Figure 3.24.

Figure 3.24 FTP files for Academia, distributed in subdirectories that correspond to user categories.

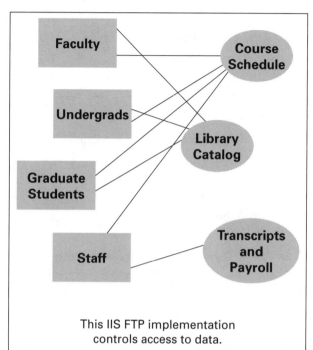

This IIS FTP implementation controls access to data.

Virtual Directories

IIS 2.0 lets you add virtual directories to your FTP file subsystem. This simply means that existing directories can be accessed under more than one name. But because of FTP's technical limitations, such virtual directories aren't readily available to users, who can browse them only if they know the virtual directory's alias. Given this restriction, you'll probably want to forgo this feature.

Managing Gopher Services

The gopher service of Internet Information Server 2.0 supports all common gopher features and, in addition, allows clients running the Gopher Plus utility to obtain additional information such as file modification date and MIME type.

Constructing an IIS-driven gopher site is similar to and as easy as configuring IIS FTP files. Initial gopher setup requires only that you copy the files that a service will make available to the root gopher directory \Inetpub\Gophroot.

Users can then browse Gophroot and its subdirectories with Windows 3.xx, by using File Manager; Windows 95, through Explorer; and under Windows NT Workstation, by means of Explorer.

The IIS 2.0 gopher service also allows you to employ what it calls **tag files**, which can be defined to do the following:

- Provide links to other computers

- Annotate gopher files and directories

- Create custom menus through which your users can navigate your gopher site

---

THE ANSWER TO THE POP QUIZ So, how *do* you delete groups? Here are the steps:

- Start the User Manager.

- Pull down User Manager's list of groups and select the name of the group you want to remove.

- Select User ---> Delete

- Respond appropriately to the resulting dialog.

Fully configuring the IIS gopher service, discussed in detail in Chapter 6, involves:

- Defining the directory or directories from which documents will be distributed and the specific files each directory will contain

- Creating any tags you plan to employ and outlining the purposes they will serve as well as how they are to be stored

- Mapping out indices, if these are to be used to speed up searches

- Configuring activity logs

- Setting connection parameters including the number of simultaneous connections allowed and the amount of time allowed for each connection, simultaneous or not

From Here

Later we will dig even deeper into using the tools just presented (we'll do that in Chapters 5 and 6). The next chapter examines relationships and interactions among those tools.

4

Nonstandard IIS
Installations

In this chapter, we consider some of the consequences for Internet services of nonstandard IIS installations. The particular scenarios we'll examine are implementing IIS on a network that includes both hard-wired and dial-up connections, implementing only the Web service of Internet Information Server, implementing a single file system for all installed IIS services, and implementing Internet Information Server on a heterogeneous network; that is, one in which both servers and clients are of a variety of hardware and operating systems.

IIS in a Dial-Up World

Providing dial-up access to your NT/IIS server implies more than extra users. Such access has as its corollary a greatly increased potential for security problems. In this section, we present examples of such problems and the actions you can take to preclude them. But first, we'll run down what must be done to add dial-up access and networking to Windows NT Server 4.0 and Internet Information Server 2.0.

Adding Dial-Up Access
Allowing a dial-up connection to your NT/IIS server, whether that connection passes through an intranet or taps into an Internet site, means updating NT Server itself.

> **TIP** You may already have dial-up access available.
>
> If, when you loaded NT Server 4.0 initially, you selected both network types that the Setup program made available to you, you've already configured modems and dial-up networking and can proceed to the section "Configuring Internet Information Server to Handle Dial-up Networking."

Adding Modems

To begin, let's review the categories of connectivity devices for which Windows NT Server 4.0 provides drivers or for which it will accept manufacturer-supplied drivers.

NT Server 4.0 can converse with and through the types of devices detailed in Table 4.1.

Table 4.1 Modems and "Super-Modems" Under NT Server 4.0 Device Category

Device	Number Possible on an NT Server	NT 4.0 Supplies Drivers?	NT 4.0 Will Accept Third-Party Drivers?
Internal modems	Equal to the combined number of free **Industry Standard Architecture (ISA)** card slots and free **Interrupt Requests (IRQs)**; a possible total of four	Yes	Yes
External modems	Equal to the combined number of free ISA card slots and free IRQs; a possible total of four	Yes	Yes
Multiport cards	Available in four- and eight-port versions, either of which occupies only a single PC slot	No	Yes
ISDN adapters	Internal or external	Yes (a specialized driver)	Yes
ISDN "multi-adapters"	Internal or external; in effect, the ISDN incarnation of multiport cards	No	Yes

Figure 4.1 NT Server can autodetect a modem or allow you to pick one from a list.

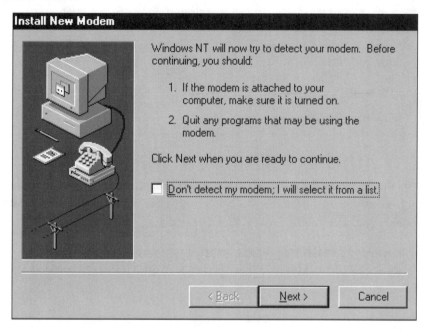

To install any of these devices, follow these steps:

1. Physically install the connectivity device, of course.

2. In NT Server, start **Control Panel** and from it, the **Modem** tool. You'll then see either the **Install New Modem** dialog (if this is the first modem you're identifying to NT Server) or the **Modem Properties** page, whose **Add** button you must then click to bring up the **Install New Modem** dialog.

3. Select a modem model by either of the means NT offers: autodetection or picking from a list (see Figure 4.1).

4. Identify a COM port for the modem.

Setting Up Dial-Up Networking

Now that NT Server knows about its modem or modems, here's how to tell it about how those modems will be used:

> **TIP** NT leads you easily through installing connectivity devices. But if you'd like to fine-tune those devices' operations, you can use the Modem tool and Properties page mentioned above to set such characteristics as:
>
> • Number of data bits
>
> • Presence or absence of parity and type of parity to be used
>
> • Maximum transmission rate

1. Choose Remote Access from Control Panel.

2. Start the Remote Access Setup dialog and highlight the modem whose operating parameters you wish to define to NT Server. Then click **Configure**. Doing that presents you with the Configure Port Usage dialog, shown in Figure 4.2.

3. After returning to **Remote Access Setup**, illustrated in Figure 4.3, click **Network**. The next thing you'll see is the **Network Configuration** dialog, shown in Figure 4.4.

> **TIP** Make sure passwords are secure.
>
> For securing password authentication, your best bet is to choose **Require Encrypted Authentication** from the dialog shown in Figure 4.4; it is independent of workstation operating system.

Figure 4.2 The default for this dialog is *Receive Calls Only*.

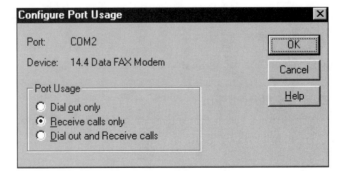

Figure 4.3 Remote Access Setup and Network Configuration work in tandem.

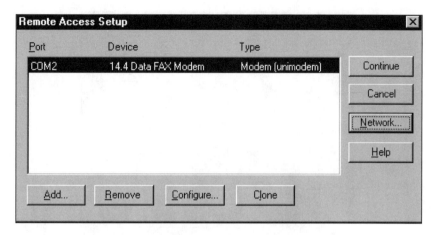

To identify remote users to NT, another tool is called for.

Take the path **Start** ---> **Programs** ---> **Administrative Tools** ---> **Remote Access Administration.** Then proceed as follows:

1. Pull down the **User** menu.

2. Click **Permissions** to display the **Remote Access Permissions** dialog.

3. Select a user from the offered list.

4. Check the Grant Dialin Permission to User box.

TIP Remote users must be users first. That is, remote access capabilities can be assigned only to existing NT user accounts. If you need to allow for the equivalent on your network of an anonymous remote session, you can do so by adding dialin permission to the default Guest account.

Configuring Remote Clients

The process to configure remote clients is quite similar to that described in Chapter 3 for setting up NT clients in general. Refer to Chapter 3 and to workstation operating system documentation for further details on the client-side aspects of setting up remote access.

Figure 4.4 Select and configure the network types appropriate to your environment.

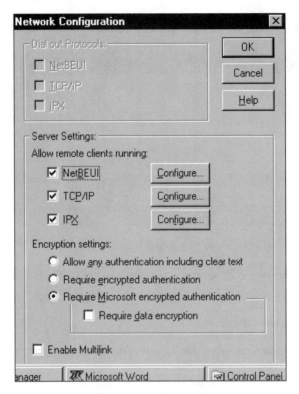

Configuring Internet Information Server to Interact with Dial-Up Networking

Inherent in Web services is the fact that access to them is essentially anonymous. When was the last time, for instance, that you had to supply a password to your browser of choice before being able to open a Web page?

If you've established remote access capabilities on your NT server, you'll have to reconfigure Internet Information Server to set up or deny anonymous access and to provide security for any password attached to such access.

Start by opening **Internet Service Manager**, with the path **Start ---> Programs ---> Internet Information Server ---> Internet Service Manager**.

Open the **Web Services Properties** page, shown in Figure 4.5, by double-clicking the **WWW** icon. Then fill out the **Anonymous Logon** and **Password Authentication** sections of this dialog as appropriate to your needs. The ramifications of the choices available to you are described in Table 4.2.

T I P Basic file access permissions still count.

If, for instance, you've defined **\Inetpub\WWWroot** and its subdirectories in such a way as to deny access to that file system to users in a given group, a user who is signed onto NT Server as a member of that group will, upon attempting to access a Web page, be denied such access, be prompted for a re-entry of user name and password, and be allowed or denied access to the IIS Web based upon the entries made in response to this prompt.

This will happen even if the user in question is using Internet Explorer.

Table 4.2 The Effects on IIS of Remote Access Profiles

Enabling the Feature	Disabling the Feature	Causes IIS to
Allow Anonymous in the **Password Authentication** section of the WWW properties page		Allow anonymous access to its Web services, through the automatically created anonymous user account **IUSR**, defined when IIS was installed, and for which NT Server creates, with each anonymous logon, a random string that serves as a password.
	Allow Anonymous	Require anyone, whether local or remote user, to have an account and explicit password under NT Server before granting access to the Web it distributes.
Basic (Clear Text) in the **Password Authentication** section of the WWW Properties page		Allows IIS to accept requests from non-Microsoft browsers. Browsers such as **Netscape** use a different method of password authentication than does **Microsoft Internet Explorer**. Checking this box is the only way users running other browsers will be able to access your IIS Web.

Continued

Table 4.2 *Continued*

Enabling the Feature	Disabling the Feature	Causes IIS to
	Basic (Clear Text)	In effect, hides your IIS Web from any browser other than **Internet Explorer**.
Windows NT Challenge/Response		Deny access to its Web to users who have not explicitly been given that access by being given appropriate file and directory permissions.
	Windows NT Challenge/ Response	Disregard NT Server file and directory access permissions in granting access to its Web.

Figure 4.5 The WWW Properties page.

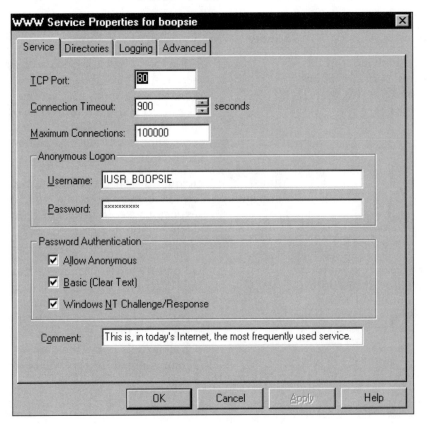

IIS as a Web Server Only

You probably recall, from the discussion in Chapter 3 of the types of data that Internet Information Server's FTP and gopher services can handle, that these seem indistinguishable from what its Web services offer. All IIS services can distribute files whose contents range from multimedia to text; the nature of the distribution makes up the difference between these services.

Given this fact, and the preponderance of users who can click effectively over those who can execute an FTP command with ease, it's worth considering making your IIS installation strictly a Web server.

By default, all three basic IIS services—World Wide Web, FTP, and gopher—are loaded along with IIS. If you have installed 2.0 and later wish to convert to a Web-only environment, take the following steps:

1. Move any intended-for-users information (as opposed to NT program files) stored under \Inetpub\FTProot, or under \Inetpub\Gophroot to the root Web directory **\Inetpub\WWWroot**.

2. Put the NT Server 4.0 distribution CD in the appropriate drive. Then either start **Control Panel** and open the **Add/Remove Programs** tool, select the **Windows NT Setup** tab, and start the reconfiguration of IIS by checking **Add/Remove Components**, or follow the path **Start ---> Programs ---> Microsoft Internet Information Server ---> Internet Information Server Setup**.

3. Navigate to the dialog box that displays the list of Internet Information Server components; clear the checkboxes for the FTP and gopher services (and any others already installed that you wish to remove).

4. Navigate to the end of the reconfiguration dialogs.

5. Through **User Manager**, modify as appropriate the file and directory access permissions of any information you moved from the now-nonexistent FTP and gopher file subsystems to the IIS Web subsystem.

> **TIP** Be careful about removing the ODBC service. Doing so would preclude your offering interactive database access to your users.

> ## The More Things Change ...
> The points made in the section "Configuring Internet Information Server to Interact with Dial-Up Networking" still apply, even in the case of a Web-only IIS implementation.

> **TIP** You can't upload without FTP. Keep this in mind, too, when mulling over the prospect of a strictly Web Internet Information Server.

IIS with a Single File System

A variation of the Web-only model of IIS just presented is to configure for additional services, but to house those services and the information they distribute in a single file system.

If you're asking yourself "What does this buy me?" consider the following:

- Dealing with a single IIS file system makes your job of assigning file and directory access through User Manager simpler.

- Establishing only one such system results in better access time and throughout for users, whether local or remote.

- Having only one IIS-related file system solves or at least clarifies many backup and disk redundancy problems.

- A single IIS file system can help streamline administrative tasks such as logging and performance monitoring.

But a monolithic Internet Information Server has its drawbacks as well. If you plan to house all three basic services in a single file system, plan the file subsystem carefully. Figure 4.6 illustrates one possible such system.

Also, check, double-check, and triple-check before checking one last time the information to be distributed by each service, because this information will be housed in a tree of subdirectories that are not as clearly set off from one another as are those of a default IIS implementation. Duplicating or misplacing files in a monolithic IIS file system would negate many of the benefits, such as improved access time, that you're attempting to establish along with that system.

If you're convinced that a single file system is the optimum storage design for your Internet Information Server, do the following to implement that design:

Figure 4.6 A Monolithic IIS File System. In this single-root IIS file system no subdirectories separate one type of content from another.

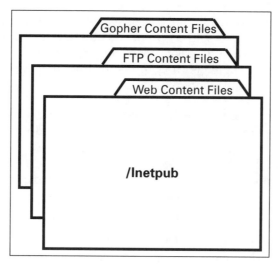

1. Put the NT Server 4.0 distribution CD in the appropriate drive.

2. By whatever means you prefer, open the **Microsoft Internet Information Server 2.0 Setup** dialog.

3. Check-select all the services you wish to make available.

4. In the **Publishing Directories** dialog, which is the next thing you'll see, enter the same directory path for all services to be installed.

5. After the reinstallation of IIS completes, move to **Disk Manager,** to create the information subdirectories you sketched out as described above and relocate to the appropriate subdirectories of the IIS monolith individual information files.

6. After finishing this construction of the IIS file system, move to **User Manager** to assign file and directory access permissions for the new file system.

IIS on Heterogeneous Networks

Networks, like so many things, evolve as much as they arise through design. Most networks have some degree of heterogeneity, certainly in their workstations and possibly in their servers as well.

> **TIP** There's a minimum required, whatever the nature of your IIS file system.
>
> In order to provide enough free disk space for that system—which, of course, in addition to the IIS program and other system files may include not only text and a relatively miserly storage hit, but also images and sound, both disk hogs—be prepared to allow at least half a gigabyte (yes, 500MB or more) to IIS.
>
> This amount isn't as grand as it might at first sound. A complete IIS 2.0 installation requires 4MB itself. A single Web page, adorned with hyper-links, graphics, and photo reproductions, could take up another 4 or 5MB. Consider that Web (and other Internet-offered) information tends to breed extremely fast.

One need only review the types of client operating systems that can connect with Windows NT Server 4.0 to realize the implications of heterogeneity for Internet Information Server. The following is only a partial list of such systems:

- Windows NT Workstation
- Windows 95
- Windows for Workgroups
- Windows 3.1
- NetWare
- Banyan Vines

Consider further that NT Server 4.0 can live comfortably on a number of hardware platforms—among them RISC-based machines and DEC Alphas—and you'll realize that you must configure the ability to deal with heterogeneity into Internet Information Server.

To do that, return to NT and, more specifically, to its reliance on domains. Like all members of the integrated NT Server 4.0 suite of software, Internet Information Server and its BackOffice partners rely completely on NT domains for security measures such as user authentication.

The remainder of this section examines the models NT's designers and programmers followed in constructing 4.0's system of domains and applies each of those models to a networking scenario, centering on the effects of the domain model on Internet Information Server configuration. It also examines the implications of those models for Internet Information Server.

Microsoft's Domain Models for NT 4.0

The first model for NT Server domains is the simplest and probably the most widely applicable. It is called the **Single Domain Model**.

Single Domain NT Networks

Microsoft recommends the single domain model for environments with:

- No more than 5000 end users

- Centralized network administration

- A relatively homogeneous information and application base

Such environments can be adequately served by a single domain. What's more, single domains simplify network management because they entail only one account- and resource-tracking database.

The Registry as Operations Database
Windows NT Server 4.0's Registry contains all information needed for the functioning of not only the operating system itself, but also of applications installed to it. The Registry also records user logon names, passwords, and access permissions.

An example of a single domain scenario is TBs Are Us, an up-and-coming chain of specialty toy stores. TBs Are Us, which carries nothing but every imaginable variety of teddy bears, has its corporate headquarters in Glen Mills, Pennsylvania. At that central office, it has 47 employees, 28 of whom have accounts on its NT Server 4.0-based LAN.

Partially because of its unexpectedly rapid growth, TBs Are Us has, on that LAN, workstations of several flavors, but only a few applications and fewer hardware resources. Therefore, it demonstrates the homogeneity of services, if not of hardware platforms, that the single domain model presupposes.

The Single Master Domain Model

The single master domain variation of the single domain provides a single master domain to which all user and group information pertains, and to which all users log on. It also provides as many resource domains as are needed, in which network resources such as files, applications, and hardware are grouped, but to which users do not connect.

As you might imagine, the single master model for domains is most applicable to environments in which:

- The critical mass of 5000 users has been closely approached if not exceeded.

- A wide variety of applications and data must be distributed.

- A similarly broad spectrum of hardware resources must be made available.

Under the single master domain model, users can access network resources, without having to log on to the domains containing those resources, because a **trust relationship** has been established between the domains. This name is quite descriptive. In a trust relationship, users from the **trusting domain** (yes, Microsoft really does use just these words to depict the situation)—that is, who seek to use resources outside the domain to which they've connected and on which they have accounts—can access such resources on a **trusted domain**.

An example of a single master domain scenario comes from Concordville Community College (CCC). This two-year school specializes in preparing its students for careers in high-tech fields or for transfer to four-year college programs in such fields. For this reason, it considers its computer labs to be among its most important facilities.

Those labs, each of which resides in a separate building, run under the NT 4.0 Single Master Domain model, as illustrated in Figure 4.7.

Although its student body usually numbers no more than 2000, CCC has a large faculty-to-student ratio as well as an extensive support staff. Together, these three categories of users give it a total network population of about 4000. Though this is significantly lower than that for which Microsoft recommends the single domain model, CCC chose single master instead because this latter model allowed it to distribute and better manage its student tools, such as the following:

- Programming environments

- CAD systems

Figure 4.7 Concordville Community College uses NT's Single Master Domain model.

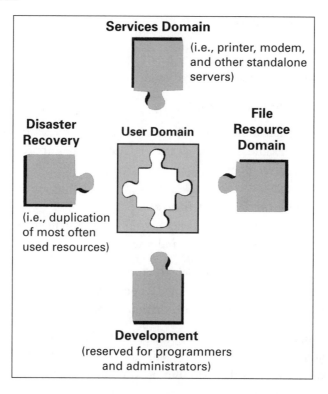

- Word processing applications

- Database applications

- Library resources, including full text online

   The single master model also allowed CCC to distribute and better manage its faculty tools, such as:

- Word processing applications

- Database applications

- FAX and modem services

- Internet research tools

The model also allowed the school to distribute and better manage staff tools, such as:

- Word processing applications

- Fax and modem services

- Spreadsheet and financial applications

- Modeling and planning packages

The network administrators at CCC set up domains for each of the above categories of applications and constructed trust relationships as appropriate from user groups to these resource domains.

The Multiple Master Domain Model

The multiple master domain model was envisioned for use in environments which combine a very large user population and a wide range of networked resources.

The multiple master domain model structures an NT network into multiple domains, each of which contains as equal as possible a share of both the network's user accounts and its physical and information resources.

Under the multiple master domain model, trust relationships are two-way. That is, users in either member of a trusting pair can not only access resources in but log on to the other member of that pair. But not all domains set up under the multiple master domain model must be members of a trusting pair.

Our example of a multiple master domain scenario is Kulicke & Soffa (K & S) Industries. This company, a major manufacturer of computer-based semiconductor manufacturing equipment, employs over 9000 people worldwide, among them nearly 3500 engineers and designers. K & S has therefore designed its intranet around the multiple master domain model for Windows NT Server 4.0, as shown in Figure 4.8.

The Complete Trust Model

At first glance, the complete trust model looks identical to the multiple master domain model, but the two differ in one significant way. All domains under the complete trust model take part in a two-way trusting relationship with all other domains.

Figure 4.8 K & S implements a Multiple Master Domain net.

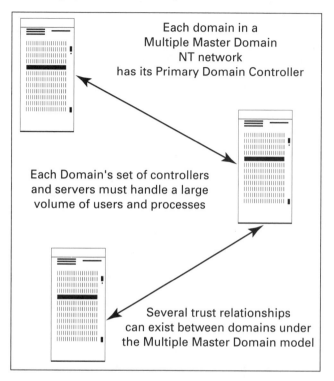

Each domain in a
Multiple Master Domain
NT network
has its Primary Domain Controller

Each Domain's set of controllers
and servers must handle a large
volume of users and processes

Several trust relationships
can exist between domains under
the Multiple Master Domain model

Under the Complete Trust model, every user can access every domain and its resources.

An example of the complete trust scenario is PA MultiList. This professional association of all Realtors in the state of Pennsylvania built its **Wide Area Network (WAN)** from the NT 4.0-based LANs of its members. Figure 4.9 sketches this WAN.

Domain Models and Internet Information Server

The scenarios just described represent a bridge between the concept of domains and the structure and features of IIS 2.0. Table 4.3, although it doesn't present the specific tools needed to configure domains so as to support Internet Information Server in heterogeneous environments, does at least begin that process. We discuss the tools involved—most applicable among them, NT Server's **User Manager**—in Chapter 5.

Figure 4.9 PA MultiList needed the all-to-all trusting relationship of the complete trust model.

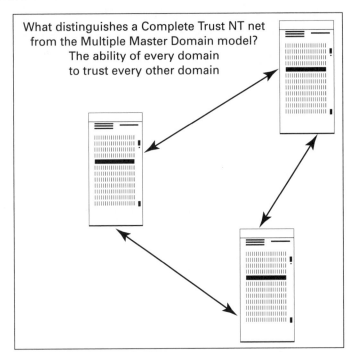

What distinguishes a Complete Trust NT net from the Multiple Master Domain model? The ability of every domain to trust every other domain

Table 4.3 Domain Models' Suitability for Varied IIS Environments

Domain Model	Applicable to
Single Domain	IIS implementations that must offer any or all of the basic services but that must serve only a limited user population.
Single Master Domain	IIS implementations that, although encompassing a relatively limited user population, must rely on a variety of hardware resources.
	IIS implementations that possess a relatively small user base and a largely homogeneous hardware base but that must distribute a wide variety of software and information.

Table 4.3 *Continued*

Domain Model	Applicable to
Multiple Master Domain	IIS implementations that must present a wide variety of physical, software, and information resources to a large user population. This population can, however, be broken down into groups according to which network resources users need.
Complete Trust Model	IIS implementations that must present a wide variety of physical, software, and information resources to every member of a large user population.

From Here

Chapter 5 provides detailed examples of uses for NT-based administrative tools. Chapter 6 does the same for IIS-based management tools.

Enhancing IIS with
NT-Based Tools

At this point, we've introduced all the tools, NT- and IIS-based, that you'll need to administer your IIS site. In this chapter, we pull out the following equipment from the NT toolbox:

- Domain management

- Group management

- User management

- File system management

- Performance management

We probe all these by putting two real-world environments—Kulicke & Soffa Industries and Delaware County Community College—under the microscope, in effect fine-tuning, if only on paper, NT LANs for each of these.

Profiles of the Environments

This chapter presents two NT LAN management scenarios. Each of these pertains to one of Microsoft's domain models. We've chosen Kulicke & Soffa Industries, the research and development arm of a semiconductor manufacturing equipment design and production firm, as the case study of a single domain network.

Delaware County Community College, a large academic institution, represents the means by which we dissect the multiple master domain template.

Kulicke & Soffa Industries

Kulicke & Soffa Industries (K & S), considered by many to be the world leader among producers of semiconductor manufacturing equipment, has its corporate headquarters in Willow Grove, Pennsylvania. At that site, it maintains an intranet that encompasses:

- An extensive Novell LAN, serving support and management staff

- An equally ample TCP/IP—Ethernet—UNIX net, made up of numerous Sun Microsystems SPARCstations and a variety of other UNIX stations, some of which (particularly those acting as testbeds) run a real-time flavor of UNIX that isn't always friendly to canned UNIX-compatible software

- A middle ground of PCs under Windows 3.11, which can connect to either of these networks

Managers at K & S have, for some time, considered establishing an intranet server and set of services that would traverse this heterogeneous software and hardware landscape. They hope to come up with a single configuration that will:

- Connect to and converse with all the OSs and NOSs just mentioned.

- Allow access to anyone with a valid account on any of its LANs by means of any Web browser to all information that must be distributed companywide.

- Allow access by engineers and developers to corporate product specifications, libraries of software and data used in ongoing product development, and test specifications and results.

Finally, the folks at K & S anticipate an intranet that will provide for the data, and to a lesser extent the application, needs of about 2500 users, in the following categories:

- Software product support engineers

- Hardware product support engineers

- Software product development engineers

- Technical managers

- Business managers

- Sales staff

- Support staff

This list of networking needs looks much like a single domain waiting to be born. Given the combination of a relatively limited number and variety of users, and the breadth and nature of the information base just described, it's quite reasonable to suppose that K & S can meet its intranet needs with a single domain rendering of Windows NT Server 4.0 and Internet Information Server 2.0.

Delaware County Community College

Referred to by many of its students as DC³, Delaware County Community College in southeast Pennsylvania has a student body of more than 10,000 on an ongoing basis, employs over 2000 full- and part-time personnel, and is distributed among six campuses. It offers a curriculum that spans 27 disciplines and makes available five types of degrees or certificates. On two distinct networks, the college maintains several hundred pieces of data processing hardware and several dozen applications, and it provides access to **Wide Area Information Services** (**WAIS**) and the Internet from several points within *each* of its networks.

Given this breadth of services and number and variety of users, DCCC is a good candidate for IIS under the Multiple Master Domain model.

Domain Management

As we've seen, NT Server 4.0 prefers to have *domains defined when the NOS is installed*. However, NT does permit the following domain management activities to take place at any time:

- Working with client stations on a domain

- Adding, deleting, or modifying domain controllers

- Establishing and administering domain-wide account policies

- Working with the **Security Account Manager,** the NT Server subsystem that oversees and manipulates NT's database of user accounts and passwords

- Attaching resources to a domain

- Setting up trust relationships between domains

- Miscellaneous tasks such as setting the speed at which clients connect to a domain, defining which portion of a domain dial-up users may access, and renaming a domain

> ## IIS Dependence on Domains
> It's worth repeating: IIS leans very heavily on domains. Most Internet Information Server configuration and management tasks are actually carried out through NT Server.

The following sections examine each of these domain-related tasks in the context of the two real-world environments we've outlined.

Management of a Single Domain

The Kulicke & Soffa implementation of Internet Information Server has only one Registry, or database of resources, one database of user and group membership and authentication information, and one primary controller. Therefore, relying as it does on the Single Domain model, the server presents no unusual situations or thorny problems.

Working with Clients

Any client station running Windows NT Workstation 4.0 receives a machine account when it is identified to Windows NT Server 4.0. This account, or **Security Identification (SID)**, is a unique number that NT 4.0 associates with the computer name of the client and makes known to all controllers on the domain, whether primary or secondary, so that they can respond to requests from any user who logs on to the domain at this client. NT 4.0 uses this unique number as an additional level of user authorization security.

A client station operating under any other OS, including Microsoft systems of all stripes, does *not* receive a machine account. Rather, such clients rely strictly on the user ID of the current session and its verification against the Registry for user-level security.

In Chapter 3, we learned the basics of associating client stations with NT Server 4.0. To recap, whatever the native operating system of the client, that includes:

- Opening a **Network** tool or dialog

- Indicating that you wish to add a component

- Indicating that you wish to add a client workstation

- Defining a computer name for the station

- Defining the networking characteristics of the station, such as protocols and network interface cards (NICs)

- Setting out login parameters for the station

In this section, we deal with a more subtle aspect of domain/client interaction, very much present at K & S: configuring what might be called nonstandard clients.

> **TIP**   Keep in mind that users in NT log on to domains, not machines.

NetWare Services Under NT 4.0   Under its out-of-the-box install of NT Server 4.0, NetWare clients at K & S *cannot* access that server. **Gateway and Client Services for NetWare**, which, like all NT 4.0 network services, can be installed with the NOS or added later, allow the opposite of what the name suggests. These services permit computers on an NT LAN to access services on a Novell net.

To accomplish the converse, Kulicke & Soffa must:

- Install the **NWLink**, or IPX/SPX-compliant, transport protocol, on its NT 4.0 server.

- Acquire from Microsoft, for about $100, a set of utilities called **File and Print Services for NetWare** and install those utilities.

- Acquire from Microsoft, for about $100, another utilities suite called **Directory Service Manager for NetWare** and install it.

If it hadn't been loaded with the initial installation of NT 4.0, the first of these three tasks would require using the **Network** tool in much the same manner as described below. Luckily, NWLink already exists on the K & S NT net. Luckily again, both of the two remaining software sets can be installed by the same method:

1. Open the **Network** tool, either from the **control panel** or by clicking the startup Network Neighborhood icon. Then click the **Services** tab.

2. Click the **Add** button at the lower left of the **Network Services** window.

3. From the **Select Network Services** box, click **Have Disk**.

4. When you are prompted, insert the disk in question and enter the full path name for the suite you're installing.

5. After completing this set of entries, choose the name of the utility set you wish to install from the list NT presents you, and either click **OK** or press **Enter** to cause 4.0 to copy the needed files from the distribution medium.

Once those files are copied, you'll see yet another dialog, this one called **Install [the name of the utility set] for NetWare.**

The first of these dialogs, and its subwindows, request the following parameters of you:

- Directory for **SYS** volume. Take the default of C:\SYSVOL that NT offers. Any Novell LAN will like this.

- Server name. NT offers a good default: **SERVER_NAME_FPNW**. Accept this value; if you enter another, you'll have to be sure the name used has nothing in common with the computer name you assigned to the server when creating your single domain.

- Password. This refers to the password for the Supervisor account on the NetWare server. You, as administrator of the entire domain, need to have access to that password.

- Minimize memory usage. This optional parameter allows you to minimize the amount of memory to be used by the NT server that will communicate with Novell. Checking this option frees up memory for use by other NT-based applications, but can slow throughput for the **File and Print Services for NetWare.**

- Balance between memory usage performance. This parameter splits the difference, so to speak, between the memory demands of NT-based applications and of **File and Print Services for NetWare.**

- Maximize performance. Choosing this option means that **File and Print Services for NetWare** will get first call on the NT server's memory—of course

> **TIP** Installing the Directory Service Manager for NetWare is not this complex.
>
> Unlike **File and Print Services** installation, loading the **Directory Service Manager** entails none of the above parameters' being supplied. Nor does **Directory Service Manager**'s setup carry with it the need to deal with connectivity questions, as does that of **File and Print Services**.
>
> To use the **NWLink IPX/SPX** dialog to configure the connections under which **File and Print Services for NetWare** will run, simply type an internal network number from the Novell side and specify appropriate parameters for every NIC through which **File and Print Services for NetWare** will be accessed—that is, for the NICs on the NetWare clients in question.

at the expense of the performance of any other applications that server might be running.

- Password. In the secondary password-related dialog you must enter and confirm, not the NetWare server password, but rather the password that will be employed by users to access **File and Print Services for NetWare.**

> **TIP** If the Novell LAN whose file and print services you're trying to offer to your NT users has been properly configured and managed, these parameters should be available from the manager of that LAN.

> ## Other Client Drivers from NT
> NT Server 4.0 provides other client drivers.
>
> These drivers, such as the one for Banyan Vines, can, like most of NT's network services, be copied to your server when it is initially loaded or added later during an upgrade of your 4.0 installation.

Adding Other Network Services In as heterogeneous an environment as Kulicke & Soffa's, it's not surprising that the need for other network services exists. The following five services were added after the initial load of NT Server 4.0, through use of the **Network** tool as described in the section "NetWare Services Under NT 4.0":

- **DHCP Server.** The people at K & S realized that their new IIS-based intranet would quickly begin to experience a **turnpike effect,** or rapid growth in the number of users and rate of usage. As part of their planning for this effect, the LAN administrators at K & S loaded NT's **DHCP Server.** Subsequently, this service kicked in during periods of high turnover in user sessions to dynamically assign, from a predetermined pool, IP addresses to clients. The name of this server of course derives from the name of the protocol that provides this ability to assign Internet addresses on the fly. That is, this server is in effect an interface to the **Dynamic Host Configuration Protocol.**

- **DNS Server.** The **Domain Name Server** and its alter ego, the **Windows Internet Naming Server** discussed below, are particularly important to any IIS implementation that includes the gopher service. Because K & S must provide its designers and engineers with desktop access to timely information such as test results and lab notes, it has included the gopher service in its IIS Intranet and therefore must install either **DNS** or **WINS.** Doing that involves not only using the Network tool and its **Select Network Services** dialog, but also specifying the domain from which **DNS** or **WINS** will run, as follows:

1. Select the **Protocols** tab of the **Network** tool.

2. Open the **TCP/IP Properties** dialog, shown in Figure 5.1, by double-clicking **TCP/IP** in the **Network Protocols** list of the **Protocols** window.

3. From the **TCP/IP** page, open the **DNS** dialog. In this dialog, you'll see the name by which your server is known on the internal network. You must supply a domain name within that network in the **Domain** field of the same window. Then, click **Add** to open yet another dialog, the **TCP/IP DNS Server** window illustrated in Figure 5.2. In this dialog, you must enter the IP address of your IIS server.

- **Windows Internet Naming Service.** The network traffic on Kulicke & Soffa's intranet arises from such a variety of sources, so the ability of WINS to resolve both TCP/IP and NetBIOS addresses—that is, to relate either type of address to a computer name—presents that net with a distinct advantage. The fact that one lookup table contains both types of addresses also improves overall network performance, because it reduces the volume of that traffic as well. To install WINS, use the **Network** tool, choose **WINS** from the **Select Network Services** list, and follow the prompts.

Figure 5.1 Here's what the TCP/IP Properties page looked like during K & S's upgrade of network services.

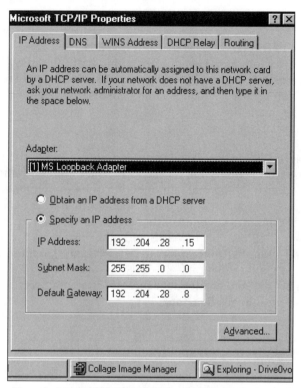

• **TCP/IP Printing.** Because many of their printers exist on the TCP/IP UNIX network, LAN administrators at K & S had to install the NT network service **TCP/IP Printing** to allow clients accessing their intranet from the Novell side of the aisle to use those printers. That load was as simple as the one of WINS. It

Figure 5.2 The TCP/IP DNS Server dialog is the last leg of the trip to expanded network services.

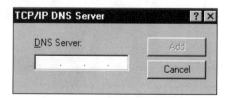

involved using the **Network** tool and the **Select Network Services** list, supplying the path name at which the files to be installed live and following the prompts once again.

Domain Name Server Defined

In effect, any **domain name service**, including that offered by Microsoft under Windows NT 4.0, is what programmers refer to as a **table lookup** utility. The **DNS** protocol keeps a small database that contains, in each line, a matched pair made up of an ASCII host name and the corresponding Internet address.

NT Server 4.0's **DNS** is essentially a spiffed-up version of the older **Windows Internet Naming Service (WINS)**. The difference is that WINS works with a lookup table that, although it can be manipulated dynamically rather than strictly manually, manages both NetBIOS and TCP/IP clients and is therefore slower to process. **DNS**, however, manages only TCP/IP clients. DNS can talk to **WINS** and make use of its lookup table, and it can, through the **Domain Name Service Manager** illustrated in Figure 5.3, manipulate that table's TCP/IP-related entries. (You can reach the Domain Name Service Manager through the path **Start ---> Programs ---> Administrative Tools.**)

Figure 5.3 Domain Name Service Manager makes NT 4.0's DNS doubly dynamic.

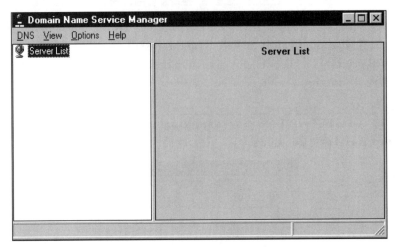

Name Service for Heterogeneous LANs
Heterogeneous LANs need some form of name service.

If left to their own devices (no pun intended), clients that have no such service available will simply broadcast a message that is in effect a request for the address of the host to which the station is trying to connect. You can easily imagine the effect such broadcasts have on network throughput.

- **SNMP Server.** Without the **Simple Network Management Protocol (SNMP) Server,** a network administrator has access to only the simplest network performance data. Forgoing the **SNMP Service** and its manager means forgoing TCP/IP statistics and IPX/SPX statistics under NT Server 4.0's **Performance Monitor,** effectively hobbling that tool. Once again, the heterogeneity of the platform base of K & S's intranet dictates that SNMP Server be included. Incorporating SNMP Server into its IIS implementation required that K & S use the Network tool and its Select Network Services list and complete the three windows that make up the Microsoft SNMP Properties dialogs.

Table 5.1 summarizes the fields presented by these dialogs.

Table 5.1 Specifying SNMP Properties

In the SNMP Dialog	The Field	Needs an Entry That
Agent	Contact (which is optional)	Gives the name or title of the individual to be notified in the event of network problems.
	Location (which is optional)	Gives such additional contact information as address, phone number, and so on.
	Services (physical)	Indicates, with a checkmark, that NT server will receive statistics on the physical health of the network; for example, the status of routers.
	Services (applications)	Indicates, with a checkmark, that NT server will receive statistics on the functioning of network applications, such as the stations from which Application X has been started.

Continued

Table 5.1 *Continued*

In the SNMP Dialog	The Field	Needs an Entry That
	Services (datalink/ subnetwork)	Indicates, with a checkmark, that NT server will receive statistics on low-level devices like NICs.
	Services (Internet)	Indicates, with a checkmark, that NT server will receive statistics on the use of TCP/IP and IPX/SPX.
	Services (end-to-end)	Indicates, with a checkmark, that NT server will receive statistics on traffic on complete sender-to-receiver (end-to-end), rather than intermediate, paths.
Traps	Community name	Supplies a generic label that will be attached to all trap messages generated by SNMP. (A **trap message** is a specific kind of alert sent by SNMP to your NT server when SNMP sees events it considers could significantly decrease the efficiency of network operations.)
	Trap destination	Supplies, as either an IP or an IPX address, where trap messages will be sent.
Security	Send authentication trap	Indicates, if checked, that NT will be notified via a trap message every time any SNMP management software starts.
	Accepted community names	Lists names for trap messages that can be used by any SNMP manager.
	Accept SNMP packets from any host	Indicates, if checked, that any computer capable of generating SNMP packets can talk to the **SNMP Server**.
	Accept SNMP packets from only these hosts	Indicates, if checked, that only the computers listed in the corresponding window may interact with **SNMP Server**.

For screen captures of the dialogs just dissected, see Figures 5.4, 5.5, and 5.6.

Figure 5.4 This SNMP Agent dialog has been filled out to meet K & S needs.

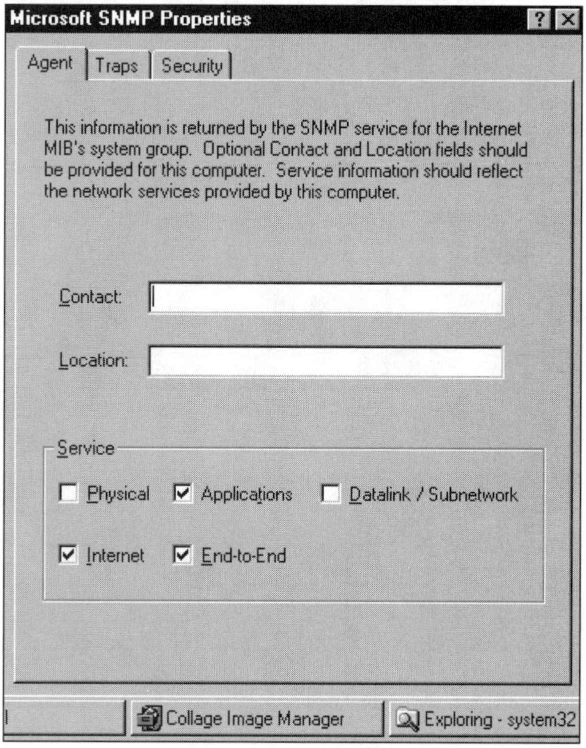

Network Administration from a Client Workstation Because their client base includes such a wide variety of hardware and software platforms, the LAN administrators at Kulicke & Soffa, in identifying those clients to NT Server, had to use 4.0's **Network Client Administrator**, first discussed in Chapter 3. In managing this diverse client base, the same dialog was again handy. For example, it established the ability to manage the NT LAN from a client station.

> **TIP** Many other network-related services can be added to an IIS/NT configuration. For a complete list of such services, refer to Chapter 2, in the section "Choosing Network Services."

Figure 5.5 These are the SNMP Traps definitions K & S will use.

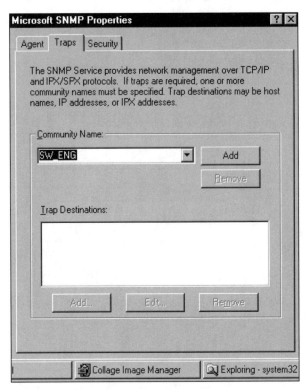

Access Denied

Client-based network administration involves the concept of shared files and directories.

We explore shares in more detail shortly, in the section "File System Management." For now, though, just be aware that, until a directory is shared, no one, not even the LAN administrator, can access the directory across the network.

Not every station can manage, nor can every LAN be managed, this way.

NT Server 4.0's **Client-Based Network Administration** tools support full management of NT, LAN Manager for MS OS/2, and LAN Manager for UNIX as well as servers from Windows 95 and Windows NT workstations.

Figure 5.6 Finally, let's look at K & S SNMP security.

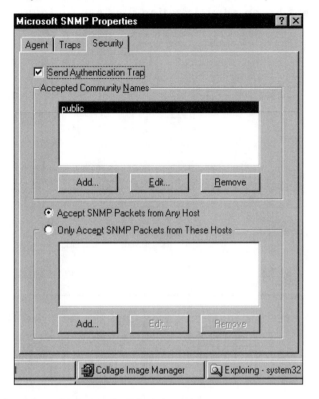

To install **Client-Based Network Administration:**

1. Follow the selection path **Start** ---> **Programs** ---> **Administrative Tools** ---> **Network Client Administrator.**

2. Click **Copy Client-Based Network Administrative Tools** and then **Continue.** Doing so will display the dialog shown in Figure 5.7.

3. In the **Path** field of this dialog, enter the full path name of the files to be installed.

4. Implement these tools on the selected workstation in one of two ways:

   • To share the files in their original path on the CD or server hard drive, click **Share Files** and type the name of the new shared directory you want to create in the field **Share Name.**

Figure 5.7 This dialog's main purpose is to supply the path through which the client-based administration files can be found.

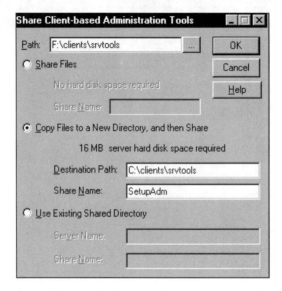

- To create a new shared directory click **Copy Files to a New Directory, and then Share.** In **Destination Path,** enter the path to which you wish to copy the files. In **Share Name,** type the name of the new shared directory you're creating.

- To use directories and files that have been set up in either of these ways, click **Use Existing Shared Directory.** In the field **Server Name,** type the name of the server where the shared directory lives, and in the field **Share Name,** enter the name of the existing shared directory. Then click **OK.**

Note that all of these steps have taken place on your NT 4.0 server. To complete the setup of Client-Based Network Administration, you must also install the remaining needed files on the client in question, using the client's software setup utilities.

Server Manager Through **Server Manager,** K & S handles the rest of its domain-dependent IIS configuration questions. **Server Manager** allows its network supervisors to add NT Workstation 4.0 clients to the single K & S domain.

To add a computer to a domain, do the following:

1. Open Server Manager by taking the path **Start ---> Programs ---> Administrative Tools ---> Server Manager.**

Multiple Computers on a Domain

Server Manager can add more than one type of computer to a domain. That includes not only NT Workstation 4.0 clients, but also domain controllers.

2. Pull down **Server Manager's Computer** menu, and click **Add to Domain**.

3. In the resulting dialog box, select the appropriate computer type: Windows NT Workstation, Windows NT Primary or Backup Controller, or Server.

4. Enter the computer name in the field **Computer Name**; then click **Add**. (Doing so automatically creates a machine account for the indicated computer name in the domain security database.)

5. Click **Close** to restore **Server Manager**'s display of computers on the domain, with the machine you just added present in the list.

To remove a computer of whatever sort from a domain, simply substitute clicking **Remove from Domain** for step 2 above.

Handling Clients from Server Manager

Server Manager can't install just any client. NT Workstation 4.0 clients can be handled from **Server Manager**; clients running other OSs cannot.

Server Manager can also move clients back and forth between domains. We review this process in the section "Management of Multiple Domains."

Adding, Deleting, or Modifying Controllers

Even in a single domain network, which by definition can and must have only one primary domain controller, several variations on the domain/controller theme can exist.

For instance, at Kulicke & Soffa, that domain spans quite a spectrum of hardware and data. In order to make the best possible use of its existing resources, the LAN group at K & S decided to establish a number of Backup Domain Controllers, each of which would correspond to a single user category. The group also settled on the notion of incorporating a number of standalone servers into its IIS Intranet, each of which would make available a particular category of applications and related data.

> ## Definitions Review
> Refer to Chapter 2 if you need to review NT's definitions of controllers and servers. The section "Defining the Server Type" covers the distinction between these.

As we saw in the section "Profiles of the Environments" at the beginning of this chapter, K & S anticipates seven categories of users on its intranet and four varieties of applications and data. However, the LAN group felt that there could be some overlap between user groups and between application/data types as well, so it arrived at a layout for backup controllers and standalone servers like that outlined in Table 5.2.

Table 5.2 A System of Backup Domain Controllers and Standalone Servers

Controller or Server Name	Affiliated with the Category
BDC1 (Backup Domain Controller 1)	Software product support engineers *and* software product development engineers
BDC2 (Backup Domain Controller 2)	Hardware product support engineers
BDC3 (Backup Domain Controller 3)	Technical Managers
BDC4 (Backup Domain Controller 4)	Business Managers and Sales Staff
BDC5 (Backup Domain Controller 5)	Support Staff
SAS1 (Standalone Server 1)	Applications required by software product support engineers *and* software product development engineers, as well as corresponding data; for example, corporate product specifications, software and data libraries, and test specifications and results
SAS2 (Standalone Server 2)	Applications and data needed by business, sales, and support personnel

---

Backup Advantage

Remember that BDCs contain a complete copy of NT's user/group database. In establishing the several BDCs outlined in Table 5.2, the staff at K & S hadn't made the mistake of thinking that each such machine would manage the accounts of only those users and groups with whom it was affiliated. Rather, their reasoning was that, because almost all K & S employees are not only computer literate but even computer articulate, having a backup controller within each major employee group would simplify the assignment of administrative tasks, allowing those tasks to be distributed.

Backup Domain Controllers Because Backup Domain Controllers can be included in an NT LAN at any time, the planners at K & S were able to phase in these machines over a period of several weeks, thereby lessening the impact on network performance of this addition of new administrative machines and databases. The process was easy, requiring only the steps outlined in the section "Server Manager" above.

Standalone Servers The same short list of tasks for server manager was all that was needed to identify SAS1 and SAS2 to the K & S NT single domain.

Promoting and Demoting The pool of PC-savvy employees at K & S realized that another factor of domain controller performance had to be taken into account in their planning. Because no known network component can be expected to avoid downtime altogether, some provision had to be made for a Primary Domain Controller's failing or simply having to be removed from the LAN for an appreciable period of time, perhaps for repair or upgrading.

NT Server 4.0 has a canned means of dealing with such scenarios. It allows the promotion of a Backup Domain controller to the temporary role of Primary Domain Controller, as well as the subsequent demotion of the new PDC to its old BDC role.

Lateral Controller Promotions

In strictest terms, there's no such thing as demoting a controller under NT. Rather, any time a machine is promoted to primary controller, the former primary controller automatically becomes a backup controller.

As you might have guessed, it is through **Server Manager** that controller promotion is carried out. Here's how the process goes:

1. Open Server Manager.

2. Highlight the name of the backup domain controller you're about to promote.

3. Pull down **Server Manager's Computer** menu.

4. Choose **Synchronize with Primary Domain Controller** from this menu, and click **OK** or press **Enter**.

5. With the name of the Primary Controller-to-be still highlighted, pull down the **Computer** menu one more time, and select **Promote to Primary Domain Controller**.

6. When you are prompted, confirm that you wish to promote a backup controller over the currently operating primary controller.

Once you click your confirmation and NT informs you, through a number of message windows, that services are being stopped and started as appropriate on the machines involved in the promotion, you'll see that the names of the primary and backup controllers displayed by **Server Manager** have shifted to reflect the new state of affairs, as Figures 5.8 and 5.9 demonstrate.

Synchronization Defined

Remember that Backup Domain Controllers have a copy of NT's user/group database, which, although not as current as the copy on the PDC, is updated regularly (the default interval being every five minutes). This updating is carried out automatically. Each BDC connects to the primary controller, sends any new information it has gathered regarding the user/group database to the primary machine, and receives from that controller whatever related information originated there in the interval.

Deleting Controllers or Servers Rule number one, the Golden Rule, and the Prime Directive of NT controller management, is this: **You cannot and will not be permitted to delete a Primary Domain Controller** from the network. (Knowing what you know about what such machines do, you should not be surprised.) However, you can easily delete a Backup Domain Controller or Standalone Server with **Server Manager** as follows:

Figure 5.8 At K & S, Server Manager first showed this Primary Domain Controller.

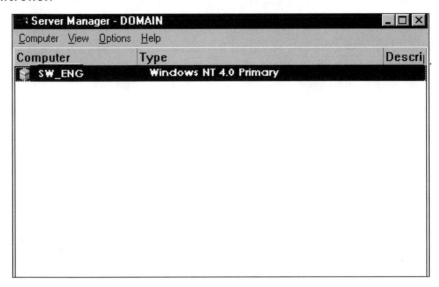

Figure 5.9 After the promotion process, we find a new PDC.

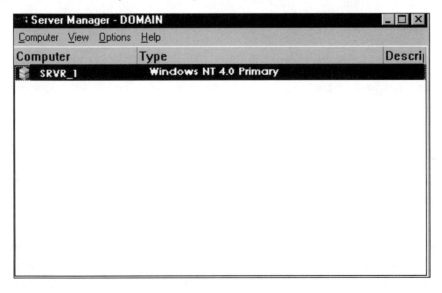

1. Pull down **Server Manager's Computer** menu, and click **Remove from Domain**.

2. Select either Windows NT Primary or Backup Controller or Server.

   (Remember, this dialog is used to add controllers and servers as well as remove them. That's why the first prompt just mentioned reads *Primary or Backup*. This *doesn't* mean that you can, by whatever hacker-conceived trickery, manage to delete a primary controller.)

3. Highlight the name of the machine you wish to withdraw from the domain in the list that **Server Manager** displays. Then click **Remove**.

4. Click **Close** to restore Server Manager's display of computers on the domain, with the machine you just removed no longer present there.

Domain Account Policies

In Chapter 2 we introduced the parameters that can be applied to user accounts. These include such characteristics as the length of time after which a password will expire, whether or not users may change their password, and how frequently users may change passwords.

A domain administrator can define ranges of values for these parameters and more. Such definitions constitute what NT Server 4.0 refers to as a domain account policy. In an account policy, the LAN administrator sets out:

- The maximum age a password will be allowed to reach

- The minimum age a password must have reached before it can be changed

- The minimum length (i.e., number of characters of whatever sort) passwords on the network must have

- Whether or not passwords may be reused, and if so, after what period of lying fallow

A domain account policy laid out in this way applies to any and all users in the domain, whether NT-generated or administrator-created.

Defining a domain account policy for a single domain network like that at Kulicke & Soffa is uncomplicated because no consideration need be given to such possibilities as the need to assign different conditions to the same user's accounts on different domains. To define a domain account policy, begin with the path: **Start** --->

Programs ---> Administrative Tools ---> User Manager for Domains. Then take the following steps:

1. Pull down **User Manager's Policies** menu.

2. Select **Account Policy** from this menu.

3. In the **Account Policy** dialog that NT then displays, fill in the values you think most appropriate to the fields discussed in Table 5.3.

Table 5.3 NT User Account Parameters

In the Area of the Dialog	The Field	Needs an Entry That
Maximum Password Age	Password Never Expires	Indicates, with a checkmark, that the pass words governed by the policy being defined will last at least until the end of this universe, if not longer.
	Expires in ...	Indicates, with a checkmark, that the passwords governed under the policy being defined will expire in the interval specified in ...
	[ ] Days	Indicates, by the integer value you enter or select from the scroll list, how long passwords governed by this policy will survive.
Minimum Password Age	Allow Changes Immediately	Indicates, if checked, that passwords operating under this policy may be changed as soon as they are created.
	Allow Changes in ...	Indicates, if checked, that a period of days, defined in the field that follows, must pass before passwords being governed by this policy may be altered.
	[ ] Days	Indicates, by the integer value you enter or select from the scroll list, how many days must pass before passwords governed by this policy may be changed.
Minimum Password Length	Permit Blank Password	Indicates, if checked, that empty passwords may exist under this policy.

Continued

Table 5.3 *Continued*

In the Area of the Dialog	The Field	Needs an Entry That
	At Least ...	Indicates, if checked, that all passwords governed by this policy must consist of the number of characters specified in the next field.
	[ ] Characters	Indicates, by the integer value you enter or select from the scroll list, how many characters must be present in all passwords governed by this policy.
Password Uniqueness	Do Not Keep Password History	Indicates, if checked, that NT Server will make no effort to prevent users from recycling passwords.
	Remember ...	Indicates, with a checkmark, that NT Server will record the number of passwords specified in the field that follows for every user of the domain for which you're creating this account policy.
	[ ] Passwords	Indicates, by the integer value you enter or select from the scroll list, how many previous passwords NT Server will record and prevent from being recycled, for every user of the domain.
Lockout	No Account Lockout	Indicates, if checked, that no user on this domain will be locked out from logging on, regardless of how many failed logon attempts he or she makes.
	Account Lockout	Indicates, if checked, that users on this domain will be prevented from logging on after a specified number of failed logon attempts.
	Lockout After [ ] Bad Logon Attempts	Indicates, by the integer value you enter or select from the scroll list, how many times a user on this domain may botch the entry of his or her user name or password, or both, before NT Server precludes logging on altogether.
	Reset Count After [ ] Minutes	Indicates, by the integer value you enter or select from the scroll list, how many minutes must pass before a user who has made a sorry attempt at logging on to the domain may try again.

Table 5.3 *Continued*

In the Area of the Dialog	The Field	Needs an Entry That
Lockout Duration	Forever (Until Admin Unlocks)	Indicates, if checked, that the domain manager must manually reset an account before its owner may attempt another logon; that is, *Forever, Sort of.*
	Duration [ ] Minutes	Indicates, by the integer value you enter or select from the scroll list, how many minutes must pass before accounts governed by this policy will unlock.
	Forcibly Disconnect remote users from server when logon hours expire	Indicates, if checked, that dial-up accounts governed by this policy will have active sessions arbitrarily terminated at the server end if those sessions extend past previously defined points on the clock.
	Users must log on in order to change password	Indicates, if checked, that users on this domain cannot change their own passwords from someone else's active session.

It's worth repeating that an account policy defined in the way just outlined *applies to every user account on a domain.* The administrators of the K & S single domain LAN therefore set up their account policy to create the greatest flexibility possible; given the variety of users their IIS Intranet is intended to serve, this was a sensible decision. Figure 5.10 illustrates the result.

Adding Resources to a Domain

Incorporating resources, whether physical or data, into a domain is done by activities such as installing printers, installing modems, and installing dedicated stand-alone servers for such functions as Faxing or for particular applications. Many of these ordinarily take place during the initial installation of Windows NT Server 4.0 and Internet Information Server. But you can, if you need to, add physical or file-based resources to a domain at any time.

Table 5.4 summarizes the steps to be taken to incorporate two of the most common resources into a domain.

Figure 5.10 This is how the K & S Account Policy was defined.

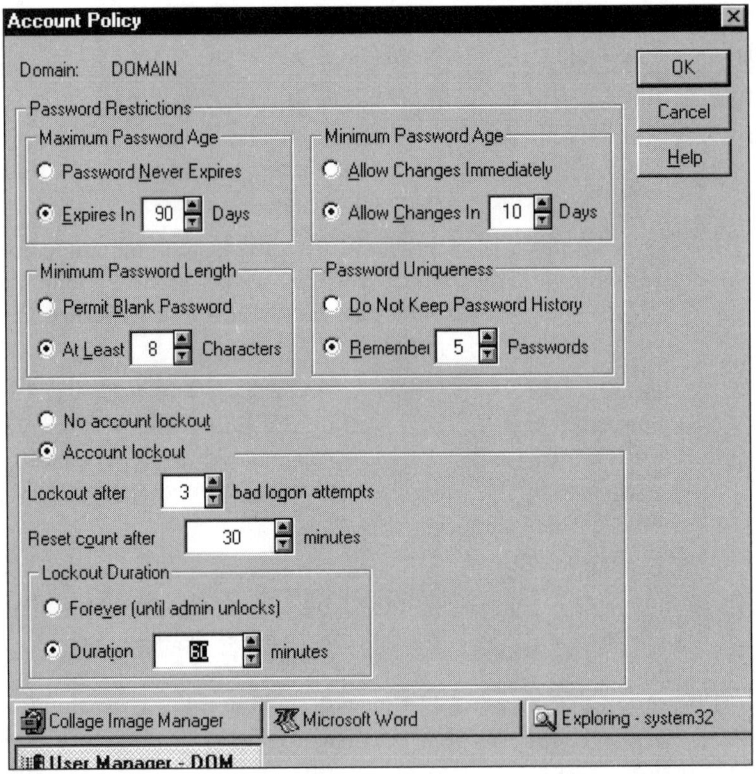

Table 5.4 Including New Resources in a Single Domain Network

To Add the Resource	Take the Path
Printer	**Start ---> Programs ---> Administrative Tools ---> Administrative Wizards ---> Add Printer Wizard.** The **Add Printer Wizard** allows you to configure either a local (that is, an unavailable-to-the-network-at-large) printer, or a network one.
	If you install the latter, **Add Printer Wizard** allows you to specify such other printer-related characteristics as physical location of the printer (so that users may view that location in order to decide whether or not it makes sense for them to send jobs to the device), intervals at which the printer will be available to users, processor priorities enjoyed by the printer's jobs, whether or not print spooling will be done by this printer, and the names of groups and users who have permission to use the printer.

Table 5.4 *Continued*

To Add the Resource	Take the Path
Modem Servers	Two possible paths exist here. You can install devices such as a multiport serial card or ISDN adapter in a primary or backup controller. Or you can scrounge an older-but-still-decent PC and convert it to a dedicated standalone print server.
	The first of these scenarios assumes the path **Start ---> Settings ---> Control Panel ---> Modem,** and your correct response to NT's prompts thereafter. The second resource addition takes the path **Start ---> Programs ---> Administrative Tools ---> Server Manager.**

Miscellaneous Domain Management Tasks

In this section, we consider a small grab bag of domain management tasks that arise only infrequently and fall into no single category.

Connection Speed With connections across some media, such as modems and T1 lines, some of NT 4.0's administrative tools experience a noticeable degradation in performance. For example, User Manager for Domains can stutter-step severely in displaying its lists of domain elements such as computers and groups. You can preclude such delays, however, by checking the box **Low Speed Connection** in the **Select Domain** dialog. To access that dialog:

1. Take the path **Start ---> Programs ---> Administrative Tools ---> User Manager for Domains.**

2. Pull down the User Manager's User menu.

3. Click **Select Domain.**

Making this choice does not affect the speed of conversation between a domain controller and network clients. Rather, it disables a number of User Manager's displays, thereby allowing it to function more smoothly.

Logon Hours and Logon Workstations Both the hours during which an active session may take place and the workstations from which logons may be done can be specified under NT 4.0 for any user or group of users. Either could be used in single- or multi-domain LANs to provide an added measure of security.

To define logon hours for individual users or groups, open **User Manager for Domains,** and then select the user or group whose network time you wish to limit from the list displayed by **User Manager.** Next, click the **Properties** tab and then its **Hours** button.

You'll see the Logon Hours dialog box illustrated in Figure 5.11.

Once NT has served up this window, you can click its column headers to specify the times at which logons will be allowed for the user or group you'd previously selected. For example, clicking the label for a particular day of the week enables logons for all 24 hours of that day.

You can access the **Logon Workstations** dialog, shown in Figure 5.16, by clicking the **Log On To** button at the lower center of the **Properties** page of **User Manager.** In this dialog, you can enter the names of up to eight clients from which the previously selected user or group may log on. Do this by checking the box **User May Log On To These Workstations** and specifying the computer name assigned to the station when it was identified to NT Server 4.0.

Figure 5.11 Restrict access times by using the Logon Hours dialog.

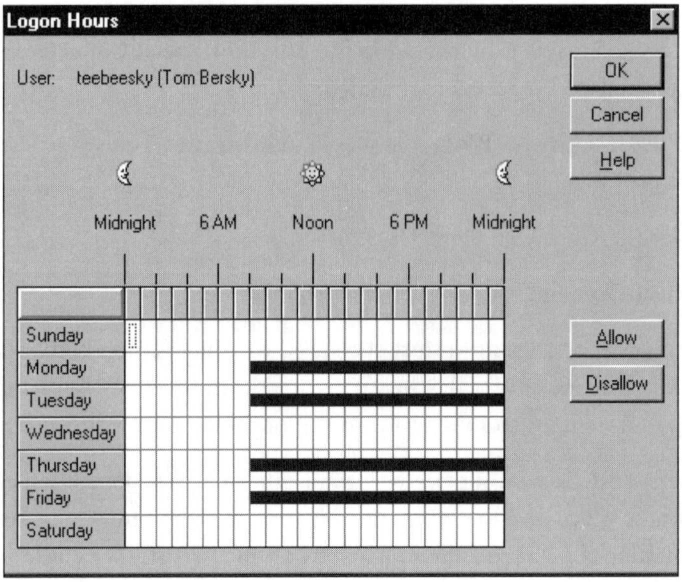

The Inside-Out Approach

It's important to remember that the selections you make in the **Logon Hours** dialog enable rather than disable logons during the indicated time period. The times left unmarked are those during which logons cannot take place.

TIP By default, NT permits logons by all users at any client. If this doesn't meet your network's security needs, specify otherwise, as Figure 5.12 depicts.

You're preventing logons not at the stations you specify, but rather at all others.

Dial-Up Connections Remote access networking as a whole is set up and managed through NT's **Remote Access Manager**. In versions of the NOS prior to 4.0, that manager also was the means by which individual dial-up accounts had to be controlled. However, the most recent incarnation of NT Server allows you to deal with such details in the same way as logon hours and stations were defined:

1. Open User Manager for Domains.

2. Select a group or user.

Figure 5.12 In the Logon Workstations window, you can tailor the number and location of clients from which users can conduct an IIS session.

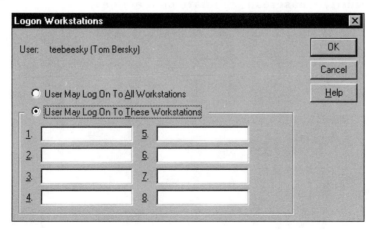

164

Part Two • Chapter 5

3. Open the Properties page, either by double-clicking the user name or by pulling down the User menu and clicking **Properties**.

4. Click the Dialin button at the lower right.

These steps result in the display of the **Dialin Information** dialog box, as illustrated in Figure 5.13.

You can use this dialog to grant or deny dialin permission, require or preclude the need for callback verification of the location from which a user dials in, require that a callback number be set to a predefined value, or allow the user to set it on the fly, so to speak.

Renaming a Domain Although the need to rename a domain should arise only rarely, a method for doing so is provided for under Windows NT Server 4.0. As you might imagine, given the discussion to this point, renaming a domain takes place through **Server Manager**. Here's how it's done in a single-domain network:

1. Open **Server Manager**. The name of the domain's one primary domain controller should be highlighted.

2. Pull down the **Computer** menu of this dialog, and choose **Synchronize Entire Domain**.

3. Close **Server Manager**, and open in its place the **Network** tool of **control panel**.

Figure 5.13 The Dialin Information window allows you to define simple security measures for remote connections.

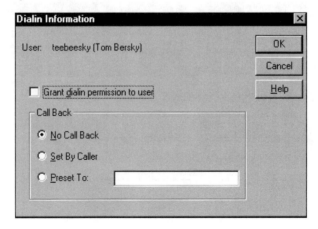

4. Select the computer name of the primary domain controller.

5. Click the **Change** button at the bottom of the **Identification tab** for the selected computer to display the **Identification Changes** dialog seen in Figure 5.14.

> **TIP** Keep in mind that, under NT 4.0, users and clients connect not to a machine but to a domain. So, if you change the domain name, you must reconfigure every user account and client station on that domain. This is not a task for the fainthearted or the overworked.

Manual Synchronization Under certain circumstances, such as the unlocking of a user account, the changes made to a primary domain controller need to be immediately relayed to any backup controllers on a domain. In such instances, waiting for the default number of minutes to elapse before synchronization of controllers takes place may not suffice.

Domain administrators of a LAN under the single domain model can manually synchronize controllers and the user databases they manage, by doing the following:

1. Open **Server Manager**. The Primary domain Controller for the one domain should already be highlighted.

2. Pull down the **Computer** menu.

3. Select one of the following:

Figure 5.14 The need to do so is rare, and the ramifications are networkwide, but you can change a domain name.

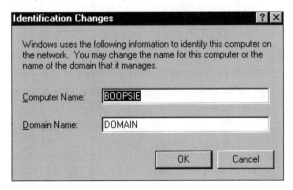

- **Synchronize the Entire Domain** (to bring all backup controllers into agreement with the PDC)

- **Synchronize with Primary Domain Controller** (to bring a previously selected backup controller into harmony with the primary)

With that, our seminar on single domains is complete. Next, we investigate domain management tasks exclusive to multiple domains.

Management of Multiple Domains

In addition to the domain-related configuration and management operations we've just carried out in a single domain network, we must still drill a few procedures relating strictly to domains under the multiple master model. All of the domain management tasks just reviewed can be carried out under models involving multiple domains. For that reason, we do not cover those functions in the sections below.

We'll use our hypothetical multiple master domain-modeled LAN at Delaware County Community College to consider management tasks specific to multiple domains. DCCC's overall environment was outlined in the section "Profiles of the Environments" at the beginning of this chapter. Figure 5.15 maps the college's computing environment.

When the Computing Services Department at DCCC decided to implement a multiple master domain-modeled, NT-based Internet Information Server, its network map changed to reflect that implementation (Figure 5.16).

Modifying Controllers

As Figure 5.16 shows, DCCC's NT/IIS implementation involves five domains and therefore five primary domain controllers. Each of its five domains has also been assigned at least one—and in three cases, two—backup domain controllers.

Shifting Controllers Among Domains In an environment like Delaware County Community College's, usage patterns and therefore the requirements for the distribution of network resources shift regularly. For instance, the college recently established two new satellite campuses, incorporating these into a sixth domain. Figure 5.17 is a snapshot representation of the part of the again-revised network map that resulted.

The college's budget is such that it could not purchase new hardware to act as controllers for this sixth domain. Therefore, it was faced with the task of shifting existing equipment into that role.

Figure 5.15 DCCC has a complex computing environment.

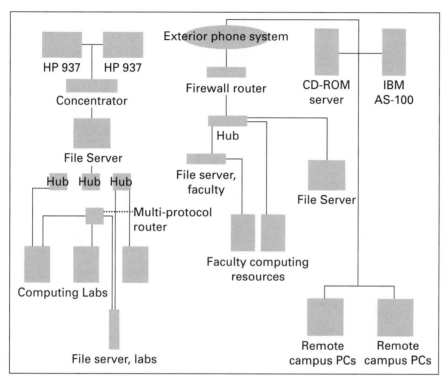

This is not a trivial undertaking. Only reinstalling Windows NT Server 4.0 on the controller to be shifted will fully disassociate it from the domain to which it was originally attached and create a new **Security Identification,** or **SID,** through which it may be uniquely and therefore correctly identified to NT on the new domain.

Before reinstallation could take place, though, the Computer Services group at DCCC had to ensure that services on the domain from which the controller was to be shifted would be uninterrupted. To do that, they opened **Server Manager,** and carried out the steps detailed in the earlier section "Promoting and Demoting" to promote one of the backup domain controllers in DomainE to its primary controller.

Having done so, the group was then able to move the now-backup controller to the new DomainF and install it there as a primary. They accomplished this by doing the following:

Figure 5.16 The College has incorporated several NT domains into its WAN.

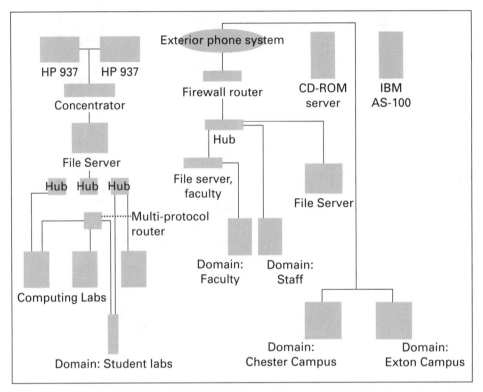

- Running a full backup of the hard drive of the now-BDC

- Reinstalling Windows NT Server 4.0 on that machine and identifying the machine as a primary domain controller for DomainF during the reload

- Restoring the new primary controller's file system

Renaming Domains on a Multi-Domain Network The possible complications of renaming a controller, discussed in the context of a single domain, grow exponentially in multiple-domain networks. For that reason, we advise against renaming domains on a multi-domain network.

However, if you cannot avoid this process, be aware that, in addition to changing the domain name for every primary and backup controller as well as for every standalone server, you need to do the following:

Figure 5.17 DCCC's newly added domain needs controllers.

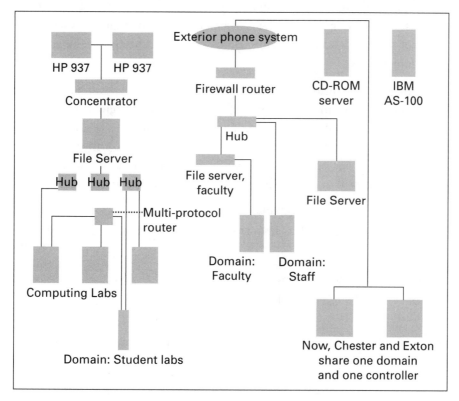

- Reconfigure clients to connect to the new set of domains.

- Reconfigure resources to correspond correctly to the new set of domains.

- Completely re-create any trusts that were established between domains (because changing a domain name destroys existing trusts).

Accounts on Multiple Domains

Account policies, user accounts, and local group membership apply only to single domains, so in a multi-domain environment like that at DCCC, the creation and maintenance of these fundamental network components is a repetitive but not a unique process. However, such tasks as managing global groups, automating the logon process, and efficiently modifying multiple user profiles do have a distinctly multi-domain flavor. We discuss each of these tasks in the following sections.

Managing Global Groups Although they may be made up only of users from the domain in which they were created, global groups can provide access for those users to resources in domains with which the originating domain shares a trust. Groups that offer such access therefore effectively, if not strictly speaking, span multiple domains.

Their doing so complicates their management. Imagine, for example, that you wish to monitor the session being conducted by a user from a global group. If that session involves the simultaneous execution of an application in the home domain, a print job generated by that application being forwarded to a printer on another domain, and an Internet connection via a modem server on a third domain, you've taken on a complicated task. Figure 5.18 shows what we mean.

Luckily, NT Server 4.0 offered a way out of such circumstances to DCCC's Computer Services group and to anyone who must manage users and groups across multiple domains.

Unlike some other of its tools, such as Windows NT Explorer, User Manager can run as several simultaneous processes or copies of itself. To cause it to do so, you must:

1. Open NT Explorer by taking the path **Start ---> Programs ---> Windows NT Explorer.**

2. Use the Edit menu of Explorer to create multiple shortcuts for User Manager.

Figure 5.18 User Manager for Domains can display only one domain at a time.

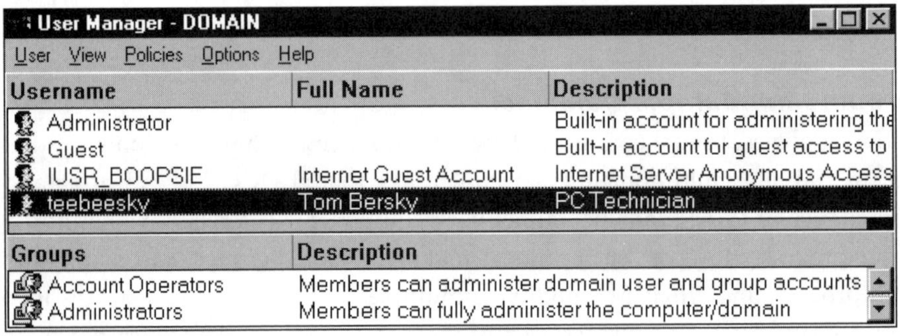

3. Right-click each of these shortcuts to display the Properties dialog.

4. Edit the Target field of that window to append the name of a specific domain to the command line associated with starting User Manager, as shown in Figure 5.19.

Once created in this way, these multiple versions or sessions of User Manager can be run simultaneously, allowing you to monitor more easily accounts that traverse domains.

User Profiles If you are familiar with UNIX, you have encountered user profiles— stylized text files that define the environment in which sessions conducted by each user will operate. Startup and operating information for every user account on an NT network is stored in an individual file similar to this UNIX *.profile* file. The default version of an NT user profile contains only the following:

- The domain of which the user is a member

- The primary group of which the user is a member

- The user's logon name

- The user's password and the characteristics of that password

You can define other details of a user's profile, such as the directory or directories where the user profile file is housed, the name of the logon script that kick-starts the user's sessions, and the local path or home directory—that is, the directory in which a user's session begins and in which the files the user generates are stored. Some of these aspects are multi-domain possibilities. Logon scripts, for

Figure 5.19 This version of User Manager has been tailored to a specific domain.

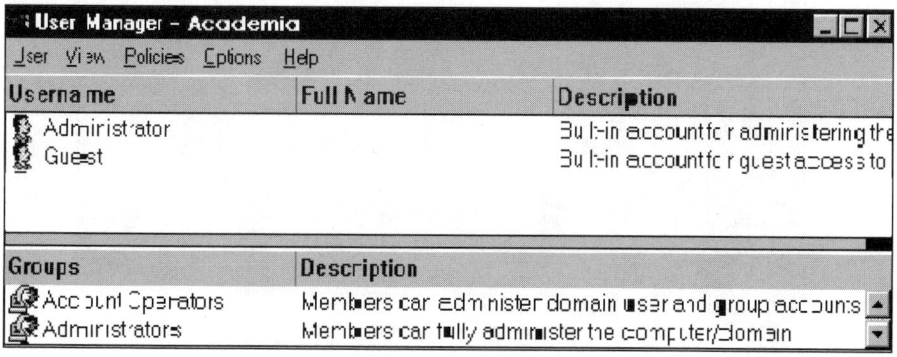

instance, can be written to apply to more than one user. And because local groups may have global groups as members, logon scripts constructed with this in mind can serve as workarounds to NT's requirement that, when one is working with a single iteration of **User Manager** to manipulate several accounts, those accounts must all be within one domain.

> **TIP** Whether you're running one copy of **User Manager** or several, the information in each pertains only to users in one domain. You may simultaneously manipulate several user aocunts in each **User Manager** session, simply by selecting several accounts and making a single set of entries that is then applied to all of them. But you cannot simultaneously manipulate a number of accounts across domains.

Figure 5.20 gives you a look at the **User Environment Profile** dialog, the key to tailoring logons in this and other ways.

Setting Up Trusts Between Domains

In Chapter 3, we introduced the three types of trust relationships that NT Server 4.0 makes available. In this section, we establish one instance of each of these types.

One-Way Trusts Within the subset of services allotted to students, not only several computer labs but also a fully automated library can be found. Therefore, the

Figure 5.20 In this User Environment Profile dialog, we've assigned the user a home directory on a network drive in another domain, which has a trust relationship with the user's original domain.

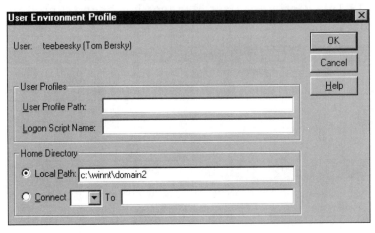

Computer Services group at Delaware County Community College reasoned that establishing a one-way trust between these labs and the library would allow students to access library resources, such as its circulation and reference services, not only from within the library, but also from the labs. Computer Services personnel worked hand in hand with the library's systems manager to establish and define the specifics of this trust under NT 4.0.

The process was straightforward:

1. Open **User Manager for Domains** from the systems manager's account on the domain of which the labs were also members.

2. Pull down the **Policies** menu and select **Trust Relationships.**

3. In the **Trust Relationships** dialog box, illustrated in Figure 5.21, click the **Add** button next to the list of trusting domains to display the subdialog **Add Trusting Domain.**

4. In the **Add Trusting Domain** dialog, enter the name of the domain to whose resources you wish to give access and the password to be supplied by users from the trusted domain when they attempt access to resources on the trusting domain.

5. Return to the **Policies** menu and again choose **Trust Relationships.**

Figure 5.21 The Trust Relationships window is navigated twice in the setup of even a one-way trust.

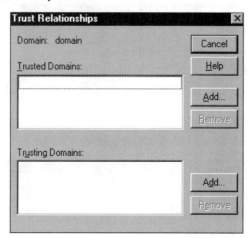

6. Click the **Add** button next to the list of trusted domains to display the subdialog **Add Trusted Domain.**

7. In the **Add Trusted Domain** window, enter the name of the domain whose users will have access to resources in the previously defined trusting domain and the password (the same one you supplied to **Add Trusting Domain**) by means of which these users will access those resources.

> **TIP** Establishing a one-way trust must begin in the trusted domain. If you begin the process from the trusting domain—that is, from the domain whose resources another domain wishes to make use of—it will fail.

Figures 5.22 and 5.23 are representations of the **Add Trusting Domain** and **Add Trusted Domain** dialogs as used by DCCC.

Two-Way Trusts Setting up two-way trusts means repeating everything you did in defining a one-way relationship, but reversing the direction of the trust the second time around.

Figure 5.24 maps out the steps involved in creating a two-way version of the one-way trust just defined.

Figure 5.22 The domain FACULTY is made the trusted member of this relationship.

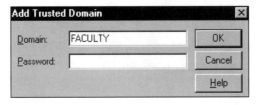

Figure 5.23 STUDENTS is the trusting member of the pair.

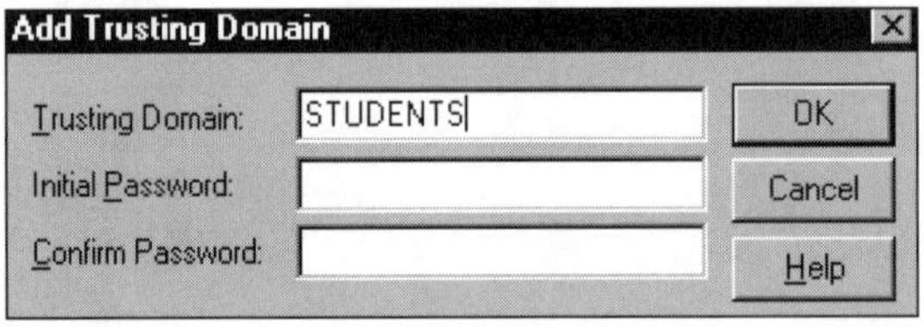

Figure 5.24 Creating a two-way trust.

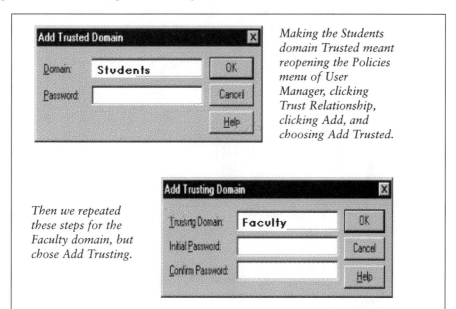

Making the Students domain Trusted meant reopening the Policies menu of User Manager, clicking Trust Relationship, clicking Add, and choosing Add Trusted.

Then we repeated these steps for the Faculty domain, but chose Add Trusting.

Complete Trusts As mentioned in the initial discussion of trusts in Chapter 3, a Complete Trust relationship is one in which every domain can access and use the resources of every other domain.

A complete trust at Delaware County Community College would result in a network schema like that illustrated in Figure 5.25.

Using Trusts to Manage Resources in Multiple Domains If trusts have been established correctly, they form, by definition, a management tool for network resources. If you find, after implementing trusts, that unanticipated or uneven usage of network resources occurs, in such forms as unexpectedly heavy demands on a resource (such as a printer or file server) and logon conflicts (if you're using DHCP) or that you have user requests for additional access to network resources, you may have to tinker with your established trusts. Before redoing them, though, consult this checklist:

• Have you used Performance Monitor to determine if there might be any other causes for these problems?

• Have you taken a look at Event Viewer to see if it has caught any unusual circumstances that might be affecting the operation of your Trusts?

Figure 5.25 The revised DCCC network map reflects the complete trusts between its NT domains.

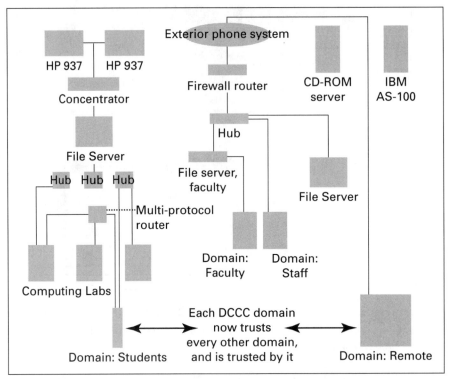

- If one of the overburdened resources is a standalone server, have you used Server Manager to check that the machine is configured properly?

- Have you talked to your users to determine if you have an accurate picture of their needs and wish lists?

Group Management

In Chapter 2, we introduced and briefly discussed the concept of and tools available for group management under NT Server 4.0. Now, we provide detailed examples of adding, deleting, and modifying the characteristics of groups that may log on to a domain.

Begin by opening User Manager. Then click the Groups button at the leftmost lower corner of that window, causing NT to display the Group Memberships dialog, shown in Figure 5.26.

Figure 5.26 With the Group Memberships dialog, you can assign users to groups, move user accounts between groups, or remove users from groups.

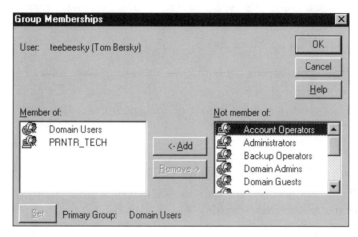

The **Group Memberships** window presents two lists at once:

- Groups of which the previously selected user is already a member

- Groups of which that user is not a member

If you, like the Delaware County Community College group, are still in the early stages of setting up your NT/IIS network, the only entry that should appear in the left of these two lists is the notation **Domain Users**.

To use the dialog to change this, in the **Not Member of** display, highlight the group or groups in which you wish to include the user in question, and click the **Add** button at the center of the window.

Groups in a Single Domain

Understandably, group management in a single domain presents fewer complications than does the same process across domains. For instance, in a single-domain IIS implementation, an administrator need not be concerned with which network-

Automatic Group for New Users

Recall from Chapter 2 that NT automatically makes group membership assignments when it is installed. The group **Domain Users**, a global one, is the group into which NT places all new user accounts.

wide resources a user must access and therefore which trusts must be taken into account. However, **Domain Users**—the default group to which all new user accounts are given membership—is, by virtue of being a global group, itself a member of another, local group, **Users**. Because the group **Users** has access to all commonly used network resources, a LAN manager must explicitly deny use of those resources to a user. **Group Memberships** won't do so.

A single-domain network is likely to have fewer resources and a smaller variety; thus, group membership, in combination with the planning of the physical distribution of those resources, has more impact on the performance that can be expected from network tools.

Adding Groups to a Single Domain

The network managers at Kulicke & Soffa came to the **Group Memberships** dialog with a list of the groups they wished to add to their NT net:

- Software product support engineers

- Hardware product support engineers

- Software product development engineers

- Technical managers

- Business managers

- Sales staff

- Support staff

However, these managers still faced one decision: whether to constitute any of these groups as global groups.

The use of global groups in a single-domain network might at first seem superfluous, because in such a net, no trusts can be established and therefore no resources shared through trusts. However, from an administrative point of view, global groups have the advantage of being unable to contain other groups as members. Thus, global groups are in effect the lowest common denominator for user accounts and can serve as a convenient way of organizing those accounts into collections that clearly share functions and needs.

Adding Global Groups K & S network staff followed the line of reasoning presented above in creating six of the seven user groups outlined as global groups. To do so, they took several steps, as follows:

1. Open **User Manager,** the first task in creating new groups.

2. Pull down its **User** menu and select **New Global Group.**

3. Respond to the **New Global Group** dialog (shown in Figure 5.27) by keying in the name of the new group and a description of its composition and by clicking the names of users to be included in the group.

Mnemonic Help

Remember, global groups *cannot* contain other groups as members. As a mnemonic to this end, the New Global Group dialog will present, in its list of potential members, only the accounts of individual users.

Adding Local Groups At Kulicke & Soffa, only the group made up of support staff was constituted a local group. This group status reflects the membership of the group—secretaries, bookkeepers, network technicians, and so on, and the job functions of those members—such tasks as maintaining and operating printers and portions of the file system.

Figure 5.27 Creating the global group SW_DEV_ENG.

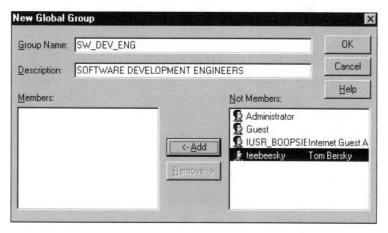

> **TIP** The procedure for creating Local Groups is nearly identical to that for creating Global Groups. Simply substitute **New Local Group** for **New Global Group** when you pull down the **User Manager's User** menu. Then respond appropriately to the **New Local Group** dialog.

If NT Server 4.0 automatically provides a number of built-in groups such as **Print Operators** and **Replicator**, which can carry out such functions, why create more?

If you wish to allow group members to carry out more than one of the tasks that by default are the purview of one of NT's built-in groups, you must create a new group and explicitly configure into it the ability to do such tasks.

You must navigate several dialogs to do so, as follows:

1. After setting up all user accounts and defining your new local group, select the group just added from **User Manager**'s scrolling list of groups by pulling down the **User** menu of **User Manager**.

2. Highlight **Properties** in this menu.

3. Respond to the **Local Group Properties** dialog by tailoring membership in the new local group through appropriate highlighting of individual user account names and use of the **Add** or **Remove** button.

Figure 5.28 shows the **Local Group Properties** about to be used to remove the account **teebeesky** from membership in the local group **PRNTR_TECH**.

After **Remove** is clicked, the Local Group Properties window reflects PRNTR_TECH's new makeup, as Figure 5.29 illustrates.

Trans-Domain Access for Groups in Multi-Domain Networks

In multi-domain networks, you can transfer users between domains and duplicate user account characteristics across domains. To do the former, simply set up accounts on additional domains for the same user or users. The latter can take place as part of that process.

However, because of the distinction between local and global groups, the need to copy or transfer groups *between* domains simply doesn't exist, nor can it. But you

> **TIP** You must select a group in order to be able to add members to it.

Figure 5.28 All that's needed now is to click Remove.

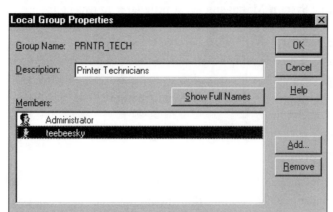

can still provide for access by members of a group on, for example, DomainZ to resources associated with another domain in one of two ways:

- Include a global group from the domain that needs to share resources as a member of a local group on the domain whose resources are to be shared. This is the easiest way to accomplish trans-domain access of resources.

- In the case of trans-domain access to file system resources, you can set up and tailor shared access to directories and files in such a way as to very closely

Figure 5.29 The local group PRNTR_TECH now has only a single member.

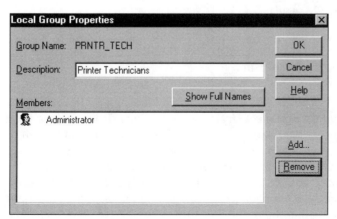

define who may use these files and directories. We'll discuss this process in the section "File System Management" a little later in this chapter.

Using the Group Membership Dialog

Rather than assign membership to groups in the way outlined in the section "Adding Local Groups," you can assign users to groups, whether global or local, in another way—by means of the **Group Membership** dialog.

To do so:

1. Open **User Manager**.

2. Highlight the account or accounts to which you wish to give membership to a particular group. Keep in mind that the highlighted items can consist of either user or group names. If you plan to add a group into the member pool of another group, though, be sure the group to be added is global and the group into which you incorporate it is local.

3. Pull down the **User** menu and choose **Properties**.

4. In the resulting **User Properties** dialog, click the **Groups** button.

Tailor the groups in which the current user can claim membership through judicious use of the **Add** and **Remove** buttons.

Deleting Groups

Whether it exists on a single- or a multi-domain network, a group can be deleted from a domain in only one way:

1. Open **User Manager**.

2. From its scrolling list of groups, select the one you wish to remove.

3. Pull down the **User** menu.

> **TIP** The dialog **Select Users** has limitations. This window, accessed via the path User Manager ---> Users ---> Select Users, results in a display that presents *only groups*. Further, you can work with only one group at a time from this list. Therefore, **Select Users** comes in handy primarily if you want to add the entire population of a group to another group, or need to establish a new group whose population will, at least initially, be made of the members of the group you've picked with **Select Users**.

4. Select **Delete**. Doing so will first produce a warning that informs you that any trust relationships enjoyed by the group in question will become kaput and must be reestablished if you proceed.

5. Assuming you're sure, click **OK**.

User Management

In Chapter 2, we discovered how to add user accounts. In this section, we reveal the fine points of adding, deleting, and modifying the characteristics of users who may log on to a domain. Remember that, to be able to log on to a domain, a user must either be a member of a local or global group on that domain, be a member of a global group from another domain that is in turn a member of a local group on the domain to which the user wishes to connect, or have a global user account defined in a trusted domain.

Figure 5.30 shows the Account Information window.

Users in a Single Domain

For accounts restricted to a single domain, you might think there would not be much management to do. But that's not the case. Even within a one-domain NT net such as that at Kulicke & Soffa, there's likely to be the need to:

1. Change the characteristics (such as logon hours) of individual accounts or the accounts belonging to entire groups.

Figure 5.30 As you can see, the user teebeesky has been specified as a global account.

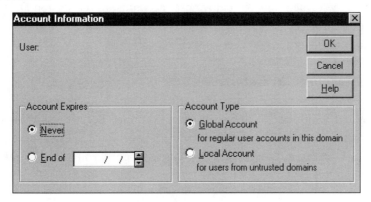

> **TIP** In Chapter 2, as part of the list of the characteristics of a new user account that can be tailored when you set up that account, we mentioned locations from which the user can connect, or Global Accounts.
>
> Characterizing a user as a **Global Account** causes any domains at the trusting end of a relationship with the domain in which the user account was created to recognize that user account.
>
> To declare a user account to be **Global**, after selecting the user name, you must:
>
> 1. Access the **Account Information** dialog by taking one of three branches of the path **Start ---> Programs ---> Administrative Tools ---> User Manager for Domains**. Those branches are three items from **User Manager's User** menu: New User, Copy User, and Properties.
>
> 2. Kick-start any of these three dialogs so that you can click the **Account** button, just to right of center at the bottom of each of these windows. That click produces the Account Information dialog, from where you can enforce recognition by other domains of the account in question, as mentioned by selecting **Global Account**, or prevent users who having accounts on domains that are not trusted by the current domain from fully accessing resources on the current domain, or restrict users on the current domain to that domain, regardless of existing trust relationships, by checking **Local Account**.

2. Copy the characteristics of an account as a shortcut to creating another account with similar traits.

3. Remove accounts from a domain.

We've already learned how to remove user accounts, in the section **Deleting Groups** a little earlier in this chapter. We'll add to that picture in a moment, but for now, let's turn to the other two account-related activities.

Changing Account Characteristics

The process for changing account characteristics is easy enough, especially after you have configured Windows NT Server 4.0 user accounts. Begin by carrying out the sequence **Start---> Programs ---> Administrative Tools ---> User Manager for Domains ---> User (menu) ---> Properties**. Doing so gives you access to the means of changing the following:

- Characteristics of a user's password

- Details of a user's profile

- Hours during which the user can conduct a session

- Domains to which the user can log on

- Nature of the account—that is, whether it is global or local

- Whether or not the account can carry out dial-up access

Simultaneous Account Changes

You can simultaneously change the traits of several accounts. Just select all the accounts you want to modify before making any of the needed changes. Do be aware, though, that if the existing characteristics of these accounts vary, only the parameters the accounts have in common can be changed in this way.

Copying User Account Properties

In many cases, the **Copy of** dialog is the most convenient way to establish new user accounts. To use this dialog:

1. Open User Manager and select the account whose parameters you wish to reproduce.

2. Pull down the **User** menu, and choose **Copy** from that menu.

3. In the resulting **Copy of [User Name]** dialog, use the by-now-familiar text-boxes, checkboxes, and buttons to define the characteristics, including such essential ones as account name and password, of the new account.

4. Complete the creation of the new user, after you've entered all the detail needed, by clicking **Add**.

No Simultaneous New User Accounts

It may be obvious, but we'll say it anyway. You cannot simultaneously create several new user accounts by copying the characteristics of one or more existing ones.

> **POP QUIZ** How do you think you should go about removing individual user accounts? (Extra credit will be given for answers that go beyond the minimum information needed. The answer is at the end of this chapter.)

Users in Multiple Domains

Users can traverse domains under only three conditions:

- They have accounts on all domains in question.

- Their accounts on their home domain have been set up to be Global Accounts.

- Their accounts confer membership in a global group that is in turn a member of one of another domain's local groups.

These conditions were discussed and illustrated respectively:

- In the section "Creating New User," in Chapter 2

- At the beginning of the major section "User Management," of which this is the last subsection

- In the section "Using the Group Membership Dialog" a little earlier in this chapter

File System Management

Of the myriad network management tools available under Windows NT Server 4.0, none bears so closely on the operations of Internet Information Server as does the group related to file management. In order to peruse these tools as closely as they therefore deserve, we first define in more detail the IIS file systems of our hypothetical environments. Then we proceed to investigate administrative questions particular to single-domain and multi-domain implementations of IIS.

> **TIP** We'll learn how to share portions of a file system in both single- and multi-domain scenarios.
>
> Unless it has been defined to be shared, no file or directory on an NT network will be available across that network. Only users logged on to the machine on which the files or directories are housed will be able to access them.

Terminology Inconsistency

NT isn't consistent in its file system terminology. Although it has made a concerted effort to adopt the term *folder* in place of the more familiar *directory*, NT occasionally forgets itself and speaks of the latter. Because the term *directory* is probably more familiar to this book's audience, we've used and will continue to use it throughout *Microsoft Internet Information Sourcebook*.

A Single Domain's File System

At K & S, with its single domain, the network staff fixed upon only one alternative to the default IIS directories. Because they wished to create an Internet Information Server environment that emphasized FTP services, they installed those services in the path **c:\ftproot,** directly under the root directory of the C drive. In addition, they set up a series of subdirectories under this FTP root. Each of these subdirectories corresponds to one of the user groups discussed at the beginning of this chapter in the section "Profiles of the Environments." After they created a few *mkdirs* (being traditionalists), the file subsystem sketched in Figure 5.31 came to life.

Figure 5.31 File subsystems can be set up to mimic systems of users.

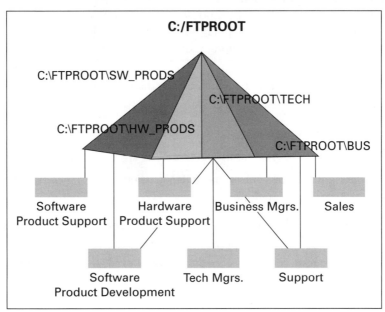

Having this clear template of their IIS file subsystem at hand, network staff members were better prepared to deal with the several file management tasks involved in establishing secure network access to that collection of information. Those tasks can be categorized as:

- Creating and modifying shares

- Assigning permissions of various types to shared directories and files

- Isolating shared information in order to view it as a group

We look at each of these in turn.

Creating, Editing, or Deleting Shares

As NT Administrator, you automatically have the ability to create shares. In addition, any user logged on as a member of the default groups—administrators, server operators, and power users—can do the same. But any of these file system architects must be logged on to a primary or backup domain controller or standalone server to carry out this task. It cannot be done from a workstation.

My Computer Versus File Manager
My Computer is functionally, if not visually, almost identical to *File Manager* of Windows 3.x fame. If you've used *File Manager*, you understand the role of *My Computer*.

Assuming you're logged on to NT as one of the users specified above, all you need do to set up a share is:

1. Open **My Computer**, and navigate it to highlight, one at a time, each of the directories you wish to make shared.

2. Click the rightmost of your mouse buttons to pop up NT's context-sensitive, file- and directory-related menu.

3. From this menu, select **Sharing**. Doing so will present you with the **Sharing** subdialog of the overall **Properties** window for the selected directory. The directory in question should appear as **Not Shared**, the default under NT Server 4.0.

Figure 5.32 In this dialog, we define sharing for one of the most frequently used tools in the K & S file system.

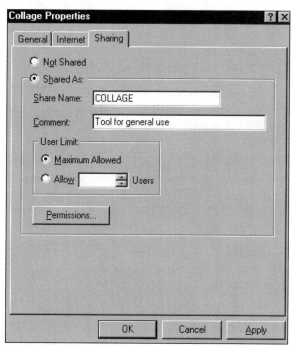

4. Check the **Shared As** box to gain access to the text and other boxes in the rest of the **Sharing** dialog. Then fill out those areas as appropriate to the needs of your IIS environment.

Figure 5.32 shows one instance of sharing as it was set up for Kulicke & Soffa.

As you might imagine, the **Sharing** window must also be used to change any of a share's defined parameters or to unshare, or make unavailable across a network, previously shared files and directories. To do the former, simply display the **Sharing** dialog as just described and change those characteristics, such as **Share Name**, that you want to modify. To make a file system or subsystem unavailable to all but locally connected users, open the **Sharing** window, and uncheck the **Shared As** box.

Assigning Permissions and Shares

Under NT, share permissions consist of the types of access outlined in Table 5.5.

Table 5.5 Understanding NT Share Permissions

The Permission	Allows Users Who Hold It to
No Access	*Do nothing whatsoever* with the files or directories to which it is attached. Users can't even read such files or see them listed under **My Computer**.
Read	Find directory, subdirectory, or file names to which this permission has been attached in listings generated by **My Computer**; open a file in the shared directory or subdirectory, *after having made that part of the overall path their current working directory*; run programs that have the **Read** permission associated with them.
Change	Everything allowed by **Read** permission, as well as creating new subdirectories or files within a shared directory that bears **Change** permission, changing existing files in such a directory, and removing subdirectories and files from shared directories tagged with Change.
All	Everything already mentioned, plus the ability to modify NTFS file or directory permissions and take ownership of NTFS files and directories.

Isolating Shared Information

To view information on shared portions of your file system, rather than on the file system as a whole, open the **Control Panel** and then its **Server** tool. In the Server window that NT then presents to you, click the button **Shares**. This in turn displays the Shared Resources window, in which you can view information on:

- Names assigned to each share

- The number of active sessions currently accessing the share

- The full path name associated with the share

> **TIP** Under NT 4.0, you have very nearly as much control over a FAT file system as over an NTFS-based one. All we were denied by running a FAT file system were the long directory, file, and share names that NTFS would have made available. We were able to allocate every one of the permissions described in Table 5.5 to a number of directories, subdirectories, and files on our FAT partition.

File Systems Across Multiple Domains

In addition to the file management tasks outlined in the section just completed, NT Server 4.0 has another group of such functions that is particularly germane to multi-domain networks. These jobs collectively carry the name *replication*.

In order to discuss replication fully, we need to introduce a few more NT terms:

- **Export folder.** The directory from which subdirectories or files are to be copied

- **Export server.** The computer housing the export folder

- **Import folder.** The directory to which information is copied

- **Import computer.** The machine on which the import folder lives

Given these terms and their translations, you can immediately see the value of replication to the administrators of multi-domain networks, such as the one established for Delaware County Community College.

Replication by the Few

Replication can be carried out only by certain users—members of the default NT groups **Administrators** and **Replicator**, to be exact.

At DCCC, as at K & S, the IIS file subsystem was designed to correspond to user groups. Figure 5.33 graphs DCCC's IIS files.

To implement this file subsystem, the Computer Services group at the college employed not only shares and access permissions as discussed in the section "A Single Domain's File System," but also used replication by:

1. Opening **Control Panel** and its **Services** tool

2. Selecting **Directory Replicator** and, if that service has not been set up to start automatically when the NT 4.0 server boots,

   a. Clicking the **Startup** button in the **Services** window

   b. Checking the box labeled **Automatic** in the resulting **Service** dialog

   c. Supplying the user name and password of the individual who will be allowed to carry out directory replications, either by typing them all in or selecting

Figure 5.33 An IIS file system can be extended across domains.

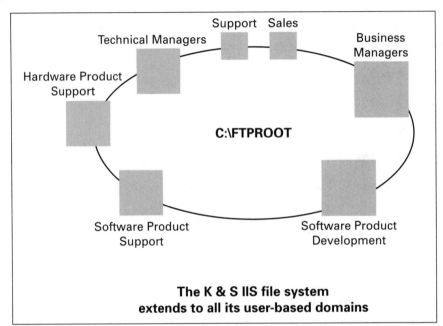

Support Sales

Technical Managers

Business
Managers

Hardware Product
Support

C:\FTPROOT

Software Product
Support

Software Product
Development

**The K & S IIS file system
extends to all its user-based domains**

the user name from the window's drop-down list of available users and then supplying and confirming the appropriate password

d. Restarting NT Server 4.0 as prompted

Figure 5.34 shows the **Service** dialog, which, again, is *not* the same as the **Services** window.

Once you've ensured that the Directory Replicator service will henceforth start when NT Server starts, you can proceed to setting up:

- The export folder or folders

- The export server or servers

- The import folder or folders

- The import computer or computers

The plurals above show that more than one directory from a given machine may be replicated to more than one machine or directory. At this point do the following:

Figure 5.34 Replicating may require the Service dialog to be filled in.

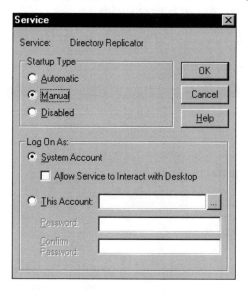

1. Open **Control Panel** and then its **Server** tool.

2. Click the **Replication** button at the bottom almost-far-right of the **Server** window.

3. In the resulting **Directory Replication** dialog,

   a. Enable exporting or importing through replication by checking the box **Export Directories** (or **Import Directories**, if appropriate).

   b. Identify the portion of the file system to be exported by entering its full path name in the **From Path** box.

   c. Identify the target domain and/or computer to which files will be sent when you click **Add** and then key in appropriate names of the list of possible destinations.

If you wish to tailor NT's handling of exported directories, click the **Manage** button immediately to the right of the **From Path** text box in **Directory Replication** to display the **Manage Exported Directories** window and respond appropriately to this latter window, shown in Figure 5.35.

The sequence of steps just given applies equally to exporting and importing.

Figure 5.35 Manage Exported Directories allows you to lock, unlock, add more, or remove export directories.

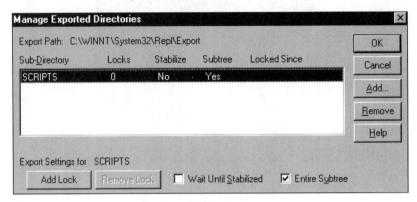

Printers

To this point, we've not walked through any of the Wizards that NT Server 4.0 makes available. To add some balance, we use no other tools in our discussions about sharing local printers and configuring network printers.

Local Printers

Open the Add Printer Wizard through any of these paths.

- **Start** ---> **Settings** ---> **Control Panel** ---> **Printers** ---> **Add Printer**

- **Start** ---> **My Computer** ---> **Control Panel** ---> **Printers** ---> **Add Printer**

- **Start** ---> **Programs** ---> **Administrative Tools** ---> **Administrative Wizards** ---> **Add Printer**

From the first screen of this Wizard, you can add a local printer (as, in this example, the first step in sharing it across the network) by checking the box **My Computer**, or add a network printer—that is, one that's physically connected to some other machine on the network—by checking the box **Network printer server**, as shown in Figure 5.36.

Then, as shown in Figure 5.37, you deal with port parameters.

Depending on the makeup of your environment, you may have to navigate several subdialogs before arriving at the next significant screen of the **Add Printer Wizard**. We outline these subsidiary windows in Table 5.6.

Figure 5.36 In this case, My Computer doesn't refer to the NT icon of the same name but rather to the machine to which you wish to attach a local printer.

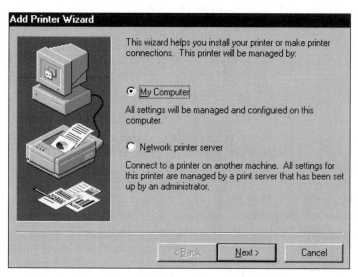

Figure 5.37 The second screen of the Add Printer Wizard allows you not only to define the port to which the local printer is connected, but also, if need be, to configure one of that port's most important operating parameters—its timeout interval.

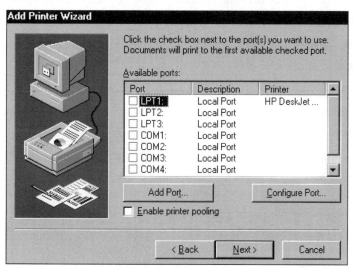

Table 5.6 Summarizing Add Printer Wizard's Secondary Screens

The Screen Titled	Allows You to
Printer Ports	Add a port, serial *or* parallel, to the list the Wizard shows you of available printer ports.
Configure LPT Port	Set the printer's timeout interval.
Ports	Choose a specific *serial* port to which to connect your printer.
Settings for COM	Define such *serial* port parameters as baud rate, parity, and so on.
Advanced Settings for COM	Define such *serial* port parameters as IRQ, base memory address, and so on.

Hardware Timeout

Timeouts occur for printers, modems, and many other pieces of data processing hardware. In other words, they stop looking for more work to do after a preset interval. So, if the computer to which a printer shared across a network is physically attached becomes bogged down, users of that printer may lose print jobs. Increasing the timeout, however, can help preclude this situation.

Screen 3 of the Add Printer Wizard, shown in Figure 5.38, is the window in which you select a printer manufacturer/model combo that best describes the printer you're installing.

In APW's fourth screen, like that in Figure 5.39, you simply name, or accept the default name, of the printer you're setting up.

Screen 5 of this process allows you to specify whether or not you want the printer in question to be shared across the network. Check **Shared**, as we did in Figure 5.40.

Before prompting you for the Windows NT Server 4.0 distribution CD, the Add Printer Wizard asks if you'd like to print a test page. This one's up to you. In any case, once you've responded to this offer and to NT's prompts for distribution media, NT copies the files your new printer needs and then takes you straight to the **Printer Properties** dialog, shown in Figure 5.41.

Table 5.7 summarizes the screens that make up **Printer Properties**.

Figure 5.38 Get as close as you can with your pair of choices to an exact definition of your printer.

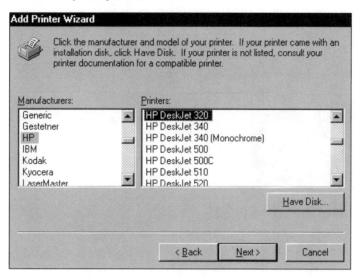

Figure 5.39 The Wizard creates the default printer name from the manufacturer/model pair you defined in the previous screen, so that name is usually descriptive.

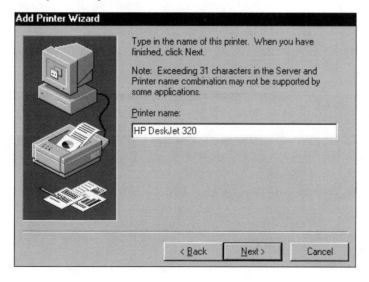

Figure 5.40 The Wizard needs to know the printer's relationship to the network.

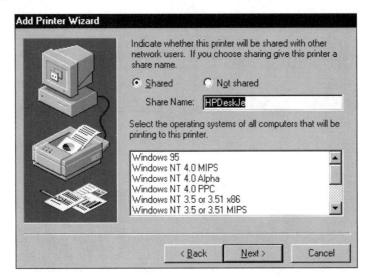

Table 5.7 NT 4.0's Printer Properties Screens

This Screen Under Printer Properties	Lets You Define Such Things as
General	The driver to be used with the printer, and whether that driver is a new or updated version of one installed earlier.
Ports	A new port or port characteristics for the current printer.
Scheduling	The hours during which this printer will accept users' jobs, job priorities, spooling, and more.
Sharing	Whether or not to continue to share this printer, and a name for the share.
Security	Access permissions for, and auditing of user and group access to, the printer as well as allows you to assign ownership of it to a user or group.
Device Settings	Printer settings, but only if you have Full Control, as do members of the Administrators, Server Operators, Print Operators, or Power Users groups.

Figure 5.41 Printer Properties—the place to go to fine-tune printer settings.

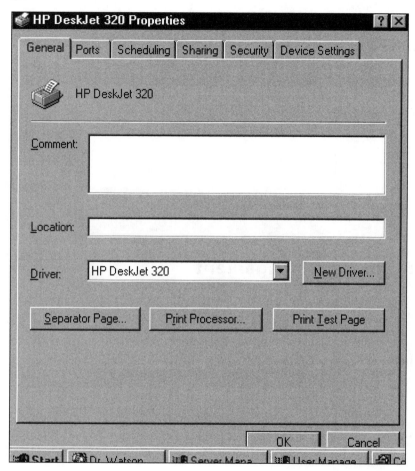

Network Printers

Setting up a remote printer to act as a print server to your NT net involves only one step in addition to those described in the section just above. After selecting **Network printer server**, you'll see a screen that asks you to define not only a print queue but also the network to which the printer will attach, as in Figure 5.42.

Figure 5.42 You must complete Connect to Printer to install a print server.

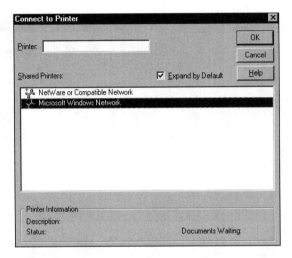

Performance Management

As we learned in Chapter 2, NT Server 4.0 offers the tools **Event Viewer** and Performance Monitor to enable you to view network performance. **Event Viewer** tracks individual instances or events; **Performance Monitor** records *trends and patterns* in network usage.

Performance Monitor relies on two more NT-specific concepts or constructs: objects and counters. Like some other NT abstractions, these need a bit of explaining.

Think of objects as a sort of generic name or label by which individual occurrences of a system resource are identified. In this sense, an object might consist of:

- A printer

- A modem

- A portion of shared memory

- An application

- A single process generated by an application

- A thread of processes

Figure 5.43 Performance Monitor sees to it that network performance parameters such as *%DPC time* **need not be a mystery.**

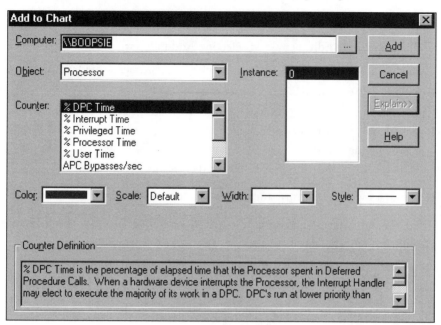

Counters are easier to define and understand. Under NT 4.0, a counter is simply a statistic of some sort, related to an object of some kind. NT has quite a few default counters available, relating to the objects:

- Memory

- Memory paging

- Hard disk

- CPU

Although it won't allow you to define your own counters or objects, Performance Monitor does supply a hefty list of statistics from which you can choose, and whose role it will explain to you, as illustrated in Figure 5.43.

Figure 5.44 is an example of one of **Performance Monitor**'s charts. We produced it by:

1. Taking the path **Start** ---> **Programs** ---> **Administrative Tools** ---> **Performance Monitor.**

2. Pulling down the **View** menu and selecting **Chart.**

3. Pulling down the **Edit** menu and selecting **Add to Chart.**

4. Selecting the parameters **% Interrupt Time,** and **% User Time** from the resulting dialog.

Had we wished to create a summary of network usage statistics in any of Performance Monitor's other three formats, we would have varied step 2 to select one of those formats and then repeated steps 3 and 4 above, which NT has kindly and automatically modified for us to reflect the format we've chosen.

To create a log using **Performance Monitor,** do the following:

1. Take the path **Start** ---> **Programs** ---> **Administrative Tools** ---> **Performance Monitor.**

2. Pull down the View menu.

3. Choose **Log.**

Figure 5.44 Here's the chart we built with Performance Monitor.

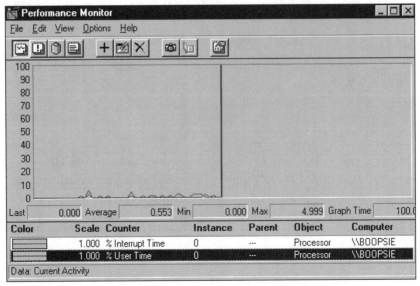

4. Pull down the Edit menu.

5. Click **Add to Log**.

Follow these steps to create an alert with **Performance Monitor**:

1. Take the path **Start** ---> **Programs** ---> **Administrative Tools** ---> **Performance Monitor**.

2. Pull down the View menu.

3. Choose **Alert**.

4. Pull down the Edit menu.

5. Click **Add to Alert**.

To define Alert options, choose the parameters you wish to use as alarm triggers from the list Performance Monitor presents you.

Table 5.8 summarizes **Performance Monitor**'s four formats, noting for each features particularly suited to overseeing Internet Information Server. Table 5.9 outlines all counters available to **Performance Monitor**'s four IIS-related objects. Table 5.10 closes this chapter by detailing **Performance Monitor** counters specific to the Global IIS object.

> **TIP** Fine-tune your IIS implementation by monitoring it with a combination of objects.
>
> In addition to the four IIS-related objects that **Performance Monitor** presents to you, creating a chart, alert, log, or report that also contains memory, processor, protocol, remote access, and server objects and their corresponding counters would allow you to tune IIS by hair's breadths.

Table 5.8 A Summary of Performance Monitor

The Format	Offers
Chart	Line charts
	Histograms
	Bar charts
	A total of 28 objects, among them four related to Internet Information Server: FTP Server, Gopher Services, HTTP (that is,

Continued

Table 5.8 *Continued*

The Format	Offers
	World Wide Web Services), and Internet Information Services Global (that is, IIS across the entire network).
	Counters that vary in number and content according to the object to which they are applied, but all of which track the parameters they represent for the objects you've selected.
	Color coding of the lines, bars, and so on to distinguish counters from one another.
	The ability to export charts to any location defined under My Computer for manipulation via applications such as spreadsheets.
Alerts	The same 28 objects as for the Chart format.
	The same object-associated counters as Chart.
	The ability to establish alerts for occurrences of an object's performance either under or over a defined threshold.
	The ability to define the interval at which performance of the selected objects will be checked against threshhold values.
	A color code to better distinguish counters from one another.
	The ability to export alerts to any location defined under My Computer for manipulation by applications.
Logs	The same 28 objects and their corresponding counters.
	The ability to define the interval at which activity of the selected objects will be monitored.
	The ability to save logs to files for later review.
	The ability to export logs to any location defined under My Computer.
Reports	The same 28 objects and their corresponding counters.
	The ability to define the interval at which activity of the selected objects will be monitored.
	The ability to save reports to files for later review.
	The ability to export reports to any location defined under My Computer.

Table 5.9 IIS-Related Counters Available Under Performance Monitor

The Counter	Applies to the IIS Service	And Gives You Information On
Aborted Connections	Gopher	Total number of connections to the gopher server that have been dropped since the server was started. Breaking a gopher connection frequently happens because the number of requests to the gopher server exceeds a limit previously defined.
Bytes Received/sec	FTP, Gopher, HTTP, Global	Rate at which data bytes are received.
Bytes Sent/sec	FTP, Gopher, HTTP, Global	Rate at which data bytes are transmitted.
Bytes Total/sec	FTP, Gopher, HTTP, Global	Total bytes transferred, equal to the sum of bytes sent and received; that is, overall throughput.
CGI Requests	HTTP	Total number of Common Gateway Interface (CGI) requests executed since WWW service startup. Such requests invoke custom executables, which can provide such features as forms processing to your Web server.
Connection Attempts	FTP, Gopher, HTTP, Global	Total connection attempts since service startup.
Connections/sec	HTTP	Rate at which HTTP requests are handled.
Connections in Error	Gopher	Total number of connections that generated gopher service errors since service was started.
Current Anonymous Users	FTP, Gopher, HTTP, Global	Total anonymous users currently connected.
Current CGI Requests	HTTP	Total CGI requests currently being simultaneously processed; includes WAIS index queries.

Continued

Table 5.9 *Continued*

The Counter	Applies to the IIS Service	And Gives You Information On
Current Connections	FTP, Gopher, HTTP, Global	Total current connections to the service; that is, the sum of anonymous and non-anonymous users.
Current ISAPI Extension Requests	HTTP	Total ISAPI extension requests currently being simultaneously processed.
Current Non-anonymous Users	FTP, Gopher, HTTP, Global	Total nonanonymous users currently connected to a given service.
Files Received	FTP	Total files received by a service since startup.
Files Sent	FTP, Gopher, HTTP, Global	Total files sent by a service since startup.
Files Total	FTP, HTTP	Total files transferred in either direction since service was started.
Get Requests	HTTP	Total number of GET requests received since service started (GET requests perform text and image file retrievals).
Gopher Plus Requests	Gopher	Total number of Gopher Plus requests received since service startup.
Head Requests	HTTP	Total number of HEAD requests received since service was started (HEAD requests involve a client's querying the state of a document already retrieved in order to determine if it needs to be refreshed).
ISAPI Extension Requests	HTTP	Total number of HTTP ISAPI extension requests received since service startup (ISAPI Extension Requests are custom code modules that can modify the HTTP service's forms and security handling, among other features).
Logon Attempts	FTP, Gopher, HTTP, Global	Total logon attempts since service startup.

Table 5.9 *Continued*

The Counter	Applies to the IIS Service	And Gives You Information On
Maximum Anonymous Users	FTP, Gopher, HTTP, Global	Largest number of anonymous users simultaneously connected to a given service since startup.
Maximum CGI Requests	HTTP	Largest number of CGI requests simultaneously processed since service startup.
Maximum Connections	FTP, Gopher, HTTP, Global	Largest number of users simultaneously connected to a given service since startup.
Maximum ISAPI Extension Requests	HTTP	Largest number of ISAPI extension requests simultaneously processed since service startup.
Maximum Non-anonymous Users	FTP, Gopher, HTTP, Global	Largest number of nonanonymous users simultaneously connected to a given service since startup.
Not Found Errors	HTTP	Total requests that could not be satisfied because requested document could not be found.
Other Request Methods	HTTP	Total HTTP requests that are not GET, POST, or HEAD.
Post Requests	HTTP	Total requests that use the POST method; most commonly applied to forms.
Total Anonymous Users	FTP, Gopher, HTTP, Global	Total number of anonymous users that have ever connected to a given service since startup.
Total Non-anonymous Users	FTP, Gopher, HTTP, Global	Total number of nonanonymous users that have ever connected to a given service since startup.

Table 5.10 Global IIS Counters

The Counter	Allows You to Monitor
Cache Flushes	Total times since service startup that the joint FTP/Gopher/HTTP cache for IIS has been flushed.

Continued

Table 5.10 *Continued*

The Counter	Allows You to Monitor
Cache Hits	Total (since service startup) file open, directory listing, or other, more service-specific request was found in the IIS cache.
Cache Hits	Ratio of cache hits to cache requests, given as a percentage.
Cache Misses	Total (since service startup) file open, directory listing, or other request was not found in the joint IIS cache.
Cache Size	Configured maximum size of the shared IIS cache.
Cache Used	Current total bytes of cached data in the shared IIS cache.
Cached File Handles	Current total open file handles cached by all IIS services.
Current Blocked Async I/O Requests	Current number of asynchronous I/O requests blocked by bandwidth throttling.
Directory Listings	Current number of cached directory listings across all IIS services.
Measured Async I/O Bandwidth Usage	Total bandwidth in bytes of asynchronous I/O; averaged over the immediately previous minute.
Objects	Current total of objects cached across all IIS services.
Total Allowed Async I/O Requests	Total asynchronous I/O requests allowed by bandwidth throttling since IIS startup.
Total Blocked Async I/O Requests	Total asynchronous I/O requests blocked by bandwidth throttling since IIS startup.
Total Rejected Async I/O Requests	Total asynchronous I/O requests rejected by bandwidth throttling since IIS startup.

ANSWER TO POP QUIZ How *do* you delete users?

You've earned yourself an A if you said, "Take the path Start ---> Programs ---> Administrative Tools ---> User Manager for Domains. Then select the user or users that have to be removed, pull down the User menu, and click **Delete**."

You earned an A-plus if you added, "Don't try to remove any of NT's default users." (Not that the NOS would let you do this in any case.)

From Here

At this point, you've accumulated quite a collection of equipment in your NT tool-box—more than enough to manage most networks. And you've learned how to construct, distribute, and administer a file system whose primary purpose is to act as the basis for an IIS-driven intranet or Internet site.

In Chapter 6, we move on to another installment of IIS tool time—working with **Internet Service Manager,** the most significant, and almost the only, management tool built into Internet Information Server.

6

Using Built-In
IIS Tools

This chapter provides a thorough walkthrough of IIS-specific tools. We examine **Internet Service Manager** (in both its NT- and HTML-based incarnations) **and Key Manager.**

Although Key Manager has as strong a relationship to Internet security as it does to IIS in general (and will be examined in even more detail in Chapter 10 for that reason), it forms an important part of Internet Information Server's toolbox as well.

We again consider the tools in the context of two hypothetical IIS implementations based on the real-world environments: Kulicke & Soffa Industries and Delaware County Community College. To that end, we repeat here the illustrations of these organizations' IIS implementations (Figures 6.1 and 6.2).

Internet Service Manager

Internet Service Manager (ISM) is the more significant, and certain to be the more heavily used, of the pair of administrative tools built into Internet Information server. ISM allows you to:

- Start, stop, or pause an Internet service.

- Change the ways in which you can view information on your IIS services (known as *sorting the view*).

- Change or fine-tune the configuration of your Internet Information Server.

- Establish a number of intranet or Internet publishing directories, which your users will be able to access as if these branches of your IIS file system were a single bough; that is, set up a system of *virtual directories*.

Virtual Identity

Virtual is a widely used data processing and data communications term that means very much the same thing to **Internet Service Manager** as it does in those larger arenas. Anything virtual—memory, sockets, or directories—is an entity that is presented in a form or under a name different from the one it actually inhabits.

- Control network use by limiting the data communications bandwidth available to your FTP, gopher, or HTTP services.

Figure 6.1 IIS at Kulicke & Soffa.

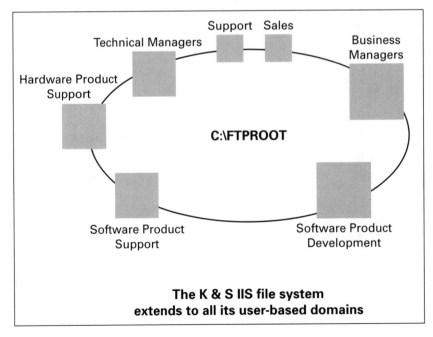

The K & S IIS file system
extends to all its user-based domains

Figure 6.2 IIS at Delaware County Community College.

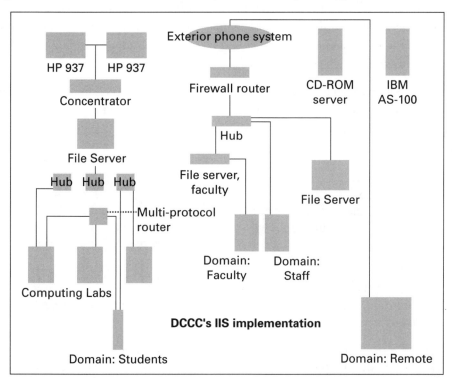

HTTP or Web?

Throughout its online Internet Information Server documentation, and in some of its **Internet Service Manager** dialogs as well, Microsoft alternates between the labels HTTP and Web. We do the same, if only to get you accustomed to the practice.

Internet Service Manager, if appropriately installed, can be run from Windows NT Workstation platforms as well as from a domain controller or server running Windows NT Server, as long as such machines can connect through the network to your IIS server and provide accounts on that server with permissions adequate to network administration.

In addition, if you've installed NT Server 4.0's remote administration capabilities, you can run **Internet Service Manager** from the IIS server itself, a workstation on the NT LAN, or a connection across the Internet.

Windows NT Server 4.0, with its several layers of control of user access, ensures that only validated administrators can work with **Internet Service Manager**. Further, because of NT's system of security and validation of user passwords, administrator passwords, like all such keys, are encrypted before they're zapped around the intranet or onto the Internet.

Internet Service Manager exists in two forms: the NT-based version whose main window is shown in Figure 6.3 and an HTML-based rendering that, according to Microsoft, can be run from any Web browser, and whose initial screen Figure 6.4 represents.

> **TIP** Why do we use the phrase *according to Microsoft*? Because of the qualifying phrase *any Web browser*. As anyone who's spent even a modicum of time cruising today's Net knows, not all Web browsers are created equal. For instance, older versions of that pillar of the browser community, Netscape, cannot handle frames.
>
> Frames are the means by which, among other things, animation can be incorporated into a Web page. A browser that cannot handle frames cannot adequately display Web pages that contain them.
>
> What's more important, many Web sites, including the Microsoft Web site, have not fully provided alternatives to their frames-laden material for those browsers that cannot handle frames. During the time this book was being written, for example, we were unable to look at, let alone download, information or software from many of the pages at Microsoft's Web site. Statements on those pages assured us that text-only versions of same were at hand for the frameless among us, but these text-based alternatives either were still under construction, or locked us out. For this reason alone, we recommend using the NT-interface embodiment of **Internet Service Manager**.

Either rendition of **Internet Service Manager** gives you access to all the **Manager**'s tools; neither offers any functionality that the other lacks. However, because the look of **ISM** differs significantly from one of its personas to another and—more important—because the physical steps you must take to use those tools differ correspondingly, we deal with each version of **ISM** individually.

Figure 6.3 This version of Internet Service Manager uses the standard NT interface.

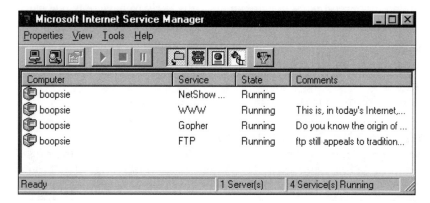

Figure 6.4 If you're more comfortable with browsers, you can use the HTML-based ISM.

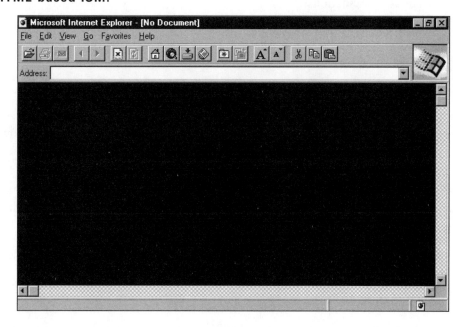

Internet Service Manager—The NT Interface

Although a single-domain NT net may have many controllers and servers, because its physical and organizational scope are limited, it is likely to have only one machine acting as an Internet Information Server. For this reason, some of the features of **Internet Service Manager** are moot in such an environment. One such feature is the need to connect to an FTP, gopher, or Web server across the network in order to administer it. If you're logged on to a single-domain NT net with administrative privileges, you're already connected to that LAN's Internet Information Server.

Automatic IIS Connection

The automatic connection to a LAN's IIS is a result of one of the most conspicuous characteristics of a domain. Remember, under NT Server 4.0, users log on to a domain, rather than to particular machines.

Another feature is the need to find servers—whether FTP, gopher, or HTTP—on the network. Once again, it's unlikely that a single-domain environment would have a number of Internet Information Servers, and therefore the need to locate these computers. By definition, such an environment is one without the following:

- A large user population

- A widely varied information base

- Heavy network traffic

- A high percentage of access from remote sites

However, even in a limited IIS implementation, the need to monitor services according to a number of criteria will exist. To monitor them, you must know how to manipulate the **Internet Service Manager View** menu.

A Manager with Several Views

Internet Service Manager makes available different graphical representations of any Internet services running on your IIS server. These are known as:

- **Report View** (the default, and the best choice for managing small IIS implementations like that at K & S)

- **Services View**

- **Servers View** (a good choice for diverse IIS environments like Delaware County Community College)

We look at each of these in more detail after investigating the abilities shared by all ISM Views.

Choosing a View

From the **View** menu, shown in Figure 6.5, you can select the display format most appropriate to your IIS administrative needs of the moment. To choose a view, simply pull down the View menu in **Internet Service Manager** and select the View best suited to your needs:

- **Servers** View, as its name implies, is most handy in isolating the display of, and managing the information pertaining to, individual machines running Internet Information Server. (Servers View is the least valuable view in a small, single-domain network.)

- **Services** View is your best bet if your IIS administrative tasks lean heavily toward the manipulation services only.

- **Report** View is a good choice if you must have available, at a single glance, information on the status of more than one IIS service or more than one computer distributing IIS within the domain. And as mentioned a moment ago, **Report** is ISM's default display format and the one best suited to small LANs.

Sorting in a View

In **Report** View, **Internet Service Manager** allows you to sort displays by four variables:

- Server

- Service

- Comment

- State

> **TIP** Only Report View allows you to sort the ISM display.
>
> As you might imagine, the need to sort by the first two criteria above is not even present in the corresponding views. What's less intuitive is that, if you're running either **Services** or **Server** view, you cannot sort by comment or state either.

Figure 6.5 Internet Service Manager's View menu offers diverse choices.

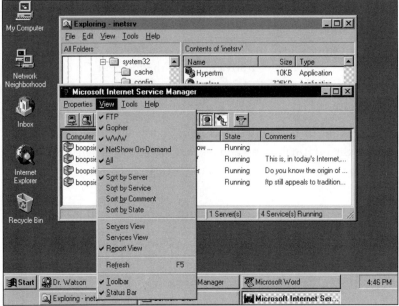

To sort **Report**'s display, follow these steps:

1. Pull down the **View** menu.

2. Select **Sort by Server** to produce a **Report** View organized like that shown in Figure 6.6.

3. Click **Sort by Service** to display a screen like that in Figure 6.7.

4. Pick **Sort by Comment** to receive a window such as the one shown in Figure 6.8.

5. Choose **Sort by State** to bring up a display of services according to their status, like that in Figure 6.9.

Hiding Services

If you're running **Report** or **Services** View, you can tailor the information presented by hiding specific services from the display. To hide a service under **Report** or **Services** View, pull down the View menu and uncheck the service or services you wish to remove from the display.

Figure 6.6   Sort by Server may prove useful to a single-domain network that has distributed its IIS services across multiple machine.

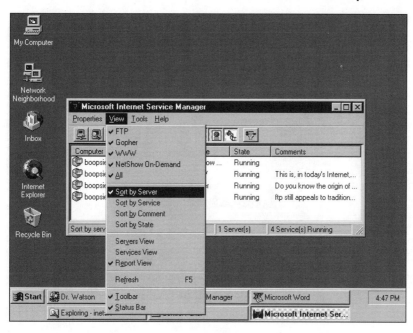

Figure 6.10 shows Report View with all IIS services running but with the FTP service hidden, and Figure 6.11 shows Services View with all IIS services running but with the WWW service hidden.

> **TIP**   Servers View doesn't hide effectively.
>
> You can hide services somewhat in **Server** View, but you cannot hide them individually. Figure 6.12 shows **Server** View with nothing hidden. Figure 6.13 shows the same view after only the FTP service was unchecked. For some reason, **Internet Service Manager** interprets this or any other single deselection as an instruction to hide all services.

A Bit More Detail on ISM Views

In this section, we deal with the miscellany of **Internet Service Manager**'s scheme of Views.

More on Report View   Report View lists selected computers alphabetically and shows every service installed on each computer, one service per line. In addition,

Figure 6.7 Sort by Service produces an at-a-glance prioritization of your service monitoring.

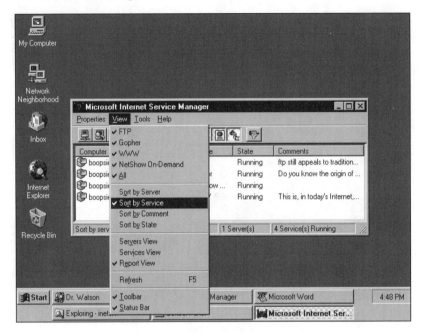

Report View shows other network- and IIS-related services, such as Network News Transfer Protocol (NNTP) and Simple Mail Transfer Protocol (SMTP).

If you wish to sort Report View's display according to the contents of one of its columns, all you need do is click the heading of the column in question. Doing so sorts the entire display alphabetically, according to the contents of the chosen column.

More on Servers View Servers View may at first seem to show you nothing more than the names of computers distributing IIS across your net. In order to see which services are running on a given machine, click the plus symbol next to that computer's name or double-click the name itself.

More on Services View Services View automatically lists all services running under IIS 2.0, whatever the computer from which they're running. If you wish to determine the name of the machine or machines that are providing a given service, click the plus symbol next to the service name or double-click the symbol for the service, or the service name itself.

Figure 6.8 Sort by Comment can be another tool for providing immediate visual focus on specific services.

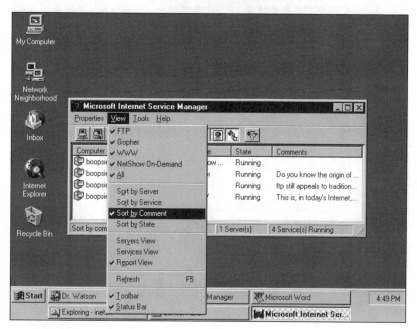

Modifying Service Properties

All Views in **Internet Service Manager** provide the IIS administrator the ability to change the operating parameters of any IIS service. Such changes are made through the **Properties** dialogs associated with each such service.

Each IIS service has its own set of **Properties** dialogs, as outlined in Table 6.1. Table 6.2 details the parameters associated with each IIS **Properties** page.

Table 6.1 IIS Services and Their Properties Dialogs

The Properties Page	Is Available to
Service	All IIS services.
Messages	Only the FTP service.
Directories	All IIS services.
Logging	All IIS services.
Advanced	All IIS services.

Figure 6.9 Sort by State zeroes in on service status.

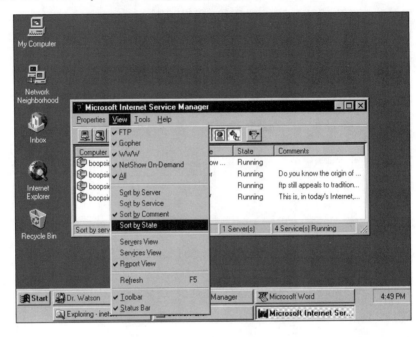

Figure 6.10 You might want to hide a service if it's one you manipulate infrequently.

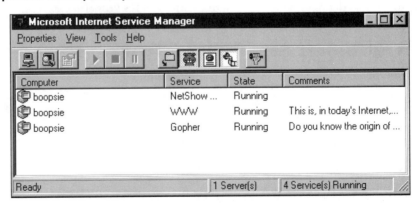

Figure 6.11 You can hide a service to help prevent "drive-by hacking."

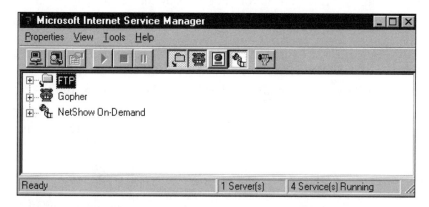

Figure 6.12 This iteration of Servers View hides nothing.

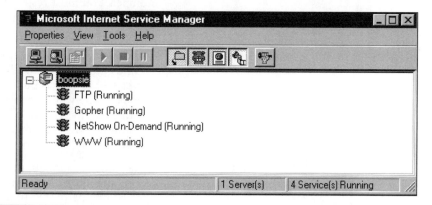

Figure 6.13 Deselecting even one service hides all IIS services in Servers View.

The Service Page Figure 6.14 shows the **Service** page of the FTP service
Properties. Table 6.2 can serve as your key to using the Service page to manipulate
those properties.

Table 6.2 The Capabilities of the Service Page

The Properties Page	Contains the Fields	Which Allow You to
Service	TCP Port	Identify the port on which a service runs. The defaults are: FTP: port 21 Gopher: port 71 HTTP: port 80 You can change any of these ports to any unique TCP port number. You must restart your IIS server for such changes to take effect.
	Connection Timeout	Determine the length of time in seconds after which an IIS server will disconnect an inactive user. The values available for this parameter range from a minimum of 100 seconds to a maximum of 32,767 seconds.
	Maximum Connections	Determine the maximum number of simultaneous connections that will be permitted to any of your IIS services.
	Allow Anonymous Connections	Enable or disable anonymous connections to the IIS service in question. When it is installed, Internet Information Server creates the account *IUSR_computername* to provide for anonymous logons. This account also exists under **User Manager for Domains**. The account was assigned a random password,

Table 6.2 *Continued*

The Properties Page	Contains the Fields	Which Allow You to
		which is the same in **Internet Service Manager** and in User Manager. Therefore, if you change the password, you must change it in both places. Neither account can have a blank password.
		IUSR_computername is granted **Log on Locally** rights by default, which is required in order to provide anonymous logon access to your site. To grant anonymous access to a specific user, you must identify that user here, as well as provide the account in question with **Log on Locally** rights in **User Manager**.
	Allow Only Anonymous Connections	Make *only* anonymous connections. When it has been selected, users *cannot* log on with user names and passwords This option prevents access by hackers or nebbers who've managed to get hold of administrative user names and passwords.
	Comment	Set out the comment displayed per service in **Report** View.
	Current Sessions	Display the current total number of active users of the service.

TIP The FTP Service Properties page has another field. Clicking the button **Current Sessions** opens another window in which details of all current FTP accesses are diplayed.

Figure 6.14 The Service page of any service's Properties set is the most detailed Properties page.

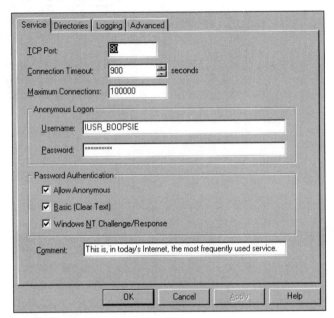

The Messages Page Figure 6.15 presents the Messages page of the FTP service Properties. Table 6.3 outlines using the Messages page.

Table 6.3 The Capabilities of the Message Page

The Properties Page	Contains the Fields	Which Allow You to
Messages	Welcome message	Create a standard message that will be displayed when users access your FTP service.
	Exit message	Create a standard message that will be displayed when users disconnect from your FTP service.
	Maximum Connections message	Create a standard message that will be displayed when users are temporarily barred from accessing your FTP service, because that service has already reached the maximum number of connections for which it is configured.

Figure 6.15 The Messages page is available only to the FTP service.

The Directories Page You can use the **Directories** page to specify which directories users of any IIS service may access and to create a Web, gopher, or FTP site made up of directories on different computers as follows:

- **In the Web service only,** to identify a default document that is displayed if a remote user does not specify a particular file

- **In the Web service only,** to enable directory browsing

- **In the FTP service only,** to specify whether full path names for files should be given in UNIX or DOS format

Directory Browsing
Directory browsing means that your HTTP service presents users with a hypertext listing of the directories and files it distributes so that users can navigate that directory tree.

Figure 6.16 presents the **Directories** page of the WWW service Properties. Table 6.4 details this page.

Figure 6.16 The Directories page is most important to the WWW service.

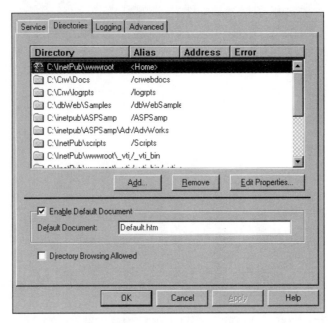

Table 6.4 The Capabilities of the Directories Page

The Properties Page	Contains the Fields	Which Allow You to
Directories	Directory listing box	Define the directories used by an IIS service.
	Directory	Define the full path names of directories used by IIS services.
	Alias	Define the full path names of virtual directories used by IIS services.
	Address	Define the IP address of the server housing the corresponding path and directory.
	Error	View a flag for system errors, such as the inability to read a file.
	Add, Remove, Edit Properties	Press the **Add** button to add a directory.

Table 6.4 *Continued*

The Properties Page	Contains the Fields	Which Allow You to
		Choose a directory in the Directories listing box and press the **Edit Properties** button to change its characteristics. Click **Remove** to remove previously selected directories.
	Enable Default Document	Place a default document in a WWW root directory, causing that document to be displayed when a remote user does not specify a particular file.
	Directory Browsing Allowed	Cause a hypertext directory listing to be sent to the user if this option is enabled and no default document is in the directory specified by the user.

TIP Virtual directories don't show up on the Directories page. Rather, users must know a virtual directory's alias and type in its URL, or click a link to it, to access such a directory.

The Logging Page The Logging dialog allows you to log service activity. You can store logs as text files or send them to an **Open Database Connectivity (ODBC)** database.

TIP Even multi-domain IIS implementations can be logged to a single file. If you're running multiple servers or services, like those envisioned for Delaware County Community College, you can log all activity to one file or database on any network computer.

This page also allows you to choose the format to be used in your IIS logs. These can be either **Standard**—that is, Microsoft's default and proprietary—format, or **National Center for Supercomputing (NCSA) Common Log File** format.

Figure 6.17 presents the Logging page of the WWW service Properties. Table 6.5 details this page.

Figure 6.17 The Logging page allows you to track all services.

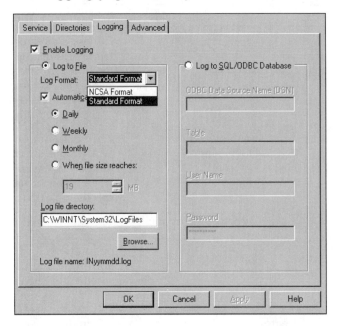

Table 6.5 The Capabilities of the Logging Page

The Properties Page	Contains the Fields	Which Allow You to
Logging	Enable Logging	Start or stop logging for the service in question.
	Log to File	Automatically cause log data to be stored in a text file.
	Log Format	Choose either Standard format or National Center for Supercomputing Applications (NCSA) format.
	Automatically open new log	Cause new logs to be created at the specified interval. If this option is disabled, a single log file will grow indefinitely and may eventually consume your IIS server.
	Log file directory	View the full path name of the directory in which log files are housed. You can change this

Table 6.5 *Continued*

The Properties Page	Contains the Fields	Which Allow You to
		directory, either by using Browse or by explicitly entering a new path.
	Log file name	Fully identify the log with the lowercase letters replaced in the indicated name as follows: *yy* with the year *mm* with the month *dd* with the day
	Log to SQL/ODBC Database	Direct logs to any ODBC data source and set the Datasource name, Table name (not the file name of the table), and the user name and password that are required by the computer on which the database resides. If you enable this option, you must also use the ODBC applet in Control Panel to create a system data source.

The Advanced Page The Advanced page property sheet allows you to prevent individuals or groups from accessing your IIS site. You accomplish such lockouts by specifying the IP address of the computers to be granted or denied access. You can also use the **Advanced** page to limit network traffic by specifying the maximum bandwidth permitted for outbound traffic.

Figure 6.18 captures the **Advanced** page of the gopher service Properties. Table 6.6 outlines the page and its fields.

Table 6.6 The Capabilities of the Advanced Page

The Properties Page	Contains the Fields	Which Allow You to
Advanced	IP Access Control	Grant or deny access to each IIS service by specifying the IP address of individual computers that may or may not use those

Continued

Table 6.6 *Continued*

The Properties Page	Contains the Fields	Which Allow You to
		services. Or, if you've given all users access (the default), you can then specify the computers from which those users may *not* connect.
	Granted Access	Select this option and then pressing the Add button to view and add to a list of computers that can access your IIS services.
	Denied Access	Click **Add** to display and begin the process of expanding the list of computers that may not access your IIS services.
	Limit Network Use by all Internet Services on this computer	Limit the network bandwidth for all IIS services involved in setting the maximum kilobytes of outbound traffic permitted.

Figure 6.18 The Advanced page—not for the network novice.

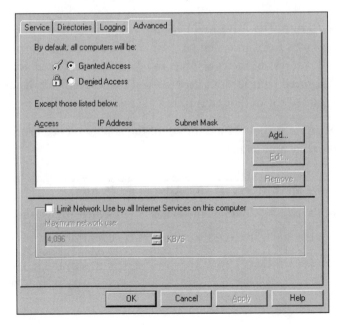

Limiting Bandwidth As the bottom right corner of the last table points out, you can limit the network bandwidth available to all IIS services you're running. Limiting IIS bandwidth is especially useful if your connection to the Internet serves several purposes, such as e-mail and remote logons. If you limit your IIS bandwidth, applications like these can use the same line as IIS services without being slowed down too severely.

To change bandwidth, follow these steps:

1. Open **Internet Service Manager**.

2. In Report View, double-click any service *on the computer for which you wish to change bandwidth allowed* in order to access the Advanced Properties page.

3. In Services View, double-click a service name or click the plus sign at its left to produce a display of computers running the service in question. Then double-click *the specific computer on which you wish to change bandwidth allowed* in order to access the Advanced Properties page.

4. In Servers View, double-click the name of the server or click the plus sign at its left to produce a display of services available on that machine. Then double-click *the service* in order to access the Advanced Properties page.

5. Enter the number of kilobytes per second you want to allocate to IIS services.

6. Click **Apply** and **OK**.

If bandwidth being used stays below the specified level, requests for information continue to be answered. If bandwidth inches too close to the value you set, requests are delayed until network traffic decreases. If the bandwidth exceeds the level you set, your IIS server will reject requests to read files and delay requests to transfer files until the bandwidth reaches or falls below the specified value.

Connecting to a Specific Server

In diverse, large IIS environments like the one we imagined for Delaware County Community College, **Internet Service Manager** may have several servers to monitor. You, as IIS administrator, must connect to a specific server to be able to view the services it distributes. To do so, simply:

1. Pull down IIS's **Properties** menu.

2. Click **Connect to Server** and enter either the host name, the IP address, or the NetBIOS computer name of the server to which you wish to connect and whose services you need to monitor.

There's another way to connect to a specific server in a multi-server or multi-domain IIS environment. After opening ISM and pulling down its Properties menu:

1. Click **Find All Servers**.

2. Double-click, in the resulting list, the name of the server to which you wish to connect.

Starting, Stopping, or Pausing IIS Services

Internet Service Manager makes it easy to start, stop, or pause specific IIS services. The easiest way to do any of these is to select the service you want to start, stop, or pause. Then pull down the **Properties** menu and click **Start Service, Stop Service,** or **Pause Service** as appropriate.

The HTML-Based ISM

The flashier rendition of **Internet Service Manager** program offers all the same tools as the NT-based version. But because by definition it works through a Web browser, the HTML likeness of ISM is particularly useful in administering Internet Information Server from somewhere in the wilds of the Internet.

Start the HTML **Internet Service Manager** by taking the path **Start ---> Programs ---> Microsoft Internet Information Server ---> Internet Service Manager** (HTML) or by using a Web browser to open a URL of the form http://computername/ iisadmin where *computername* is the name of the IIS server you need to manage.

> **TIP** URLs alone aren't all that's required by the HTML **Internet Service Manager**. To administer services across domains or the Internet, you must be logged on to a user account that has Administrator privileges on the server you wish to manage.

Microsoft cautions those using HTML **Internet Service Manager**, and in particular anyone using it across the Internet, regarding the scenarios outlined in Table 6.7.

Table 6.7 Precautions Needed with HTML Internet Service Manager

This Condition	Requires This Precaution
Using a browser that supports only Basic authentication	Do *not* turn off Basic authentication while you are working with **HTML Internet Service Manager.**
Deleting the *Iisadmin* directory on the server you're managing	*Don't delete the Iisadmin directory.* If you forget and delete it, the HTML **Internet Service Manager** will be unavailable on the machine in question.
Stopping a service	*Don't do it.* If you stop a service while working with HTML **Internet Service Manager,** you'll be disconnected from the service and be unable to restart it with HTML Internet Service Manager.

Internet Publishing from Multiple Servers and Directories

All IIS services can make use of multiple directories. Each of these directories can be housed on a local drive or a drive on a server somewhere on the network. This scheme is, in a nutshell, what is meant by the terms *virtual directories* and *virtual servers.*

Supply a name that follows the Internet **Universal Naming Convention (UNC)** format of **xx.yy.com** (or **.gov**, or **.org**) and a user name and password to connect to the server.

Decoding UNCs
The *xx* and *yy* segments of UNC names usually represent department and organization. For instance, the group of software design engineers who contributed many answers to our questions regarding the technologies presented in this book share the UNC **swdesign.kns.com**.

A machine that distributes IIS services can have one home directory and any number of publishing directories, the latter being virtual directories.

To simplify users' entry of URLs, the entire set of publishing directories is presented to clients as a single directory tree. The home directory is at the root of this virtual tree; each virtual directory is dealt with as if it were a true subdirectory of this home directory, *regardless of where the subdirectory actually is.* (Of course, actual subdirectories are also available.)

TIP Only the WWW service of IIS supports virtual servers.

Its FTP and gopher services can have only one home directory. In the FTP service, virtual directories can exist, but must be explicitly noted as such with directory annotations. In the gopher service, virtual directories must be accompanied by explicit links contained in what are called tag files. Without these, users cannot access virtual gopher directories.

Whatever service it is associated with, an IIS virtual directory must be defined in **Internet Service Manager** and have an alias associated with it as part of that definition.

The alias is the subdirectory name that users will supply to access the virtual directory.

No Alias?
Don't worry if you've neglected to supply an alias name. If one hasn't been specified, it will be generated automatically by **Internet Service Manager**.

Home Directories
The **Directories** page of the Properties of any IIS service is the point from which all directories and subdirectories distributed by the service must be defined. Directories not identified to this page are not available to users of the service in question.

Further, every IIS service must have a home directory, which is also the root directory for that service. A root directory cannot have a name other than one of the form **whatever-the-service**root. By default, a service's home directory and any subdirectories it contains are always available to users.

Changing a Home Directory If for some reason you need to change an IIS service's home directory, as was the case with the Kulicke & Soffa IIS installation pictured at the beginning of this chapter, do the following:

1. Open **Internet Service Manager**, select the service whose home directory must be changed, and then display that service's **Directories** Properties page.

2. In the **Directory** list, select the directory with the label <home>.

3. Click **Edit Properties**.

4. In the Directory Properties dialog, shown in Figure 6.19, either type the name of the new home directory, or select a new home directory by means of the **Browse** button.

5. In the **Access** box, select the access that you want to give users who connect to that directory.

6. Click **OK, Apply,** and then **OK** once more.

Adding a Subdirectory to a Home Directory Large, diverse multi-domain and multi-server IIS implementations like the one we've envisioned for Delaware County Community College might often need to enhance their IIS services by adding new information to be distributed by those services. Probably the easiest way to accomplish this is to add subdirectories to a home directory. To do that, do the following.

1. Open **Internet Service Manager,** choose the service to whose home directory you wish to add a subdirectory, and then display that service's **Directories** Properties page.

2. Click **Add.**

3. In the **Directory** box, either type the name of the new subdirectory, or create a subdirectory by using the **Browse** button.

4. If you need to restrict or otherwise closely define access to the new subdirectory, click **Access** and then select the access type you want to supply to users who will connect to the new directory. Finally, click **OK, Apply,** and then **OK** one last time.

Deleting a Subdirectory from a Home Directory Just as the people at DCCC might need to enhance their IIS services with new information housed in new subdirectories, they might also need to make those services more timely or accurate by deleting service subdirectories. Doing that requires starting **Internet Service Manager** and navigating to the subdirectory to be removed, clicking **Remove, Apply,** and then **OK.**

Virtual Directories Whatever the IIS service, you can create a theoretically unlimited number of virtual directories for it.

Virtual Directories Limited
Take care in creating virtual directories that you don't define too many. IIS performance, and overall network performance as well, may suffer if you do.

Figure 6.19 The Directory Properties dialog is available to all IIS services.

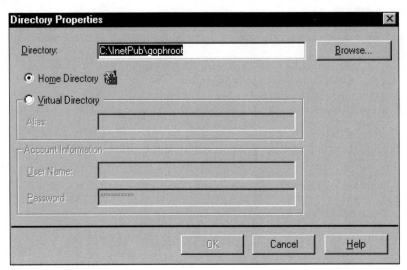

To create a virtual directory, open **Internet Service Manager**, select the service to which you wish to add a virtual directory, bring up that service's **Directories** Properties page, and then proceed as follows:

1. Click **Add**.

2. Select an *existing* directory from the **Directory** box; this is the directory from which the virtual directory being added will seem to branch.

3. Click **Virtual Directory**, and then enter the name for the virtual directory in the **Alias** box.

4. Click **Access** and set permissions.

5. Click the by-now-familiar sequence **OK**, **Apply**, and **OK**.

Setting Up a Virtual Server

Virtual servers must be defined through the **Directories** Properties page. To define one, do the following:

1. Click the **Directories** tab, then click **Add**.

2. In the **Directory** box of the resulting dialog, either select a directory by clicking the **Browse** button, or manually enter a full path name.

3. Click **Home Directory**.

4. Check the box **Virtual Server**.

5. Enter an IP address for the virtual server, and then click **OK**.

Internet Identity

IP addresses are typically supplied by an Internet service provider (ISP). Remember, any IP addresses used in conjunction with Internet Information Server must be configured through use of the **TCP/IP Properties** dialog, which can be most easily accessed through the **Network** tool in **Control Panel**.

Directories on Virtual Servers

If your virtual server has been assigned more than one IP address, you must specify which of these addresses corresponds to each directory on that server. Any directory for which definition of this sort is not done will be visible to *all* IIS servers.

To correlate directories and servers in this way, do the following:

1. Open **Internet Service Manager**, and select the server in question.

2. Click the **Add** button, and either type the path in the **Directory** box of the **Directory Properties** dialog, or use the **Browse** button to pick a directory.

TIP Deleting a virtual directory doesn't get rid of the actual files to which the virtual directory pointed. Because every IIS service must have a home directory and all subdirectories and files stored under that home directory will always be accessible, removing a virtual directory simply removes links to it—that is, its alias.

Key Manager

As part of the process of enabling Secure Sockets Layer security on an IIS server, you need to generate what is known as a key pair and then acquire something called an SSL certificate. The **Key Manager** application within Internet Information Server allows you to do both.

The **Secure Sockets Layer,** or **SSL,** is a set of protocols that provides for encryption and decryption of traffic traveling the Internet. As you might imagine, this dual process of encrypting and decrypting requires a key at either end of the conversation. What might not be as obvious is that such keys are not valid on the Internet until they receive the blessing of a type of organization known as a **Certificate Authority.**

VeriSign Authority

VeriSign is the company that is probably the best-known Certificate Authority. Our discussion of **Key Manager** relates to working with VeriSign.

Our discussion of **Key Manager** covers the following topics:

- Generating a key pair

- Generating a key pair on another server

- Acquiring a certificate

- Installing the new certificate with a key pair

- Setting up a directory to require SSL

- Moving a key pair to another server

- Backing up keys

- Loading backed-up keys

All these tasks must be run from IIS's **Key Manager,** illustrated in Figure 6.20. You can open **Key Manager** through the path **Start ---> Programs ---> Internet Information Server ---> Key Manager,** by opening **Internet Service Manager,** pulling down its **Tools** menu, and clicking **Key Manager,** or by opening **Internet Service Manager** and clicking the **Key Manager** icon on its toolbar.

Once **Key Manager** is open, you can proceed.

Creating a Key Pair

Create a key pair by pulling down the **Key** menu and clicking **Create New Key** in the **Create New Key and Certificate Request** dialog box, depicted in Figure 6.21. Fill in the requested information as outlined in Table 6.8.

Figure 6.20 Key Manager controls SSL on your Internet Information Server.

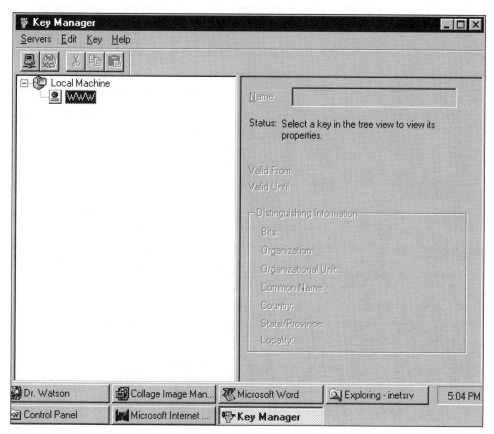

Table 6.8 The Keys to Creating SSL Keys

Using the Field	Results in
Key Name	A unique name to be associated with the key you're creating.
Bits	By default, **Key Manager** generating key pairs of 1024 bits. To specify a key of 512 or 768 bits, make the appropriate selection here. But be aware that the longer the key pair in bits, the greater the security they will provide.

Continued

Table 6.8 *Continued*

Using the Field	Results in
Organization	A top-level organization or company name as opposed to a departmental or group one.
Organizational Unit	A department or group within a company or organization.
Common Name	The domain name of the server, such as www. mycompany.com.
Country	Two-letter ISO Country designation, such as US, FR, AU, UK.
State/Province	PA, MD, and so on.
Locality	The city or town where your organization is located.
Request File	The name of the certificate request file that will be created.

As the key is being created, **Key Manager** displays a small icon. When creation of the key pair is complete, a screen giving you information about new keys and how to obtain a certificate is displayed.

To save the key pair you've just created, pull down the **Servers** menu and click **Commit Changes Now.** Confirm the request to commit changes by clicking **OK.**

Key Manager will display the newly created key under the name of the computer for which you created the key.

TIP Keep these points in mind when creating keys.

The default for new keys is to associate them with the local server. Also, **Key Manager** doesn't like commas in any field. Commas are interpreted as the end of a field, so using them will result in an error.

Remote Key Pair

Defining a key pair on a remote IIS server involves no more than connecting to that server and then following the steps outlined above in *Creating a Key Pair.*

Figure 6.21 The entries you make in the Create New Key ... dialog will be the basis for the authorization you eventually receive for the key.

Acquiring a Certificate

As mentioned earlier, before a key pair can be used on the Internet, it must be associated with a valid certificate from a Certificate Authority such as VeriSign. To obtain such a certificate, you need only send the certificate request file created by **Key Manager** as part of the process of generating a key pair to the Certificate Authority.

> ### Certificate Request Protocol
> Microsoft recommends consulting VeriSign's Web site before sending off your certificate request. That site is at http://www.verisign.com/microsoft.

Installing a Certificate and Key Pair

After you receive a signed certificate from the Certificate Authority you've chosen to work with, install both certificate and keys, as follows:

1. In the **Key Manager** window, select the key pair that matches your signed certificate.

2. Pull down the menu and select.

3. Select the appropriate Certificate file from the resulting list and click **Open**.

4. When prompted, type the password used in creating the key pair; this will cause the key and certificate to be stored in the registry of the appropriate server.

5. Pull down the Servers menu, click **Commit Changes Now**, and then click **OK**.

Setting Up a Directory to Require SSL

Once you have installed certificate and key pair, enable SSL from **Internet Service Manager's** Directories Properties page. Simply select the WWW service, open its Directories Properties page, and then:

1. Choose the directory to which you wish to add SSL security.

2. Click **Edit Properties**.

3. Click the **Require secure SSL channel** option and then **OK**.

Figure 6.22 gives an example of getting a file subsystem ready for SSL.

Moving a Key Pair to Another Server

You can save yourself the effort of creating new keys through Key Manager's ability to move a key pair to another server. Just take these steps:

1. Open **Key Manager** and pull down its **Servers** menu.

2. Select **Connect to Server**, and enter the name of the server to which you wish to move the key pair; then click **OK**. The server name will, as a result, appear in **Key Manager's** list of servers.

3. Next, highlight the key you want to move, pull down **Key Manager's** Edit menu, and click either **Copy** or **Cut**.

4. Reselect the server to which the key pair will be moved, pull down the **Edit** menu once more, and click **Paste**.

Backing Up Keys

Key Manager allows you some flexibility in your handling of keys. For instance, it permits you to copy keys from the NT registry into a file on your hard disk, and

Figure 6.22 SSL further secures any directory in your IIS environment.

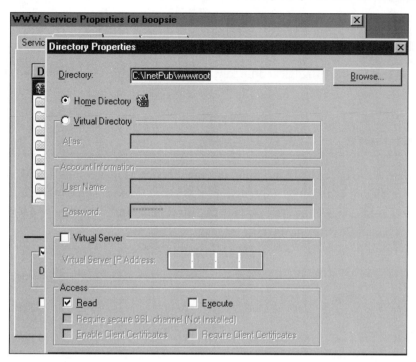

from there to a floppy or tape. You can back up either an uncertified key pair file or a key with a valid certificate.

Backing up a key means doing the following:

1. Open **Key Manager,** and pull down its **Key** menu.

2. Select **Export Key,** and then **Backup File** (to indicate that you want to send the key to a file).

3. Read the warning, then click **OK.**

4. Identify the key in the **File Name** box, and click **Save.**

The file in question receives the extension **.req** and is saved to your hard drive; from there, copy it wherever you like.

With its **Import** command, **Key Manager** also provides you the means of loading previously backed-up keys. Loading such a key means:

1. Opening **Key Manager** and pulling down its **Key** menu.

2. Picking **Import Key** and **Backup File** from that menu.

3. Choosing a file name from the displayed list of key files, and clicking **Open**.

These steps restore the backed-up key, whether uncertified or certified, to the Registry.

From Here

Now that we've unearthed everything **Internet Service Manager** and **Key Manager** have to offer, we can turn to a discussion of what to do with some of the information these tools, as well as **Performance Monitor**, generate. We provide that discussion in Chapter 7, when we investigate logging.

Part Three
Beyond the Basics: Advanced IIS Features

7

Logging and
Databases

In Chapter 6, we had our first encounter with logging IIS activity. In this chapter, we consider that topic in more detail, examining setting up logging, storing log information in text files and converting such files between available formats, and interpreting text log files. In addition, we look at using **SQL Server** or other ODBC-compliant databases as the storage medium for logs of IIS activity and at manipulating and interpreting database-housed log files.

Setting Up Logging in IIS

The activity of each service offered by Internet Information Server can be logged; the information in these logs can help you fine-tune your site, plan for future enhancements and expansion, review the value of areas of content, and monitor security.

Internet Information Server's logging abilities are flexible in that they provide you with choices in several areas, as outlined in Table 7.1.

Whether you do it when you set up Internet Information Server or at some point after that, enabling and configuring IIS's built-in tracking allows you to monitor which users have accessed which service, and how often.

Table 7.1 Flexibility in IIS Logging

The IIS Logging Characteristic	Is Available in the Forms
Where log information is stored	File system
	SQL Server
Log file format	Standard (that is, Microsoft default) format
	European Microsoft Windows NT Academic Centre (EMWAC) format
	National Center for Supercomputing (NCSA) Common Log File format
Location of log files	The default of C:\WINNT\System32\LogFiles, which may be changed
Creation of new log files	New log files that can be created whenever the files achieve a particular size, or whenever the day, week, or month changes

IIS Logging Considerations

Before you can make so much as one click on the path to establishing IIS logs, you need to have thought through and made decisions in the following areas:

- Where will log files be stored? It goes without saying that system information of the sort collected into IIS logs is not for general consumption. Plan to place IIS logs in a portion of your file system accessible only to you, the network administrator, and to members of the group Administrators. If anyone else needs to see these logs, assign read-only access to specific log files to each such user individually.

- How frequently should new logs be created? Almost more than any other type of information on your server, log files are guaranteed to grow far more quickly than it's even possible to anticipate. Consider this scenario:

The manager of a small NT LAN decides—upon implementing Internet Information Server as a Web server only and within the organizational intranet only—to log only users and sessions that request a single HTML page that contains information on using the Web server. Thinking that such limited monitoring need not be configured further, our hypothetical manager neglects to define the frequency at which new logs should come into existence and old ones should be archived. As a result, after several weeks, this solitary log takes up several hundred kilobytes, making it not only an example of poor use of disk space but also turning it into an inefficient tool. (Try quickly finding a single fact in a file this size.)

- IIS allows you to renew logs daily, weekly, or monthly, or when a log file has reached a specified size.

- What tools do you anticipate using to analyze the data in your IIS logs? If yours is a small or infrequently used IIS implementation, text files may suffice to store your logs, and a simple search with an editor or word processor may do to scrutinize the information they offer. However, if you wish to fine-tune your IIS services, or if your server is a busy one, you might want to consider using a database not only to store log data, but to provide you the ability to search it according to varying sets of qualifiers.

- In what format would log files be most useful?

Table 7.2 summarizes the log formats available under Internet Information Server.

Table 7.2 IIS Log File Formats

The Format	Offers the Fields	Which Indicate
Standard	Client IP address	The IP address at which the request for services from your IIS implementation originated.
	Client Username	The user name under which the request for IIS-based information originated.
	Date	The date of the request for IIS-distributed information.
	Time	The time of the request for IIS-distributed information.
	Service	The service to which the request for IIS-distributed information was directed.
	Computer Name	The name by which the station where the request for IIS services originated is known on the network.

Continued

Table 7.2 *Continued*

The Format	Offers the Fields	Which Indicate
	Server IP Address	The IP address of the IIS server to which the request was directed.
	Elapsed Time	The total time in seconds that receiving and fulfilling the current request has occupied.
	Bytes received	The total number of bytes received from workstation by server during the current request.
	Bytes sent	The total number of bytes sent by server to workstation during the current request.
	Service status code	An indicator to the service being accessed of the status of the current request for IIS services—successful or not, complete or not, etc.
	Windows NT status code	An indicator to the operating system of the status of the current request for IIS services—successful or not, complete or not, etc.
	Name of the operation	The specific nature of the current request, such as read, post, and so on.
	Target of the operation	The entity (file or other network resource) that the operation manipulated.
NCSA Common Log File format	Remote Host	The name or IP address of the machine from which the request for IIS services originates.
	User Name (on the remote system)	The name under which the user making the request logged on to the machine indicated by **Remote Host.**
	Authentication Name (User Name under which IIS is accessed)	The user ID used to connect to the IIS server.
	Date (and time of request)	Not only date and time, but also a factor by means of which the time in question can be converted to Greenwich Mean Time.

Table 7.2 *Continued*

The Format	Offers the Fields	Which Indicate
	Operation (a catchall describing the nature of the request)	The action to be performed, the file to be accessed, and even the version of HTML involved.
	Status (of request)	Success or failure, basically.
	Size in bytes (of the result of the request)	The size of the Web page displayed.

Configuring Logging

In the section "The Logging Page" in Chapter 6, we canvassed the basics of logging as controlled by **Internet Service Manager**. In this section, we walk through setting up such logs. The steps follow:

1. Open Internet Service Manager.

2. Double-click the service for which you wish to establish logging, in order to display its property sheets. Select the Logging tab.

3. Check the **Enable Logging** checkbox to turn on logging.

4. Choose **Log to File** to place the results of logging in an ASCII text file.

5. From the Log Format dropdown menu, choose the logging format you wish to use. You can select either Standard format or NCSA format.

6. Check the box **Automatically open new log** if you need to create new iterations of the service log according to specific parameters. The conditions under which you can roll logs over are:

   - Daily

   - Weekly

   - Monthly

   - When file size reaches ... (NT allows you to choose a file size from a list, or to enter one directly.)

> **TIP** EMWACS is indeed one of the three formats IIS logging makes available. However, the initial configuration of a log does not present this option. Rather, if you need EMWACS-formatted logs, you must convert to that format. To learn how to carry out such conversions, turn to the section "Converting Logs from One Format to Another" later in this chapter.

7. If any of the first three options is selected, the log file in question is closed, and a new one opened, when a log record is generated after midnight on the last day pertaining to the current log file. When maximum file size is the trigger for closing an old and creating a new log, that dual process takes place as soon as the indicated file size has been attained. Log records created simultaneously with or after that breakpoint will be placed in the new file.

Choosing any of the automatic log generation triggers also causes log file names to be assigned automatically, according to the following patterns:

- **Inetsv*nnn*.log**, where *nnn* is a number, incremented in units of one, that indicates the iteration of the log
- **In*mmddyy*.log**, where *mmddyy* indicates the month, day, and year the log file was created

Accept the path name indicated in the field **Log file directory**, or enter a new path name if you wish to store IIS logs at some point in the file system other than the default C:\WINNT\System32\LogFiles.

The Logging page shows you, but does not allow you to change, an IIS log file name. As Figure 7.1 illustrates, the field **Log file name** simply reflects the file generation options you've selected.

> **TIP** Rolling logs over based on file size involves some additional constraints. The maximum length permitted for a single line, or record, in an IIS log is 1200 bytes. Fields in a log line may not exceed 150 bytes. The 100-byte difference between the cumulative total of 14 150-byte fields, or 1100 bytes, and the maximum of 1200 is being reserved for header information.
>
> Keep these factors in mind when deciding upon a maximum log file size.

Figure 7.1 Become familiar with log file naming conventions; you won't be able to change them.

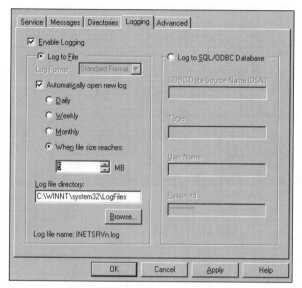

Converting Logs from One Format to Another

You can convert Internet Information Server log files configured to use standard format to either the EMWAC or Common Log File formats by using the **Internet Log Converter** utility. This tool exists only as a command-line program called **Convlog.exe**. Making use of this tool means doing the following:

1. Open either Windows NT Explorer or, from the control panel, a DOS session.

2. Using the techniques appropriate to your choice in step 1, add **Convlog.exe**, which by default lives in the directory path **C:\WINNT\Inetsrv** to your default search path.

3. Open a DOS session from the control panel.

4. At the DOS prompt, type **convlog**, followed by the parameters suitable to the conversion you wish to carry out. A command line of this sort would have the syntax: **convlog -s f|g|w -t emwac | ncsa:GMTOffset | none -f temp file directory -o output directory -d<m:cachesize> <i> -h logfilename**.

Table 7.3 details the syntax of convlog.exe. Figure 7.2 illustrates a convlog command.

Table 7.3 The Syntax of convlog

The Parameter	And Its Corollary	Indicate
-s		The service for which the log file conversion will be carried out. If no service is specified, the logs of all services will be converted.
	f, g, or w	That it is the log of the ftp, gopher, or Web service, respectively, that is to be converted.
-t		The format in which the destination file will exist. The default is to convert to EMWAC format.
	emwac	That it will tell convlog to produce an output file in EMWAC format.
	ncsa	That it will tell convlog to produce an output file in Common Log file format.
	GMTOffset	That it will tell convlog to include, in the output file it produces, time-related data stated as a number of hours before or after Greenwich Mean Time. This parameter applies only if the Common Log File format has been specified for the output log file.
	none	That it will tell **convlog** to apply no format conversion.
-f		That you wish to specify the directory in which convlog will place its temporary working files.
	temp file directory	The full path name of the directory you wish **convlog** to use to house its working files.
-o		The directory where converted files will be placed; by default, the current directory.
	output directory	The full path name where you wish **convlog** to place its output.
-d		That it will tell convlog whether to convert IP addresses to computer or domain names. The default is to perform no such conversion of IP addresses.
	m:cachesize	That IP addresses should be converted to computer names. Also allows you to define the size of the memory cache to be used to hold such names. The default cache size is 5000 bytes.

Table 7.3 *Continued*

The Parameter	And Its Corollary	Indicate
	i	That convlog's IP addresses cannot be converted to computer names.
-h		That Help for convlog will be displayed.
logfilename		The name of the log you wish to convert. *Don't mistake this for the name of the output file*; convlog will automatically create and display the latter.

Table 7.4 clarifies three sample **convlog** command lines.

Interpreting Log Files

Whichever text log file format you've selected, don't expect Internet Information Server to display the log information in a readily understandable way. IIS makes little effort to do that. Rather, it outputs nearly raw data and assumes you have the ability to interpret that data.

In the sections "Interpreting Standard Format Logs" and "Interpreting Common Log File Format Logs," we'll gain that ability.

Table 7.4 convlog Command Lines in English

The Command Line	Means
convlog -sf -t ncsa -o c:\logs in*.log	Convert all logs, but with reference only to information regarding the FTP service, to output files that use the Common Log File format. Place those output files in the directory c:\logs.
convlog -o \stats\logs c:\logs\in*.log	Convert all logs in the path c:\logs, and all information they contain, regardless of the service to which that information pertains. Place all output files in the directory c:\stats\logs. Use the default output format of EMWAC.
convlog -m *.log	Convert all log files. Use the defaults for output format, temp file directory, and output directory. But do convert IP addresses to computer names, reserving the default cache of 5000 bytes for the process.

Interpreting Standard Format Logs

In their crude form, IIS log files in standard format are not a pretty sight. An example of one line or record in such a file might be:

10.75.176.21,_,12/11/95,7:55:20,W3SVC,TREY,110.107.1.12,4502,163,3223,2,000,GET,small.gif,

About the only thing that's even fairly obvious at first glance is that the commas in it separate one item of information from another. Use Table 7.5 as your key to decrypting the rest of this murky amalgam.

Commas at the End

All fields in standard-format log files end in commas. That's why the sample record dissected in Table 7.5 ends with one too.

From this example, it's plain to see that records in standard format log files contain everything but the kitchen sink. If you prefer a more terse yet equally useful IIS log, consider converting standard format files to Common Log File format, as reviewed in the section "Converting Logs from One Format to Another," earlier in this chapter. As for interpreting NCSA logs, the next section, "Interpreting Common Log File Format Logs," gives you all the clues you'll need.

Figure 7.2 This convlog command is explained fully in Table 7.4.

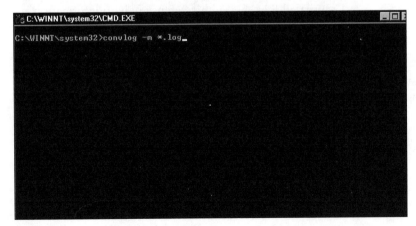

Table 7.5 Understanding a Standard Format IIS Log File

In the Example Log File Record, the Item	Corresponds to the Parameter	And Translated into English, Means
110.75.176.21	Client IP Address	A request originating at the IP address 110.75.176.21, ...
-	Client User Name	From an anonymous user, ...
12/11/95	Date	On December 11, 1995, ...
7:55:20	Time	At 7:55 and a few odd seconds in the morning, ...
W3SVC	Service	To the World Wide Web service, ...
TREY	Computer name	Running on the server called TREY, ...
110.107.1.12	IP address of server	The server that has the IP address 110.107.1.12, ...
4502	Elapsed time	Took 450 milliseconds to complete, ...
163	Bytes received	Sent 216 bytes to the server, ...
3223	Bytes sent	Received 332 bytes from the server, ...
2	Service status code	Was seen as successful by the HTML service, ...
000	Windows NT status code	And by NT, and ...
GET	Name of the operation	Involved the download, or GET, from the server to the client of ...
small.gif	Target of the operation	A file called small.gif.

Interpreting Common Log File Format Logs

As Table 7.2 and our discussion to this point have indicated, Common Log File Format or NCSA logs are far more compact than standard format log files. One record in an NCSA log might consist of the text 157.55.85.138 — REDMOND\doug [07/Jun/1996:17:39:04 -0800] "POST /iisadmin/default.htm, HTTP/1.0" 200 3401.

In NCSA-format logs, spaces, rather than commas, are used to separate fields in a record. The single comma in this sample NCSA record separates not fields but segments within a single field.

For the translation to the rest of this line, turn to Table 7.6.

Logs and Databases

Internet Information Server's online help regarding logging IIS activity to databases makes the following cautionary statements before even beginning to discuss how to go about accomplishing that task:

Table 7.6 Interpreting a Common Log File, or NCSA, Log

In the NCSA Example Record, the Item	Corresponds to the Parameter	And Translated into English, Means
157.55.85.138	Remote Host	A request originating at this IP address, ...
-	Remote User Name	From an anonymous user, ...
REDMOND\doug	Authentication Name	Who logged on to our IIS server under the name REDMOND\doug, ...
[07/Jun/1996:	Date	On June 7, 1996, ...
17:39:04:	|	At 5:39 and a few odd seconds in the afternoon, ...
-0800]	|	Which time includes an eight-hour, zero-minute correction for Greenwich Mean Time, ...
"POST	Operation	Consisted of a POST, or write operation, ...
/iisadmin/default.htm,	|	To the file /iisadmin/default.htm, ...
HTTP/1.0"	|	Which operation was carried out under HTML version 1.0, ...
200	Status	Completed successfully, ...
3401	Bytes	Involved sending 3401 bytes to the requesting user.

> ## Delimiting Characters
> NCSA-format logs contain characters such as square brackets and double quotes that delimit areas within single fields. That's why, for example, the one field known as date both is enclosed in square brackets and contains a minus sign indicating that the time in question is eight hours slower than, or behind, Greenwich Mean time.

- For best results, use an SQL Server version 6.5 database.

- Install ODBC drivers and SQL Server before defining database-housed logs.

- If you do not want to log to a database or use the **Internet Database Connector (IDC)** on a Web server, do not install any ODBC drivers.

- On the Logging page of a service's Properties display, select Log to SQL/ODBC Database only if you wish to send information on IIS activity to any ODBC-compliant database.

- On the Logging page, properly define the **ODBC Data Source Name (DSN)** and **Table Name** to be used for the log in question in order to send information on IIS activity to any ODBC-compliant database.

- On the Logging page, indicate the user name and password required to initiate logging to the indicated database before such logging can commence.

- When ODBC is used for logging, each field in a log record is limited to 255 bytes.

- Logging to a database increases the time and demands on IIS resources needed to fulfill requests for IIS services. Therefore, if yours is a heavy-traffic site, log not to a database, but rather to the file system.

Let's use Table 7.7 to examine each of these caveats more closely.

Table 7.7 The Basics of Logging IIS Activity to Databases

The Caution Referring to	Alludes to
SQL Server 6.5	Microsoft's own **Remote Database Management System (RDBMS)** application. SQL Server is, as you might expect, ODBC-compliant.

Continued

Table 7.7 *Continued*

The Caution Referring to	Alludes to
Installing ODBC and SQL Server	(We discuss these tasks in detail in Chapter 12. For now, assume you already know how to achieve such feats.)
No Logging to Databases or Use of IDC	ODBC drivers serve no purpose and take up disk space unnecessarily if you load them and never log to a DB or use IDC.
Log to SQL/ODBC Database	That you can log not only to databases constructed and managed through SQL Server but also to DBs built and administered with any ODBC-compliant database management system. In effect, any DBMS for which you have a 32-bit ODBC driver qualifies as ODBC-compliant. ODBC DBMSes that will coexist quite peacefully with IIS logging include: Access (from Microsoft) dBase Excel FoxPro Jet, from Access 95 Oracle Paradox SQL Server ODBC DBMSes for which the NT Server 4.0 distribution CD provides drivers include: Access dBase FoxPro Paradox
Data Source Name	A name associated with the template, or schema, for a database, as well as with the driver and any other information required to access the data, such as server name or location of the database. The data source name allows Internet Database Connector to tell Internet Information Server where to find data.
Table Name	The name given to a particular database that follows a particular schema or blueprint. There may be more than one table that follows a given pattern as defined in a single schema.

Table 7.7 *Continued*

The Caution Referring to	Alludes to
User Name and Password	The user ID information that will kick-start ODBC action.
Field Length	(Refer to Table 7.8.)
Effects on Traffic	"Heavy traffic," "demands on resources," "response time."

The Internet Database Connector

Access by Internet Information Server to distributed databases takes place through an IIS component called the Internet Database Connector (IDC). This tool is an ISAPI DLL that uses ODBC to gain access to databases. For a refresher on ODBC, turn to the section "What Is ODBC?" in Chapter 3.

> **TIP** Chapter 10 discusses using ISAPI to customize the activities of IDC.

IDC uses two types of files to control database access and the creation of the Web page that is to be returned to the user:

- Internet Database Connector (.idc) files, which contain the information needed to connect to an ODBC data source and execute a Structured Query Language, or SQL, statement. .idc files also hold the name and location of the HTML extension file that will control the construction of the Web page to be displayed in response to the user request.

- HTML extension (.htx) files, which serve as the templates for the HTML document that will be returned to the Web browser *after the database information has been merged into it by IDC.*

Figure 7.3 contains one of the sample .idc files that are nestled in the innards of the NT Server 4.0 distribution CD and illustrates the relationship among the components mentioned in that file.

> **TIP** SQL Server has requirements for the length and data types of the fields that you may incorporate into an IIS log file contained in one of its databases. These requirements are stated in Table 7.8.

Figure 7.3 Mapping out the components of a .idc file.

```
Datasource: web sql

Username: sa

Template: sample.htx

SQLStatement:

+SELECT au_lname, ytd_sales from pubs.dbo.titleview where ytd_sales>5000
```

Table 7.8 Requirements for Log File Fields under SQL Server

The Field	Represents the Parameter	Must Be of the Data Type	And Can Be No Longer Than
ClientHost	The station from which the request for IIS service originated	Character (that is, able to contain both letters and numbers)	255 characters.
UserName	The authentication name of the user who initiated the request for IIS services	Character	255 characters.
LogTime	The date and time at which the request for IIS services took place	Datetime	The format mm/dd/yy; you enter the parameter in this fashion, but SQL Server stores it internally as a long negative integer.
Service	The specific IIS service to which the request was made	Character	255 characters.
Machine	The computer name of the IIS server	Character	255 characters.
Server IP	The IP address of the IIS server	Character	255 characters.

Table 7.8 *Continued*

The Field	Represents the Parameter	Must Be of the Data Type	And Can Be No Longer Than
Processing Time	In milliseconds, the total time needed to fulfill a request for IIS services	Integer	In theory, values from −32,768 to 32,767. In practice, values in the tens or hundreds should be the only ones needed or used.
Bytes Received	The size in bytes of the request for IIS services	Integer		
Bytes Sent	The size in bytes of the response, whatever its form, to the request for IIS services	Integer		
Service Status	Success, failure, or pending	Integer		
Windows NT Status	Success or failure	Integer		
Operation	The specific IIS-related task to be carried out, such as a READ from or POST to a database	Character	255 characters.
Target	The entity, usually a file, on which the task defined by **Target** is carried out	Character	255 characters.
Parameters	The task defined in **Target,** tweaked	Character	255 characters.

Establishing Logging to a Database

As was the case with text log files, you must explicitly instruct Internet Service Manager on how you wish it to carry out logging to a database. Here's a rundown of such a conversation with ISM:

Familiar Formats

The resemblance between SQL Server's requirements for log file fields and the standard log file format should come as no surprise. Each is, after all, a Microsoft product and pattern.

TIP For Microsoft Access, the Data Source Name is the same as the database file name.

1. Open Internet Service Manager.

2. Double-click the service for which you want to set up a log housed in a database.

3. Open the Logging page for the service in question.

4. Check the box **Enable Logging.**

5. Choose the option **Log to SQL/ODBC database.**

6. In the field **ODBC Data Source Name (DSN)**, enter the computer name of the source of the information to be logged.

7. In the field **Table**, identify, by SQL table name, the database table, *not the database file*, that will structure the information to be logged.

8. In the **User Name** and **Password** fields, enter a name and corresponding password that are to be used to access the log database and that are also valid for the computer on which the database will be housed.

9. Click **Apply** and then **OK.**

TIP If you've designed your IIS log database according to the specifications in Table 7.8, you'll be able, through Internet Database Connector, to view log data from a Web browser.

Figure 7.4 illustrates one definition of database logging.

From Here

Now that you understand logging IIS actions, Chapter 8 explains what will certainly constitute one of the most significant such activities—working with ODBC databases. Specifically, it addresses using the dbWeb Administrator to create and

Figure 7.4 We've elected to use the Microsoft Access database Server1 as the ODBC database here.

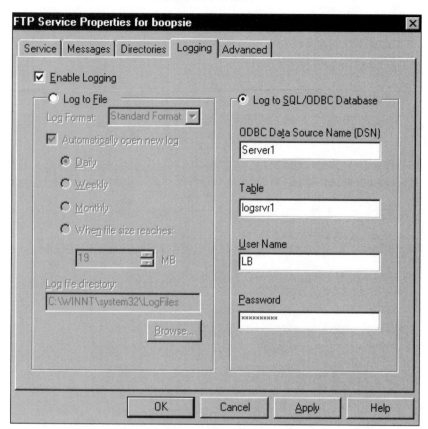

publish a database; quickly design Web pages that include the ability to retrieve, read, or write database information; control which data a user may access; and determine which fields can be subject to queries.

The chapter also examines the NT-related portion of dbWeb, called **dbWeb Service**, that conducts the exchanges of data between an ODBC data source and Internet Information Server. (This service processes data retrieval requests and formats and displays the results of those requests, based on the specifications made in **dbWeb Administrator**.)

dbWeb

I t's a safe bet that the bulk of the material you publish by means of Internet Information Server will be presented through Web pages. It's also safe to assume that much of this material will involve interaction, whether through taking in data from a user or massaging material to be presented, with a database.

Database management systems represent an area of expertise unto themselves. Whether you are a novice or db expert, **dbWeb**, one of the most significant add-ons to IIS, will allow you to create and manipulate Internet-ready databases after only a brief tutorial.

In Chapter 8, we conduct that tutorial, based on Microsoft's online version included with dbWeb. We examine and work with the two major components of this application:

- **dbWeb Service,** which handles the interactions between an ODBC data source and Internet Information Server.

- **dbWeb Administrator,** which defines and applies schemas to control database queries and the resulting HTML pages that are displayed on the Web. No HTML or ISAPI programming expertise is needed here; **dbWeb Administrator** provides an interactive **Schema Wizard.**

The lessons make use of sample Microsoft Access databases, but don't require that you have Access installed.

dbWeb Service

dbWeb Service, the workhorse of the dbWeb application, processes data retrieval requests and formats and displays the results of those requests. You can, through appropriate use of the Service's partner, the dbWeb Administrator, specify the manner and look of the display of such results. Further, and probably more important, this combination of Service and Administrator allows you to control how much of your data a user sees, what fields can be subject to queries, and whether a user, remote or local, can insert, update, or delete records.

Figure 8.1 represents the interaction between dbWeb Service, dbWeb Administrator, and clients.

dbWeb Administrator

The sections below probe the advantages of using dbWeb over struggling through the stages of database setup and orchestration from scratch.

dbWeb Creates Pages Quickly

dbWeb permits the publication of information in HTML format without the need for an understanding of how to program in HTML or the **Internet Server Application Programming Interface (ISAPI)**.

Figure 8.1 dbWeb's architecture.

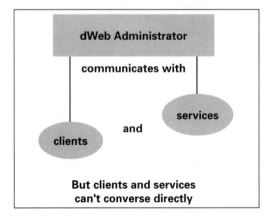

> **TIP** If your experience with databases is more traditional, use Table 8.1 to translate Microsoft db-speak into ordinary DBMS terminology.

Web pages produced by dbWeb may include dynamic data queries. This means that requests for information need not be drawn only from a predefined set of queries. Such pages can also, as you might expect, carry out basic row manipulation.

A subset of dbWeb called the **DBX editor** allows you to customize not only Web pages you've come up with but also the methods that manipulate those pages, by entering HTML code directly into the specifications for Web pages dbWeb Administrator creates.

dbWeb Administrator Offers Assistance

First and foremost among the tools with which dbWeb presents you is the **Schema Wizard**. Like all such Microsoft applications, the Schema Wizard can be used by anyone with a basic understanding of the English language and PCs. This wizard asks you a number of questions and then uses your answers to create a schema, or blueprint, for a database, based on the information you've supplied to it.

dbWeb's main window on your world is its **Schema** window, which includes separate pages (or tabs, in Microsoft terms) for creating and modifying a schema. Other dbWeb pages allow you to:

- Choose data sources (from the **Data Sources** menu item of its main window).

- Set properties for fields (in the **Query-by-Example [QBE]** page).

- Set properties such as **Automatic Links** (in the tabular page).

Table 8.1 Microsoft DBMS Terms and Traditional Database Terminology

When Microsoft Says	Substitute the Term
Column	Field or collection of fields
Drill Down	Jump directly to
Method	Process
Row	Record
Schema	Data dictionary
Table	Data file (as opposed to index or schema)

> **TIP** You may call Microsoft for information on this or other purchases at 1-800-426-9400. Navigate through the menus till you arrive at Technical Sales. The representatives are very helpful and will answer not only sales, but also many technical and support questions.

Downloading and Installing dbWeb

At the time we started this book, **dbWeb 1.1** and its upgrade **dbWeb 1.1a** were *not available commercially*, but could be obtained from Microsoft's Web or FTP sites via free download. However, by early spring 1997, dbWeb became available on CD for purchase directly from Microsoft. It listed on the company's Web site at $995.

According to the MS Web page, to run the dbWeb utility, you must have the following:

- A PC with an Intel Pentium or higher microprocessor

- 10MB of free disk space

- Windows NT 3.51 or higher, with Service Pack 4 (SP4)

- Internet Information Server (IIS) 1.0 or higher

- Open Database Connectivity (ODBC) version 2.5 or higher

- Microsoft Internet Explorer or other Web browser, preferably Netscape Navigator

Note that dbWeb was not developed by Microsoft, and probably for this reason, the downloadable version is *not supported* by Microsoft.

Downloading dbWeb

Because of the application's ample size, Microsoft gives you the choice of grabbing a single downloadable file or downloading a group of several such files. In either case, the contents are identical, and are available both at the URL http://www .microsoft.com/develops/msdn/dbweb and at the FTP site ftp://ftp.microsoft.com/ developr/msdn/dbweb.

If you've downloaded the single dbWeb file, take the following steps after that download completes:

1. Run **DBWEB11A.EXE** to unzip the files you've grabbed.

2. Run through **README.TXT** to get further setup information.

> **TIP** On our PC—a Pentium 133 with 32MB EDO RAM and an at-least-adequate modem (running at 38,400Kbps), the download of dbWeb by means of the single file from the MS FTP site took about three hours. We ran this transfer very late at night, when traffic could be expected to be light. This information should give you an idea of the time you'll need to allot to this task.

3. Run **SETUP.EXE**, and simply follow the instructions it presents on your screen.

If you've downloaded dbWeb via multiple files, follow these steps:

1. Put the .EXE files you've garnered into the same directory.

2. Run **DISK1.EXE** through **DISK6.EXE** *in that order*. Each of these executables unpacks and writes to the **\dbWeb149** subdirectory it creates beneath your system's temporary folder.

3. After you have run all six executables, simply allow dbWeb setup to start automatically.

> **TIP** Microsoft suggests 10MB free disk for downloading dbWeb. We suggest 30MB, primarily because the download and install don't clean up after themselves.

Starting the dbWeb Service

Before you start dbWeb Administrator or work through any dbWeb tutorials, start dbWeb Service and verify that **data source names** (**DSNs**) exist for the sample databases that have been placed in the ODBC directory by the load of dbWeb.

To start dbWeb Service:

1. Open **Control Panel**.

2. Choose **Services**.

3. In the Services dialog box, select **dbWeb Service**, and click **Start**.

4. Click **Close**.

Avoid Redundancy

After we installed dbWeb, starting dbWeb Service and verifying data source names proved to be redundant. The last instruction given us during that installation was to restart our PC. After we did so, logging back into NT and opening dbWeb from the path **Start ---> Programs ---> Microsoft dbWeb**, we simply had to click through the appropriate sequences within the application to confirm that dbWeb Service was running and that the correct data sources, correctly named, existed.

Verifying Data Sources

dbWeb provides you with two sample Microsoft Access databases called **dbnwind** and **dbpubs**. In addition, the application includes the internal **dbWebSchema** database, in which you store schemas. During installation, dbWeb also creates system data source names (DSNs) for each of these databases. But Microsoft insists that the user verify that these DSNs are associated with the databases to which they properly pertain.

To verify DSNs:

1. Open **Control Panel.**

2. Select the b program group.

3. Choose **ODBC Administrator.**

4. In the resulting **Data Sources** dialog, click **System DSN.**

5. In the **System Data Sources** dialog you see next, choose **dbnwind.**

6. Click **Set Up.**

7. Scan the Setup dialog box to verify that dbwind is indeed listed in the database area of the window.

8. Click **OK.**

Once you're assured that dbWeb Service is up and running and that the correct databases have the correct DSNs, you're ready to begin dbWeb's tutorials.

Sample Database Locations

Typically, dbWeb's sample databases get placed in the path c:\winnt\ system32\inetsvr\dbweb\samples. But this location may vary if you've specified directories different from those suggested during installation.

Using dbWeb

dbWeb allows you to connect to a variety of data sources, such as:

- SQL Server

- Access

- Visual FoxPro

- Oracle

- Other databases that support 32-bit ODBC

The application's Schema Wizard helps you to create schemas that can access these DBMSs and more. In the following sections, we create a schema by using Schema Wizard and then, through a Web browser, view the Web pages the schema defines.

Schema Wizard

The schema we're about to build with Schema Wizard uses the **dbpubs** data source. To begin the exercise:

1. Open dbWeb Administrator.

2. From the Data Sources window, select **dbpubs**.

3. Click **New Schema**.

4. In the New Schema dialog, click **Schema Wizard**.

5. Select **Authors** from the **Choose a Table** list (Figure 8.2).

6. Click **Next**.

7. At **Choose the data columns to query**, click the single right arrow button to add all available data columns to the list being compiled at the right of the window (Figure 8.3).

8. Click **Next**.

9. On the page **Choose tabular form data columns**, click the single right arrow button to add all data columns to the tabular data column list (Figure 8.4).

10. Click **Next**.

11. In the **Specify a Drilldown Automatic Link** page, select **au_id** (Figure 8.5).

Figure 8.2 With this dialog, you tell dbWeb to work with the database table called authors.

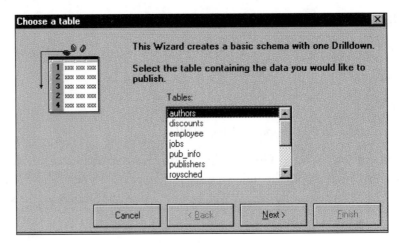

12. Click **Next**.

13. Type **Authors_All_Columns** in the text box **Enter schema name** (Figure 8.6).

14. Click **Finish**.

Schema Wizard now takes the information you've supplied it and creates a new schema based on that information. dbWeb will make available in a Query By

Figure 8.3 As this screen demonstrates, author id, or *au_id*, will be the first data item against which dbWeb will query.

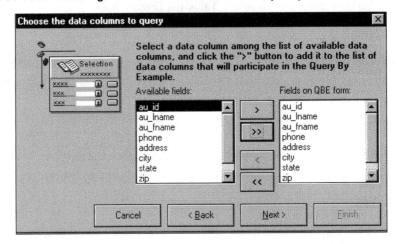

Figure 8.4 Here, we've specified that the query includes *au_id* will take place via a tabular form.

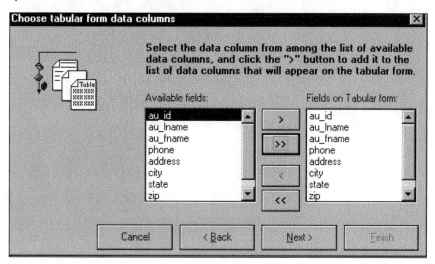

Example form the columns you selected in step 7 (Choose the data columns to query). It will employ the columns you picked in step 9 (Choose tabular form data columns) in tabular versions of the results of queries of this database. Finally, columns you identified in step 9 will also act as a hyperlink by making the value of the item available as a new query criterion.

Figure 8.5 By completing this screen, we've ensured that *au_id* will be the basis not only of a query but also of a link.

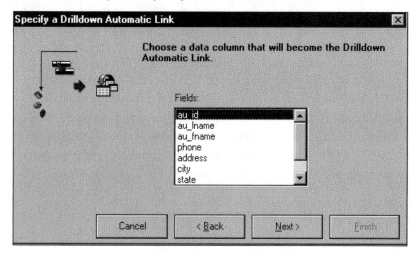

Figure 8.6 Finally, you must name the schema you're creating.

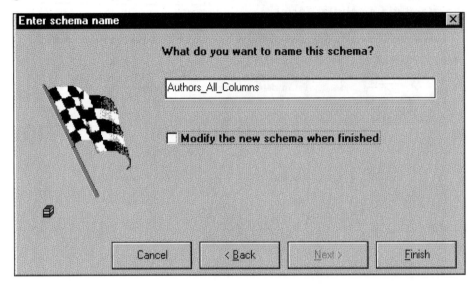

> **TIP** Each dbWeb schema requires a unique name. The schema name must begin with a letter, but you may use a combination of letters, numbers, the underscore character(_), and the hyphen (-) for the rest of the name.

Browsing Data

Once a schema is defined, you can browse the database it outlines with a Web browser, either by entering a URL that directly starts the dbWeb executable or by supplying a link in an HTML document, which link points to the executable's URL.

The correct syntax for specifying the dbWeb executable's location by means of a single URL is http://machine-IP address/scripts/dbweb/dbwebc.dll/schema-name/method. Replace *machine-IP address* with the computer name or IP address of your IIS server, and substitute *getqbe* for *method*. getqbe is the dbWeb process that displays the QBE form designed during the tutorial to appear as the first form in browsing sessions for this database. Figure 8.7 illustrates that form.

The form shown in Figure 8.7 will also be used in the next step in our dbWeb tutorial, testing schemas.

Figure 8.7 The Author QBE form, created during the first dbWeb tutorial session.

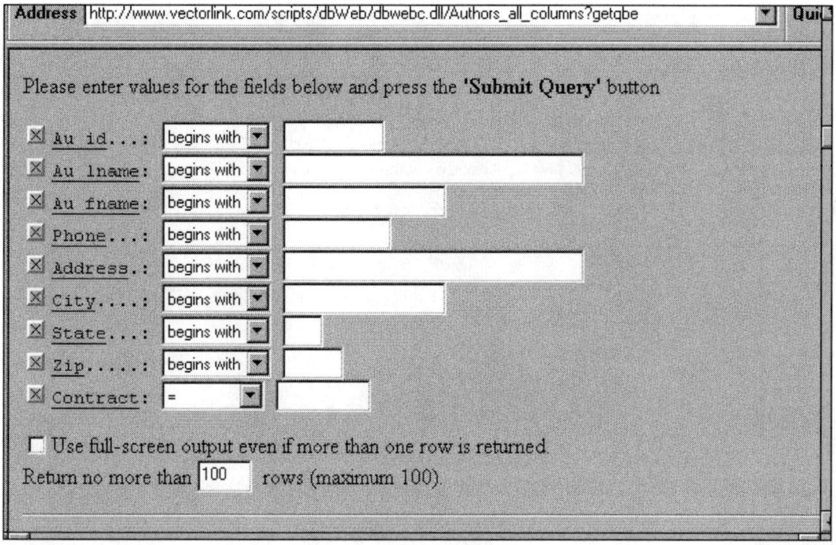

Testing dbWeb Schemas

The best way to test the schema just established is simply to start using it. Only a few steps are needed to do so:

1. Open dbWeb Administrator.

2. In the **Data Sources** window, select **dbpub**.

3. Choose the **Authors_all_columns** schema.

4. Click the **QBE** tab.

5. In the **State** field of the **Author QBE** form, type **CA**.

6. Click **Submit Query**.

The next thing you should see is a tabular form similar to the one in Figure 8.8.

If you've started dbWeb via a browser, as described in the section "Browsing Data" a little earlier in this chapter, you can, by using your browser's horizontal scrollbar, look at more of the Authors Tabular form. You should be able to see that the values listed in the column labeled **Au_id** are identified as hyperlinks. These are the same links you created as drilldown automatic links when you used Schema Wizard to define this database's parameters.

Figure 8.8 The Authors Tabular form gives you the results of your request to see information on authors in the state of California.

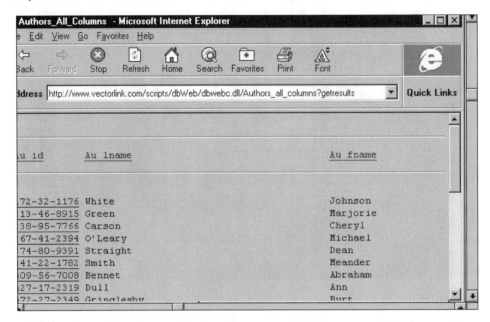

You can activate one of these links by clicking the item **172-32-1176** in the first row. This item is a value for the field Author ID, or Au_id; clicking it should display a form like that shown in Figure 8.9.

Manually Creating and Using Schemas

Next, we create a dbWeb schema manually. We start with an order summary schema, then add an order detail schema and links between them, relying on the sample dbnwind database.

Specifying Schema Information

Users need to be able to ask questions like, "Who placed an order for 50 cases of Rye Crisp Bread?" or "How many cases of Cajun Seasoning did the Mom and Pop Food Market order?" of the database you administer. Answers to such questions can, for our purposes, be found in the **Orders, Customers, Order Details**, and **Products** tables of the dbnwind sample database.

Therefore, our next task is to build schemas that query all these tables and present the results of those queries in a way even PC-phobic users can understand.

Figure 8.9 This display of Author's data was produced through hyperlinks.

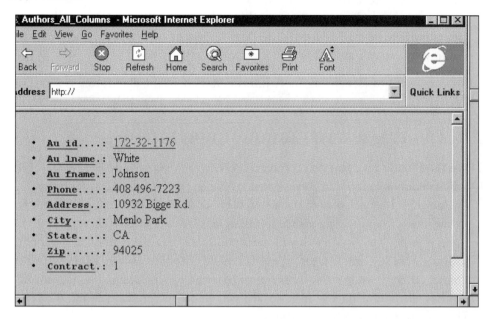

These schemas employ a tabular form in which customer orders are sorted by order ID. Selecting a row of this table in turn allows users to view details of the order in question.

In other words, we're about to create two schemas, **Order_Summary** and **Order_Details**, that will accomplish two-level queries based on customer information. Here's how we'll go about it:

1. Open dbWeb Administrator.

2. In the **Data Sources** window, choose dbnwind.

3. Click **New Schema**.

4. In the New Schema dialog box, click **New Schema**.

5. Type **Order_Summary** in the **Schema name** text box.

6. Press **TAB** to move to the next text box.

7. In **Browser title bar**, type **Northwind Customer Orders**.

8. Once again, press **TAB** to advance to the next field.

9. If you would like anyone browsing your data on the World Wide Web or your company's internal network to provide feedback through electronic mail, enter an appropriate e-mail address in the **Mail comments to** box. The address you supply will appear at the bottom of all forms.

10. If you want browsers to see more information about the data forms you're designing, enter appropriate path information in the **Page help URL** box. Such information need not be limited to Web sites; it can also include ftp, gopher, and Telnet sites, as well as remote sites on the Internet.

11. In the **Default max rows** box, enter a sensible number, such as 100, to specify the maximum number of rows returned from a query of this schema. If the value given here is less than the actual number of rows obtained in response to your query from the data source in question, dbWeb will go with what you've told it to do. That is, dbWeb will return no more than the maximum number of rows you've just defined, for all queries made with this schema. If, on the other hand, the max you just set turns out to be greater than the number of records retrieved from the data source, dbWeb will ignore the preset max and display instead as many rows as it grabbed.

12. In the **Allow actions on data** area, *leave all checkboxes unmarked* to prevent users of the dbnwind database from changing its data. If you do check any of these boxes, you'll enable any or all inserts, updates, and deletes for users of this schema.

13. In **Database object type**, be sure **Table(s) or view(s)** is selected. The underlying data objects used in the tutorial Order_Summary schema are database tables; you must inform dbWeb of this fact.

14. Choose **Select distinct records only** in the **SQL** portion of this dialog. dbWeb's default queries do not contain the DISTINCT option in their SELECT clauses. This default therefore means that a query might return duplicate records.

The Schema window should now look like that shown in Figure 8.10.

Adding Tables dbWeb allows you to choose which tables in your data source users may browse. We do that next, by adding the **Customers** and **Orders** tables from the dbnwind database to the Order_Summary schema.

Figure 8.10 Schema query information has been supplied to dbWeb.

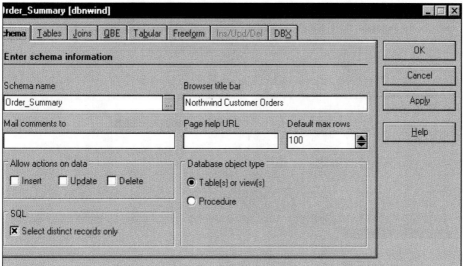

Once in the Order_Summary schema, add tables by taking these steps:

1. Click the **Tables** tab.

2. From the **Tables in datasource** list, select **Customers**.

3. Click **Add**.

4. Once again from the **Tables in datasource** list, choose **Orders**.

5. Click **Add**.

The Schema window you're looking at should now resemble Figure 8.11.

Joining Tables Including more than one table in a schema, as we just did, carries with it a corollary—the need to join all tables referenced by that schema. This latter process isn't as simple as its name might seem to imply. For instance, one of the constraints upon joining tables is that *only columns of a similar or the same data type may be joined*. So, you can join a column of type **smallint** (small integer) to another of type **integer**, or join two columns whose datatype is **varchar** (variable-length character). dbWeb doesn't stop you from joining columns of dissimilar type, but doing so most frequently produces not usable information, but a data type mismatch error from the underlying database.

Figure 8.11 In this Schema window, we've used the Tables tab to add sources of information available to our users.

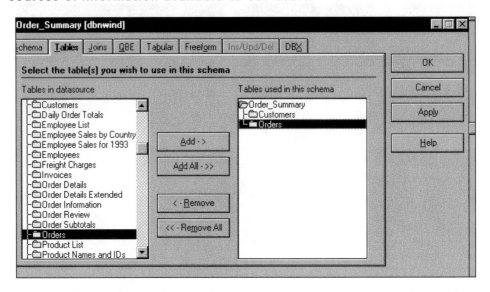

In addition to defining the relationship between tables in a schema, joining lets you create filters for data. Filters in turn permit you to control the information presented to users browsing your site, by, for example, making only specific records within a table available to such browsing.

From the Order_Summary schema, complete the following to join tables:

1. Click **Joins**.

2. Click **New Join** to display the **Joins dialog** box, shown in Figure 8.12.

3. From the **Tables** list, double-click **Customers** to display the list of data columns in the **Customers** table.

4. Select **Customer ID**.

5. From the **Related table** list, double-click **Orders** to display a list of its data columns.

6. Choose **Customer ID**.

7. From the drop-down list box between the boxes displaying the two fields just selected, choose the **equal sign** (=) to represent the relationship between **Customers:Customer ID** and **Orders:Customer ID**.

8. Click **OK** to complete joining.

Your screen should now contain a **Schema** window like that depicted in Figure 8.13.

Defining the Query Form A **Query by Example** (QBE) form is another means of browsing a dbWeb-established database. Through this form, users send queries to a database and receive results from it, both in real time. Building a QBE form boils down to compiling a list of data columns that will be subject to queries. dbWeb also allows you to create new data columns that are computed from existing columns in the schema and that can be incorporated in results of queries. Computed columns, or field categories, can be based on simple arithmetical expressions or functions, can manipulate character strings, can call ODBC database functions, or can call native database functions.

In any case, you must set the properties—that is, define the characteristics of— every dbWeb field that will be subject to a query.

Figure 8.12 The Joins dialog box: the place to go to establish relationships between tables.

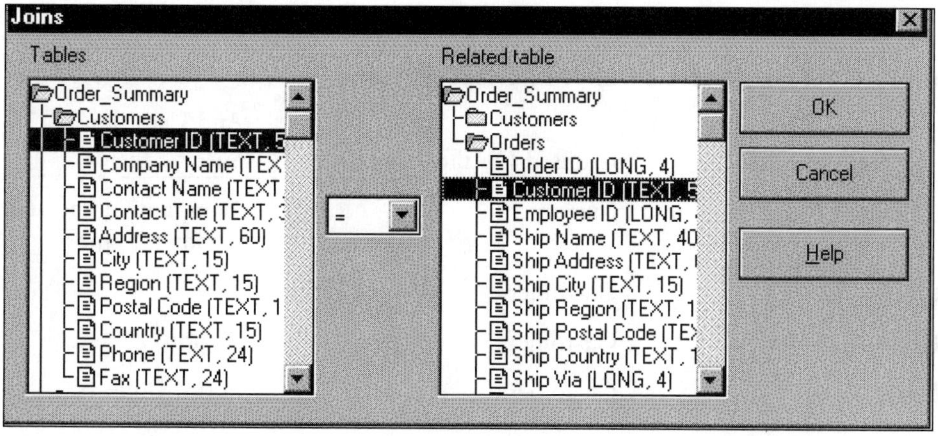

Figure 8.13 In this Schema window, Joins information has already been supplied.

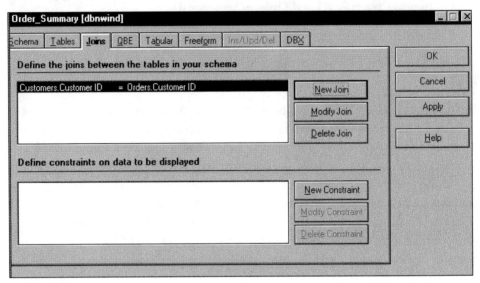

Table 8.2 outlines some of the conditions that will be incorporated into our tutorial QBE form.

> **TIP** In pure dbWeb terminology, Table 8.2 would have had only two columns and look more like Table 8.3.

Table 8.2 Five Filters in dbWeb's Query Form

The Generic Filter	Is Based On the Table	And Uses the Specific Fields
Customer Name	Customers	Company Name and Contact Name
City	Customers	City
Region or State	Customers	Region
Postal Code	Customers	Postal Code
Country	Customers	Country

Table 8.3 Using dbWeb Terminology to Understand Filters

The Generic Filter	Uses the Fields
Customer Name	Customers.[Company Name] and Customers.[Contact Name]
City	Customers.[City]
Region or State	Customers.[Region]
Postal Code	Customers.[Postal Code]
Country	Customers.[Country]

To establish data filters, from Order_Summary do the following:

1. Click the **QBE** tab.

2. From the **Data columns in selected tables** list, double-click **Customers** to display its data columns.

3. Choose **Company Name**.

4. Click **Add** to add Company Name to the QBE data columns list.

5. Repeat steps 3 and 4 for **Contact Name, City, Region, Postal Code,** and **Country**.

Taking these steps produces a Schema window that resembles Figure 8.14.

Setting Column Properties Rather than move directly through the tutorial to defining tabular output, we now examine the steps to establish greater control over who can access which of our data columns. That is, we discover how to set column properties in dbWeb.

Such properties control not only the way a tabular form will appear when it is displayed through a Web browser, but also what information that form can display. We'll work with settings that influence:

- The way data appears in the form

- The width of every column

- The label of every column

- Whether values in a column can act as Automatic Links

Figure 8.14 In this Schema window, we've completed QBE information.

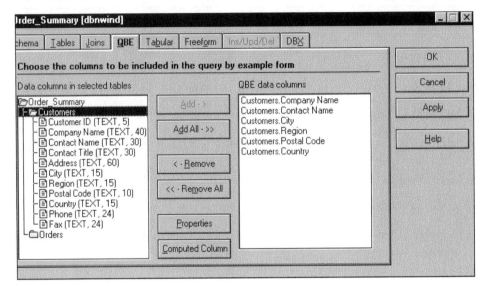

To set column properties, from the Order_Summary schema, proceed as follows:

1. Click the **QBE** tab.

2. From **Data columns in selected tables**, double-click **Customers** to display a list of its data columns.

3. In **QBE data columns**, choose **Customers.Company Name**.

4. Click Properties to display the properties page for **Customers.Company Name**, or access that page by highlighting **Customers.Company Name**. Figure 8.15 shows this column's properties.

5. While keeping the mouse pointer on the data column, hold down the right mouse button. Doing so produces a shortcut menu.

6. From this menu, click **Properties**. (Double-clicking the data column name produces the same effect.)

7. From the **Properties** drop-down, select **All Properties**.

8. Set **Display when** to **Always.**

9. Change the width of a column by selecting the box on the right of the Column width box and typing a sensible value, such as 40. Then press ENTER.

Parameters for "Display When"

The **Display when** property is associated only with the Tabular form. If you select a column to appear in the Tabular form, but do not include that column in the QBE form, the column in question will always be presented by the Tabular form. If the column appears in both the QBE and Tabular forms, dbWeb Administrator makes available several settings for this parameter. In either case, users browsing your data can override the setting you've chosen for Display when by selecting or clearing the checkbox next to the column name in the QBE form. Only setting Display when to **Always** disables the checkbox and forces the column to be displayed in a Tabular form.

You can also change characteristics of a column such as header title. To modify this parameter, simply check the box on the right of the Column label, type an appropriate name, and press ENTER. Then, to force dbWeb to use this new column header as the primary sort key for query results, check the box to the right of **Sort Priority**, type **1** (the digit) and press ENTER.

TIP You needn't close and reopen properties pages after editing the properties for one column, in anticipation of setting those of another in the same form. Just move the current properties sheet aside to expose the **Tabular data columns** box. Then select the data column whose properties you wish to set next. The properties page will be visible all the while and will automatically display the characteristics of the data column you've just chosen.

POP QUIZ #1 How would you go about making a column the second sort key dbWeb would use in ordering query results? (The answer appears at the end of this chapter.)

Figure 8.15 This properties sheet reflects the characteristics of Customer.Company Name before carrying out the alterations we've just run through.

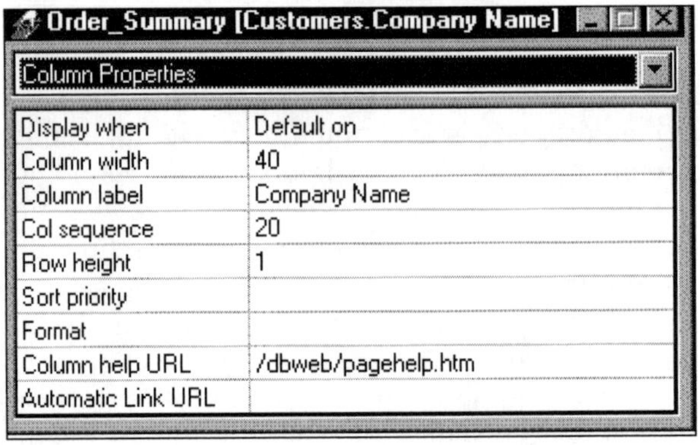

Defining Tabular Output Tabular forms allow users browsing your database to see the information they requested in table format. To create a tabular form, put together, from the available columns in the schema, a list of fields that can appear in the tabular form. As was the case with QBE forms, defining a Tabular form can involve creating new columns that are computed from existing ones. Finally, producing a Tabular form means setting the properties for each column in that form.

Our Northwind lesson in generating Tabular forms will result in such a form for the Order_Summary schema. This Tabular form lists the orders Northwind customers have placed with this hypothetical company. For now, we won't include much detail, saving that for another schema to be called, appropriately enough, Order_Detail. In this section, we deal only with general order information presented according to customer and order ID.

To create a Tabular form for the Order_Summary schema, do the following:

1. Click the **Tabular** tab.

2. From the **Data columns in selected tables** list, double-click **Customers** to display the data columns that make up that table.

3. Double-click **Company Name**.

4. Click **Add** to move **Company Name** to the **Tabular data columns** list.

5. From **Data columns in selected tables**, double-click **Orders**.

6. Select **OrderID**.

7. Click **Add** to move this second column to the **Tabular data columns** list.

8. Repeat steps 3 and 4 for **Order Date** and **Required Date**.

Setting Format Properties A **format property** is that characteristic of a dbWeb form that controls the way numerical, date, and string values look in Tabular and Freeform forms. dbWeb Administrator provides a list of display formats in a drop-down menu. In addition, the Administrator allows you to specify your own output formats by typing strings that define those formats directly into the **Format property** box.

Format codes for numeric data (integer, small integer, money, float, double, and so on) use the pound sign (#) and zero (0) as a place identifier. The semicolon (;) separates the different formats for positive, negative, and null values. Any other character is considered a literal and will be displayed as is. Table 8.4 gives two examples of numeric format code strings and explains those examples.

Among the things you can do to practice working with format properties for the Order_Summary tabular form are:

- Changing the label of the column **Order_Date** to **Needed by**.

- Pulling down the drop-down format menu and setting the display format for this column to 9/03/97.

- Changing the label of the column **Shipped Date** to **Shipped on** and using the drop-down format menu to define this column's format as 10/06/97.

Displaying Computed Values As we've mentioned a few times, dbWeb does not limit you to the columns in a schema's tables—you can create as many computed columns as you like. Such columns will be derived from existing columns or from arithmetical expressions that evaluate some value. Computed columns behave just

Table 8.4 Two Typical dbWeb Format Specifiers

The Format String	Tells dbWeb to
$#,##0.00;($#,##.00);None	Format as a monetary value. If the value is negative, enclose it in parentheses.
#,###;#,###;#,###	Add comma separator to thousands place.

like regular columns, so you'll still be able to set their properties or define them as being subject to queries.

In the next step in our Northwind dbWeb tutorial, we include a computed column in the Tabular form for the Order_Summary schema and define this column as an **Automatic Link** to the **Order_Details** schema, which we have yet to set up.

Creating a computed column for the Order_Summary schema's Tabular form means you must:

1. Click the **Tabular** tab.

2. Click **Computed Column** to open the **Computed column** dialog box, shown in Figure 8.16.

3. In **Computed Column**, type '**detail**', being sure to encase the word in single quotes.

4. Click **OK**.

5. Set **Column width** to 8 and **Column label** to **Expand**.

Once you've carried out the steps just outlined, the Schema window should look like Figure 8.17.

Figure 8.16 In the Computed Column Expression Builder dialog, you can define quite complex conditions that will form the basis of computed columns.

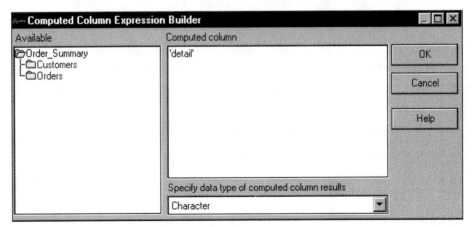

Figure 8.17 This Schema window shows a Tabular page that reflects the use of the Computed Column Expression Builder; we double-clicked the column name *detail* to produce this layered display.

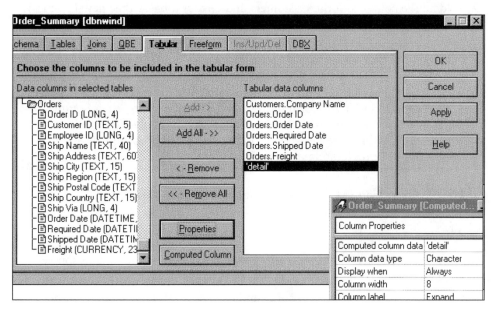

Defining an Expanded View The information contained in a row of the Tabular form is sometimes better presented through a dbWeb Freeform. (That's how Microsoft spells it, so from here on out, we'll do the same.) A Freeform uses an entire Web page to display a single data record vertically. Therefore, in a query result that will be displayed via Freeform, you can include as much information as you care to.

When designing a schema around Tabular and Freeforms, however, you have no choice in one area: the number of rows in a query result will decide which form dbWeb uses to display such data. If a query produces two or more rows (records), dbWeb automatically employs a Tabular form to display these rows. If, on the other hand, a query dredges up only a single record, dbWeb will display that record by means of the Freeform.

Going back to our Northwind example, we'll use a Freeform for the Order_Summary schema to display additional information about particular orders. These details will include the customer name and customer address as well as details about the order, such as date shipped.

We set up our Order_Summary Freeform as follows:

1. Click the Freeform tab.

2. Add all the columns in the **Customers** and **Orders** tables to the new Freeform by clicking **Add All**.

Completing these steps should show you a Freeform page like that in Figure 8.18.

> **TIP** To ensure that a Freeform works smoothly, set column labels and format properties in this form to the same values used by their counterparts in Tabular forms. In similar fashion, switching between Freeform and Tabular within a schema should affect only the properties that those forms share. Don't change any others.

Linking Information At this point, the basic forms for the Order_Summary schema are set. Our next job will be to create the **Automatic Links** that connect these forms.

Automatic Links accomplish hypertext-style navigation within a data source. Such links are actually hypertext data that can in turn be linked to World Wide Web resources such as other Web pages and even other (ODBC-compliant, of

Figure 8.18 We're done with this Freeform page for now.

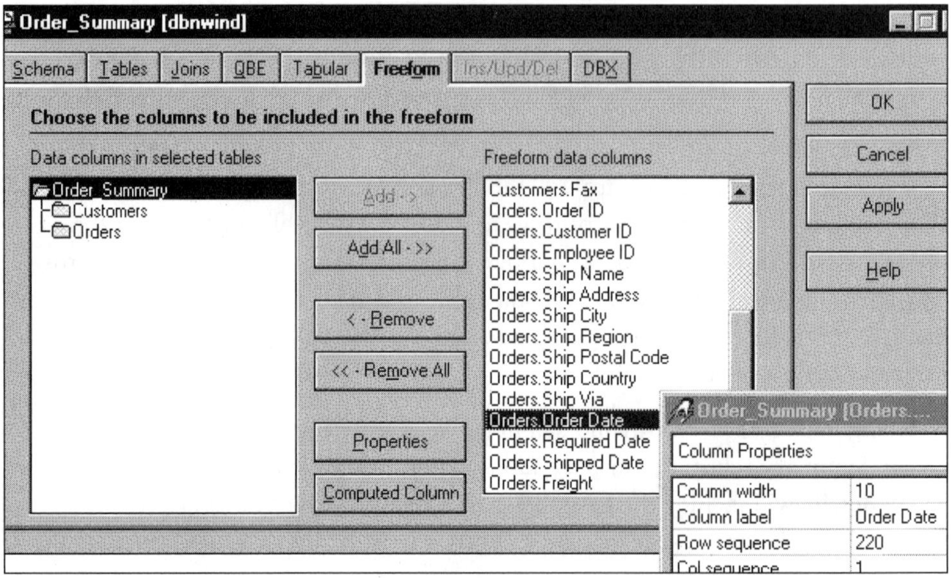

course) schemas. Incorporating Automatic Links into a schema enables users to browse your data simply by clicking on the links. Automatic Links can exist in either the Tabular form or Freeform.

In our next Order_Summary tutorial exercise, we first build Automatic Links that narrow a query, causing it to produce not several rows of results, but only one. By doing so, we'll have implicitly defined a link between this schema's Tabular form and its just-created Freeform and will also have inherently enabled users to peruse the details of orders displayed in the Tabular form simply by clicking on an Automatic Link.

From Order_Summary, creating an Automatic Link means taking the following steps:

1. Click the **Freeform** tab.

2. Select **Customers/Company Name**

3. Click **Properties**.

4. Choose the **Automatic Link URL** property.

5. Click **... to display the Automatic Link** dialog box shown in Figure 8.19.

6. Choose **Drill down** from the Automatic Link type drop-down.

Figure 8.19 The Automatic Link dialog box allows you to define link types.

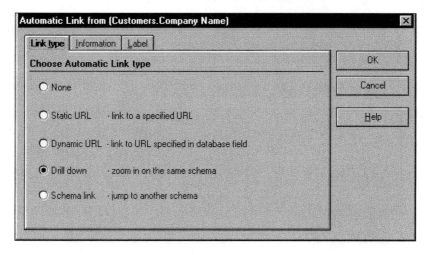

7. Click the **Automatic Link Information** tab (Figure 8.20).

8. Click **New Criteria** to open the Automatic Link Drill down criteria builder.

9. Select **Company Name** from the **Customers** table.

10. Use the equal sign (=) as the comparison operator.

11. Click **OK**, and then **OK** again, to close the Automatic Link dialog box.

12. Repeat steps 2 through 8 to set up another Automatic Link for the Order ID column from the Orders table, once again using = as the Drilldown Automatic Link criterion.

13. Close the Properties dialog.

14. Click **Apply** in the **Schema** window.

Creating the Order_Detail Schema

The **Order_Detail** schema that we'll create next is similar to Order_Summary, except that Order_Detail makes use of the Order Details and Products tables of the sample Northwind database. Once Order_Detail is set up, we'll also work with a Schema-to-Schema Automatic Link to connect the Order_Summary and Order_Detail schemas, as described in the section "Defining Tabular Output" earlier in this chapter.

Figure 8.20 The Information tab of the Automatic Link dialog lets you define the data item that will be the basis of the link.

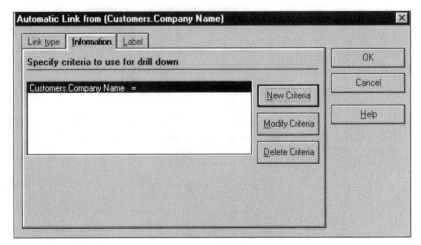

Building the Order_Detail schema means taking the same steps we did in creating Order_Summary, with the following differences:

- Replacing the schema name Order_Summary with the schema name Order_Detail

- Including the tables Order Details and Products instead of Customers and Orders

- Joining the Order Details.Product ID and the Products.Products ID columns

- Including the English Name field from the Products table and the Unit Price and Quantity columns from Order Details in the QBE form

- Creating a computed column in the QBE form based on the expression [Order Details.Unit Price * Order Details. Quantity]

> **TIP** Microsoft Access uses **square brackets** ([ ]) as delimiters for expressions. If yours is a different ODBC data source, you may have to use delimiters appropriate to it. You can create the expressions that form computed columns in either of two ways: by typing the expression in the **expression** text box or by double-clicking the data columns you want to place in the expression. Doing the latter automatically puts those columns' names in the **expression** text box. Then just edit the expression to add the **multiplication operator** (*) between the field names.

Linking Schema-to-Schema

Once you've created the Order_Detail schema, you can link it with Order_Summary through a schema-to-schema Automatic Link. Like all such links, schema-to-schema relies on relating columns.

Recall that in the Order_Summary schema, we set up a computed column called detail in the Tabular form. This detail column differs from the other computed columns we've worked with in that it is not derived from an existing data column but rather exists as a constant—that is, as a character string. It is through this unusual computed field that we link Order_Details and Order_Summary, following these steps from the Order_Summary schema:

1. Click the **Tabular** tab.

2. Look at the **detail** column's properties.

3. Select **Automatic Link URL.**

4. Click **. . . to display the Automatic Link** dialog.

5. In **Automatic Link type,** choose **Schema link.**

6. Click **Automatic Link Information,** as shown in Figure 8.21.

7. In **Specify schema to jump to,** click **...** and select **Order_Detail.**

8. Click **OK.**

9. In **Specify criteria to use for schema link,** click **New Criteria.**

10. Choose **Order_Summary.Orders.Order ID** in **From current schema.**

11. Pick **Order_Detail.Order Details.Order ID** in **Links to** schema.

12. Select the equal sign as the comparison operator.

13. Click **OK.**

Figure 8.21 Schema-to-schema: A different kind of Automatic Link.

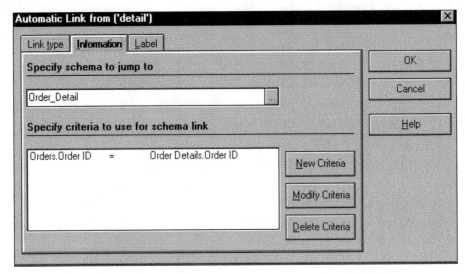

14. Click **Automatic Link Label** and type 'detail'. This computed column does not contain data; therefore, the label you just defined acts solely as a placeholder for the detail column in the Tabular form.

15. Click **OK** twice in succession to close all open schema windows and save your changes. Only **the Data Sources** list should remain open.

> **POP QUIZ #2** Now that you have manually built and linked two complete schemas with no help whatsoever from **Schema Wizard**, how can go about testing these schemas? As always, the answer is at the end of this chapter.

Customizing Schemas

Users' needs will undoubtedly require you to customize queries and forms created through dbWeb. Luckily, the application contains all the tools you need to change the appearance of all query and data display forms. Those tools in effect create **database format** (.DBX) files written in HTML.

> **TIP** dbWeb's DBX file editor does have the ability—which the more simple HTML editors sometimes lack—to generate and insert into HTML code tags that influence form controls.

> ## Undisturbed Properties
> dbWeb will not disturb any properties you've set. Rather, it preserves all properties you've defined for columns that will be used by the .DBX editor.

Customizing a QBE Form

You can change the look of QBE forms without using the DBX editor, by setting certain properties pertaining to columns involved in the query and to the entire form. Properties such as **Row sequence** and **Col sequence**, if manipulated, alter the placement of column labels and their controls. The property **Control type** offers several types of entry controls, beyond the ubiquitous textbox.

dbWeb also allows you to predefine, or populate, selection controls such as combo and list boxes by specifying the **#autofill#** or **#autofill+#** markers.

The first of these tags permits you to define data that will appear automatically in the indicated control as soon as the form in question is displayed. The marker #autofill+#, on the other hand, causes the selected control to display a blank value, by which dbWeb means to say "all rows by default."

You can also specify comparison operators through the **Data operator** property. For instance, dbWeb will accept such values as *begins with*, *contains*, and *is less than* here.

Customizing a Delete Form
In a Freeform, simply clicking **Delete** executes dbWeb's delete method. dbWeb does not use special forms to delete records from databases, but employs the value in the key field of a displayed row to carry out an SQL **DELETE** operation and inform the user whether or not the delete attempt was successful.

Other dbWeb Customization Features
If you have a background in HTML and database programming, you may want to investigate the more technically demanding customization tools that dbWeb offers:

- Maintaining the Menu Tree

- Exporting topics

- Multiple-choice questions

- Hint messages

ANSWER TO POP QUIZ #1 How *would* you go about making a column the second sort key dbWeb would use in ordering query results?

Set Sort Priority to 2, forcing dbWeb to use the indicated column as the secondary sort key for query results.

ANSWER TO POP QUIZ #2 How *do* you test manually built schemas?

In your Web browser, open a URL that accurately represents the location of the QBE form. Then, once your browser has displayed that form, type in the field and click Submit Query.

Customization Support

dbWeb supports customization of single-record forms like its Freeform. The method for creating single-record .DBX files is very similar to that for creating multi-record .DBXs. Check the online dbWeb tutorial for more details.

From Here

Chapter 8 provides a solid grounding in dbWeb's role as a tool for IIS publishing of database-related information. In Chapter 9, we move on to a discussion of protecting those and all other content areas of our Internet Information Server installation. We talk about Internet security issues in general and Microsoft's Proxy Server in particular.

Chapter

9

Securing Internet
Information Server

The primary purpose of your IIS implementation may be Internet publishing, but your IIS server must still interact and perhaps even share data with
other services such as mail management and real-time chat. The factors
involved in securing IIS are not limited to IIS parameters. For instance, a
small to midsized IIS server may be housed on the same machine that distributes other Internet-related tools such as DNS or finger. Whatever the nature
and distribution of your Internet services, though, in addition to giving your
users some desirable features, those services give hackers and computer
crooks a wider range of backdoors into your information.

Computer break-ins remain a significant source of financial loss to companies worldwide. The number of such incursions reported to the Computer
Break-In Task Force in 1990 was 130. By 1994 the number had risen to
2300. A survey conducted in the same year by the firm Ernst and Young
determined that over 200 of the organizations questioned suffered financial
losses as a result of computer break-ins. A 1991 study by USA Research cited
losses of $164 million resulting from unauthorized computer access.

Security on the Internet

Now that we've scared you, we'll present means by which you can secure
your Internet Information Server installation and your NT network as a

whole. Although it's beyond the scope of this book to give detailed instructions for so doing, in this chapter we acquaint you with some of the tools you'll need:

- Packet filtering and filtering routers

- Firewalls

- Proxies and proxy servers in general, and the Microsoft Proxy server, formerly code-named and still nicknamed Catapult, in particular

Packet Filtering and Filtering Routers

Packet filtering is a technique offered by many high-end routers. It denies access from outside your network, wherever such access may originate, to services with obvious break-in potential, like telnet and ftp. Packet filtering accomplishes this by examining the protocols involved in a given access attempt.

Packet filtering can also restrict access to or from specific IP addresses. Figure 9.1 depicts an example of packet filtering.

Until about 1994, filtering routers were essentially the only off-the-shelf way to secure a LAN. Filtering routers, such as those from Cisco and Proteon, permit the definition of often complex tables that allow some OSI application-layer protocols through the router and keep others out. However, filtering routers simply can't

Figure 9.1 A sketch of packet filtering.

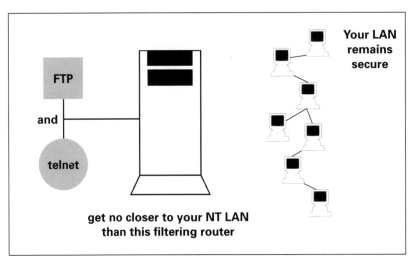

Filtering Routers versus Firewalls

The use of packet filtering is not restricted to routers. Many of the best commercial firewalls employ various forms of packet filtering. The difference between filtering routers and firewalls is that the latter don't rely solely on this single technique.

offer the same degree of security as do firewall applications. Table 9.1 summarizes some of the differences between filtering routers and firewalls.

Table 9.1 Shortcomings of Filtering Routers

Filtering Routers Lack	Which Means That
Application Server Protection	A filtering router passes packets from anywhere on the Internet directly into your servers. If these machines have security weaknesses, hackers or criminals can exploit those soft spots via the Internet.
	For example, many UNIX e-mail servers have security bugs. Firewalls can eliminate these either by providing a true application-level server and protocol for e-mail or by making available an intelligent proxy that can screen out potentially dangerous commands.
Upper Port Protection	For applications like FTP to work transparently through a filtering router—that is, to appear to a user to be unimpeded in any way—that router must be configured to allow remote connections to high-number serial ports on LAN servers. Because it is not always possible to know which services are accessible through such ports, important applications like database services may be unprotected.
	Firewalls, on the other hand, can screen not only specific protocols but also specific IP addresses, so they can be oblivious to port numbers and still be secure.
Address Translation	A filtering router cannot protect unregistered IP addresses, or those not associated with DNS names. Most firewalls, in contrast, handle all IP address-to-DNS name conversion automatically. Some firewalls even let you access sites whose IP addresses are duplicated in some way, like those managed by DHCP.

Continued

Table 9.1 *Continued*

Filtering Routers Lack	Which Means That
Network Masking	Filtering routers do not in any way hide or even disguise packets that originate *within* a network. Therefore, an educated hacker can get a pretty clear picture of the structure of a LAN, including its layout and traffic patterns, simply by analyzing the packets that *leave* a net. Such tricksters have even been able to access Domain Name System tables and steal internal host names and addresses.
	Most firewalls eliminate such threats by translating all network traffic leaving the firewall so that it seems to have originated at the firewall itself. Some firewalls even include a DNS server that provides only the information you want it to provide to the Internet.
Encryption Capabilities	Filtering routers, by virtue of dealing solely with incoming traffic, do not have encryption capabilities.
	Most commercial firewalls, on the other hand, allow you to set up "virtual private networks." These are in reality simply the encryption of traffic between designated entities, such as firewalls themselves or firewalls and specific clients. Such encrypted traffic does not depend on a specific physical transmission path, hence the term *virtual private network*. This traffic instead represents conversations between defined entities, regardless of physical path, thereby earning another jargon-label: *encrypted tunnel*.

Firewalls

A firewall must prevent hackers or other intruders from accessing an organization's confidential information via the Internet. At the same time, a firewall would be of little use if it interfered with internal or external users' ability to perform other necessary functions such as these:

- Browse Web pages

- Transfer files

- Send and receive e-mail

- Carry out remote logons

Each of the common categories of Internet applications has unique characteristics that in turn present specific security problems. A good firewall must overcome all of these. In doing that, commercial firewalls rely on proxies, application gateways, and/or DMZ networks.

Proxies

A proxy does just what its name suggests. It allows a firewall to act on behalf of another computer when it is making a connection. For example, if a user tries to connect to an external computer, a firewall that employs proxies would itself make the connection. To the machine being accessed, the firewall would appear to be the remote user. This ability to shield internal machines from examination by external ones, delineated in Figure 9.2, makes proxies valuable security tools.

> **TIP** There's a similarity between proxies and another type of data protection software; as is the case with anti-virus applications, firewalls and the proxies upon which they rely need to be updated frequently. When considering the purchase of a commercial firewall, be sure to ask: Does its manufacturer release upgrades quickly enough to handle new protocols, which multiply only a little less rapidly than viruses?

Figure 9.2 A mail proxy might look like this. Users accessing your NT LAN through this e-mail proxy server won't be able to tell the difference between the server and your LAN.

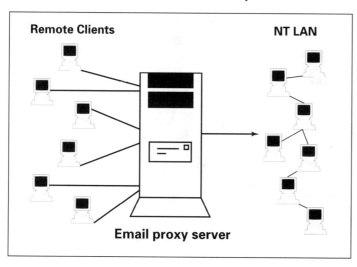

Many commercial firewalls offer what are referred to as *transparent proxies.* Such software allows client applications to disregard the nature and even the existence of the proxies and parent firewall. In other words, once the firewall itself is successfully installed and appropriately configured, no tweaking or reconfiguration of client applications is needed.

However, not all over-the-counter firewalls rely on transparent proxies. Some support only the nontransparent proxy SOCKS. Such firewalls will protect only those client applications that have been written specifically to work with SOCKS. Many, but not all, commercial TCP/IP suites will do so.

Proxies most frequently point outward. That is, they protect an internal network from unsecure external access. Proxies such as the one represented in Figure 9.3, which attempt to keep traffic within a network from traveling outside it in unspecified ways, often provide a lesser degree of protection.

In an attempt to avoid the security risks that can be inherent in inbound proxies, some firewalls include what are called *intelligent proxies.* Such software understands enough about the operations of the OSI Application layer protocols coming to it from the outside world to make it an effective tool in securing inbound traffic.

Figure 9.3 The direction in which a proxy server operates affects its reliability. This intelligent e-mail proxy allows certain remote clients access.

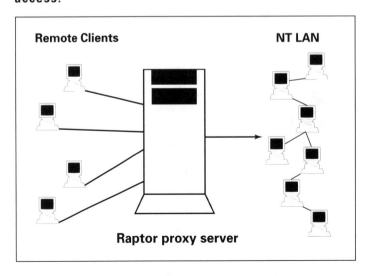

Companies Securing E-Mail Traffic
A company called Raptor uses an intelligent inbound proxy to secure e-mail traffic. Another, called BorderWare, uses an application gateway, which we discuss in the next section.

Application Gateways

By using a type of software known as an *application gateway*, a firewall can completely shield a network from a specific protocol, whether that protocol is entering or leaving the network. An application gateway is without a doubt the most effective tool a firewall can have. Unfortunately, as Figure 9.4 shows, it can also be the most intrusive, even though application gateways typically filter only specific protocols.

Application gateways most frequently deal with the network activities and related protocols outlined in Table 9.2.

DMZ Network

The final firewall-related tool we'll examine is known in data communications parlance as a *DMZ network*. This title, borrowed from the military jargon *demilitarized zone*, aptly describes this type of software.

Figure 9.4 Application gateways are single-minded. This application gateway blocks access to your Domain Name services from remote clients by filtering the protocol DNS.

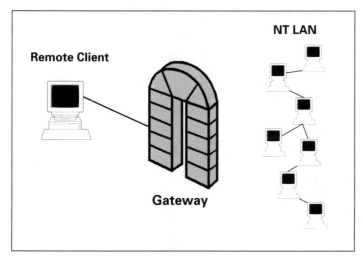

Table 9.2 Application Gateways Monitors and Their Protocols

The Intranet or Internet Activity	And Its Protocol
Domain Name System Management	DNS
E-mail	SMTP
News Services	NNTP
Web Browsing	HTTP

A DMZ network is one which is neither an unsecured, external network, nor a secure internal one. Rather, it is a unique if often virtual entity that sits between these two.

A DMZ can access, and be accessed from, both the internal and external networks it separates. But as Figure 9.5 makes evident, internal and external users have different access rights to a DMZ. Although this feature gives DMZ networks their security, it also complicates their configuration.

DMZs are most frequently used to house servers for applications that are not only Internet accessible but that also can be expected to carry high traffic. Therefore, you might find a DMZ protecting a Web or e-mail server.

Figure 9.5 Its control of access rights is the DMZ network's ace in the hole.

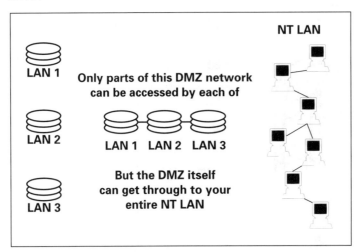

Many commercial firewalls take a simple but effective approach to providing DMZs. They do that simply by making available a third network interface to the firewall.

Microsoft Proxy Server: A Firewall with a Difference

Microsoft Proxy Server was designed to offer the best available firewall security. In addition, it can be run in conjunction with packet-filtering routers and other firewalls.

Proxy Server—or Catapult, as it was known for so long and is still called—has offers two types of proxy service: CERN-style proxying and Remote Winsock (RWS), an enhancement to WinSock. CERN-style proxying can be applied to just about any client OS and hardware platform known to humanity. RWS, on the other hand, can monitor and protect only Windows 3.x, Windows 95, and Windows NT clients.

What does the addition of RWS offer? For one thing, RWS anticipates our multimedia, MMX future by being able to handle Internet services other than the traditional FTP, gopher, and World Wide Web. For example, among the Internet exotica with which RWS can work are protocols based on the User Datagram Protocol (UDP) suite, such as Real Audio. In addition, RWS is completely transparent to WinSock applications—that is, it does not in any way interfere with them. RWS even enables IPX-based, or NetWare, clients to access Internet resources formerly available only through TCP/IP.

RWS does have its drawbacks. Unlike the SOCKS proxy mentioned in the section *Proxies* earlier in this chapter, RWS supports only Windows clients of some flavor. SOCKS, on the other hand, has capabilities similar to those of RWS and in addition supports every popular PC platform. As serious a flaw, and less understandable, is RWS's lack of support for WinSock 2.0 applications, which are, if not now the current standard, rapidly becoming so.

Table 9.3 summarizes some of the other significant characteristics of Microsoft Proxy Server.

Web Proxy

Proxy Server is not organized, as you might have thought, into separate proxies for each Internet Information Server service—that is, for FTP, gopher, and Web. Rather, Proxy Server has two major components: a Web Proxy and a WinSock Proxy.

Table 9.3 MS Proxy Server Features

The Feature	Means
Security Certification	Microsoft Proxy Server was subjected to extensive security testing, including penetration attacks.
Resistance to Common Security Attacks	Microsoft Proxy Server resists attacks such as IP Spoofing. This characteristic is not always found in commercial firewalls.
Masking of Internal Network	Through IP address aggregation, the MS Proxy Server ensures that a network's topology and internal addressing are never available to outside users.
Support for both plain-text and NT C2 encrypted authentication	Microsoft Proxy Server transmits passwords in either clear text or encrypted form.
Site Filtering	Microsoft Proxy Server allows administrators to select a list of sites whose users can be exclusively permitted or denied access.
Access Control	Administrators are allowed to set detailed user and group permission lists per protocol in both the Web and WinSock proxies.
Logging to Text and ODBC	Extensive logs that can be processed by text parsers or database queries are generated.
SSL Tunneling	Web Proxy supports SSL tunneling to provide an encrypted path between client and Web server.
DMZ Capabilties	The proxy server is placed between the main LAN of an organization and a more tightly controlled subnetwork.

The Web Proxy supports the industry-standard CERN-Proxy protocol, thereby requiring that that client programs be configured specifically to use the proxy server if they are to be able to access the Internet through it. CERN-Proxy and therefore

Proxy Support for the Most Popular Browsers
Web Proxy documentation specifically mentions certain browsers. It refers to Microsoft Internet Explorer 3.0, Netscape Navigator 3.0, and PointCast Network. Of course, this doesn't mean that Proxy Server won't coexist nicely with other browsers. But you might want to check yours for CERN-Proxy support in any case.

Web Proxy rely on a modified version of the HTTP protocol. Finally, CERN-Proxy and therefore Web Proxy are supported by most popular Web browsers.

Web Proxy Service supports quite a variety of server and client operating systems, including:

- Windows NT Server

- Windows NT Workstation

- Windows 95

- Windows for Workgroups/Win 3.1

- UNIX

- Macintosh

Web Proxy, despite its name, can handle many protocols besides HTTP. Among the other protocols Web Proxy supports are FTP, gopher, and the Secure Sockets Layer (SSL) protocols HTTPS and SNEWS, which in turn offer encryption of Web and News service traffic.

WinSock Proxy

Proxy Server's WinSock Proxy component does more than provide transparent monitoring and protection of the FTP, gopher, HTTP, and SSL protocol suites. It also manages a wide range of less common protocols such as streaming audio and video. WinSock Proxy differs from Web Proxy in another very significant way. Although Web Proxy requires its clients to be configured specifically to work with it, WinSock Proxy needs no modifications to a client program's protocols.

The WinSock Proxy functions by means of remote calls made by Internet clients to the WinSock 1.1 on the proxy server. Any client/server protocol that relies on WinSock 1.1 can be enabled or disabled from WinSock Proxy. WinSock Proxy goes even a step beyond this flexibility, in being preconfigured with a wide range of other protocols such as RealAudio, NetShow, and IRC. WinSock Proxy has the additional very attractive feature of being upgradable; new protocol suites can be identified to it via a graphical tool.

Unlike other proxies, WinSock Proxy supports connectionless protocols. The v4-based proxies used in SOCKS firewalls, for instance, work with what are called connection-oriented transport protocols and therefore exclude not only such contemporary suites as streaming audio and video, but even old standbys like TCP.

Finally, WinSock Proxy is capable of full access control and transaction logging and of encrypted authentication.

Network Compatibility

One of Proxy Server's strengths lies in its ability, through WinSock Proxy, to act as a gateway between IPX networks or subnets and TCP/IP-based network services. Unlike some commercial firewalls, Proxy Server doesn't require that existing IPX/SPX LANs or segments be replaced with or migrated to TCP/IP. In addition, by operating in transparent cooperation with Windows NT Server 4.0 and Internet Information Server, Proxy Server offers a comprehensive degree of control over access to your IIS site.

Caching

Although they do not relate directly to security, Proxy Server's caching abilities increase its effectiveness in helping to maintain the health of your intranet or Internet site.

Caching has been instituted at many such sites as one means of controlling the growth of information bases and the increase in their impact on server and network resources. Proxy Server caches frequently used documents to disk. By doing so, Proxy Server can significantly reduce a site's overall bandwidth usage, thereby producing not only significant savings on connectivity costs, but also fewer opportunities for unfriendlies to invade.

Web Proxy carries out Proxy Server's caching, storing local copies of popular Internet materials on whatever machine it is associated with. Through such caching, Web Proxy can achieve hit rates as high as 50 percent. In other words, Web Proxy can allow an organization to forgo as much as half the Internet-related connection time it might otherwise have incurred.

Web Proxy's caching offers other benefits. Cached information, which may include not only text and other files, but applications, sound, video, and so on, is retrieved at the best speeds of which a LAN is capable. Remember, the cache is internal to the site. Therefore, clients on a LAN that enjoys Web Proxy caching have better throughput and less delay than clients to whom this advantage is unavailable. What's even more impressive is Web Proxy's proactive caching.

By performing on-the-spot statistical analyses of network usage trends, Web Server can proactively retrieve material from the Internet. In other words, *it gets what you want before you even ask for it*. Proactive caching is intelligent caching, too. It takes the current load on its server into account in making individual decisions to retrieve Internet material. As a result, proactive caching and retrieval tend to take place during periods of low demands on a server. Therefore, it can free server and network resources and help to preclude traffic-generated problems.

Auto Online Connect and Disconnect

Perhaps the most intriguing tool offered by MS Proxy Server is its automatic connect/disconnect feature. Called the Auto Dial tool, this Proxy Server utility automatically connects to an Internet service provider (ISP) whenever a user needs information not already stored in the local cache. When the desired information is retrieved from the ISP and stored, Auto Dial disconnects from the ISP, which can not only save online costs, but significantly reduce hack-in opportunities.

Bigger Drive, Better Proxy

The size of Proxy Server's cache is limited only by Windows NT Server resources. So, if you have a gargantuan hard drive on your NT/IIS machine, Proxy Server's proactive caching will operate even more effectively.

Proxy Server Requirements and Installation

To run its firewall, Microsoft says you need a machine that has the characteristics outlined in Table 9.4. We disagree with some of the company's recommendations And have noted those with an asterisk. Discuss follows in this section.

Table 9.4 What You Need to Run Microsoft Proxy Server

Category	Requirement
Hardware	
Intel and compatible PC systems	486/33MHz, 32-bit processor, or higher* 15MB free disk
RISC-based systems	RISC processor compatible with Windows NT Server version 4.0 20MB free disk

Continued

Table 9.4 *Continued*

Category	Requirement
All systems	16MB of RAM* CD-ROM drive* VGA, Super VGA, or video graphics adapter compatible with Windows NT Server 4.0
Software	Microsoft Windows NT Server version 4.0 Microsoft Internet Information Server version 2.0 Windows NT Server 4.0 Service Pack (provided on the Proxy Server CD)

Our objections to Microsoft's Proxy Server list of requirements are as follows:

- *System with 486/33MHz, 32-bit processor, or higher*. In our opinion, Microsoft does the public a disservice by using this statistic in all its NT Server and Internet Information Server requirements list. If you'd like Proxy server to do more than groan along, we'd suggest nothing less than a Pentium 100.

- *16MB of RAM*. This small amount of RAM will cause your system to run extremely slow. We'd suggest at least 32MB.

- *CD-ROM drive*. Make sure this is at least a four-speed if you want to avoid spending hours on end installing and configuring.

Catapult's installation is straightforward; Figure 9.6 shows its initial screen.

The next step in installing Proxy Server is a clone of one of NT Setup's early steps: supplying NT product ID number as shown in Figure 9.7.

Now Proxy Server setup gives you the opportunity to change installation options such as directory, as Figure 9.8 illustrates.

Proxy server installation includes supplying information such as Internet address ranges to a dialog like that in Figure 9.9.

When Proxy Server installation is complete, two additional servers appear in Internet Service Manager: Proxy Server and RWS. Each has its own dialogs for Permissions, Logging, and Filters. For instance, you might want to use the Properties tab on the Proxy server to allow all users access to your World Wide Web and FTP services through Proxy Server.

Figure 9.6 Proxy Server installation began with this welcome.

On the RWS side, you can configure access to such resources as RealAudio and Internet Relay Chat (IRC). And as mentioned in the section "WinSock Proxy" earlier in this chapter, RWS comes with definitions for a wide range of recent protocols, among them IRC, VDOLive, and Lightweight Directory Access Protocol. In addition, you can at any time add new protocols to RWS simply by specifying protocol name, connection type, and port number.

No Firewall Is Impenetrable

It's worthwhile once again to draw a parallel between those hackers who create viruses and those who invade a network. Both types of pranksters seem to live for devising new and more subtle ways to sabotage your server.

> **TIP** Microsoft offers a Filters option with Proxy Server that accomplishes server-based access permissions and exclusions that rely on a machine's domain name or IP address. However, such fine-tuning can be done not on a per-user, but only on a per-site basis.

Figure 9.7 You must identify your copy of NT Server when installing Proxy Server.

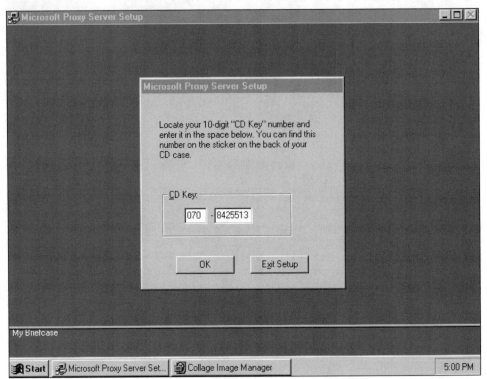

To reinforce the truth of this section's title, we present a summary of several papers we found on the Internet that describe some of the kinds of damage such jesters can do. Keep in mind that the pranks presented here date from early January 1997. No doubt these folks have devised more in the meantime.

The tricks documented pertain to attacks on SSL authentication as implemented in browsers such as Microsoft Internet Explorer 3.0 and Netscape Navigator 3.0. Attacks like the ones we review in this section can persuade such browsers to connect to the wrong server, but to give the appearance of a normal session. Because users taking part in such a session would suspect nothing, they might be persuaded to reveal such information as credit card numbers, PINs, and so on. Another risk: users may download and try to run applications from the fake server, believing them to be from the real server and therefore safe.

Figure 9.8 Clicking Installation Options allows you to change some of them.

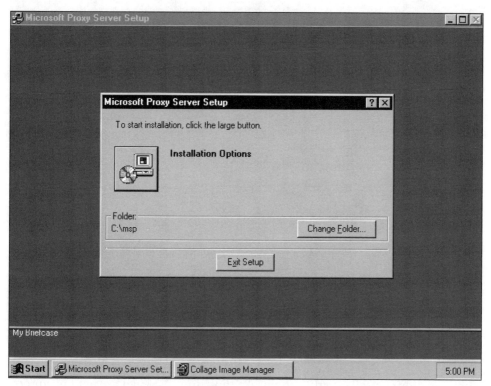

These tricks do not attempt to attack the cryptography or the lower-level workings of the SSL protocol itself. Rather, they toy with the various certification methods SSL and browsers use.

Microsoft Internet Explorer 3.0, Netscape Navigator 3.0, and Netscape Communicator Preview are all susceptible to what's called *server spoofing*. Any SSL server that either follows that suite's defaults or can be accessed by the browsers just mentioned, or both, can be impersonated through server spoofing.

> **TIP** Although the sources we consulted hadn't specifically tested either earlier versions of these browsers or any commercial firewalls and their proxies, their consensus was that all such software would be fair game to spoofing too.

Figure 9.9 Identifying addresses to Proxy Server.

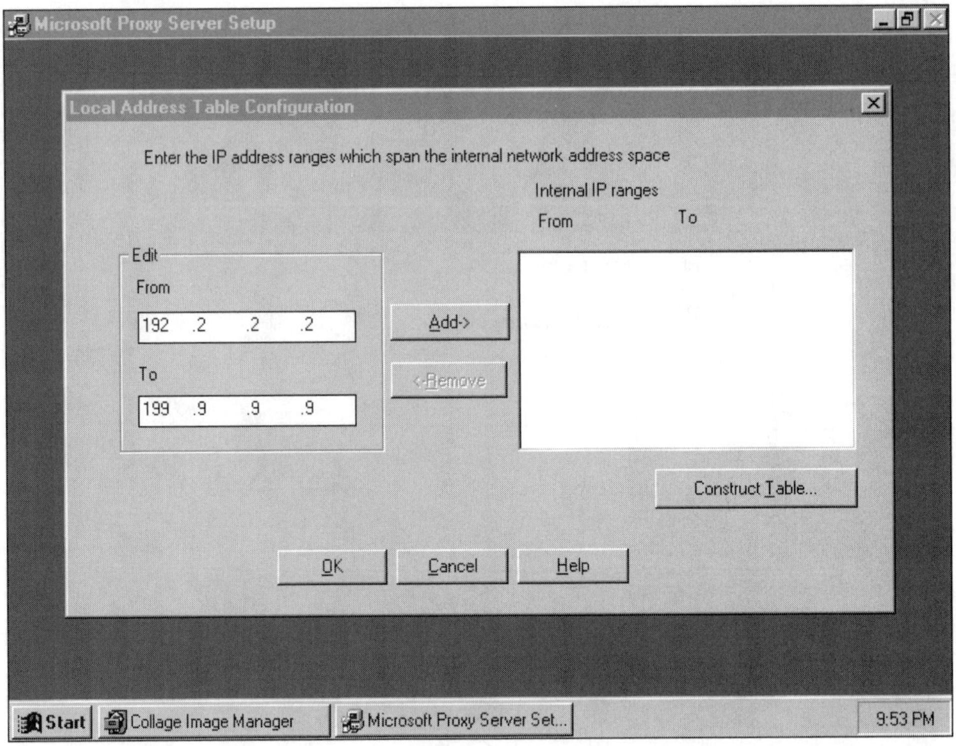

Even tightly controlled certifications like those from VeriSign are not bulletproof if they're working with and under the Big Three browsers. Only through modifications to both the certificate file and the configuration of the browser can a dependable degree of impenetrability be achieved.

The Loophole in SSL Connections

When an SSL connection is made, a protocol sits between browser and server, trying to identify and authenticate the server. To pass muster, the server presents to the protocol a certificate, or digital structure, which associates a server's public identity with certain attributes. Most frequently, such certificates use DNS names. Further, these names may be wildcarded so that a particular certificate may read something like *.ddata.gov.

By responding correctly to this conversation through SSL and by presenting a valid certificate that the client recognizes and accepts, a server can demonstrate that it has the right to use the DNS name under which it is operating.

Unfortunately, most users don't know DNS or even URL, but operate largely through hyperlinks. Current versions of SSL only confirm a server URL and not any hyperlinks a user may have clicked on to get there. DNS names can themselves be subject to a form of spoofing in which a DNS server provides incorrect information about the Internet address of one of the hosts it monitors. URLs are spoofed in a different way, with a page misrepresenting a DNS name. Both forms have the same effect: misdirecting you to a wrong Internet site. URL server spoofing, however, may be more dangerous in that it requires little technical expertise.

For instance, if the line of HTML code in Figure 9.10 can be fed to one of the three browsers subject to server spoofing, that browser's user will see a line on his or her screen that looks like a legitimate hypertext link, but that leads only to the server the prankster intends it to lead to.

In short, clicking on this link would result in your being sent to the wrong site but your browser being unaware of the misdirection, and maintaining that your session is secure and private. Other than through page content, which even the least-sophisticated attacker would remember to doctor, nothing might exist in such a scenario to give you a clue that you are in the wrong place. You probably would get no help from a URL. If, for example, you clicked on the link produced by the line of code above, and arrived as a result at a page with the URL http://www .libnet.net/~ddata, how would you know that this address was not the legitimate one for the company in question?

The Lack of an Audit Trail

Spoofs like the one just imagined leave few if any tracks. Server logs might show an http or https GET to a legitimate server, followed by another GET, this time to the fake server. But to have the ability to recognize the latter as fake, you'd already have to have recognized that you'd been spoofed. *You* may know that the second GET happened because of the first GET's result having been altered. It might also have come from your bookmarks, from a local cache or one at your ISP's site, or simply as a replay of the first GET. Although it's reasonable to infer that the fake site belongs to the attacker, you'll have a tough row to hoe in trying to prove it.

Figure 9.10 Here's one example of spoofing.

```
<A HREF=https://www.dd.com/>Click here to visit Desktop Data.</A>
```

Attackers might also use server spoofing to send you somewhere within a site other than the location to which you actually wanted to go. Although this would be less easy to do under schemes of virtual directories, like those made available by NT Server 4.0 and IIS, such internal misdirection is possible even there.

Closing the Loopholes

If you use your Internet Information Server site to distribute material that relies on server authentication and any of the Big Three browsers, you would be wise, while waiting for a patch from the browser's manufacturer, to ensure that every user session begins on a secure page. Such a page should do the following:

- Consist of a local HTML file or an SSL-served page.

- Have its URL publicly advertised, if it is an SSL-served page, to make it less susceptible to attack.

- Have all links it contains monitored regularly, to ensure that they lead to secure and legitimate servers.

- Display the server certificate, thereby enabling users to see who owns the site they've connected to.

- Have access to something along the lines of a trusted bookmark—that is, a mapping from hyperlink text or images to DNS names and/or URLs stored by the browser, thereby enabling the browser to determine whether links led to legitimate domain members.

Third-Party Add-ons

Another subset of security software—add-ons to firewalls and proxy servers—is worthy of scrutiny. We examine three such packages:

- SurfWatch from Spyglass Corporation

- Proxy Server 2.5 from Netscape

- Cyber Patrol from Microsystems

SurfWatch

SurfWatch for the Microsoft Proxy Server is a standalone product that allows Proxy Server to access Internet content filtering services through a centralized server.

Once installed under Proxy Server, SurfWatch blocks unwanted material whose nature a network administrator may define from every client connected to the network, while at the same time preserving users' Internet access rights. SurfWatch does not remove any material from the Internet or any server, but prevents defined categories of information from ever reaching clients or LANs to which it is installed. SurfWatch screens Web, FTP, gopher, and other Internet services, and it can block a number of types of material, among them the following:

- Sexually explicit

- Violent

- Drug related

- Alcohol related

- Tobacco related

- Gambling related

In devising SurfWatch for Microsoft Proxy Server, Spyglass continues a relationship with Microsoft that began in December of 1995, when Microsoft licensed Spyglass Mosaic Web client technology for use in Internet Explorer.

At $495, SurfWatch for Microsoft Proxy Server is an effective and relatively inexpensive solution to the problem of inappropriate Internet material. This price includes a full one-year subscription to updated filtering lists.

TIP You can try SurfWatch at Spyglass's Web site at http://www .spyglass.com/products/surfwatch/mproxy.html.

Proxy Server 2.5

In January 1997, Netscape announced its Proxy Server 2.5, whose key features include the ability to block transmission of specific MIME types, such as Java or ActiveX components, and a secure reverse proxy, which is the ability to protect outbound as well as to monitor inbound traffic.

However, this product lacks many of the features of MS Proxy Server, including proactive caching and a WinSock proxy. Despite such shortcomings, though, Netscape's Proxy Server is worth considering if yours is an environment that encounters and must monitor unusual MIME formats or high levels of outgoing Internet traffic.

Cyber Patrol

Microsystem's Cyber Patrol, which, like SurfWatch, is a content filter, allows organizations to effectively and consistently enforce information content policies by blocking access to undesirable Internet addresses.

Cyber Patrol Proxy blocks access based on a list of addresses, called the CyberNOT list, that includes sites groups by category such as Sports and Leisure. Network managers can choose the material they wish to lock out from the application's menu of 13 categories. In addition, sites can be filtered based on time of day. In this way, a company wanting to block sports sites during business hours can open the sites up to employees at the end of the business day. Cyber Patrol also offers its users the option of developing their own lists of sites to be filtered.

From Here

In Chapter 10 we take a largely algorithmic, but still guaranteed-to-stretch-you-a-bit, look at customizing Internet Information Server by means of ISAPI programming.

10

ISAPI

I SAPI, or the Internet Server Application Program Interface, contains the programming tools needed to customize not only Internet Information Server but even NT Server itself. Although the text that follows is heavily algorithmic, it explores ISAPI's most basic features: filters and extensions.

This chapter assumes that you have at least a nodding acquaintance with programming in some high-level language. In addition, a familiarity with HTML and CGI is helpful. (We don't write code here, but you need a context into which to place the information we present.) Also, some of the tools Chapter 10 discusses are ones we haven't encountered to this point, such as Microsoft Visual Basic and Microsoft Visual C++.

Introducing ISAPI

The **Common Gateway Interface** (**CGI**) scripting standard allows the creation of simple applications in any number of languages. CGI scripts run on Web servers and send output to Web browsers. Input from the user passes through the browser by means of environment variables or standard input to the CGI-driven program. The program then does its work, and finally, it sends HTML-formatted information back to the user through the browser, usually by means of standard output. CGI scripts using this simple design and programs written in languages like Perl and TCL made CGIs very easy to develop.

The one bad thing about CGIs is that they perform poorly. There are ways of making CGIs faster, such as constructing them so that they can be run as compiled executables rather than interpreted scripts. However, even in such cases, CGIs are still slow. Each time a CGI is accessed in a Web request, the executable or interpreter must create a new process. In high-traffic sites, this can put quite a burden on a server.

When Microsoft began to develop Internet Information Server, it realized that CGIs posed a major problem for the product in large production Web environments. That's when Microsoft began to develop ISAPI.

Instead of relying on executables—or even worse, an interpreter—ISAPI uses **Dynamic Linked Libraries** (DLLs). DLLs are loaded into server memory and stay there, and as a result they greatly improve performance by keeping code cached in memory instead of having it reloaded for each process that needs it.

Thus, ISAPI has distinct advantages over CGIs, including a considerable gain in speed of execution, as well as the ability to create specialized filters for customized processing of requests to a Web or other IIS server. In addition, ISAPI DLLs are completely integrated with Microsoft C and Visual C++, thereby allowing these applications to act as development environments for ISAPI code.

Like anything, though, ISAPI has its disadvantages too. One is that it lacks standardization; only a few third-party applications currently support ISAPI, although the number is growing. In similar fashion, it is much easier to find tech support in general for CGI than it is for ISAPI. Documentation for the latter is sparse, to say the least, and writing and debugging ISAPI code can therefore be laborious.

The Basics of ISAPI

ISAPI applications rely on the CHttpServer class of DLLs. This group or library of modules controls all interaction with an IIS server and contains all functions needed to satisfy client requests. Only one instance, or use, of a CHttpServer module can exist in a given ISAPI application. However, such an application can process any number of simultaneous requests. In order to accomplish this, the active CHttpServer instance creates what's called a CHttpServerContext for each request. CHttpServerContext is in effect a clone of CHttpServer that contains all data specific to a request, as well as all HTML to be returned to the user through a browser by the ISAPI application.

ISAPI DLLs are called by a client in the same way it might have called a CGI script—that is, by using ether a GET or a POST process. For instance, an ISAPI application might make the following request:
http://www.mysite.com/myisa.dll?name=lb&id=15248.

The fields *name* and *id*, and the data associated with these fields, are passed into an ISAPI application. But before that application can use the data in question, it must be placed into data structures. To facilitate this latter process, ISAPI uses what's known as a request mapping system.

Each request that can be made has a parse map, which is a table in memory that directs data accompanying a Web request to an appropriate data structure. The parse map accomplishes this by defining the data type under which, and the order in which, the data will be received form the client. Once again referring to the request example just shown, the parse map would show a character string and integer respectively for the field/value combinations name=lb and id=15248. In addition, the values, lb and 15248, would be parsed out, cut and placed in appropriate data structures.

The parse map system also allows ISAPI applications to direct requests to specific member functions within the application. A request string like the example we just dissected can contain a command that the parse map uses to direct the request to the proper member function or Command Handler.

Because ISAPI uses this command-driven approach to handling requests, developing applications under it may proceed haltingly at first. However, once a degree of ISAPI programming expertise has been attained, this language/technique can be a very powerful customization tool.

Filters versus Extensions

ISAPI filters, as their name suggests, are code modules that accomplish such non-standard tasks as these:

- Custom authentication schemes

- Compression

- Encryption

- Custom logging

- Traffic or other request analysis, such as logging requests to a specific Web page

IIS can support multiple filters. The order in which multiple filters will be executed and will notify the server of their results is based upon both the priority specified by a specific filter and the ordinal position it occupies in NT Server's list, maintained in the Registry, of the order in which modules should be loaded.

When a filter indicates interest in a network request, the filter will obtain the information involved in the request, whatever the nature of that information. So, a filter can take in data that originated with a text file, a Common Gateway Interface application, or an ISAPI application.

ISAPI filters can be used to enhance the Microsoft Internet Information Server with custom features such as enhanced logging of HTTP requests, custom encryption, compression schemes, or new authentication methods. The filter applications sit between the network connection to the clients and the HTTP server. Depending on the options chosen by the filter application, it can act on several server actions, including reading raw data from the client, processing the headers, communicating over a secure port (for example, Private Communication Technology [PCT] and Secure Sockets Layer [SSL]), or several other stages in the processing of the HTTP request.

Using ISAPI Filter Functions

Using ISAPI filters requires that the filter be installed as described in the section "Filters versus Extensions." When an IIS server is started, it reads the indicated value from the Registry and loads the DLLs listed. The IIS server then calls the GetFilterVersion entry point in order to exchange and verify version information and to determine the information, or notifications, the installed filters need, as well as the priorities at which these notifications must be delivered. As server events such as the termination of a client TCP/IP session occur, the server informs each filter application that registered an interest in the event in question, in the order specified by GetFilterVersion, by calling the second ISAPI entry point, HttpFilterProc.

Every ISAPI filter, therefore, must, at a minimum, employ the entry points GetFilterVersion and HttpFilterProc. GetFilterVersion itself receives an HTTP_FILTER_VERSION structure that must be loaded with version information, requested events, and priority level.

After the exchange between GetFilterVersion and HTTP_FILTER_VERSION, a server will, each time it processes an event, automatically call any filters that have expressed an interest in that event. (Remember the definition of DLL? Now you can

> **TIP** ISAPI filter applications should register an interest only in events that are truly significant to them. Poking into ancillary events can, as you might imagine, have a significant negative impact on server performance.

better appreciate its significance.) The order in which the server calls filters depends first on the priority loaded into the dwFlags member of the HTTP_FILTER_VERSION structure by GetFilterVersion. On the relatively rare chance that two or more filter applications have expressed an interest in—or in ISAPI parlance, registered for—the same event at the same priority, the Registry's record of the order in which the filters were loaded breaks the tie and determines the order in which they will be executed.

When HttpFilterProc is called, the filter using it will typically examine the notificationType parameter in order to decide what action to take. For example, an encryption filter might register to read and write raw data, while a logging filter would probably register only for directly log-related activity. Most filter applications, as you might imagine, also register to be notified of an end-of-net-session event, because such breakpoints are excellent opportunities to recycle any server buffers that had been used by the client in question.

For performance reasons, filters probably should be written to keep a pool of server memory buffers, and only to allocate or to free those buffers when the pool becomes either empty or too large to manage efficiently. One useful tool in this context is the AllocMem routine in the HTTP_FILTER_CONTEXT structure. AllocMem allocates memory that is automatically freed when communication with a client ends. If used improperly, tools like AllocMem might destroy a server. But if used judiciously, such tools can improve performance.

DLL Entry Points

The makeup of ISAPI's filter entry points is detailed in Figure 10.1.

GetFilterVersion GetFilterVersion function is the first entry point called by Internet Information Server. Its parameter pVer points to the structure HTTP_FILTER_VERSION. This structure contains version information for the server and fields for the client, which together indicate version number, notifications, and priority desired. The structure also includes space for the filter application to register a description of itself.

Figure 10.1 These are the units of code that plug an ISAP filter into a larger application.

```
BOOL WINAPI GetFilterVersion(
HTTP_FILTER_VERSION *pVer
);


DWORD WINAPI HttpFilterProc(
HTTP_FILTER_CONTEXT *pfc,
DWORD notificationType,
VOID *pvNotification
);
```

If GetFilterVersion loads properly, it will return a value of TRUE to the calling module. If GetFilterVersion returns FALSE, the filter application executing it will be unloaded and will not receive any server activity information.

In addition to having access to the flags described in the section on the HttpFilterProc function later in this chapter, GetFilterVersion has priority flags through which you may specify the order in which the filter should be called. Table 10.1 outlines these priority flags.

HttpFilterProc The HttpFilterProc records notification of events from the server. The code below is that for HttpFilterProc.

```
DWORD WINAPI HttpFilterProc(

PHTTP_FILTER_CONTEXT pfc,

DWORD notificationType,

LPVOID pvNotification

);
```

Table 10.1 GetFilterVersion's Priority Flags

The Value	Tells IIS to
SF_NOTIFY_ORDER_DEFAULT	Load the filter at the default priority; this is the recommended load order.
SF_NOTIFY_ORDER_LOW	Load the filter at the lowest available priority.

Table 10.1 *Continued*

The Value	Tells IIS to
SF_NOTIFY_ORDER_MEDIUM	Load the filter at a medium priority.
SF_NOTIFY_ORDER_HIGH	Load the filter at the highest available priority.

The parameter pfc is a pointer to the structure HTTP_FILTER_CONTEXT. This structure contains context information and can be used by a filter to associate explanatory information with an HTTP request. After such information has been used, HTTP_FILTER_CONTEXT may be cleared of it by using the flag SF_NOTIFY_END_OF_NET_SESSION.

The field notificationType within HTTP_FILTER_CONTEXT may have the values described in Table 10.2.

Table 10.2 Notification Types for HTTP_FILTER_CONTEXT

The Value	Indicates to the Filter	And May Be Used in Order to
SF_NOTIFY_ SECURE_PORT	A session is taking place over a secure port.	Monitor traffic on secure ports.
SF_NOTIFY_ NONSECURE_PORT	A session is taking place over a nonsecure port.	Prevent access through nonsecure ports.
SF_NOTIFY_ READ_RAW_DATA	The application may see raw data; the data returned will contain both headers and data.	Allow the filter to read header information as a form of context filtering.
SF_NOTIFY_ PREPROC_HEADERS	The server has preprocessed request headers.	Allow the filter to monitor the amount of preprocessing a particular server must carry out.
SF_NOTIFY_ AUTHENTICATION	A server is authenticating a client.	Allow the filter to monitor the number of client authentications a particular server must carry out.

Continued

Table 10.2 *Continued*

The Value	Indicates to the Filter	And May Be Used in Order to
SF_NOTIFY_URL_MAP	A server is mapping a logical URL to a physical path.	Allow the filter to log the number of times a server must transfer a user to a virtual location or page.
SF_NOTIFY_SEND_RAW_DATA	A server is sending raw data to a client.	Permit the filter to attach header or other information to the data stream being sent to the client.
SF_NOTIFY_LOG	A server is writing log information of some kind.	Allow the filter to duplicate the log information.
SF_NOTIFY_END_OF_NET_SESSION	A client session is about to end.	Allow the filter to keep statistics regarding the length of client sessions.
SF_NOTIFY_ACCESS_DENIED	A server is about to deny access to a client.	Allow the filter to log and keep statistics regarding unsuccessful access attempts.

The structure pvNotification, also a member of HTTP_FILTER_CONTEXT, points to a number of other ISAPI structures, as outlined in Table 10.3.

Table 10.3 pvNotification Values and the Structures to Which They Point

The Value	Points to the Structure	And Can Be Used to
SF_NOTIFY_READ_RAW_DATA	HTTP_FILTER_RAW_DATA	Allow the filter to remove selected components from the raw data.
SF_NOTIFY_PREPROC_HEADERS	HTTP_FILTER_PREPROC_HEADERS	Allow the filter to customize preprocessing of request headers.
SF_NOTIFY_AUTHENTICATION	HTTP_FILTER_AUTHENT	Allow the filter to customize authentication.
SF_NOTIFY_URL_MAP	HTTP_FILTER_URL_MAP	Allow the filter to monitor or log location mapping.

Table 10.3 *Continued*

The Value	Points to the Structure	And Can Be Used To
SF_NOTIFY_LOG	HTTP_FILTER_LOG	Allow the filter to customize logging.
SF_NOTIFY_ ACCESS_DENIED	HTTP_FILTER_ ACCESS_DENIED	Allow the filter to customize access denial, with a special message, for instance.

Return Values for HTTP_FILTER_PROC Return codes for this structure indicate how the filter application handled the event in question. Possible return codes are summarized in Table 10.4.

It is through these return codes that ISAPI filter applications do their real work.

Developing ISAPI Extensions

Unless you're a software development engineer, probably the best, and certainly the most painless, way to develop an ISAPI extension is to use the wizards provided by Visual C++. Doing so involves the following steps:

1. Open Visual C++.

2. Select **New**, and then **Project Workspace** from its **File** menu.

3. Choose **ISAPI Extenuation Wizard** from the resulting dialog. This choice defines the type of project you will have Visual C++ build for you.

4. Type a name, such as **Hello World**, for the new project.

5. Click **Create**.

This five-part process produces a dialog that asks what type of ISAPI application you want to build. The default settings are already configured for an ISAPI extension.

> **TIP** If you do not have all needed development DLLs loaded on the machine on which you're developing your ISAPI code, that code may have to be manually linked.

At this point, all you need to do is click **Finish**. Visual C++ keeps you informed as it proceeds to create various files and to generate a class called CHelloWorldExtension. This created class is a derivative of CHttpServer, the basic class for all ISAPI applications. That's it; you've built a project. Now you're ready

Table 10.4 Return Codes for HTTP_FILTER_PROC

The Return Code	Indicates
SF_STATUS_REQ_ FINISHED	The filter has handled the HTTP request. The server should disconnect the session.
SF_STATUS_REQ_ FINISHED_KEEP_CONN	The filter has handled the HTTP request. However, the server should keep the TCP session active.
SF_STATUS_REQ_ NEXT_NOTIFICATION	The next filter in the chain, if any, should be called.
SF_STATUS_REQ_ HANDLED_NOTIFICATION	The current filter completely handled the need for service. Therefore, no subsequent filter should be called.
SF_STATUS_REQ_ERROR	An error of some sort has occurred. The server should notify the client of this error.

to work through Visual C++ tutorials by using the class CHelloWorldExtension you (and the software) created.

ISAPI/IIS Interactions

The relationship between an ISAPI application and Internet Information Server can become quite complicated. For instance, an ISAPI application, whether extension or filter, runs as a service under IIS. IIS in turn runs as an NT Service. This chain of statuses complicates debugging ISAPI applications. The Visual C++ debugger cannot take control of an ISAPI application while IIS is itself seen as a service by NT Server. As one solution to this problem, Microsoft, shortly before this book was written, shipped IIS in two forms: service and standalone executable, the latter of which allows you to control the server from a command line. But even if you're running IIS as a standalone executable, you still have some configuring to do to allow the Visual C++ debugger to operate.

When you are in a debug session, Visual C++, and IIS as a whole, will run with the default permissions available to your account. Because IIS needs to do things that many users' permissions won't allow, you or your network's manager may have to do the following:

1. Open **User Manager for Domains**.

2. Select **User Rights** from the Policies menu.

3. Check **Show Advanced User Rights**.

4. Select **Act as part of the operating system**.

5. Click **Add** to access the **Add Users and Groups** dialog.

6. Click **Show Users**.

7. Choose the account you'll be using while working with Visual C++.

8. Click **Add**.

9. Repeat steps 4 through 8 to generate security audits.

10. Log out of and then back in to NT Server to make the changes you just defined take effect.

Keep in mind that IIS actually consists of three services: FTP, gopher, and Web. You, through Visual C++ and the ISAPI code it's attempting to debug, will be working from and manipulating IIS through a command line. Because they're not intended to run in such an environment, you must stop all three IIS services before using the Visual C++ debugger on your nascent ISAPI code. You can stop the IIS services either with the Services tool in control Panel or by using Internet Service Manager.

Once IIS services are halted, you can proceed to configure your project workspace as the first step in testing your ISAPI application. To do so, just do the following:

1. Start Visual C++.

2. Select **Settings** from its **Build** menu.

3. Click **Debug**.

4. Choose **General Category**.

5. Type the location of your IIS (that's Internet Information server, not ISAPI) executable—most likely, c:\winnt\system32\inetsrv\server\inetinfo.exe—in the field **Executable for debug session**.

6. Type -e w3svc in **Program arguments**.

7. Click **Link**.

8. Type the path and filename where you want the compiled DLL to be placed in **Output filename**.

Figure 10.2 This message means your extension has been built.

```
This default message was produced by the Internet Server DLL Wizard. Edit your
CHelloWebExtension::Default() implementation to change it.
```

> **T I P** The path name you supply in step 8 should be somewhere under your Web root directory, so that the ISAPI application can be accessed by a URL.

Now log out and log back on. The source code generated by ISAPI Extension Wizard has everything needed to compile a working ISAPI application. It won't do much, but it will compile. You've finished configuring your development environment; now you can build and run your project. Here's how to do that:

1. Press **F5** to start your ISAPI application.

2. Press **yes** when asked if you want to build the project.

3. IIS should be running in the background, so enter the URL of your just-created DLL into a Web browser. But be sure to add a question mark at the end, as in this example: http://www.mysite.com/helloworld.dll?

Connecting to your ISAPI application for the first time may take several seconds. However, DLLs are cached after their first execution, so this delay should be a one-time proposition. After the DLL loads, the message shown in Figure 10.2 should appear. Congratulations! If you see this message, you have a working ISAPI application.

From Here

We have now taken a detailed look at ISAPI and even touched on using it to customize IIS. In Chapter 11, we examine some of the add-ons to Windows NT Server that can significantly enhance your IIS implementation.

Add-Ons, Upgrades, and Internet
Information Server

The only absolute is that the life expectancy of software releases has an inverse relationship to the complexity of the software involved. Applying this premise to Internet Information Server yields no surprises or contradictions. In the time it took to write this book, the current release of IIS changed once and was announced to be about to change again.

In addition, the number of software suites that can be added into an IIS configuration grew, during the same period of time, only slightly more slowly than interest in the Internet. Among the add-ons that Microsoft makes available for download at its FTP site are:

- Development kits for ActiveX, alx, and directx3

- Extensions to Exchange and FrontPage

- A beta version of MediaManager

- The 6.5 release of SQL Server

- A beta version of NetMeeting

- A beta version of Normandy, the MS catchall for Internet-related tools such as a chat server, an Internet locator server, and a news server

The list represents an embarrassment of riches indeed, especially when you have to decide which to incorporate into your IIS implementation. Our rule of thumb in deciding which of these and other add-ons to present in this book was to choose only those we felt most enhanced IIS operations. So, in this chapter, we examine SQL Server and NetMeeting.

SQL Server

Microsoft began to produce its own versions of SQL Server with release 6.0 of this application, after it dissolved its relationship with Sybase about two years ago. Since then, MS has come up not only with release 6.5, but also with the beta version of release 7.0. In this chapter, we discuss the enhancements to SQL Server contained in the former.

In SQL Server 6.5, Microsoft provides:

- Distributed Transaction Coordinator

- Compound indices

- New commands: Cube and Rollup

- SQL Server Web Assistant

- New administrative tools

Distributed Transaction Coordinator

Distributed Transaction Coordinator (DTC) manages remote database operations that involve more than one server and has been implemented as an **OLE COM (Object Linking and Embedding component object model)**. DTC, also known as **Transaction Manager**, works with the transaction objects that a network administrator may create, by means of OLE, to control distributed transactions. Targets of such transactions may, at this time, consist only of SQL Server 6.5 servers.

Transaction objects can be executed both from client applications and from an SQL Server stored procedure. But because DTC exists solely as a 32-bit application, clients that may use it are limited to Windows 95 or Windows NT Workstation nodes.

DTC accomplishes transparent multisite updates of remote databases by carrying out server-to-server tasks within the scope of a single distributed transaction. Quite a few DBMS programming interfaces support DTC, among them:

- Transact-SQL

- ODBC

- DB-Library

- OLE Transactions

Compound Indices

SQL Server 6.5 is the first release of SQL Server that allows you to create compound indices. Such tables may, under this release, be up to 600 bytes in size, as opposed to the limit in release 6.0 of 256 bytes.

In effect, what this buys you is a database index that can include a greater number of fields. Queries that reference a relatively high number of fields (or columns) can therefore, if based on compound indices, execute more quickly.

New Commands

Two new commands, **Cube** and **Rollup**, permit SQL Server 6.5 to aggregate easily the results of a single query.

Cube and Rollup allow you to create result sets with running totals. These commands differ from the others such as **compute by**. Cube and Rollup display only cumulative information, such as subtotals. (Cube and Rollup are very nearly identical. However, Rollup allows you to be more selective in how you group reported information.)

The listing in Figure 11.1 illustrates the use of Cube.

Figure 11.1 This piece of code will display cumulative totals for items sold.

```
Query:
SELECT model_num, qty
FROM inventor, sales
WHERE inventor.model_num = sales.model_num
GROUP BY model_num WITH CUBE
```

If we had used Rollup in this example, it would have produced rather different results. Rollup never tallies the column to the immediate left of the field in which it is specified, unless that column is itself an aggregate.

Other command-related new features of SQL Server 6.5 include:

- The ability to replicate TEXT and IMAGE datatypes, with support for the commands INSERT, UPDATE, and DELETE. However, *only data that has been subject to previously logged text operations can be replicated.*

- The ability to disable predefined constraints on the types of operations that may be carried out on particular fields during replication and the corollary precluding of the need to drop or add constraints before and after duplicating data.

- The use of the **INSERT...EXEC** statement to enable remote stored procedures to return results from remote databases that populate local tables. Results from such procedures can be stored in permanent or temporary SQL Server tables.

Web Assistant

SQL Server Web Assistant helps you format the results of an SQL query as an HTML file, which in turn allows you to distribute such data by means of Internet Information Server's Web service. HTML files created in this way can be updated automatically through use of a trigger from within SQL server, which modifies the output HTML file whenever relevant data in the SQL Server-managed database changes.

The first step in using Web Assistant is to specify the source of the data that will be used in the HTML document. Three options are available for specifying such a source:

- Selecting columns from a specific table through point-and-click.

- Using SQL statements supplied directly to Web Assistant.

- Using stored procedures that contain such statements or that explicitly point to the data source for the HTML output.

After a data source is defined, Web Assistant can schedule the production of the HTML output document. This output can be generated immediately, at defined intervals, on specific dates, or when particular data items change.

Finally, Web Assistant can tailor the format of output HTML document and even set up links to other HTML files.

Managing SQL Server 6.5

SQL Server 6.5 includes several administrative tools:

- Database Maintenance Plan Wizard

- SQL Trace

- SQL Enterprise Manager

The following sections look at each of these.

> **TIP** Web Assistant consists of five screens. Working with these for an hour or two is all the training you'll need in this new SQL Server tool.

Database Maintenance Plan Wizard

Database Maintenance Plan Wizard is the tool that sets up and automates many of what had previously been the most tedious and time-consuming DBMS management tasks, including backups and **database consistency checks (DBCCs)**.

The Maintenance Wizard prompts you for information that helps it to determine the percentage and rate of change of data. After being supplied this information, Maintenance Wizard suggests intervals at which backups should be run. Maintenance Wizard also allows you to specify when to run DBCCs, where backups should be housed, and how long backups should be retained.

Maintenance Wizard, upon being fed all the information it requests, automatically creates, and stores in Task Manager, a maintenance plan that it can thereafter access or change as needed.

Curiously, though Maintenance Wizard doesn't run the maintenance tasks it creates. Indeed, no window or dialog does. Rather, these jobs are carried out by a command-line utility, sqlmaint.exe. SQL Server passes off to NT's Task Manager a cmdExec option, which is then used by Task Manager to call sqlmaint.exe, with the specific options needed to carry out the tasks defined by the Maintenance Wizard already in place.

> **TIP** As you might expect, you can kick-start sqlmaint.exe yourself, at any time, from a command line.

SQL Trace

SQL Server 6.5 offers another graphical-based tool, SQL Trace, with which the execution of code written from SQL Server can be traced and debugged. SQL Trace permits you to create and save filters with which you can grab the results of any SQL statement or remote procedure call. Once you've obtained such statistics, you can either view them immediately in the SQL Trace window or save them to a log for later analysis.

SQLTrace is installed with SQL Server 6.5. You can also, if you care to, install it as an option on any 32-bit SQL client.

SQL Enterprise Manager

SQL Enterprise Manager contains many useful features, including a transfer management interface that can transfer some or all objects from one database to another. Using this interface, you can:

- Copy all or only some of the types of objects your database contains.

- Copy all or only selected ones of the objects of a specific type.

- Move only schema, only data, or both.

- Transfer data to the tail end of a remote database (that is, append the transferred data) or to anywhere within such a db, thereby overwriting existing records.

- Delete objects in the destination database, most likely because they don't match the schema you're about to transfer, before copying that schema, thereby saving yourself the need to modify it once it gets to where it's going.

- Include dependent objects when transferring an object (for instance, a middle initial, should one exist, when transferring first names).

- Execute a transfer immediately or according to some schedule.

In any of these tweaks of transfer, the destination server must also be running SQL Server 6.5. The source server, on the other hand, can run any of SQL Server 4.x, SQL Server 6.x, or Sybase.

Under SQL Server 6.5, Enterprise Manager can execute any application, whether SQL Server-based or external. The latter can be added and run from the Server's Tools menu.

In addition to Enterprise Manager, SQL Server 6.5 offers another administrative tool: support for Simple Network Management Protocol (SNMP) monitoring. This support includes the ability to raise SNMP traps.

An SNMP trap notifies the SNMP agent (or utility) that some predefined condition has occurred. The SNMP agent then can pass this information along to workstations that are running SNMP-based monitoring applications.

NetMeeting

NetMeeting is, as the Microsoft Web site phrases it, "at the core of Microsoft's real-time Internet communication strategy." In other words, this suite—which offers real-time voice and data communications, application sharing, file transfer, a virtual whiteboard, and text-based chat—will be around and developing for some time.

NetMeeting is based on the standards of the **International Telecommunications Union (ITU)**, which governs much of data and voice transmissions. In its current beta release, NetMeeting uses the T.120 specification for data conferencing, which is in turn part of the larger H.323 standard. Microsoft expects that future releases of NetMeeting will be fully compliant with H.323. The gist is that NetMeeting supports a more limited set of audio and video protocols now than it will in future.

Internet conferencing in general can work with several transport-level protocols, among them IP and IPX. In addition to these, vendors sometimes create and provide proprietary transport-level protocols to handle such conferencing. Most conferencing applications allow users to connect to different types of connections simultaneously. So, if you're using one of these packages, you might be a triple threat, in that you could take part in a conference over an intranet, another over the Internet, and one dialed in over a modem, all at the same time.

Right now, NetMeeting is available only for Windows 95 and Windows NT platforms. However, Microsoft plans, at some unspecified date in the near future, to port this application to the Macintosh.

Compatibility through Shared Standards
Remember, NetMeeting follows ITU standards. Therefore, almost any product that does the same should be able to use it.

In a section from one of its white papers, Microsoft presents the following scenarios as examples of situations in which NetMeeting might be found.

- A customer is using your product but is having trouble. The customer clicks the Support button or menu item you've added to your application and gets connected to a member of your support staff, who can control the customer's application remotely and can talk the customer through the problem.

> **TIP** Microsoft's white paper states that all the user needs are a sound card, microphone, speakers, and a network connection; no additional hardware or software is required. That's not quite correct. The customer would also need NetMeeting, which would add another expense to the cost of the features just ticked off.

- You create a Web page that can function as the joint forum for a group of people with similar interests. One of them can, from that page, see a roster of those individuals currently participating in the conference and click a button to join in.

- Business associates, from their separate offices, can collaborate on a report, taking turns talking and editing the report in real time.

> **TIP** Note that in scenarios like the report collaboration example, a user at each machine must explicitly select an application to be shared. NetMeeting's not magic; it doesn't help a machine see an application running on a remote peer unless that application has been opened by the remote user.

Installing and Configuring NetMeeting

NetMeeting looks like Figure 11.2.

Despite its being a beta, the load of NetMeeting went smoothly. It began with a typical Microsoft setup screen, like that in Figure 11.3.

After a couple more install screens—including one into which you must enter your name, address, phone number, and other identifying information for use by NetMeeting confreres—the load completes, and Net Meeting starts automatically. The application presents a window like that shown in Figure 11.4.

Figure 11.2 When it's installed, NetMeeting presents this tool group.

Figure 11.3 Here's the first step in loading NetMeeting.

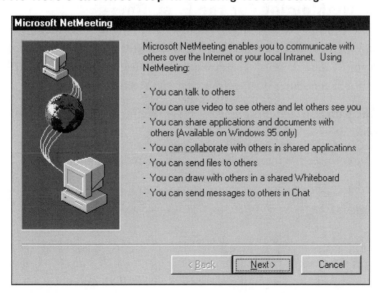

Figure 11.4 This is NetMeeting's main window.

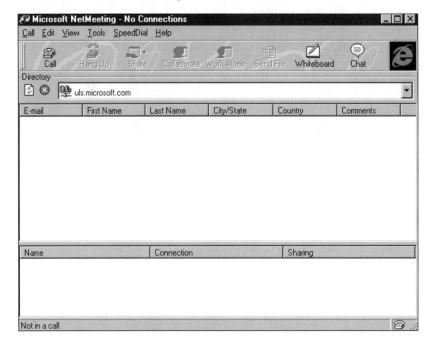

Running NetMeeting for the First Time

The first time you run NetMeeting, it prompts you to enter information about yourself and the **User Location Service** (**ULS**) that you want to connect to. Then it runs the Audio Tuning Wizard to automatically configure your sound card. Here's what you should encounter during your first NetMeeting session:

1. Take the path **Start** ---> **Programs** ---> **NetMeeting** to display the application's Welcome/informational screen.

2. Click **Next** to see the Internet User Location Service dialog box.

3. In this dialog, enter appropriate information in First Name, Last Name, E-mail Address, City/State, Country, and, if you care to, Comments.

4. Click **Next**.

5. Click **Yes** if you want your name to be included in a ULS directory. If you choose this option, you also supply the name of the ULS. If you do not want your name to be included in a ULS directory, but do want to use such a directory to find other NetMeeting participants, type the name of the ULS after clicking **No**.

6. Click **Next,** and follow the instructions in the Audio Tuning Wizard.

7. Click **Finish**.

Once you've completed the steps, you'll be ready to conference; placing a call to begin a net get-together would involve using NetMeeting's Call menu, illustrated in Figure 11.5.

> **TIP**   Not only **Comments** but also **City/State** and **Country** are optional entries when you are setting up NetMeeting.

As one would hope, you can enter information about yourself or a ULS, or rerun Audio Tuning Wizard, at any time; these tasks aren't restricted to the first go-around with NetMeeting. To repeat any of these functions, use NetMeeting's Tools menu.

Figure 11.5 NetMeetings begin at the Call menu.

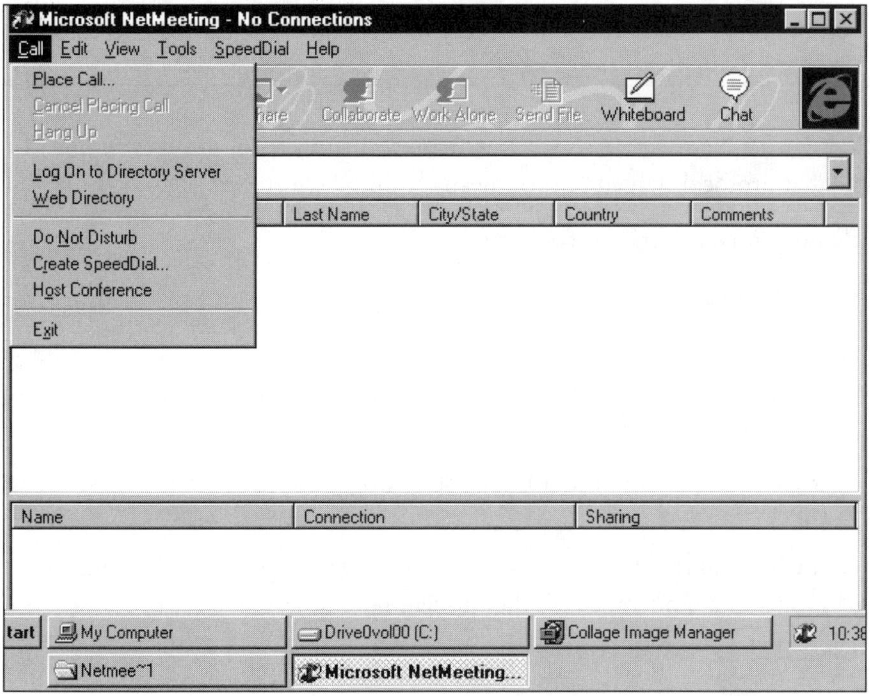

NetMeeting and Specific Types of Connections

NetMeeting can run over any of the following:

- A LAN

- The Internet

- A modem, on standard telephone lines

- An Integrated Services Digital Network (ISDN) line

If you run it across a LAN, you can use either TCP/IP or IPX/SPX to establish the connection. However, if you run NetMeeting across the Internet, only TCP/IP will do.

THE ABCs of Running NetMeeting on TCP/IP

There's a good reason for NetMeeting's being limited, in some situations, to working with TCP/IP. Under IPX/SPX "A" can initiate a conversation with "B," and vice versa. The same holds true for "C/B" exchanges. But "A" cannot talk to "C," or "C" to "A."

On the other hand, under TP/IP, any node can contact any other node, or even the outside world.

Configuring NetMeeting to work with a specific protocol means you must first enable that protocol, which in turn means taking these steps:

1. Pull down NetMeeting's **Tools** menu.

2. Click **Options**.

3. Click **Protocol**.

   a. If you want to establish a LAN or Internet connection under TCP/IP, select **Network (TCP/IP)**.

   b. If you want to establish a LAN connection under IPX/SPX, choose **Network (IPX)**.

   c. If what you're setting up is a connection over a standard telephone line by means of a modem, check the **Modem** box.

4. Click **OK**.

If you've set up NetMeeting so that you participate in remote conferences via a modem, you can change the operating parameters of the modem in question from within NetMeeting by doing the following:

1. Pull down the **Tools** menu.

2. Click **Options**.

3. Click **Protocols**.

4. Click **Modem**.

5. Click **Properties**, and change the parameters that NetMeeting then displays, as appropriate.

It's possible to modify the mirror image of this situation, too. If you'd like remote users to be able to access your Internet Information Server or NT server via a NetMeeting dial-up, follow steps 1 through 5 just outlined, and then click Use Modem To Answer Incoming Calls, and then specify the number of rings NetMeeting will wait before answering incoming calls.

To tell NetMeeting to use a new, that is, a different, modem, select the new modem from the list displayed in the **Connection** area of the NetMeeting window.

> **TIP** Whatever the nature of your NetMeeting connection, common sense still applies. For modem or ISDN, run at 28,800Kbps if you expect acceptable performance. For TCP/IP, make sure the protocol is installed to all stations you want to allow into the NetMeeting conversation.

Modifying NetMeeting Audio Settings

You can change NetMeeting's audio settings only if you're running it across a LAN or the Internet, with TCP/IP. You can't even use, let alone reconfigure, NetMeeting's audio capabilities on a modem-to-modem or IPX/SPX connection.

NetMeeting's audio is set up automatically when you run NetMeeting for the first time, or any time you run Audio Tuning Wizard. This results in audio compression settings being based on the connection speed you've specified and microphone sensitivity settings being based on the reading sample you've recorded.

> ## Enabling Full-Duplex Audio
> Audio Tuning Wizard is smart enough to be able to figure out if your sound card can handle full-duplex audio.
>
> But the Wizard doesn't automatically enable such audio. You must do so manually, through NetMeeting's Tools menu.

You can also set audio compression and microphone sensitivity manually, with these steps:

1. Pull down NetMeeting's **Tools** menu.

2. Click **Options**.

3. Click **Audio**.

4. Click **Manually Configure Compression Settings**.

5. Click **Advanced**, and make appropriate entries.

6. Click **Let Me Adjust Sensitivity Myself** in **Microphone Sensitivity**.

7. Click **OK**.

Modifying Other NetMeeting Parameters

You can further customize NetMeeting through its **Properties** dialog as follows:

- Cause NT Server to include a NetMeeting icon on its taskbar.

- Refresh the NetMeeting window after accepting a call.

- Cause Help messages to be displayed next to the NetMeeting cursor.

- Cause NetMeeting to be started when NT Server starts and to automatically notify you of incoming calls.

- Cause NetMeeting to accept calls automatically when you're not participating actively in a conference or when you are taking part in one.

- Use the entire screen as the scroll area if a shared window does not fit on your display otherwise.

- Disable scrolling of shared windows that don't fit your screen.

- Specify the directory in which NetMeeting will save files sent during a conference.

Changing or even establishing any of these properties is simple. Just pull down NetMeeting's **Tools** menu, click **Options,** and follow the application's lead.

NetMeetings through a Firewall

When you use NetMeeting across the Internet, NetMeeting in turn may use any one or all of several IP ports. If there's a firewall anywhere between you and your NetMeeting confreres, that firewall must be configured so that the ports NetMeeting expects to use are available to it, not blocked.

NetMeeting uses the IP ports described in Table 11.1.

Any firewall through which you want NetMeeting to pass must be set up to allow TCP connections on ports 522, 1503, and 1731. What's more, the firewall must pass through secondary UDP connections on dynamically assigned ports.

Audio Ports for NetMeeting

Ports used to transfer NetMeeting's audio stream are chosen on the fly by a call to its audio control module.

The two ports needed for this task are picked at random from the collection of ports that can be dynamically assigned. NetMeeting sends its audio stream over secondary UDP connections to these ports, by means of the additional protocol RTP.

TIP Not all firewalls offer the degree of flexibility in configuration that Table 11.1 implies. If yours doesn't, you may not be able to use NetMeeting audio or to use it fully.

Table 11.1 NetMeeting's IP Ports

Port Number	Is Used by NetMeeting for
522	Its ULS server, via TCP/IP.
1503	T.120, under TCP/IP.
1731	Audio control, by means of TCP/IP.
*** (that is, whatever port is available)	Audio Stream, through the RTP and UDP protocols.

Transferring Files with NetMeeting

During NetMeeting conferences, you can transfer a file to everyone taking part simply by dragging the file's icon to the NetMeeting window. If you want to send the file only to specific NetMeeting participants, select those individuals from NetMeeting's list of conferencing users, then drop the file's icon on each highlighted name.

In addition, NetMeeting offers the following ways to carry out global (i.e., to all participants) file transfers:

1. Click the **Send File** button in the NetMeeting window, and specify the file to be transferred.

2. Click the **NetMeeting** icon in the taskbar, if one has been established there, and then click **Send File**.

3. Pull down NetMeeting's **Tools** menu, click its **Send File** item, and specify the file.

However you tell NetMeeting to transfer a file, it tells the recipients of that file something too. NetMeeting presents these people with a virus-warning dialog box, which gives the recipient the options of opening, not opening, or deleting the file after it is transferred.

NetMeeting's Whiteboard and Chat Features

Move aside, Magic Markers! With NetMeeting, you can, along with all the participants in a conference, use a virtual whiteboard to create or to discuss ideas. Here's how:

1. Pull down the **Tools** menu.

2. Select **Whiteboard**.

3. Pull down the **Options** menu.

4. Choose **Stencils**.

5. Pick the type of line or shape you want to draw.

6. Click the whiteboard surface.

7. Drag the mouse pointer across the whiteboard surface.

These seven steps should display the Whiteboard on the screens of everyone in the conference.

NetMeeting Chat involves only three steps:

- Pull down the **Tools** menu.

- Click **Chat**.

- Key in your message to the Chat window, and press **ENTER**.

Your message will then wend its way to all conference participants.

From Here

In Chapter 12, we take a detailed look at Internet Information Server 3.0.

Internet Information
Server 3.0

Microsoft released the 3.0 version of Internet Information Server in January of 1997. The company plans a release for IIS 4.0, as well as Windows NT Server 5.0, sometime in the final quarter of this year. So for the next several months, at least, what you'll glean from this chapter will be the most up-to-date information.

We explore IIS 3.0, examining additional system requirements, enhancements to IIS 2.0 features, and installation and configuration. In addition, we look at the five add-ins to IIS 3.0 that distinguish it from the 2.0 release:

- Active Server Pages
- Index Server
- NetShow
- Front Page Server Extensions
- Crystal Reports 4.5

Additional Requirements for IIS 3.0

We part company once again with Microsoft on the question of requirements for Internet Information Server 3.0. MS states that the minimum hardware characteristics of NT Server 4.0 will support IIS 3.0 and its components adequately.

Consider, however, that a single one of those components, Index Server, requires 3MB to 30MB free disk simply for its data files. Or probe another point. It was our experience, during the upgrade to IIS 3.0, that temporary files alone required 3MB to 5MB *and were not removed by Windows NT after the install*. Finally, we offer this piece of evidence. NetShow, the multimedia Internet arm of IIS 3.0, should be run, even according to Microsoft, under a Pentium 200 and 48MB RAM to perform *adequately* (as opposed to just barely).

Save yourself some angst. Don't consider running Internet Information Server 3.0 on a platform that offers any less than the hardware parameters outlined in Table 12.1.

New in IIS Proper

Unlike its immediate predecessor, IIS 3.0 supports both SSL 2 and SSL 3. In addition, IIS 3.0 offers an **Internet** tab in Windows NT Explorer, which allows the use of this NT tool in managing Web-related virtual and physical file systems, sharing, and permissions. IIS 3.0 also supports multiple default documents.

Installing IIS 3.0

The evaluation copy of IIS 3.0 forwarded to us by Microsoft contained two compact discs, the first holding IIS 3.0 itself and the second, NT Server 4.0. The contents of each CD were set to cease functioning 120 days after installation.

Microsoft provides the NT Server 4.0 CD in this evaluation kit only to make the NOS, the necessary underpinning of IIS, available to those who might not otherwise be able to look at the latter. This copy of NT Server provides no upgrades or add-ons

Table 12.1 What You Need to Run Internet Information Server 3.0

For This Component	Plan on a Minimum of
Bus	PCI
CD drive	An 8-speed drive
Hard disk	A 1 gigabyte drive
Processor	A Pentium 200
RAM	32MB

whatsoever to NT itself. Nonetheless, Microsoft points out, in the CD's onboard notes, that all products offered through the evaluation kit will time out (that is, quit working) 120 days after being loaded. We were also told that we could not disclose any results of any benchmark or performance testing we might conduct on the evaluation kit's contents without the prior written approval of Microsoft.

The following sections walk through installing IIS 3.0.

Installation Options

In carrying out the upgrade of Internet Information Server, you may install any or all of its features. To help you decide which of those you'll load, we review them briefly here. For a fuller discussion of these features, refer to later sections in this chapter, as well as to the individual chapters about them.

Active Server Pages

Active Server Pages is Microsoft's compile-free application environment. With it, you can combine HTML files, scripts in various languages such as Perl, and ActiveX server components into Web-based applications. Active Server Pages supports two Microsoft scripting languages: Visual Basic Scripting Edition (VBScript) and Jscript (one of MS's answers to Java).

Active Server Pages should be—and will be if your copy of IIS 3.0 uses the same setup procedure as did our evaluation copy—the first IIS 3.0 component loaded to your server; the setup routine for Active Server also copies features required by IIS 3.0 itself. During the installation of Active Server Pages, simply accept all defaults. In this way, you can be assured that those components of IIS 3.0 that draw on the install information you provide at this point will have usable, sensible path and setting data with which to work.

Microsoft Index Server 1.1

Microsoft's Index Server 1.1 is not a database. Rather, despite any confusion its name might cause, Index Server is a search engine designed to allow full-text indexing and searching of information in intranet or Internet formats such as HTML or simple text.

Microsoft NetShow

Microsoft NetShow, sure to be the star of IIS 3.0, accomplishes one-to-many multimedia communications and information distribution over Internet or an intranet. NetShow offers both live and on-demand audio and video distribution. Microsoft also claims that NetShow reduces resulting impact on network bandwidth (but we can't imagine how). This add-in is impressive, but it's also demanding.

Microsoft tacitly acknowledges this by asking, in the IIS installation CD's onboard documentation, that you review NetShow release notes carefully before installing it. We concur, especially because most of the fairly beefy hardware requirements we cited in Table 12.1 are there primarily because of NetShow.

FrontPage 97 Server Extensions

FrontPage 97 Server Extensions provide not only Web-page building but also Web-site management tools. Among other things, for example, FrontPage 97 Server Extensions can locate, by means of a graphical interface, broken links on a Web site or create links between HTML and MS Office files.

Crystal Reports 4.5 for IIS 3.0

Version 4.5 of Crystal Reports is a report generator that can create reports from IIS Web Server log files. Crystal Reports for IIS 3.0 includes canned, preformatted Web log report templates. Its HTML publishing capabilities can, in addition, convert reports to presentation-quality Web documents. Crystal Reports' setup, like that of IIS 3.0 as a whole, allows you to select components to install.

Installation

It's much more difficult and time consuming to load NT Server than to install IIS 3.0. Assuming that you have NT up and running by now, you won't have much more to do in upgrading Internet Information Server than stick the CD in the drive and respond to prompts.

We'll point out a few things, though. Very early on in our upgrade to IIS 3.0, we were disconcerted at one of the messages generated by the load of Active Server Pages. A snapshot of this message is shown in Figure 12.1.

But don't be alarmed; go ahead and click **Open**. We did so and no disasters ensued. Rather, we saw, as the next step in the install, the License Agreement for IIS 3.0, as Figure 12.2 shows.

Without your having to tell it so, IIS's install routine starts with Active Server Pages, warning you to close all applications before proceeding, as we've illustrated in Figure 12.3.

Figure 12.1 Apparently even Microsoft distribution media aren't immune.

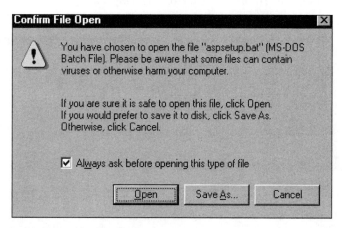

Next, you'll be given the opportunity to select the Active Server Pages (ASP), components to install. We grabbed them all, as Figure 12.4 depicts.

Now Setup asks you to select the path to which at least some of the chosen ASP components will be loaded. We took the defaults offered, as Figure 12.5 portrays.

Even as the load of IIS 3.0 proceeds, you'll have the chance to bail out, as Figure 12.6 indicates in its lower right corner.

After only a few minutes, installation was complete; we were presented with a summary of the process like that in Figure 12.7.

We still have some configuring to do, though; both NetShow and Crystal Reports require additional setup.

Configuring NetShow

When IIS 3.0 finishes loading, NT reminds you that you still have some work to do. Specifically, it advises you to run setup for NetShow by clicking the Setup icon in the new program group NetShow it's just established.

We did that and saw, as the first step in the NetShow setup process, the screen depicted in Figure 12.8.

NetShow configuration progresses quite quickly to more demanding material. First, you're asked to define bandwidth for the server as a whole and for individual files in particular. Figure 12.9 shows you our responses.

Figure 12.2 It's even more important than usual to read the License Agreement because of terms it contains regarding such things as benchmark testing.

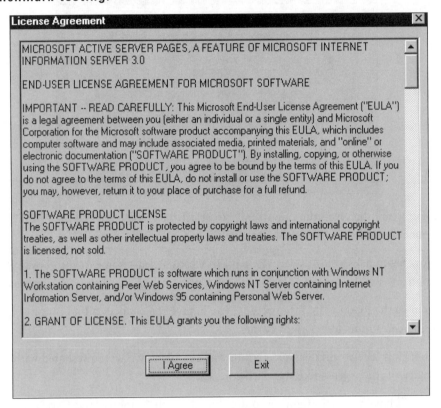

Now comes a point in the NetShow setup process that might induce some confusion. You're asked to select a virtual root directory for NetShow On-Demand content files, as Figure 12.10 illustrates. What might throw you momentarily is the earlier choice, shown in Figure 12.5, of a path for Active Server Pages. Don't worry about the latter interfering with the former. However similar the dialogs presenting them and the default paths referred to might be, there's no overlap.

Not all NetShow files will live under its virtual root, though. As Figure 12.11 indicates, program (as opposed to content) files are placed in quite a different part of the overall file system.

Next, as Figure 12.12 depicts, we provided yet another path to the setup program, this time for NetShow demos.

Figure 12.3 Active Server Pages installation starts with this screen.

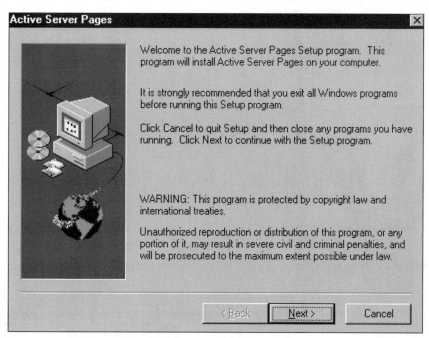

After you've supplied this last bit of information, NetShow setup proceeds to completion.

Configuring Crystal Reports

During IIS 3.0 installation, the part of the process that loads Crystal Reports, like all segments of the install, displays the amount of disk space the components you've decided upon will require. Figure 12.13 outlines our selections.

As you proceed through the installation of Crystal Reports, you're made aware that this product was not developed by Microsoft; Figure 12.14 presents a snapshot of this information.

In installing Crystal Reports, you're required to fill out a personal/product information sheet like that in Figure 12.15.

Once you have completed the registration form and setup as a whole, Crystal Reports starts automatically, producing a window like that in Figure 12.16.

Figure 12.4 We chose to install all ASP features.

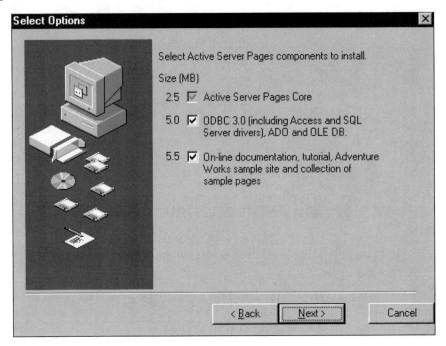

That's the end of the IIS 3.0 installation and setup. Now we take a closer look at the new features you've just implemented.

Active Server Pages

Because Active Server Pages is fully integrated into Windows NT Server, it knows when a file has changed. As a result, ASP will automatically recompile changed scripts when such scripts are requested after a change. This in turn means that you can immediately preview when developing—quite a nice feature.

Active Server Pages can be created with either VBScript or Jscript. In addition, with plug-ins, you can incorporate REXX, PERL, and Python into your Active Server toolkit.

Active Server Pages work with any Web browser. The output of ASP in turn produces vanilla HTML content. In addition, Active Server Pages maintain state; that is, they can be configured, through application and session variables, to carry the same parameters across multiple pages on a Web site.

Figure 12.5 Taking the defaults helps ensure a smooth installation.

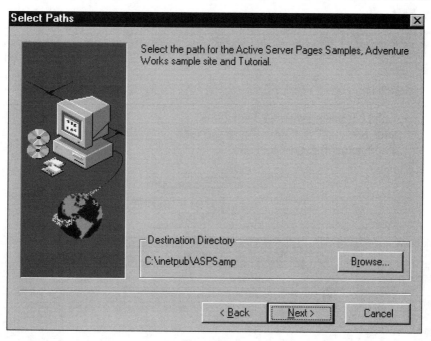

A Thumbnail Sketch of ASP Operations

Unlike CGI, Active Server Pages runs as a multithreaded process. In effect, this means that ASP can maintain and manipulate, simultaneously, several different series of low-level tasks.

A Root by Any Other Name

NetShow's *Virtual Root* isn't virtual in the sense of being an alias. Rather, it represents a point in the file system from which all NetShow content file resources will branch.

Maintain State for Security

The ability to maintain state is a handy one in many Web applications. For example, a bookstore's online catalog might want to allow a shopper to record his or her name and credit card number only once, for obvious security reasons, but to have that information available to purchases drawn from widely separated sections of the catalog.

Figure 12.6 IIS keeps you informed of its progress and provides an early Exit.

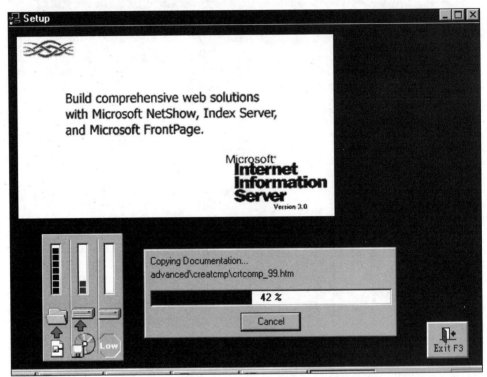

ActiveX components were known as OLE automation servers in their previous incarnation. Such components, or objects, are basically anything you can access from a Web page. IIS 3.0's ASP implementation ships with a core set of ActiveX components including an Ad Rotator and Browser Capabilities.

Active Server Pages runs ActiveX components by means of ASP-executed scripts. For example, to retrieve records from a database, a script passes the request to the Active Database Object (ADO). The ADO is the compiled code that talks to the database and produces the desired results. But another ASP script, not the Database Object, retrieves those results and displays it as an HTML page.

Did You Notice the Discrepancy?

Even though Figure 12.6 was created during the installation of IIS 3.0, the promo it includes refers to IIS 2.0. Take it as an example of the way in which software releases build on their predecessors.

Figure 12.7 Here's what we installed.

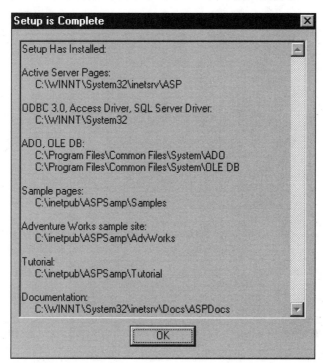

> ## ADO's Flexibility
> ADO can carry out operations on any ODBC-compatible data source. Among these are Microsoft Access, Microsoft SQL Server, Oracle, Informix, and Sybase.

> **TIP** It's ASP's use of ActiveX that broadens the former's range. ActiveX components can be written in any number of programming languages, including Visual Basic, C++, Cobol, and Java.

It's one of Active Server Pages' greatest strengths that it prepackages much of what would otherwise have to be programmed from scratch, through its use of ActiveX components. Even if your information needs are somewhat unusual, there are probably components available, albeit not bundled with the IIS 3.0 implementation, which will meet them. For instance, a number of software vendors have created ActiveX components that can access databases on IBM mainframes.

Figure 12.8 As you might expect given its content, NetShow offers some interesting components.

Figure 12.9 We took the default bandwidths NetShow setup presented.

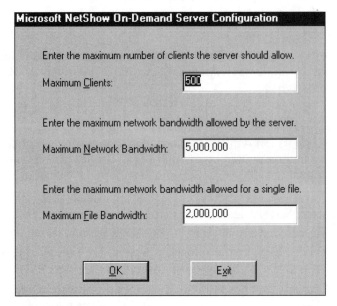

Figure 12.10 NetShow setup allows you not only to specify the application's virtual root, but also to enable security for its content files from the start.

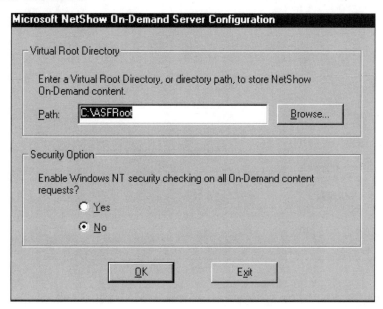

Figure 12.11 Once again, we took the defaults and put NetShow program files in their own path.

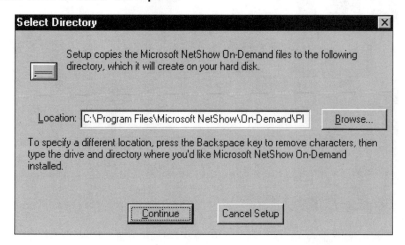

Figure 12.12 NetShow demos have their own subsystem too.

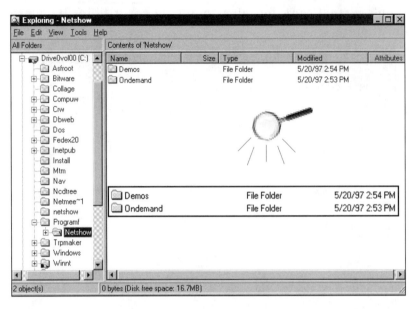

Figure 12.13 We chose to load all aspects of Crystal reports.

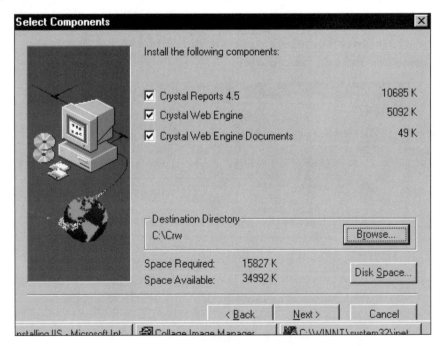

Figure 12.14 Seagate Software also lets you know that there's already an upgrade to Crystal Reports.

Anatomy of an ASPage

An Active Server Page file is a simple text file that can be edited with any text editor. An ASP file can begin life as HTML and only later have server-side script commands inserted and be saved as .asp rather than .htm or .html.

> ### GUIs on the Horizon
> If you prefer a graphical interface, be patient. Microsoft tells us that it has quite a few visual tools under development that will allow you to create Active Server Pages in a GUI-based environment.

Active Server Pages can access all HTTP server variables, such as browser type and referring page, thereby simplifying Web page development, even to the point of allowing you to customize pages for specific users. Because the output of an ASP file is standard HTML, Active Server Pages works with any Web browser. They're stored as plain text, so ASP files can also be customized to make optimum use of

Figure 12.15 Completing this information is part of the process of registering Crystal Reports.

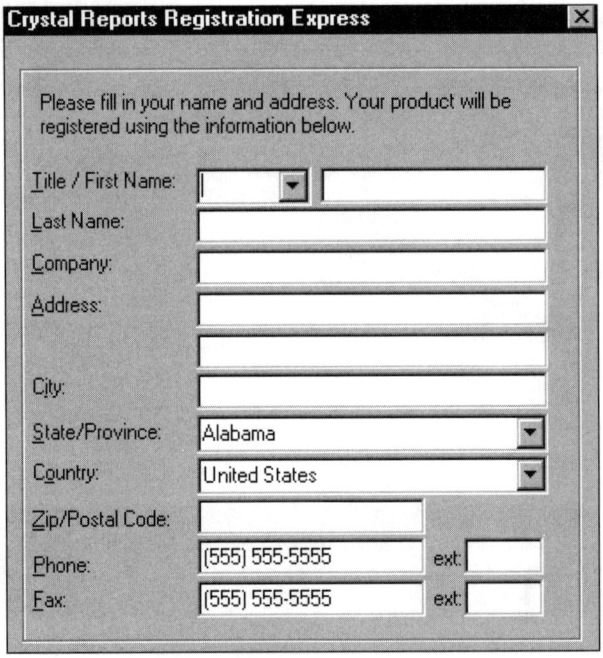

the capabilities of each browser. This flexibility in the makeup of ASP files in turn grants flexibility to your information base, allowing content files to exist in any form and to be housed on any server in your IIS implementation.

More Active Server Technologies

Other Microsoft Active Server technologies to look forward to include the Distributed Component Object Model (DCOM), Transaction Server, once called Viper, and message queue server, which used to be known at Microsoft as Falcon.

At the time this book was written, Transaction Server was about to begin shipping. The Message Queue Server, on the other hand, was still unavailable as of early 1997.

ASP Implementation Issues

The implementation issues associated with ASP are discussed in the following sections.

Figure 12.16 Here's Crystal Reports' home base.

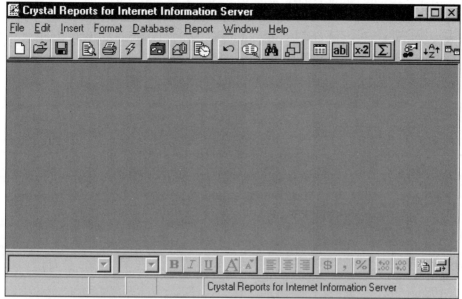

Platforms Supported

Active Server Pages will run under Windows NT Server 4.0, Windows NT Workstation 4.0 with Peer Web Services, and Windows 95 with Personal Web Server. However, Windows NT Server 3.51, Windows NT Workstation 3.51, and Windows NT Server 4.0 on MIPS do not support Active Server Pages.

ASP Security

As a component of Internet Information Server 3.0, ASP draws on Windows NT security measures. Therefore, access to ASP files can be restricted to specific users or groups by a number of means, including Windows NT authentication, basic Web authentication, client-side certificates, and SSL.

ASP and Databases

Active Server Pages applications can interact with not only ODBC-compliant databases such as SQL Server, Oracle, Sybase, Informix, and DB2, but also with the output of OLE 2 applications like Lotus Notes or Microsoft Excel. With the inclusion of objects programmed in languages like C++, ASP applications can even access online data feeds or mainframe and supercomputer databases.

ASP versus LiveWire

Netscape LiveWire employs JavaScript as its programming tool, thus providing a more limited development environment than Active Server Pages, which can incorporate not only VBScript and Jscript but also compiled objects written in any programming language, including Java. In addition, LiveWire applications must be recompiled manually each time they are modified, whereas Active Server Pages recognizes ASP file changes and can automatically recompile as a result.

Index Server

As was the case with ASP, we begin our overview of Index Server with what we consider to be its best feature. Index Server can search information formatted as HTML, text, or Microsoft Office documents. That information can be in any of seven languages:

- Dutch

- English

- French

- German

- Italian

- Spanish

- Swedish

Once installed, Index Server automatically builds an index of your IIS Web service; that index can be searched from any Web browser, simply through use of the sample query forms included with Index Server.

Index Server builds its index to include all virtual roots and subdirectories on your Web server, as well as indexing the physical file system. In addition, a network administrator can choose directories and file types that should *not* be indexed.

Index Server automatically updates its content index whenever a content file is added, deleted, or modified. The Server uses Windows NT security to control the searches users may perform on this index. Users receive only those index search results that pertain to documents they have permission, under NT, to see. Index

> **TIP** When the Index Server setup has completed, you can test your installation by connecting to the URL http://your-server-name/Samples/ Search/Queryhit.htm. Of course, substitute the actual name of your IIS server for the parameter *your-server-name* shown here.

Server can index documents not only on an NT Server, but also on any host accessible to that Server and IIS 3.0, such as NetWare and UNIX platforms. This IIS 3.0 feature is designed to operate with low overhead on its multipurpose NT server, but to retain the ability to scale up to more powerful servers like UNIX supercomputers and the very large numbers of documents they house.

Index Server also makes available to third-party developers an ISAPI-based hook called IFilter, through which programmers can tweak Index Server to index and search any document type. An IFilter routine might, for instance, read a target file generated by WordPerfect, extract the text to be indexed, and return that text to Index Server.

Index Server Search Characteristics

Index Server indexes not only the text but also the properties of documents. Properties that can serve as the basis for one of its indices include:

- Author
- Date of last modification to file
- File name
- File size
- Properties set in documents, such as HTML tags

Index Server supports stemming and inflection in all seven of the languages it understands. That means that it can carry out fuzzy searches on, for example, all tenses of a verb or all forms (masculine, feminine, neuter, singular, and plural) of nouns and pronouns.

Searches under Index Server can include queries made up of single words, phrases, or complete sentences and can incorporate proximity relationships as well as the more familiar Boolean ones. Results of an Index Server search can be displayed in full or as abstracts, in text or HTML format. Index Server can also make use of custom search forms in order to accept prefab or limited queries.

Fuzzy Advantage

Fuzzy searches may not be employed to their fullest in English. For example, our language doesn't assign such characteristics as gender to every noun. Others do. So, Index Server can distinguish between the French nouns la femme and l'homme (meaning woman and man respectively) even if the articles indicating gender that accompany them are misspelled.

Finally, Index Server searches can be run under any Web browser, because its search and results forms are simply standard HTML pages. Therefore, Index Server provides any Web browser the ability to search documents for key words, phrases, or properties such as author's name.

"Traditional" Index Server Searches

Index Server can, in its fuzz-free searches, find:

- Words

- Phrases

- The proximity of a word or phrase to another word or phrase

- A word or phrase that exists within a textual properties such as a document's abstract

- A word or phrase within unusual document types such as a PowerPoint presentation

- A document that contains a value whose relationship to a constant (such as date or file size) is defined by any of the common relational operators such as greater than and less than

- A document that contains combinations of values defined by the operators AND, OR, and AND NOT; for example, *'tree' AND NOT 'three'*

- A document that contains ranges of values defined by wild card operators like * and ?, as in *AUTHOR='THI?H NHAT HANH'*

Fuzzy Queries

Through its support for fuzzy queries, Index Server can generate words that are similar to the ones entered by users and then use those generated terms in searches of its index. Thus, your entry of the word *cat* might return not only references to cats but also to cathartic and category. Index Server's ability to conduct fuzzy queries also relies on its linguistic analysis abilities, through which it matches the user-entered *flex* with flexing, flexed, and will flex, as well as the user-specified *swum* with swim and swimming.

Inflection and Stemming
Working forward from a basic term through its variations, as we did with *flex*, is called *inflection*. Working backward as our *swum* example did is referred to as *stemming*. You'll see these two terms used frequently in any discussion of indexing.

Index Server Constraints

Index Server is designed for use on a single Web server on an intranet or the Internet. It requires Internet Information Server 2.0 and Windows NT Server 4.0 or Windows NT Workstation 4.0 and Peer Web Services. Index Server is limited to indexing a single machine; however, because a single Internet Information Server can contain many Web sites, Index Server can reference every one of those sites.

Index Server does not have a Web crawler, or intermediate agent. Instead, it works directly with the file system. If that system is composed of NTFS volumes, Index Server will respect all NTFS security constraints, unlike other search engines, many of which display hits to users whether or not the user in question has the file access permissions needed to read or retrieve the documents in question.

Because Internet Information Server itself logs all traffic to and from its clients, it automatically gathers information related to index queries, such as the IP address at which the query originated. For this reason, Index Server does not include a separate logging facility. However, Index Server does include a set of counters for NT Server's Performance Monitor. These counters allow Performance Monitor to track the performance of both major components of Index Server: its content index engine and its search engine.

NetShow

NetShow is made up of two major components, NetShow On-Demand and NetShow Live. NetShow On-Demand sends audio, illustrated audio, and video over networks. NetShow Live pushes audio out over intranets.

NetShow On-Demand relies on a technology called *streaming*. Streaming allows a user to see or hear multimedia-based information that has been transferred across the Internet or an intranet before the transmission of that material is complete. In other words, you don't have to wait for all of a file—whether it's JPEG, WAV, or something more exotic—to arrive at your station; you see or hear it as it's coming in.

NetShow Live, on the other hand, broadcasts rather than transmits. More correctly, it multicasts. IP multicasting like that used by NetShow relies on standards that govern the simultaneous distribution to multiple users of the same information. In this context, ordinary TCP/IP transmissions can be viewed as a form of broadcast too, but one called *unicast*, which, although it may send the same information to a number of individuals, must make an individual copy of that information for each user involved.

The NetShow Server can accommodate a wide range of streaming needs. For instance, it can simultaneously stream different multimedia content files, some at low bit rates such as at 14.4Kbps and others at rates as high as 6Mbps. NetShow therefore makes possible productions in which graphics, photographs, videos, and other visual material can be synchronized with audio, or with each other.

It is through this ability to allow a large number of users to access a single multicast transmission that NetShow gains some efficiency in the use of overall bandwidth. Such single-point transmissions take up much less of a network's path than would the transmissions of individual copies of the same material. In other words, multicasting is well suited to those presentations that simultaneously forward the same content to many people.

NetShow archives multimedia content before streaming it, under the ASF format. When structured as ASF files, multimedia content can be delivered at varying rates. Even more impressive is the ability conveyed by ASF files to insert markers into the NetShow-delivered stream to allow users to fast forward through the material. ASF files can contain material from a variety of sources, such as video, audio, and the contents of URLs.

Using what Microsoft calls Forward Error Correction (FEC) information, appended to its content material by the NetShow server prior to transmission, NetShow can compensate for less-than-perfect network conditions such as traffic jams. Along these same lines, NetShow can recover, without any intervention on your part, from transmission problems like lost packets.

In addition to having its own built-in administrative tools, NetShow integrates fully with those of NT Server, making it possible for you to use, for instance, Performance Monitor and Event Viewer to track its performance. Just as important is NetShow's integration with Internet Service Manager, which allows an administrator to configure and manage a NetShow Server with one tool. Through Internet Service Manager you might, for instance, set such NetShow operating parameters as maximum content throughput per file.

NetShow supports Windows' standard ACM/VCM, or Audio/Video Compression Modules, thereby offering another tool for efficient use of transmission paths. By virtue of being based on Internet standards such as IP multicast, it can distribute audio to such "foreign" applications as MBONE.

Finally, NetShow client software is fully ActiveX compatible, so it can be used with Internet Explorer 3.0 and even Netscape Navigator, if you have the NCompass ActiveX Plug-In. What's more, because it is in effect an ActiveX object, the NetShow Player can be embedded within any application that itself employs ActiveX, such as those generated by Visual Basic and Microsoft Office.

> **TIP** Files in WAV, AVI, QuickTime, PowerPoint, JPEG, GIF, and URL formats can, with the use of NetShow's built-in tools, be used to generate illustrated audio.

FrontPage 97 Server Extensions

FrontPage Server Extensions are not the same as FrontPage. FrontPage 97 Server Extensions form a collection of components and APIs that exist and run solely on an IIS 3.0 server and through which Web sites may be built and managed. FrontPage 97, on the other hand, also includes a client application that itself provides a visual HTML and site management environment.

FrontPage 97 Server Extensions for IIS 3.0 are ISAPI applications, not CGI. As such, they provide significant performance benefits.

Crystal Reports 4.5

Crystal Reports is a report writer through which you can, in an HTML environment, create presentation-quality reports *and* integrate them into database applica-

> ## Additional Server Extensions
> Native Alpha and PowerPC versions of the FrontPage Server Extensions
> for IIS 3.0 were not available at the time this book was being written.
> However, Microsoft anticipates that they will be ready sometime in the
> second half of 1997.

tions. Crystal Reports for Internet Information Server 3.0 also includes preformatted Web log reports for analyzing Web log files.

Crystal Reports offers its version of Wizards, called Experts. Specifically, Crystal Reports provides Experts for:

- Database Table Selection

- Graphing

- Report Creation

- Report Distribution

- Style

- Visual Linking of reports

It also offers what it calls its Private Tutor, through which it provides on-screen, context-sensitive, step-by-step help.

Crystal Reports uses two distinct windows to view its output. Its Preview Window presents live data from reports-in-the-making; its Design Window, on the other hand, displays templates. The application also includes features important to the quality of a report, such as:

- Twelve graphing styles

- A library of styles

- A number of right-mouse-button menus

- Box drawing

- Grid control options

- Integrated e-mail capability, with support for both VIM and MAPI

- Line drawing

- Macro language with more than 140 functions and operators, which may be extended through user-programmed DLL functions

- Sorting on groups

- Support for Paradox and xBASE bitmap formats

- Support for a number of image formats, including BMP, GIF, TIF, PCX, and TGA

- Support for heterogeneous data sources; that is, the ability to link data from a number of types of databases in a single report

- Support for OLE 2.0

- The ability to browse database field contents

- The ability to export to other analysis tools

- The ability to save component data with its report as a means of providing for after-the-fact analysis

- The ability to sort and subtotal in a single step

Crystal Reports can access data from PC, SQL, and ODBC databases. Its analysis tools include the capacity to integrate graphs and drilldowns of various levels of detail in information into reports, as well as a search function by means of which you can locate specific pieces of information in even very long reports.

Distributing reports can also be handled by this IIS 3.0 add-in. Crystal Reports enables you to export its output to formats like:

- 1-2-3

- Excel

- Quattro Pro

- Word

- WordPerfect

Crystal Reports for Internet Information Server 3.0 is a special version of the product that was developed specifically for the IIS environment. Crystal Reports for Internet Information Server allows you to report on only IIS Web Server log files, Microsoft Access databases, and Microsoft SQL Server databases. You can export these reports to HTML. But if you wish to use any other PC or SQL data sources or to enjoy full development and distribution functionality, you'll need to upgrade to Crystal Reports Professional 5.0. Doing so would allow you to, for example, distribute reports through a much wider variety of communication applications, such as cc:mail, Lotus Notes, and Microsoft Exchange.

On the development side, Crystal Reports 5.0 allows you to integrate reports directly into applications through a number of programming tools such as its ActiveX Control; these tools can be obtained in either 16-bit or 32-bit implementations.

Another upgrade to Crystal Reports 4.5 you might want to consider is Crystal Info 4.5. This add-on to Crystal Reports allows you to:

- Automatically update the content of predefined reports

- Offload all report processing

- Refresh report data according to any schedule

Both Crystal Reports 5.0 and Crystal Info 4.5 can be purchased from resellers such as Programmer's Paradise and Egghead Software or directly from Seagate Software and its distributors.

From Here

After this quick run-through of IIS 3.0, we'll examine some of its components more thoroughly. In Chapter 13, we explore Active Server Pages, Front Page 97 Server Extensions, and Crystal Reports. In Chapter 14, we look at Index Server in detail, and in Chapter 15, we investigate NetShow On-Demand Server.

Active Server Pages, FrontPage 97 Server Extensions, and Crystal Reports 4.5

It's indicative of the emphasis Microsoft places on the Web that not only Internet Information Server itself but even the new features added to it in the 3.0 release lean heavily toward Web-based distribution of information. None of what we discuss in this chapter or the remaining two touches in any way on IIS ftp or gopher services.

We begin our examination of IIS 3.0's additional features with a look at those that are most overtly Web-related:

- Active Server Pages

- Crystal Reports 4.5 for Internet Information Server

- FrontPage 97 Server Extensions

This chapter won't teach you how to create Active Server Pages, nor will it delve deeply into applying Front Page 97 Server Extensions to dress up your Web site. It won't even provide details for creating reports under Crystal Reports. What it will do, though, is acquaint you with some of the more significant administrative and configuration considerations that apply to each of these new IIS features.

Active Server Pages

Active Server Pages (ASP) can be found not only under Internet Information Server 3.0, but also as an adjunct to Microsoft Peer Web Services 3.0 on Windows NT Workstation 4.0, and under Microsoft Personal Web Server version 1.0a on Windows 95. ASP can, on any of these platforms, create applications that can then be distributed by Internet Information Server.

Before Installing ASP

In the documentation regarding installing ASP provided on the Microsoft Web site, we're given a number of before-you-begin caveats about this process. Those cautions include a need for the following:

- A minimum of 30MB free disk to install ASP

- A Microsoft Web server already installed, as follows:

  - Internet Information Server 2.0 or higher under NT Server

  - Peer Web Services 2.0 or higher under NT Workstation

  - Personal Web Server 1.0a or higher under Windows 95

- Stopping all applications and services that might even consider accessing ODBC data sources

- Reinstalling both Internet Information Server and Active Server Pages, if you've tried to load the latter to a backup domain controller and (as should have been the case) failed

- Installing Microsoft VM for Java on your HTTP server, if you intend to incorporate Java elements into your Active Server Pages

Now we'll add a caveat of our own: Active Server Pages' samples, included with the application, require Microsoft Access to be present. Further, although you can also run those samples in conjunction with SQL Server, doing so requires some tweaking on your part.

> **TIP** VM is available for download from www.microsoft.com and is included in Windows NT version 4.0 Service Pack 2 and higher.

> **TIP** Other bits of exotica that can be incorporated into Active Server Pages are **Active Data Objects** (**ADO**s). Files called **Adovbs.inc** and **Adojavas.inc**, for VBScript and Jscript respectively, define some values for ADOs. So, if you want to use these values, you'll also need to install, or identify the path to, a sample ASP site called **Adventure Works**, which can be found in the directory **Inetpub\Aspsamp\Samples directory**.

Loading Active Server Pages

Active Server Pages can be installed as part of the overall upgrade to IIS 3.0 or as a separate process. Our installation of ASP was from the IIS 3.0 evaluation CD forwarded to us by Microsoft, so if you're working from a purchased copy, some of the details of what we're about to tell you may differ. But the load as a whole will follow these steps in either case.

With the distribution CD in the drive, take the path **Start ---> Programs ---> Administrative Tools ---> Windows NT Setup or the path Start ---> Settings ---> Control Panel ---> Add/Remove Programs.**

Navigate to the installation routine. In our case, this was easy. As soon as the eval CD was in our drive, its Welcome window displayed automatically under Internet Explorer. From there, we had simply to scroll to the link in the page for installing Active Server Pages.

ASP Documentation

Active Server Pages documentation installed with the application is, as you might expect, in HTML format. Probably the easiest way to navigate through this documentation is to start Internet Explorer. Assuming you've installed IIS 3.0 in the default directories, open the URL illustrated in Figure 13.1: http://yourserver/Inetsrv/docs/aspdocs/ipmain.htm.

For instance, it not only points out that the ASP samples you've just loaded are designed to work with Access, but also gives you instructions in tweaking SQL Server to act as a partner to ASP. In any case, following the link in this page will lead you to the Active Server Pages Roadmap, as depicted in Figures 13.2 and 13.3.

Figure 13.1 This page of ASP documentation describes the application.

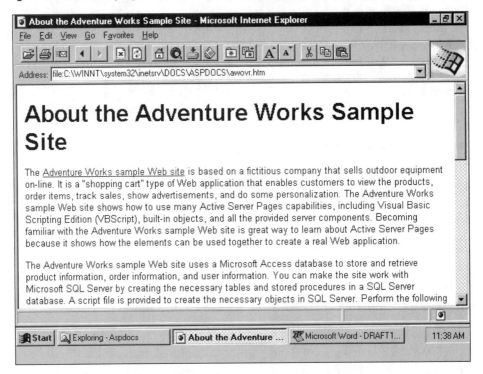

Touring with ASP Roadmap

The ASP Roadmap starts you off on a tour of the Adventure Works sample Web site. Although meandering through that site isn't a tutorial per se, it will give you a clearer idea of what's involved in scripting Active Server Pages. You'll even find some sample ASP code at this site, which can also be reached by opening the URL http://yourserver/iasdocs/aspdocs/roadmap.asp with a frames-capable Web browser.

We found the VBScript and Jscript material included with ASP quite informative. Figure 13.4 gives you a look at the curriculum.

POP QUIZ Describe the purpose and nature of the parameter *yourserver* in the URL listed in the section "ASP Documentation."

Figure 13.2 The ASP Roadmap has numerous links.

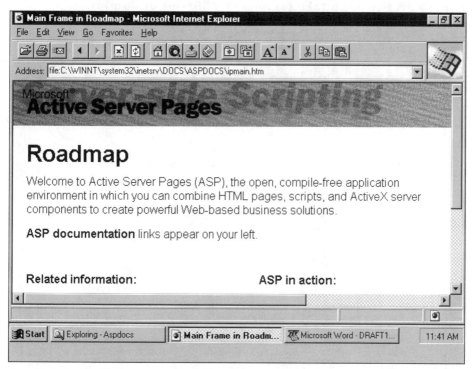

ASP and SSL

Using SSL client authentication on a server to which you've added or will shortly add ASP has implications for the latter (and for all applications running in conjunction with SSL, for that matter).

SSL maintains something called *session state*, which is in effect the conditions applied to a user session after that user has been successfully authenticated and allowed to conduct a session in the first place. Unfortunately, if you've not designed your virtual path names sensibly, and the name of one such path contains the name of another, session state may inadvertently but incorrectly apply to all applications in both virtual file systems, even if SSL would not have so applied it had it been explicitly asked to do so.

Out-of-Process Components and ASP

Left to itself, Active Server Pages will not acknowledge out-of-process components—that is, OLE components that run in a process other than ASP, such as Excel. Further, Microsoft dissuades us from using out-of-process components. Once

Figure 13.3 You can use the links from ASP Roadmap to explore the sample ASP site or to take lessons in VBScript or JScript.

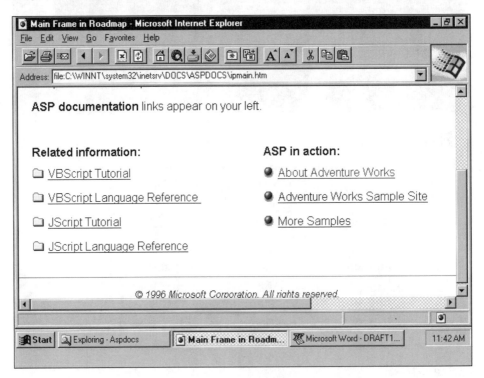

again, there's a security question involved; using out-of-process components in ASP makes it possible for later users of that component to inherit the original security context of the component. This is another example of the kind of loss-of-security-by-osmosis situation we encountered in the section "ASP and SSL."

If you choose to use out-of-process components, you'll have your work cut out for you if you also hope to avoid the security loophole these components add to ASP. You'll need to run the command line utility dcomcnfg.exe to define a specific identity under which the component will run. Only setting such an identity precludes the possibility of users inheriting other users' security contexts.

> **TIP** The Win32 Software Development Kit from Microsoft has, in its documentation, some excellent tips on working with out-of-process components. The OLE Programmer's Reference is similarly helpful on the topic of defining identities for components.

Figure 13.4 As you can see, ASP gives you the chance to learn a great deal about VBScript.

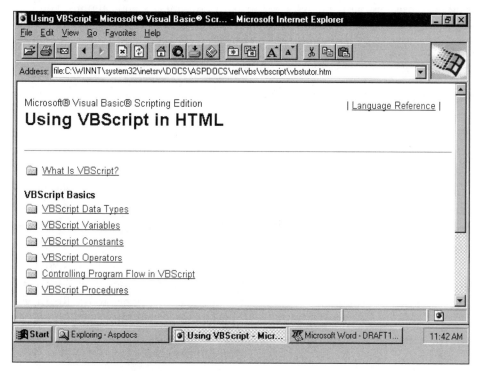

SQL Server and ASP

The most significant issue between SQL Server and ASP is a performance-related one involving threads. Ordinarily, ASP would expect a threading model of Apartment to be used in conjunction with the Database Access component, if that component is stored in the Session object. If it is, but you're not using any databases other than SQL Server, you can improve Active Server performance by manually changing the threading model associated with ASP in the Registry from the Apartment value to one of Both.

One easy way to make this change is to follow these steps:

1. Start Windows NT Explorer.

2. Double-click the directory \Program Files\Common Files\System\Ado folder.

3. Double-click the file Makefree.bat.

4. Manually make the edit needed.

Be aware also that Microsoft isn't sanguine about the whole idea of storing instances of the Database Access Component in the Session object. So, if you're using databases other than SQL Server or if you're simply being cautious, you'll take Microsoft's advice and consult the section called "Connection Pooling" in its *Component Reference* for ASP to learn better ways than stuffing the Session object to interweave components and Web pages.

Improving ASP Performance

Tweaking a few factors can result in appreciable performance improvements for ASP. We consider two such tweaks now.

Disabling Checks for Virtual Roots

By default, every time it receives a request, ASP checks for virtual roots nested within other virtual roots. Attention to detail is commendable, but this fastidiousness can cause ASP performance to degrade. If you don't anticipate the need to create new virtual roots, you can set the Registry parameter CheckForNestedVroots to 0, precluding ASP's doing this check from then on. Doing so will improve your Active Server's performance. The only problem such a procedure might cause is to blind nested virtual roots that might be created while this change to the Registry is being made to the existence of global ASP configuration files. So be careful that no such roots are created while you're massaging the Registry.

Allocating Virtual Memory

Another Registry parameter, MemFreeFactor, whose default value is 50, is the basis for the allocation of virtual memory to Active Server Pages. If it's heavily loaded down with requests and processing, the HTTP server on which you've installed ASP might exhaust its supply of virtual memory.

Setting MemFreeFactor to 100 or even more will force ASP to cache more memory, making it less likely to run out, but also leaving less for other applications. So, you probably want to take this step only if your IIS Web service is to be devoted largely to Active Server Pages.

ASP and Your Choice of Database

In the small print at the bottom of the page (so to speak) Microsoft tells us that ASP was extensively tested with and designed to work alongside SQL Server. This is after informing us that the sample Web site that accompanies ASP uses Access. MS states further, "We recommend that Microsoft Access be used solely for development purposes and not for production. Microsoft Access was designed as a single-user desktop database, and not for server use. When multiple, concurrent users make requests of a Microsoft Access database, unpredictable results may occur." That's good enough for us.

Here are two more excerpts from a list of glitches involving Access and ASP:

- Using the ODBC driver for Access foils attempts, made by setting the MaxRecords property of the RecordSet object, to limit the number of records returned.

- Attempting to insert a record into an Access database with the AddNew method sometimes fails. But at least there's a workaround for this one: rather than dealing with the record as a whole, include *only the fields into which you wish to insert a new value* in a SELECT statement when opening a record set.

Browsers and ASP

Scripts that create or manipulate Active Server Pages must check a file called **Browscap.ini** for the definitions of properties that browsers seeking to retrieve those pages must have. Because the properties of browsers change frequently, Microsoft updates Browscap.ini as frequently. To obtain the most recent version available for this file, check the Microsoft Web site at the URL http://www.microsoft.com/iis.

Notepad and ASP

If you're using **Notepad** to create ASP script files—which require the filename extension **.asp** but which are made up of ASCII text in the same way HTML files are—you might think you'd use the Text Documents (**.txt**) file type in the Save or Save As dialogs. Although well-reasoned, that would be a poor choice. It would simply add the extension .txt, rather than the needed .asp, to whatever file name you've entered in the File Name box. Even if you try to force your way around this by typing, for instance, firstfil.asp into File Name, that's not what you'll get. Instead, Explorer would find something called firstfil.asp.txt if you're working under NTFS, or simply firstfil~.txt if you're running FAT. The only way to avoid such confusion is either to select **All Files** from the Save As Type list or to enclose the file name you've entered in single quotes before you save it.

Server-Side Includes under ASP

The newest release of Internet Information Server includes enhancements to the capability known as **Server Side Includes** (SSI).

> **TIP** You can bone up on SSI by opening its documentation at the URL http://yourserver/iasdocs/aspdocs/ssi/isiall.htm with your Web browser.

The gist of these enhancements is as follows. If you change an included file, that change will *automatically and immediately* be reflected in output sent to a browser that has requested the including file *if the included file is in a virtual root or one of its subdirectories*. If the included file is not in such portions of the file system, changes you make to it will not be reflected in output involving the included file until the HTTP service of IIS is stopped and then restarted.

Crystal Reports 4.5

Crystal Reports 4.5 for Internet Information Server allows you to create and view reports based upon the logs IIS itself generates. Reports created with this application may draw upon log files in Microsoft standard log file format and in NCSA (common log file) format that have been stored in an ODBC-compliant database such as SQL Server.

Crystal Reports can export any report you create under it, including any graphics that report might contain, to HTML. Crystal Reports 4.5 for Internet Information Server can also create reports dynamically if those reports are intended to be housed on the HTTP server. Doing so involves:

- That CR component called the Crystal Web Reports Engine

- A sample Active Server Page that can launch six predefined Web log reports

- The concurrent need to have ActiveX Server installed before attempting to use any of these prefab reports

The easiest way to kick-start this tool, assuming ActiveX is installed, is to use your browser to open the URL http://yourserver/logrpts/.

The Crystal Web Reports Engine is itself made up of four other components:

- Crystal Web Publishing Interface

- Crystal Web Activity DLL

- Crystal Reports Engine

- Crystal Web Application Interface

The following sections look at each of these in turn.

Crystal Web Publishing Interface

Using the Crystal Web Publishing Interface, developers and end users can create presentation-quality reports already formatted for HTML, which can therefore be viewed immediately by most Web browsers.

Crystal Web Activity DLL

Crystal Web Activity DLL allows the Crystal Reports Engine to treat all the fields in an HTTP server log as database fields, thereby permitting more in-depth reports because of the corollary ability to include greater detail in queries.

Crystal Reports Engine

Crystal Reports Engine is a subset of Crystal Web Reports Engine. Crystal Reports Engine retrieves selected data from a database, sorts and summarizes it, and groups it in any way you like and specify before presenting a final report. Such abilities allow the addition of reporting capabilities to a Web server with little if any coding.

Crystal Web Application Interface

Crystal Web Application Interface is the intermediary between Web server applications and Crystal Reports Engine. The Web Application Interface passes parameters to that Engine that specifies the nature and structure of a report.

If a database to be accessed by the Reports Engine requires a password, Crystal Web Application Interface will generate a Database Logon page to obtain that password. Once the password has been verified, the Application Interface will pass the specified report parameters to the Reports Engine and return the completed report.

Sample Log Reports

There's a constraint on reports based on IIS log files: reports created in Microsoft Standard Log format can't be combined with information in NCSA formats, and vice versa. It's for this reason that Crystal Reports 4.5 contains, in its logrpts directory, six sample reports for each of these formats.

English Wizard

Crystal Reports Pro, Release 5.0, available as an upgrade from Seagate Software, has an interesting feature—support for a third-party application called English Wizard.

English Wizard allows users to access relational databases with queries expressed in ordinary English. English Wizard then translates that English into SQL-ese, retrieves the response, and returns it. So, if you have English Wizard available, you can ask your SQL Server 6.5 database something like, "How many of the sunflower seeds I attempted to start last year germinated before the end of April?" Literally. What's even more intriguing is that English Wizard can handle either typed or spoken input. English Wizard will even work with a user to resolve ambiguities in a question.

Installing and Playing with Crystal Reports

The process of installing Crystal Reports also can take place as part of the overall load of IIS 3.0 or autonomously. In either case, it involves no more than running the installation routine from the CD and responding sensibly to the setup prompts.

When Crystal Reports has loaded successfully, there will be a new directory on your hard drive, called CRW, right beneath the root. This is where the application's program files as well as data will be housed. You can begin to get to know Crystal Reports just by diving into it. It's *extremely* friendly. Probably the quickest way to get to get into Crystal Reports is to take the path **Start ---> Programs ---> Crystal Reports**, When we did so, we were led to the main window of Crystal Reports, shown in Figure 13.5.

Pulling down the **Edit** menu and clicking **Log on Server** brought us to the dialog in Figure 13.6, which allowed us to select the log files that would be the basis of the reports we were about to create.

We took the defaults in filling out this form. Crystal Reports responded by telling us, as Figure 13.7 illustrates, that the operation had succeeded.

Next, we pulled down the application's File menu and clicked **New** to begin creating a report, as shown in Figure 13.8.

We chose listing from these formats and thereby opened the application's Create Reports Expert. Figure 13.9 is its snapshot.

Front Page Server Extensions

Front Page 97 Server Extensions form a set of components and APIs that run on an IIS server and make building and managing Web sites simpler.

Figure 13.5 This simple-looking screen is the starting point for creating sophisticated reports.

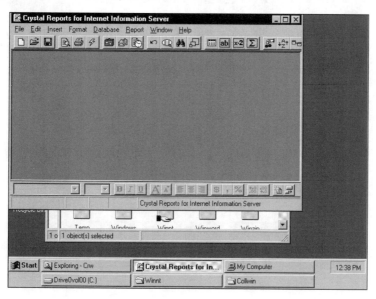

Figure 13.6 Before creating reports, you must choose the logs that will serve as their foundation.

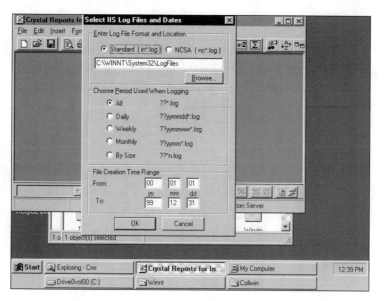

Figure 13.7 Crystal Reports liked what we told it.

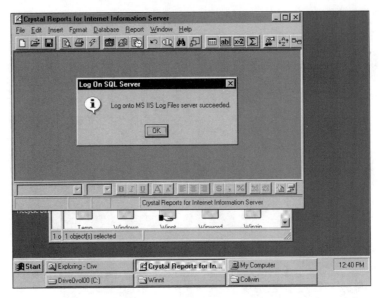

Figure 13.8 You can see that Crystal Reports offers a variety of report formats.

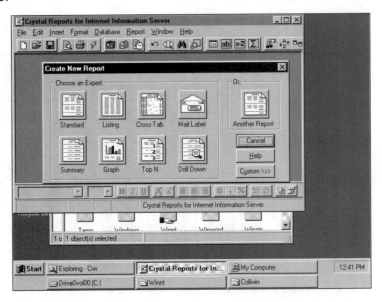

Figure 13.9 A Listing-format report can be set up starting here.

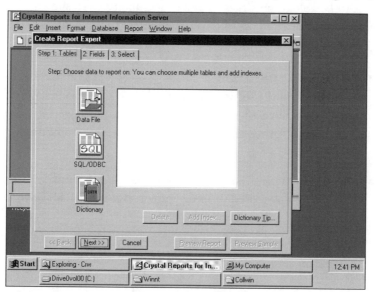

The Client Side of Front Page

Front Page 97 also has a client-side application. This client application runs a GUI-based HTML and site management environment on NT workstations.

Front Page 97 Server Extensions for IIS are ISAPI applications under release 3.0; they had been CGI under earlier releases. This shift in composition brings with it more efficient performance.

> **TIP** At the time this book was written, native Alpha and PowerPC versions of Front Page 97 Server Extensions had not yet been made available by Microsoft, but they were anticipated in the second half of 1997.

Front Page 97 Server Extensions are used by Front Page as a whole to help manage Web sites. These extensions can also be used to customize existing Web pages. The extensions are what we like to call programming tools for nonprogrammers in that they allow the insertion of interactive features without programming.

Front Page 97 Server Extensions must be present if the Front Page 97 client application is to be able to post files to and to maintain a Web site on a remote IIS server. Such applications can post to IIS HTTP servers running either the Front Page 97 Server Extensions or the Front Page 1.1 Server Extensions.

Installing the Extensions

Review the information in the section "Loading Active Server Pages," and, with a few substitutions, you'll have a template for installing Front Page 97 Server Extensions. Our doing so proceeded smoothly. Early on in the process, we saw a screen like that in Figure 13.10.

Next, we were told that setup had all the information it needed to proceed, as Figure 13.11 depicts Setup advised us to be patient. But it need not have; the next stage of installation took only a few seconds.

Figure 13.10 The installation of Front Page 97 Server Extensions automatically detects your Internet server.

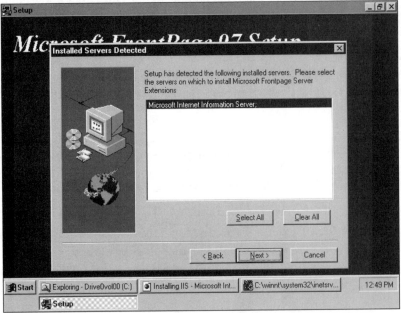

Figure 13.11 Just click Next.

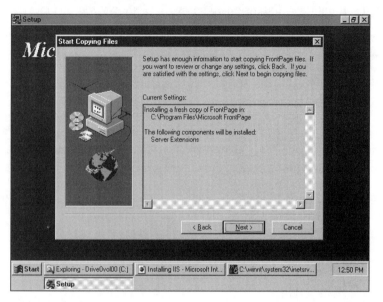

Figure 13.12 This step, too, took only a few seconds.

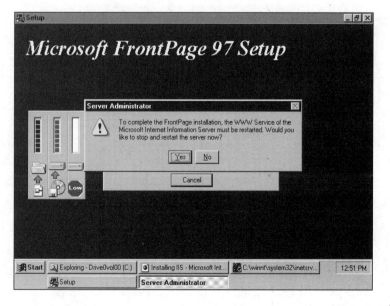

Setup then stopped and restarted Internet Information Server as the next step needed in installing these Extensions. Figure 13.12 shows you this message.

Now we had a chance to be a bit bold. Despite setup's advice to the contrary, shown in Figure 13.13, we chose not to convert our file system to NTFS.

With that, we were able to complete the installation of Front Page 97 Server Extensions, as Figure 13.14 points out.

We then discovered that taking the path **Start** ---> **Programs** ---> **FrontPage Server** resulted not in our being able to create a Web page, but rather in our accessing the application's Administrator, shown in Figure 13.15.

Assuming you have Front Page 97 itself running, you're now ready to roll into Web site management, and even a little Web authoring with it.

Figure 13.13 Depending on the nature of your IIS information, you may not want to stay with FAT and forgo NTFS file security.

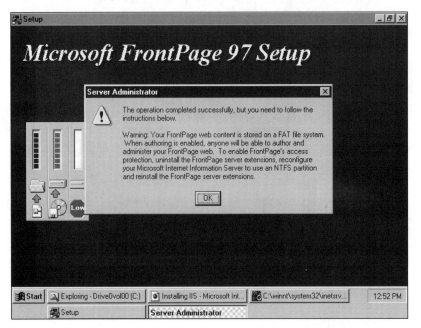

Figure 13.14. Click Finish.

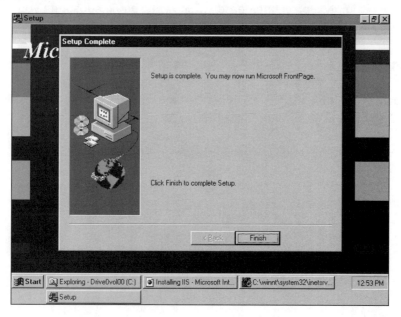

Figure 13.15. You can very closely configure the Server Extensions with this tool.

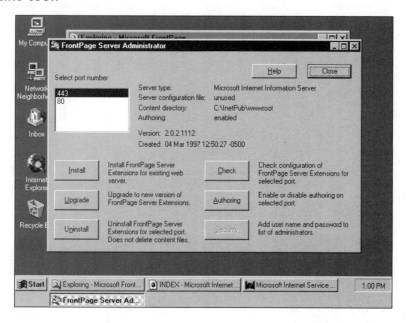

> **ANSWER TO POP QUIZ** If you said that the parameter your
> server is simply a placehholder for which you should substitute your IIS
> HHTP server's computer name, give yourself an A+.

From Here

In Chapter 14, we investigate what is perhaps the most significant new feature of Internet Information Server 3.0: Index Server.

Index
Server

Don't be confused by its name: Index Server has little to do with databases. It is that part of Internet Information Server 3.0 that handles context indexing and searching of Web sites.

As was the case in the previous chapter, this one won't give you extensive instructions in using its topic. What it will do, though, is provide a solid introduction to the concepts underlying Microsoft Index Server, looking at the makeup of Index Server, the nature of its queries, and the characteristics of its indices.

We also run through its installation and point out some of the tools it includes for becoming Index Server savvy.

What Is Index Server?

Index Server allows IIS 3.0 clients to construct queries regarding Web-published material simply by using a browser to complete an HTML-based form. The HTTP server of IIS forwards the contents of the query to Index Server's query engine. That module identifies relevant documents and returns the results to the client, via the browser, in the form of a Web page.

The jargon for this sort of thing is *context indexing*. In doing its content indexing, Index Server can use either document text or document properties.

Index Server Queries

Index Server enables the managers of a Web site to create custom forms through which users can locate documents. Such forms are set up as standard HTML files.

Defining Queries

Three factors—scope, restriction, and the nature of the result set—must be taken into account in designing a query form for use under Index Server.

Scope, another word for *path*, doesn't tell the query engine how many records to retrieve or how close to exact a match should be to be considered a hit. Scope defines where, within a Web site, the query engine should search.

Query Engine Confines

Index Server can index only within a single site such as a corporate intranet. It can't go out across the Internet to do its job.

Once the "where" has been defined, restrictions kick in. A restriction tests the indexed information regarding a document to determine if that document satisfies the parameters of the query. Only if it does will the document be returned.

Finally, a result set describes the body of information that will actually be returned by a query. More specifically, the list below outlines some of the things you can do to define queries to Index Server:

- Search document contents for words or phrases.

- Search document contents for words or phrases that occur *near* another word or phrase.

- Search the text of document properties for words or phrases.

- Search the text of document properties for some relationship to a constant; for example, look for a file whose size is greater than 15.37Kb.

- Use the logical conditions—that is, the Boolean operators AND OR and NOT in refining searches—as in, for instance, a file whose last date of modification is after March 3, 1997, AND NOT before April 27, 1997.

- Use wild cards, including not only the ubiquitous * but also ? and regular expressions.

- Rank hits by quality.

Regularity in Expression

The term *regular expressions* arose in UNIX. In a nutshell, it applies to shorthand that represents ranges of values. For example, the regular expression ab*[a-d]* would match any text string that:

- Begins with the lowercase letters ab.

- Has, following those letters, any number of characters as its second term.

- Has any of the lowercase letters a through d as its third term.

- Has, as its final portion, any number of any characters.

Query Scope Once again, the scope of a query refers not to its size, but to its extent through the file system. To put it another way, scope defines the collection of documents that will be searched. This means that the usual way to specify scope is simply to supply a directory path on a device, such as F:\Docs.

Just as Index Server can index any or all Web sites on a given machine, Index Server queries can be run against several, one, or a selected few of those sites or even against a single portion of a file system housed in a site.

Restrictions on Queries Index Server allows you to inquire about several document format types:

- HTML

- Microsoft Word

- Microsoft Excel

- Microsoft PowerPoint

- Text

> **TIP** If you must index documents in other formats through Index Server, there is a way—through custom programming centered on the ISAPI tool **Ifilter**. Microsoft suggests, in its Index Server documentation, that you contact the company for more information on such customization.

Free-Text Queries

Free-text queries are among the most useful features of Index Server. With them, sets of words or phrases, or even a complete sentence, act as the query restriction. Index Server examines this text, plucks out all the nouns and noun phrases it contains, and constructs a query on that basis. So, you might supply the sentence below to Index Server: *A large part of the reason for the continuing popularity of Star Trek is its stubborn optimism.*

Index Server would notice the nouns *part, reason, popularity, Star, Trek,* and *optimism* as well as the phrases *large part, continuing popularity, Star Trek,* and *stubborn optimism.*

Index Server would then weight these nouns and phrases, combine them into a restriction, and execute the resulting query.

Queries Based on Document Properties

Document properties about whose makeup and condition Index Server allows you to inquire include:

- File size

- File creation date

- File modification date

- File name

- Author of file

- All ActiveX properties, including custom ones

Now we arrive at the first functional distinction between queries. In looking into text, you can search for both numeric and textual entities that meet any of these conditions:

- Equal to

- Not equal to

- Greater than

- Greater than or equal to

> **POP QUIZ #1** What do you think is the opposite of *greater than*? A correct answer means far fewer logic errors and corollary debugging. But even professional programmers often miss this one.

- Less than

- Less than or equal to

However, searches conducted against document properties, although they also may use any of these operators, can use them only to compare the property in question with a constant. Index Server does not allow you to compare one document property with another.

Finally, Index Server allows you to fine-tune restrictions through the use of the Boolean operators AND, OR, NEAR, and NOT and by employing parentheses to delimit terms. It would, therefore, enable you to differentiate all files whose modification dates were either March 3, 1997, or April 27, 1997, and all files that were modified on both March 3 and April 27 from all files that were modified on both March 3 and April 27, but not after the latter or before the former.

The restrictions you'd construct using the relational and Boolean operators we've just introduced would look like the following:

- All files whose modification dates were either March 3, 1997, or April 27, 1997: write = 03/03/97 OR write = 04/27/97

- All files that were modified on both March 3 and April 27: write = 03/03/97 AND write = 04/27/97

- All files that were modified on both March 3 and April 27, but not after the latter or before the former: write = 03/03/97 AND write = 04/27/97 AND NOT (write < 03/03/97 OR write > 04/27/97)

> ## Boolean Overseas
> How do the various language versions of Index Server handle Boolean operators? Simply by translating them, as, for example, the German version does, turning *OR* and *AND* into *ODER* and *UNT*.

Fuzzy Queries

Index Server's fuzzy queries make use of both standard wildcards and regular expressions, applying queries built with these to textual document properties. Index Server can also conduct fuzzy queries against document content. In doing so, it employs:

- Simple-prefix matching, thereby returning, for example, not only *peace* but *peaceful* and *peaceable* for the query term *peace*

- Stemming, thereby returning *swim* and *swimming* for the query term *swimming*

- Inflection, which would return *swim*, *swimming*, and *swam* for the term *swim*

Rules for Constructing Queries

When it comes time for orientation to Index Server, make those attending the session, be they developers or users, aware of the rules of query syntax. (Although users of Index Server query forms won't need to apply these rules explicitly—that's done in constructing the forms—their use of those forms will be constrained by and reflect the nature of these standards.) Query syntax rules are as follows:

- Index Server sees multiple consecutive words as a phrase. To qualify as a hit, those same words must appear in the same order in a document.

- The operator NEAR resembles AND in returning a match if both operands are in the same page. But NEAR differs from AND in assigning rank to hits based on the proximity of words. So, to NEAR, the rank of a page that contains the query terms closer together is at least equal to and may be greater than the rank of a page in which the terms are farther apart. Further, NEAR will ignore as a possible hit pages in which the search terms are more than 50 words apart.

- The operator NOT can be used only after the operator AND in content queries. What's more, in such queries, NOT can be used only to exclude pages that match a previous restriction. But in property value queries, NOT can be used apart from AND.

- AND has a higher precedence than OR, meaning queries or parts of queries containing the former will be executed before queries or portions thereof with the latter. However, you can use parentheses to override this precedence of execution.

- Queries are case insensitive, so don't concern yourself with the differences in, for instance, Genardi, GENARDI, genardi, and GenARDi.

- Words in Index Server's exception list—which in English contains a, an, and, as, the, and more—are ignored by Index Server in conducting queries. However, Index Server considers such words to be delimiters in phrase and proximity queries. So, a user searching for *Beaches in Nova Scotia* would receive a result set containing *beaches*, *Beaches*, *Nova Scotia*, *Beaches in Nova Scotia*, and *beaches in Nova Scotia*.

- Index Server ignores punctuation in conducting searches. So, if you need to include these or other special characters in your search terms, enclose the entire query in single quotes. For example, if you want to search for the phrase *Ikky & Skratchy*, indicate it to Index Server as *'Ikky & Skratchy'*.

- Property names used in queries must be preceded by an at sign (@) in relational queries or by a pound sign (#) if regular expressions are to be part of a query.

- Relational operators that may be used in property queries include:

  - lt (for *less than*)
  - = (for *equal to*)
  - != (for *not equal to*)
  - gt (for *greater than*)

- Free-text queries must begin with the string *$contents*.
  - The properties that may be searched for in any type of file include contents, filename, size, and write (that is, the last time the file was modified).

- If no property name is specified, @contents is assumed.

- ActiveX property values that may be queried for by Index Server are DocTitle, DocSubject, and DocAuthor.

- The components of vector queries—that is, queries that look for ranges or lists of values—must be separated by commas and can be ranked by means of the [weight] syntax.

- Date and time values must be supplied to Index Server queries in the form *yyyy/mm/dd hh:mm:ss*. Such strings represent Greenwich Mean Time (GMT). Therefore, to correct dates and times to local terms, you must use a minus (–) character followed by the needed number, if any, of integer unit and time unit pairs.

- Currency values must be fed to Index Server in the form *x.y*, where *x* is dollars and *y* is cents.

  - In supplying Boolean constants to Index Server, only limited formats and values may be used: *t* or *true* to indicate TRUE and *f* or *false* to indicate FALSE.

International Values

Microsoft's documentation on Index Server states that currency value formats make no assumption about units. So, although our definition of them in this list assumes American usage, we could as easily and correctly have worded it to read *"x is lira "* or *"y is pfennigs."*

- Index Server will accept numeric values presented in either decimal or hexadecimal form. If the latter is used, the value in question must be preceded by the character 0x, as in *0x10B* to indicate what, in decimal notation, would be represented as *49*.

- Relational operators may not be used in queries regarding the contents property. If you try to use them, you'll get an empty results set. For example, a query that includes *@contents Taoism* can find documents whose contents contain the word *Taoism*. But a query containing the term *@contents=Taoism* will return nothing.

Index Server Query Results

Once it's unearthed all matches within a Web site for your query, Index Server gathers those matches—or hits, as search slang calls them—into result sets. Only then are the hits returned to the requester, as a set.

A network or system administrator can limit or otherwise structure the number of hits that will be returned. For instance, a result set of 210 hits might be returned to a client session in 21 pages of 10 hits each. Although users, through their response to a query form, may specify the number of hits returned per page, it is the administrator who configures that form to provide this option to the user in the first place.

Sorting and Ranking Results

Index Server always sorts result sets before returning them. It will always sort by rank, which means by degree of relevancy to the query. Index Server can also sort results according to any document property you specify.

If it's working with an NTFS file system, Index Server will check all security restrictions that might apply to a result set before returning it. In this way, a user who does not have read access to a given document will not see that document listed as part of a result set.

Result sets may include document properties as well as content. Users may specify which document properties they wish to have returned. Further, an administrator may restrict the properties that may be displayed as part of a result set. The administrator's restrictions override a user's specifications.

Index Server can also produce thumbnail summaries of the contents of a document, called *abstracts*. Abstracts may make up part of a result set.

Characteristics of an Index

Beyond the qualities we've already examined, the indices created by Index Server have the following characteristics:

- They can be refreshed, or updated, incrementally. Index Server's default practice is to refresh an index by indexing only changed files. Its performance is therefore unimpeded by any effort to reindex all documents in a scope simply to reflect a handful of changes.

- The index for each virtual path can be controlled separately. An index applies only to a defined set of directories and any subdirectories branching from that set.

- Access for the index can be viewed through Performance Monitor and other tools. Index Server offers several means of measuring criteria like the number of documents that require indexing or the rate at which queries are being processed. Applying these tools, as well as NT-presented ones like Performance Monitor, can help optimize query service.

- Best of all, once they've been configured, Index Server operations are automatic. This means that updates, index creation, index optimization, and even the recovery of an index after a power failure or some other disaster will take place without intervention on your part.

A Multilingual Index Server

Index Server was designed not only to offer modules that can handle languages other than English, but also to load and unload language-specific utilities such as stemmers on demand. This design gives Index server the ability, for instance, to index a French paragraph, switch to index a German paragraph, switch once again to French, and finally move to English.

Installing Index Server

The Prime Directive of Index Server installation is this: it can't be done unless Internet Information Server 2.0 or higher is already present.

Assuming that's the case, still pause for a moment before loading Index Server to ensure that the platform waiting for it meets the Index Server program files' need for 3 to 12 megabytes of disk storage, depending on the languages installed. The amount of disk storage needed for Index Server data depends upon the size of the body of documents, or corpus, to be indexed and the type of documents to be indexed. Index Server needs an amount of free disk equal to about 40 percent of the amount the corpus occupies.

Although it acknowledges that they're not required, Microsoft states that the more memory and the speedier the processor on your Index Server platform, the faster indexing and querying will run.

Table 14.1 recaps Index Server's memory requirements; Table 14.2 summarizes the languages that can be installed with Index Server. Note that the RAM requirements for workstations in Table 14.1 assume that the station is running under NT Workstation 4.0 and is acting as the platform for Index Server.

Table 14.1 Index Server Memory Requirements

Number of Documents	Minimum Server RAM (MB)	Recommended Server RAM (MB)	Minimum Workstation RAM (MB)	Recommended Workstation RAM (MB)
Fewer than 10,000	16	32	16	16
10,001–99,999	32	48	32	32
100,000–250,000	64	128	32	32
250,001–500,000	128	256	64	64
Over 500,000	256	>256	128	128

Table 14.2 Languages Support by Index Server

The File	Provides Support for
Idxsvall.exe	All supported languages
Idxsvdeu.exe	German
Idxsveng.exe	International English
Idxsvenu.exe	U.S. English
Idxsvesn.exe	Spanish
Idxsvita.exe	Italian
Idxsvnld.exe	Dutch
Idxsvsve.exe	Swedish

Installation

This is another simple installation that requires you merely to stick in the CD and respond to the resulting prompts. We began it at the window shown in Figure 14.1.

Clicking **Yes** brought us to yet another copy of the License Agreement and then to beginning to define the paths that Index Server files would occupy. Figure 14.2 is the first in this latter series of windows.

After a handful of **Nexts,** we were informed that Index Server had been successfully installed and that we could begin to work with it, as Figure 14.3 shows.

Turning now to Internet Explorer, we took the advice given us in Figure 14.3 and opened the indicated sample file. Figure 14.4 shows the result.

From this page, we navigated, by means of its links, to more complicated queries, such as that illustrated in Figures 14.5.

Where Index Server Lives

Index Server resides in a few places, as we saw in some of the figures dealing with installation. What's more, Index Server is accessed in still other spots, including the sample pages in the virtual path /Samples/Search and the sample query scripts in the virtual path /Scripts/Samples/Search.

Starting Index Server

Starting Index Server is easy. Once it's successfully installed, you can start Index Server simply by issuing a query against one of its sample pages, as we did under

Figure 14.1 Loading Index Server starts with a simple question.

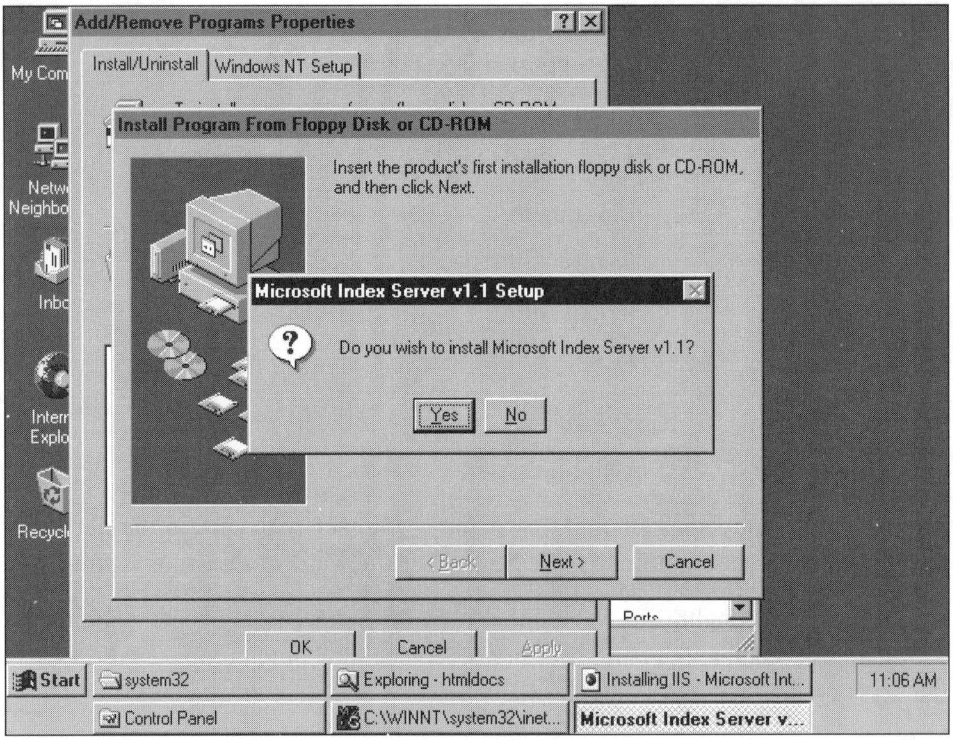

Internet Explorer with the sample form shown in Figure 14.4. As easy as it is to start the Server, it might be just as easy to forget that it *doesn't* start automatically when IIS kicks in. It takes a query to get Index Server going.

Stopping Index Server

There's only one way to stop Index server: stop Internet Information Server.

Index Server Performance Details

This section delves into some of the more technical aspects of Index Server.

Interaction with the Web Server

Index Server's queries interact closely with Internet Information Server. What's more, Index Server's querying process uses the same model that IIS does for searching an Open Database Connectivity (ODBC) data source.

Figure 14.2 We took the defaults here and in the next few dialogs.

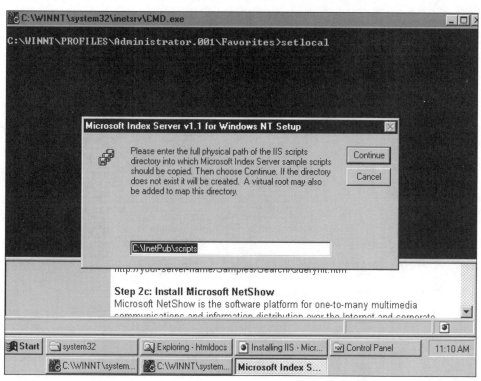

The Internet Database Connector (IDC) converts a query from an HTML file into a search string that can be understood by ODBC. When a database receives a query, it sends the results to IDC to be reconverted into an HTML page.

Files known as *.idc* files help IDC carry out this conversion/reconversion task. A category of Index Server, as opposed to IDC, files, *.htx*, defines how query results should be formatted and displayed. Another such Index Server file type, *.idq*, also gets involved in converting queries. In the remainder of this section, we examine IDQ and HTX files more closely.

IDQ Files

An Internet data query, or *.idq* file, defines query parameters such as the scope of your search, any restrictions, and query results sets. Figure 14.6 represents a basic .idq file.

Table 14.3 elaborates on this .idq file.

Figure 14.3 We exited the installation.

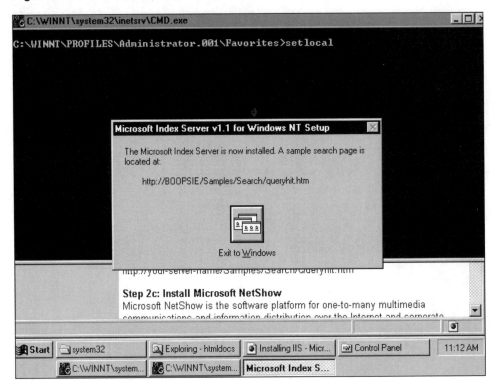

Table 14.3 Anatomy of an IDQ

This Line in the .idq File	Tells Index Server
[Query]	What follows in this file is a query restriction.
CiColumns=filename,size,rank	What information should make up the result set.
CiFlags=DEEP	To search all subdirectories within the scope.
CiMaxRecordsInResultSet=375	To return no more than 375 records.
CiMaxRecordsPerPage=25	To display results in groups of 25 per Web page.
CiScope=/	To start the search at the root of the indicated storage device.

Table 14.3 *Continued*

This Line in the .idq File	Tells Index Server
CiTemplate=/scripts/spdc1.htx	To use the format specified in the file *spdc1.htx* in presenting results
CiSort=rank[a]	To sort the results in ascending order
CiCatalog=f: \	To use the index stored in the root directory of drive f:

Microsoft even uses Index Server to help you navigate IIS online documentation. When you open that documentation and begin to push through it in Internet Explorer, Index Server is in the background, locating and returning material to you. The actual .idq file it uses is shown in Figure 14.7.

Figure 14.4 This is the first of a few sample Index Server query forms we played with.

Figure 14.5 Filling in this query form would kick-start a search not only of the material within documents but also of document characteristics.

Figure 14.6 Among other things, this file tells Index Server that it wants an index stored on drive F.

[Query]

CiColumns=filename,size,rank

CiFlags=DEEP

CiMaxRecordsInResultSet=375

CiMaxRecordsPerPage=25

CiScope=/

Figure 14.6 *Continued*

CiTemplate=/scripts/spdc1.htx

CiSort=rank[a]

CiCatalog=f:

Figure 14.7 This .idq file was drawn from Microsoft's online documentation.

#<HTML><Body BGCOLOR=#FFFFFF><Font size=4><Font color=white>

#</font><Font color=white>

#</font><P>You must install Microsoft Index Server 1.1<Font color=white>

#</font>
<a href="http://www.microsoft.com/iis"><Font color=white>

#</font>(http://www.microsoft.com/iis)</a><Font color=white>

#</font>
before you can search the online documentation.<P>

#<Font color=white>

#</font>

<Font color=white>

#</font>

<Font color=white>

#</font>

<Font color=white>

#</font>

<Font color=white>

#</font>

<Font color=white>

#</font>

<Font color=white>

#</font>

<Font color=white>

#</font>

<Font color=white>

#</font>

<Font color=white>

#</font>

<Font color=white>

#

Continued

Figure 14.7 *Continued*

```
# This is the query file for the query.htm query form.

#

[Query]

CiColumns=filename,size,rank,characterization,vpath,DocTitle,write

CiFlags=DEEP

CiRestriction=%CiRestriction%

CiMaxRecordsInResultSet=300

CiMaxRecordsPerPage=%CiMaxRecordsPerPage%

CiScope=%CiScope%

CiTemplate=%TemplateName%

CiSort=%CiSort%

CiForceUseCi=true

#</font></body></html>
```

HTML Extension Files

In Index Server, a *.htx* or HTML content file is an HTML file that contains variables that refer to a results set. The .htx file is a template that formats results before they are returned. This file is written in HTML format, but it also contains extensions supplied by IIS and Index Server. These extensions constitute codes for processing results.

Creating Indices

Index Server builds its indices largely through filtering. Document content filters dissect documents to create word lists, which in turn make up the raw material of indices. Filtering has three steps:

1. A filter DLL extracts text and properties.

2. A word-breaker DLL parses—that is, structures—the text and properties into words.

3. Noise words are removed and the remaining words stored in the word list.

The CiDaemon Process

CiDaemon (pronounced dee-mon) is a child process or spinoff of Index Server engine. Index Server then passes a list of documents to CiDaemon, which manages their filtering by associating the appropriate filter DLL and word-breaker DLL with each document. Filtering runs in background.

Filter DLLs

Filter DLLs are bright; they understand document formats and can therefore extract text and properties out of documents made up of those formats. Filter DLLs use an ActiveX tool, *Ifilter*, to extract text from a document.

Index Categories

Index Server has three types of indices:

- Word lists

- Shadow indices

- A master index

   Words and properties extracted from a document go to a word list first. From there, they are transferred as needed to a shadow index and finally to the master index. But even though Index Server has several internal indices, users never know it, but rather see only a list of documents that satisfy their query.

Word Lists Word lists are small indices that never leave memory for disk storage. Each such list refers to only a very few documents. And these lists don't hang around long. When the number of word lists exceeds the value defined in the Registry parameter *MaxWordLists*, all word lists are merged into what's called a *shadow index*.

Persistent Index

An index that has been stored on disk is called a *persistent index*. Unlike word lists, a persistent index can survive shutdowns and restarts. The data in persistent indices is highly compressed before it's stored as either a shadow index or a master index.

   Shadow indices are created when word lists, and occasionally shadow indices, are merged into a single entity. Index Server provides for the presence of several simultaneous shadow indices.

Memory-Resident Wrinkle

An interesting wrinkle attaches to word lists being solely memory-resident. Because they are so, documents to which word lists refer must be refiltered if IIS is restarted.

A master index, of which there can be only one, holds indexing information for a large number of documents. As you can imagine, therefore, its contents are highly compressed.

One last point about persistent indices: their aggregate total, which is the combined number of shadow indices and the master index, cannot exceed 255.

Merge Categories

Shadow indices are combined into a master index through a process called *merging*. Merging manages indexing and makes it more efficient by removing redundant data and therefore freeing up resources. Index Server carries out three types of merges:

- Shadow

- Master

- Annealing

Shadow Merges

A shadow merge joins multiple word lists and/or shadow indices into one shadow index. Shadow merges free up memory used by word lists and prepare index data for disk storage.

A shadow merge, usually very quick to execute, takes place automatically if the number of word lists exceeds MaxWordLists and the combined size of all word lists exceeds the value defined in the related Registry parameter *MinSizeMergeWordLists*.

Master Merges

Master merges can't take place until a shadow merge has combined all existing word lists into a shadow index. Although the master merge hogs both CPU time and disk space, it ultimately releases more system resources than it gobbles because it removes redundant index data, allowing queries to run faster. Probably the only significant performance detriment associated with master merges is that, if the source indices fed to them are very large, master merges may take quite a while to run.

ANSWER TO POP QUIZ #1 The opposite of *greater than* is not, as first pops into many of our minds, *less than*. Instead, it's *less than or equal to*. Think about it.

ANSWER TO POP QUIZ #2 To stop Internet Information Server as a whole, you must use the **Services** tool in Control Panel.

Annealing Merges

Annealing merges are variants of shadow merges that are carried out automatically if the following two conditions pertain:

- Index Server has not had to use the CPU for an interval equal to the value defined in the Registry parameter *MinMergeIdleTime*.

- The total number of persistent indexes exceeds the value defined in the Registry parameter *MaxIdealIndexes*.

From Here

In Chapter 15, we attend a show—a NetShow. We explore NetShow On-Demand Server, the multimedia, and the multicasting tool provided with Internet Information Server 3.0.

NetShow

In this chapter, we learn the basics of NetShow On-Demand, one of two multimedia applications in Internet Information Server 3.0. Specifically, we examine configuring an On-Demand server, determining appropriate bandwidth, monitoring NetShow performance, and logging NetShow activity.

Configuring a NetShow On-Demand Server

NetShow On-Demand is no lightweight. Table 15.1 outlines Microsoft's recommendations for an On-Demand server.

Table 15.1 NetShow's Appreciable Requirements

For the Component	Use at the Minimum	But Microsoft Recommends
Processor	486/66	Pentium/133
Bus	EISA	PCI
Memory	24MB	48MB
10Mbps NIC	Any Ethernet NIC	Compaq NetFlex 2 ENET TR or Intel EtherExpress Pro 10/100B(PCI)

Continued

Table 15.1 *Continued*

For the Component	Use at the Minimum	But Microsoft Recommends
100Mbps NIC	Any Ethernet NIC	SMC EtherPower 10/100, DEC DE500, or Compaq NetFlex 3
Content Storage	A dedicated disk partition	Two or more identical disk drives configured as stripe sets

NICs for NetShow

Microsoft has tested and approved the NICs in Table 15.1 for use with NetShow. Although these aren't the only network interface cards that can be used with the application, be advised that its performance may suffer if NIC throughput is insufficient.

TIP In addition to hardware requirements, NetShow On-Demand has some for software too. Windows NT Server 4.0 and Internet Information Server 2.0 or higher must already have been installed, because NetShow relies heavily on the latter, particularly for its administrative tools.

Previewing NetShow

As a preliminary to configuring the application, as a means of gaining a better appreciation of why NetShow is a bit of a hog, and simply as a way of learning if it will meet your needs as you may have envisioned, we recommend you look at the NetShow demo that is automatically installed with the product. Doing this is simple; just take the path **Start ---> Programs ---> Microsoft Internet Information Server ---> NetShow ---> NetShow Demo.**

The first thing you'll see during this demo is the opening NetShow screen shown in Figure 15.1.

Once in the demo, you can explore a bit; you're not limited to a strictly linear progression through it. Our next stop was at the definition of *streaming* illustrated in Figure 15.2.

Figure 15.1 NetShow's opening window conveys a sense of lots more to come.

Wondering where to motor to next, we opened the NetShow Demo documentation to review the tours available to us, as Figure 15.3 depicts.

Figure 15.2 This demo window uses a tried-and-true teaching technique: reinforcing a concept through more than one sense.

Figure 15.3 NetShow is almost as heavy in demos as it is in demands on your server.

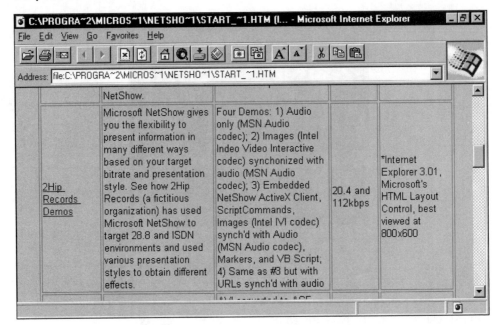

It's a good thing we stopped to read the documentation; it led us to some more of the same without which we wouldn't have gone much further. Take a look at Figure 15.4 and you'll see why.

In case you're wondering, we did have to download the controls mentioned in Figure 15.4. But they came down and installed readily, allowing us to walk through more of the demos unimpeded.

RAID and NetShow

In its NetShow documentation, Microsoft several times recommends the use of dedicated, redundant disk drives in an On-Demand server. MS further suggests striping as the RAID technique to be employed.

Disk striping is a RAID technique that, like all RAID methods, seeks to improve server performance. Like any other RAID method, striping requires at least two identical drives. Drives to be included in a striped set must be from the same manufacturer and must be of the same model and capacity. But you don't have to stop at two. RAID level 0, striping, can accommodate as many as 32 drives.

Figure 15.4 Some of the NetShow demos can't be run unless your server is configured in specific ways.

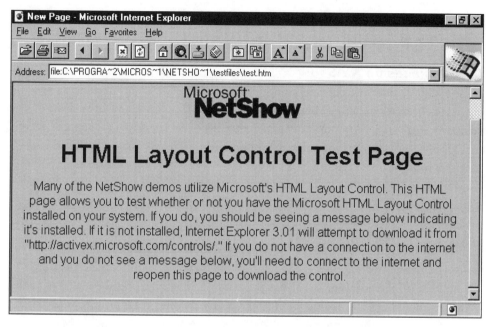

Determining Bandwidth Needed by NetShow

One of your most important NetShow configuration tasks will be to get a good handle on the bandwidth your On-Demand server will need. That total will be affected by:

- The maximum number of simultaneous client connections your On-Demand server must support.

- The total number of bits per second your server is capable of streaming.

- The maximum rate in bits/second at which any single file can be streamed.

You must do more than make sufficient allowance for each of these factors individually. You must also take into account their interaction. Let's say, for example, you set the maximum number of clients to 30, the total bit rate to one **megabit per second** (**Mbps**), and the maximum stream per file to 30 **kilobits per second** (Kbps). Based on such a total bit rate, and assuming the file bit rate specified to represent a typical user session, an On-Demand server configured with these parameters could actually handle a maximum of 33 clients.

Total bit rate, as you can see from this example, is the key to deciding on a NetShow server configuration. As a rule of thumb, Microsoft suggests the following:

If the total bit rate exceeds the capacity of one hard drive, you can consider this a high-demand environment, and you may need to enhance your hardware.

Low Demands on NetShow

As an example of a low-demand configuration, MS documentation suggests an environment that has only (Microsoft's phrasing) a 10Mbps LAN. In such cases, the company suggests limiting the streaming capacity of a NetShow On-Demand server to 1Mbps to prevent NetShow from hobbling normal network traffic. Table 15.2 uses this total bit throughput (1Mbps) and a variety of file bit rates to extrapolate the number of clients an On-Demand server operating under these conditions might support.

Of course, the bit stream a given file will need must likely vary, which is the reason the most important On-Demand server parameter is maximum total bit rate. Once you define this parameter, the load on the server will still vary according to the number of players trying to access the server at one time and the bit rates of the materials they request. For this parameter, specify the best total bit rate your server can push out onto the network.

Your best tool for determining that optimum is Performance Monitor. It will allow you not only to benchmark-test your server as it is currently configured, but also to examine other possible constraints to On-Demand performance, such as the throughput of various hardware components.

Table 15.2 Some Examples of Low-Demand NetShow Configurations

Assuming a File Bit Rate of	Would Allow for This Number of Clients
20Kbps	50
30Kbps	33
40Kbps	25
50Kbps	20
75Kbps	13

NetShow and Heavy Demands

If yours is a 100Mbps network, you're already in high-demand territory. Such a network automatically assumes high stream bit rates and bulky content. To ensure that your clients can access such heavy volume without degradation of performance, you must configure a well-balanced server.

A high-demand, 100Mbps network might, for instance, readily support an overall bit rate of 30Mbps, which would allow client-to-file ratios like those outlined in Table 15.3.

Given scenarios like those sketched in Table 15.3, a maximum server disk throughput of 20Mbps, which is, if not high-end, at least respectable, would still be insufficient to the demands on your NetShow server. You might seek to solve this problem by adding a second 20Mbps drive. But if all your clients need or try to access the same file at once, you've paid out all that money for a second drive to no real purpose.

Here's where the role of striping becomes paramount. Striping improves the performance of both disk reads and disk writes, because many I/O commands can be active simultaneously on drivers controlling striped drives. If you configured your two 20Mbps disks to support striping, you would create a functional total bit rate of 40Mbps. Equally as important, every file could be distributed across both disks, thereby allowing all clients to access the same bit stream.

NetShow Performance: Other Constraints

No matter how carefully you configure the maximum bandwidth demand on your NetShow On-Demand server, that machine may still run into problems caused by what are known as bursty applications. Perhaps the classic example of this category is ftp and its brother file transfer programs, which require a sudden shot of high bandwidth when they execute. The bandwidth demands of bursty, and even of

Table 15.3 Projections of High-Demand NetShow Environments

Assuming a File Bit Rate of	Would Allow for This Number of Clients
1.5Mbps	20
3.0Mbps	10
4.0Mbps	8

more prosaic applications must be taken into account when you plan the configuration of your On-Demand Server. In other words, realize that you will be spending a lot of time with Performance Monitor.

Monitoring NetShow

Performance Monitor allows you, among so many things, stream bit rate and client/file bit rate demands. Performance Monitor can also be used to fine-tune your On-Demand server, and NT server in general, to make the best use of the resources you have. Then, if NetShow and your other NT-based applications still can't coexist comfortably, you can consider a more powerful NetShow On-Demand platform, perhaps even a dedicated one.

NetShow On-Demand has its own set of counters that become available to Performance Monitor once NetShow is successfully installed. These parameters include:

- Active streams

- Aggregate read rate

- Aggregate send rate

- Allocated bandwidth

- Connection clients

- Connection rate

- Late reads

- Scheduling rate

- Stream errors

- Stream terminators

The section "Using Counters" later in this chapter goes into these parameters in more detail.

Windows NT/ NetShow
Interactions That Affect NetShow Performance

Interestingly enough, the architecture of Windows NT can itself put a crimp in NetShow's style. NT uses a single Cache Manager to carry out caching for *all* of its I/O system. But the whole reason for caching—the practice of keeping in memory frequently used data—has little significance to an application like NetShow On-Demand; most data streams aren't reused. Therefore, assuming it won't degrade the performance of other applications on your NT server, you could turn off Cache Manager as a means of improving NetShow performance. Here's how to go about it.

1. Right-click **Network Neighborhood.**

2. Click **Properties.**

3. Select **Services.**

4. Choose **Server.**

5. Click **Properties.**

6. Select **Maximize Throughput for File Sharing.**

Managing NetShow

You have several tools available to you for monitoring and managing NetShow on demand:

- Internet Service Manager Add-In

- Windows NT Performance Monitor counters

- Windows NT Event Viewer log entries

- NetShow On-Demand Trace Facility

- NetShow On-Demand Log Facility

Table 15.4 provides an overview of the tools available to you for NetShow management.

Table 15.4 Tools to Administer NetShow

This Tool	Does This Task
IIS Internet Service Manager Add-In	Starts and stops the NetShow On-Demand server, monitors server performance, and sets server configuration parameters.
Windows NT Performance Monitor	Tracks and charts NetShow On-Demand performance counters.

Continued

Table 15.4 Continued

This Tool	Does This Task
Windows NT Event Viewer	Stores event alerts from the NetShow On-Demand system. The Event Viewer's Event Log tool is used for logging critical system errors or failures.
NetShow On-Demand Trace Facility	Monitors the NetShow On-Demand system for the occurrence of irregular events, based on the types of events the network administrator selects to be logged—Administrative, Client, Alert, or Server events.
NetShow On-Demand Log Facility	Receives events from a NetShow On-Demand server and redirects them to a Data Access Objects (DAO) object for data analysis. The resulting .mdb file can be opened in Microsoft Access.

Using IIS Internet Service Manager Add-In

The IIS Internet Service Manager Add-In is fully integrated into Internet Service Manager when you install NetShow. The Add-in allows you to use Internet Service Manager to track and administer NetShow in the same way you use it to oversee other IIS services. With it, you can:

- Start, stop, or pause an On-Demand server.

- Keep track of the status of all NetShow On-Demand servers within a domain.

- Set server parameters for client systems.

- Create and manage virtual root directories.

What you learned in Chapter 6 about Internet Service Manager, and in particular in the section of that chapter called Modifying Service Properties, applies to NetShow as well. We recap a little of that material in the section "Fine-Tuning a NetShow On-Demand Server."

> **TIP** Internet Service Manager uses the Windows NT security model, so only validated administrators are allowed to administer services, and administrator passwords are transmitted in encrypted form over the network.

Fine-Tuning a NetShow On-Demand Server

Following are the steps for using Internet Service Manager to calibrate NetShow On-Demand:

1. Take the path **Start ---> Programs ---> Internet Information Server ---> Internet Service Manager.**

2. Depending on the View you're using in the Manager, click as appropriate your On-Demand server or the NetShow service itself.

3. Pull down ISM's **Properties** menu.

4. Click **Service Properties** to display the **NetShow On-Demand Service Properties** dialog.

5. Key in the options of your choice.

6. Click **OK** or **Apply** to save your settings, but keep the dialog open.

Table 15.5 outlines the NetShow On-Demand parameters that can be set in this way.

Table 15.5 Behind the Scenes in a NetShow

The Option	Controls	And Has a Minimum Value of	And a Possible Maximum of
Maximum Clients	The number of clients that can be connected to the server at any given time.	0	10,000
Maximum Aggregate Bandwidth	The amount of bandwidth that the server will stream in bits/second. The upper limit should not exceed 85% of the throughput capacity of your NIC.	0	100Mbps
Maximum File Bitrate	The amount of bandwidth at which any one file can be streamed in bits/second.	0	6Mbps

Continued

Table 15.5 *Continued*

The Option	Controls	And Has a Minimum Value of	And a Possible Maximum of
Enable File Level Access Checking	That the client accessing the .asf file has the appropriate access rights under Windows NT.	–	–
Comment	The 260-byte field reserved for comments regarding the selected server.	–	–

Configuring Logging Options

One of the most important features of the NetShow-related Internet Service Manager Add-Ins is the Logging property. In setting up this logging, you can specify the directory in which logs relating to NetShow will be stored and the frequency at which those logs should be rotated. However, NetShow, at the time this book was written, did not support logging to SQL or ODBC databases or to NCSA Common Log Format.

To set NetShow logging options, follow these steps:

1. Start Internet Service Manager.

2. Select **NetShow On-Demand**.

3. Pull down the **Properties** menu.

4. Click **Service Properties** to display the Service Properties dialog.

5. Click **Logging** to open the Logging dialog.

6. Enter the logging options you need.

7. Click **OK**.

Table 15.6 sketches out the options that you can set in this way.

Table 15.6 NetShow's Logging Options

This Option	When Applied
Enable Logging	Starts or stops logging. By default, logging is disabled.
Log to File	Logs data to a text file, in which maximum log line length is 512 bytes.
Automatically open new log	Generates new logs using the specified frequency. If it is not selected, the same log file will grow indefinitely. The default option for this field is Daily. In any case, a new log file is generated each time the service starts, regardless of this setting. The service will close the log file and create a new one with a different name in the same folder when the appropriate interval or file size is reached. The log file name is NSOSrv .yymmddnnn.log, where yymmdd represents the year, month, and day when the log file is created, and nnn is a sequentially increasing number that represents the number of logs generated so far on the current date.
Log file directory	Specifies the server directory containing the log file. By default, the directory used is C:\winnt\ System32\Logfiles. Even if you are using a remote machine to store logs, the path you enter here must be a NetShow On-Demand server path.

One bit of Microsoft phrasing regarding the structure of On-Demand server log entries demonstrates that this product is still evolving. As MS says, such log records "currently" have the structure 22:17:00, 11, 5, 87500, 157.56.138.81, c:\asfroot\ 100.asf, 31, 0, 44, 0x0, 31, 0, 0, 20, 42, 60, MSCCORE NT 4.0.1381, 90, 5, 5, 1, 95.

Table 15.7 dissects this entry.

Table 15.7 Probing a NetShow On-Demand Server Log Entry

The Log Entry Field	Is a Value for
22:17:10	Server local time
11	Number of connected clients

Continued

Table 15.7 *Continued*

The Log Entry Field	Is a Value for
5	Number of active streams
87500	Allocated bandwidth
157.56.138.81	Client and Stream Statistics
c:\asfroot\100.asf	Name of streamed file
31	Number of packets sent to client
0	Number of packets skipped
44	Ideal packet duration in msec; = packet size / rate
0x0	HRESULT for the termination of the streaming session; an error code
31	Number of packets received by client
0	Number of erasures detected by client; = number of packets recovered from transmission
0	Maximum number of contiguous erasures detected by client; contiguous erasures = contiguous packets dropped by server
20	Minimum packet period; = minimum interval in msec between packet arrivals
42	Average packet period; = average interval in msec between packet arrivals
60	Maximum packet period; = maximum interval between packet arrivals in msec
MSCCORE	Name of client module returning these statistics
NT	Client operating system abbreviation (currently supports only Windows NT or Windows 95)
4.0 1381	Operating system version, expressed as major .minor.build number
90	Total number of packets received during current playback
5	Total number of packets recovered through error correction during current playback

Table 15.7 *Continued*

The Log Entry Field	Is a Value for
5	Total number of packets lost during current playback
195	Number of times the client buffered during current playback
	Minimum reception quality (percentage of non-lost packets over the last 30 seconds) recorded during current playback

Using Counters

In addition to viewing NetShow On-Demand performance counters through NT's Performance Monitor, you can track these system indicators by means of the Performance Monitoring Settings in the NetShow program group. To do so, take only two simple steps:

1. Follow the path **Start ---> Programs ---> Microsoft NetShow**.

2. Click **On-Demand Performance Monitoring Settings** to display the **Performance Monitor** window, which displays, among other measures, the NetShow On-Demand Service counters.

Table 15.8 details these counters and the information they provide.

Table 15.8 On-Demand Performance Counters

The Counter	Represents
Active Stream	Number of active files, or streams, currently being sent to NetShow On-Demand players. Note that a NetShow On-Demand Server maintains bandwidth per client for 60 seconds after a client stops playing. This interval, the Client Inactivity Timeout, is followed by the server checking client status and the server maintaining a client connection as long as the client responds within three minutes. The latter interval is referred to as Client Terminal Timeout.
Aggregate Read Rate	Total, in bytes per second, of read rates for all files being sent to players; indicates speed at which server reads from disk.

Continued

Table 15.8 *Continued*

The Counter	Represents
Aggregate Send Rate	Total, in bytes per second, of send rates for all files. A jagged graph may indicate contention with other applications for bandwidth.
Allocated Bandwidth	Amount of bandwidth server allocates, based on currently connected players.
Connected Clients	Number of client programs currently connected; indicates all players and includes clients streaming, clients in paused and connected states, and clients that the server has not yet detected as being disconnected.
Connection Rate	Rate at which clients are connecting to the server; handy for correlating client connections with system resource utilization.
Late Reads	Number of late reads per second. A late read is one that takes significantly longer than expected to complete. This counter should be greater than zero only when a server carries a very heavy load.
Scheduling Rate	Rate at which requests are being made for tasks to be scheduled, in tasks per second. Roughly proportional to the rate at which packets are being sent by the server, but not an exact one-to-one correspondence.
Stream Errors	Per second. Indicates number of stream data packets discarded by server when it cannot keep up with the demand for data and must throw some packets away to avoid running behind schedule indefinitely. Stream errors reflect an improperly configured system or too high a degree of competition for system resources.
Stream Terminations	Rate per second at which streams are terminated because of errors. Stream terminations indicate an improperly configured system or a corrupted file being streamed.

Using Windows NT Event Viewer Logs

Event Viewer may not be as flashy as Performance Monitor, but it doesn't miss critical happenings. Event Log is designed to catch crucial system errors, failures, or changes.

Event Viewer will tell you that the On-Demand service started and that the On-Demand service stopped.

NetShow On-Demand's Trace Facility

NetShow On-Demand's Trace Facility looks for unusual events or the response of the server to specific actions.

> **TIP** You must have administrative permissions on the server to use the NetShow On-Demand Trace Facility.

Trace has as unassuming an appearance as Event Viewer. The trace log looks like nothing so much as an old-fashioned console window; the events Trace monitors simply scroll through this window.

Here's how to start the Trace Facility:

1. Through **Internet Service Manager**, connect to the On-Demand Server whose activity you must monitor.

2. Pull down the **Tools** menu.

3. Click **On-Demand Trace Facility** to display the **Trace** window.

4. To prevent log messages from scrolling off your screen, click the **Up scroll arrow** of the vertical scroll bar. This will stop the window from scrolling but still allow new messages to be added to the bottom of the list.

To save Trace's log as a text file, take these steps:

1. Pull down the **File** menu.

2. Click **Save As** to display the Save As dialog. By default, NetShow On-Demand saves logs as .txt files with line breaks, simply by taking a snapshot of the entire NetShow On-Demand Trace Facility window. To save only selected messages, highlight the messages you want to save and click **Save As**.

To print a Trace log:

1. Pull down the File menu.

2. Click **Print** to display the Print dialog. Here, you can define print options for the log.

> **TIP** Clicking the Print icon on the toolbar to print the contents of the NetShow On-Demand Trace Facility window will cause that window to be printed under the current print settings you're using. These may or may not be appropriate for Trace.

To filter trace log messages:

1. Pull down the Option menu.

2. Click **Properties** to display the NetShow Trace Properties dialog.

3. Click **Filter**.

4. Select the message types you want to display:

   • General Server Events

   • Client Events

   • Administrative Events

   • Alerts

5. Click **OK**.

> **TIP** By default, the foreground color for the system is set to black, but you can change that to associate an event with a particular color. To change the color associated with an event, click the color bar next to the event type to display the Color dialog box. You may then select the color to be associated with an event.

The NetShow On-Demand Log Facility

NetShow's Log Facility makes use of a type of file called **.mdb**. Such files can be manipulated through Access and Excel, among other applications.

Log Facility can do the following:

• Connect to any On-Demand server in the domain.

• Write to an .mdb file for a user-configurable number of hours before beginning to overwrite.

• Filter messages according to their type.

- Connect users to On-Demand servers.

- Allow users to open or create .mdb files.

> **TIP** You must explicitly configure and enable the On-Demand Log Facility; its default is to be disabled. The section "Configuring the Log Facility" later in this chapter describes this task.

The Log Facility writes to a default access database called **Nslog.mdb,** which lives in the \Microsoft NetShow\On-Demand\Admin directory. Table 15.9 gives an overview of the structure of this database.

Configuring the Log Facility

During NetShow installation, the Log Facility icon is placed in the Windows NT Startup group, which means that the Log Facility starts automatically when you boot NT. But to actually begin logging, you must enable logging, as follows:

1. Right-click the NetShow On-Demand Log Facility icon in the Windows NT task bar.

2. Click **Properties** to display the NetShow Log Facility dialog.

3. Once you've entered the parameters you have in mind, click **OK.**

Table 15.10 summarizes the fields in this dialog and the values that pertain to them.

Table 15.9 The Log Facility Information Report

Field Name	Data Type	Description
EventDate	Date/Time	Date and time a log entry was made
ClientID	Text—field size: 15	Client IP address
Event Type	Text—field size: 20	Can be any of Administrative, Client, Alerts, or Server
Event Description	Text—field size: 255	

Table 15.10 Configuring the On-Demand Log Facility

Field Name	Value
Enable Logging	Check to enable logging. By default, logging is disabled.
Server to monitor	Name of the NetShow On-Demand server you want to monitor.
Select or create an Access database	Displays default database name. To change, click **Change** and type full path name of an Access database. If the database doesn't exist, the Log Facility will create it. Also enter table name here.
Set length of logging time	Default = 48 hours. A value of 0 will cause logging to continue indefinitely. Maximum nonzero value permitted = 1,000 hours.
Categories of events to log	Types of events you want to log.

Starting the Log Facility

After you've configured and enabled the On-Demand Log Facility, you can connect to an On-Demand server by following these steps:

1. Right-click the NetShow On-Demand Log Facility icon in the task bar.

2. Click **Properties** to display the Log Facility dialog.

3. Key in an appropriate server name at **Server to monitor**.

4. Click **OK**.

From Here

To this point, the information we've offered has pertained to the 2.0 and 3.0 releases of Internet Information Server. In Chapters 16 through 20, we'll examine the most recent 4.0 release, which differs from its predecessors in a few ways.

- IIS 4.0 offers added functionality, such as a Transaction Server that allows you to create, distribute, and manage network applications.

- The 4.0 release communicates with you through a new interface, whose look and structure will characterize Windows NT 5.0 as well.

- IIS 4.0 provides new and enhanced Web publishing tools. One example of this is Posting Acceptor, which enables you to place HTML content files on a server automatically.

Part Four

IIS 4.0

16

Internet Information
Server 4.0

In the context of Internet Information Server, versions crowd one another at ever-increasing rates.

Even though IIS 3.0 has been in official release less than a year, the folks in Redmond have already brought version 4.0 into the world. In this chapter, we'll examine this new version, focusing on those features that distinguish it from its antecedents.

IIS 4.0 Features

Microsoft considers IIS 4.0 to have 17 unique functional areas. However, a few of these features are carried over from earlier releases. Table 16.1 summarizes the new and old of Internet Information Server 4.0.

Now let's walk through each of IIS 4.0's new features.

Active Directory Service Interfaces

The **Active Directory Service Interfaces (ADSI)** is based on the **Component Object Model (COM)**, the foundation of so many Microsoft products. As Figure 16.1 illustrates, ADSI allows IIS clients to use a single-user interface while traversing such differing directory services as LDAP, Netware 3.x, NDS, and Windows NT.

Table 16.1 Getting to Know Internet Information Server 4.0

Feature	In IIS 3.0?	In IIS 4.0
Active Directory Service Interfaces	No	Provides a single-user interface for different directory systems
Active Server Pages	Yes	Samples and templates offered
Authentication Server	No	Uses the RADIUS (Remote Authentication Dial-In User Service) protocol
Data Access Components	Yes	As in IIS 3.0, includes ActiveX and ODBC
FrontPage Server Extensions	Yes	As in IIS 3.0, presents FrontPage as a Web publishing tool
Index Server	Yes	Indexes Web and other content
Mail Server	No	Provides mail management through SMTP
Microsoft Management Console	No	The new look for Internet Service Manager
News Server	No	Is the newsgroup analog to Mail Server
Posting Acceptor	No	Takes in Web pages or entire Web sites
Script Debugger	No	Works with several languages, including Java, Perl, VBScript, and JScript
Site Analyst	No	Creates and maintains Web site maps
Transaction Server	No	Allows the creation, configuration, and installation of server applications
Usage Analyst	No	Massages IIS logs
VBScript and JScript	No	Are presented with complete Programmer's Guides
Web Publishing Wizard	No	Carries out automatic, a-bit-more-than-one-button Web publishing
Windows Scripting Host	No	Related both to Web page scripts and to administrative batch files

ADSI is organized into components, each of which provides, on a per-interface basis, the interface itself, the objects and methods upon which it rests, and all properties related to those objects and methods (see Figure 16.2). ADSI also has a set of definitions through which such common file system elements as computer, service, and organizational terms may be represented in the final interface. Through ADSI's Schema Management arm, programmers can create new properties for existing interfaces, or even entirely new interfaces.

An ADSI client communicates with a directory service through the ADSI router and support component. This component relies on the Windows NT registry to identify the appropriate interface for the client. Once this interface has been determined, a client can communicate directly with the directory service in question.

Figure 16.3 shows a sample ADSI from the ADSI **System Developer's Kit (SDK)**.

Authentication Server

Internet Authentication Server (IAS), once considered part of Windows NT Server's Distributed Security Services, functions under IIS 4.0 to carry out authentication, authorization, and accounting of users connecting to your Internet or intranet server by dial-up from a remote site. IAS is built on the protocol **RADIUS (Remote Authentication Dial-In User Service)**. By handling access requests locally, IAS becomes, in effect, a server for the RADIUS service.

Figure 16.1 ADSI allows clients to talk to several directory services.

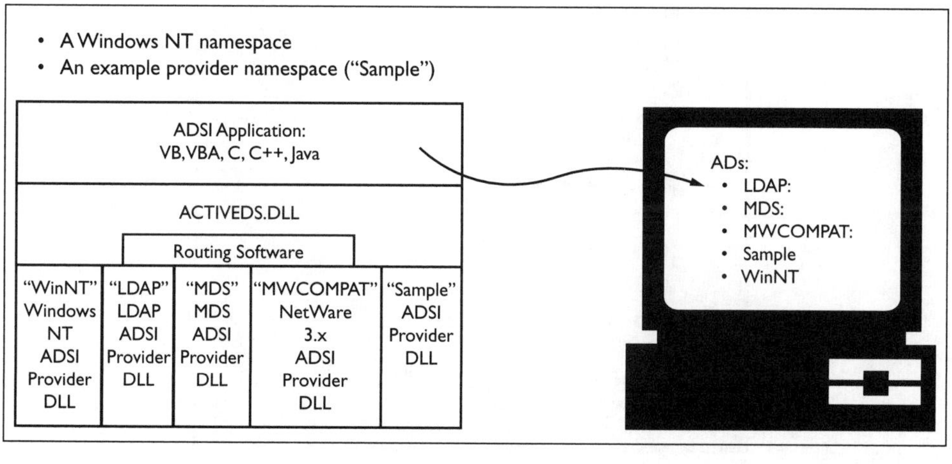

Figure 16.2 ADSI's architecture makes a lot out of a little.

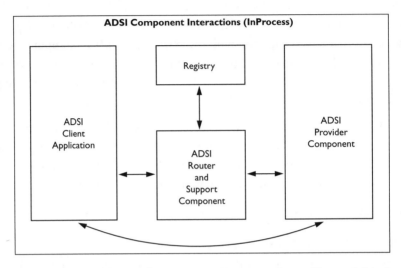

You can tailor much of IAS's functioning. For example, as Figure 16.4 shows, you can fine-tune the ports the service uses, as well as the threads it will handle.

Those logs can be precisely defined, and can be run at intervals most efficient for your environment. Figure 16.5 takes a look at configuring IAS logging.

Figure 16.3 This ADSI was written in Visual Basic.

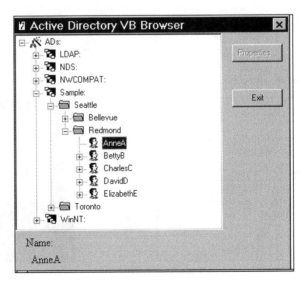

Figure 16.4 IAS even allows you to fine-tune its logs.

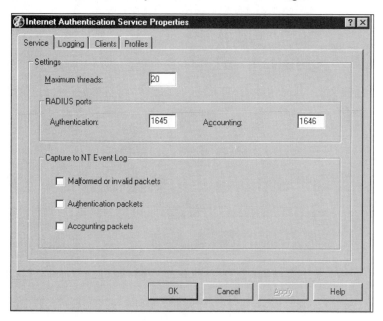

Under IAS, you can define both passwords for client devices (see Figure 16.6) or profiles for users of those clients (see Figure 16.7).

Mail Server and News Server

Internet Mail Server, like its mirror image News Server, uses the application-layer, TCP/IP-based **Network News Transport Protocol** (**NNTP**). (One of NNTP's most significant functions is to provide a client/server command set for access to newsgroups.) Mail Server also relies on a beefed-up, heavy-traffic incarnation of the **Simple Mail Transfer Protocol**, or SMTP. Among Internet Mail Server's most significant features are:

- Access to **Microsoft Management Console** (**MMC**) for administration

- Routing configuration to customize delivery options

- Support for secure transmission through support for the **Secure Sockets Layer** (**SSL**) protocols

- Transaction logging, which can track messages, usage numbers, and usage patterns

Figure 16.5 IAS logs can be run at any of several intervals.

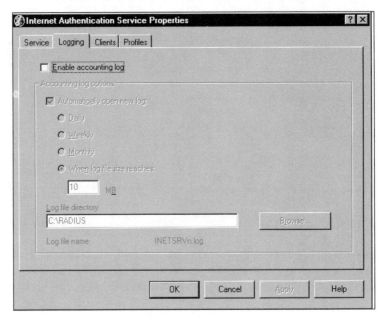

News Server provides similar functions, including:

- Local, remote, and moderator-approved article posting

- Newsgroup searching

- SSL support

- Support for both private and public newsgroups

- Transaction logs like those available to Mail Server

Microsoft Management Console

Microsoft Management Console (MMC) isn't one management tool, but many. Through a single interface, it presents several NT Server and IIS administrative tools, including Internet Service Manager. MMC also allows you to configure additional administrative programs (which it refers to as Snap-Ins), and then run them through this common interface. Future releases of Windows NT and all BackOffice products will use MMC Snap-Ins as their administrative programs. Figure 16.8 shows an MMC Snap-In serving Internet Information Server.

Figure 16.6 Logging in from a client device will require a password defined here.

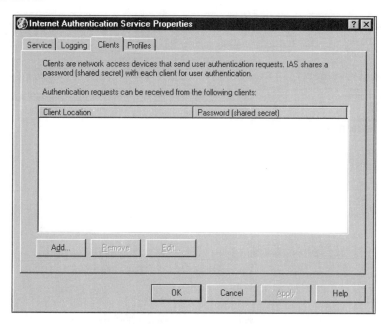

Figure 16.7 Remote users log in under profiles set up here.

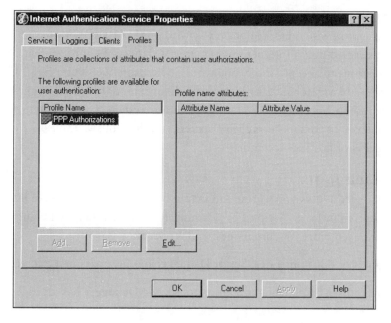

Figure 16.8 Under MMC-based administration, every management tool can be considered a Snap-In.

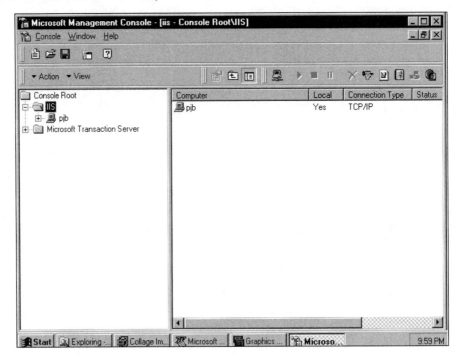

Posting Acceptor

Posting Acceptor, which works not only with IIS 4.0 but also with recent releases of Microsoft's scaled-down Internet server's Peer Web Services and Personal Web Server, functions to accept Web content from Microsoft Web Publishing Wizard/API and Netscape Navigator 2.02 or later through any standard HTTP connection. In conjunction with Microsoft's **Content Replication System (CRS)**, Posting Acceptor can also distribute content to multiple servers simultaneously. Table 16.2 sketches a quick likeness of Posting Acceptor.

Script Debugger

Script Debugger allows you to test and debug both server- and client-side scripts, whether written in Java, JScript, Perl, Python, REXX, or other CGI coding languages with even more obscure names, and VBScript.

As Figure 16.9 demonstrates, Script Debugger has an unassuming look about it.

But as you can see by glancing at Figure 16.10, the Debugger has an eagle eye.

Table 16.2 There's a Lot to Posting Acceptor

This Component	Consists of
Active Server Pages	A file that determines the type of client browser and activates the appropriate content-uploading form
ActiveX Upload Control	An ActiveX control that can be used to post content files
ASP PostInfo File	A file that configures client software for posting
CRS Mapping Module	A module that maps URLs to physical locations on a hard drive
File System Mapping Module	Another URL-mapping module
Posting Acceptor ISAPI	The ISAPI application, which is the heart of Posting Acceptor

TIP At the time this book was being written, Script Debugger was available only in an early Preview release.

Figure 16.9 Script Debugger packs a lot into this little package.

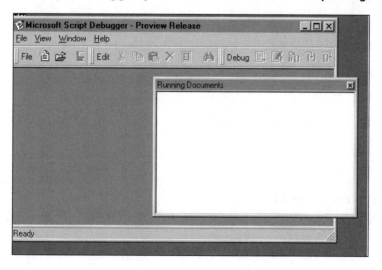

Figure 16.10 Script Debugger flags coding errors line by line.

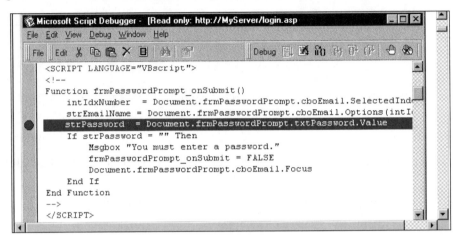

Site Analyst

Site Analyst, whose initial screen we've illustrated in Figure 16.11, is one of the Site Server suite of tools.

The Analyst lets you create Web maps, that is, graphical representations of the resources on a Web site. Further, Site Analyst allows you to view these maps in either Tree view, a linear, hierarchical presentation, or Cyberbolic view, a more HTML-like display.

Site Analyst's toolkit is packed full; it includes the Link Info window shown in Figure 16.12, as well as the ability to:

- Import usage data from a server's common log, combined log, or from a log report

- View and modify the Analyst's properties

- View or modify the set of automatically generated, linked HTML-based reports that are created by the Analyst when you define a map

Transaction Server

One of the most impressive IIS 4.0 add-ons, Transaction Server is an application development and deployment environment. The Server defines a programming model for creating component-based distributed applications. We feel its neatest feature is its runtime module, which allows you to configure, install, and manage these applications. Among the many things Transaction Server's runtime enables

Figure 16.11 Start here to follow your Web map.

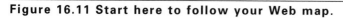

you to do are to manage processes and threads, and to oversee the use of objects and object instances. Such tasks can be carried out through the graphical interface Transaction Server provides for system and component administration.

Figure 16.12 No more broken links with this tool.

Figure 16.13 shows you one of the sample applications provided as a get-started tool within Transaction Server.

Usage Analyst

Usage Analyst bears some resemblance to Site Analyst. However, Usage Analyst, while it is chock-full of useful tools, is not primarily graphically oriented. Rather, Usage Analyst lets you sift through the information IIS and NT Server record in their log files, and create reports based on the grains that result. Usage Analyst offers three primary jumping-off points for such garnering. Figure 16.14 depicts Usage Analyst's report creation and viewing interface.

In Figure 16.15, we see one of the steps involved in importing data from a log into Usage Analyst.

Figure 16.16 illustrates the tools available within Usage Analyst's report generator.

VBScript and JScript

Those of you who live to Web-author can take heart. IIS 4.0 provides two Web page creation and configuration tools to die for: VBScript and JScript. These two client-side scripting languages are among the most powerful and widely used Web scripting tools. What's even nicer is that by providing JScript, IIS 4.0 in effect pro-

Figure 16.13 While its underlying code is written in Visual Basic, this application was configured and distributed through Transaction Server.

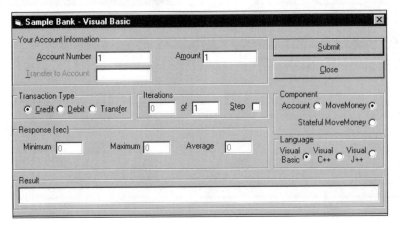

Figure 16.14 Here's where Usage Analyst reports originate.

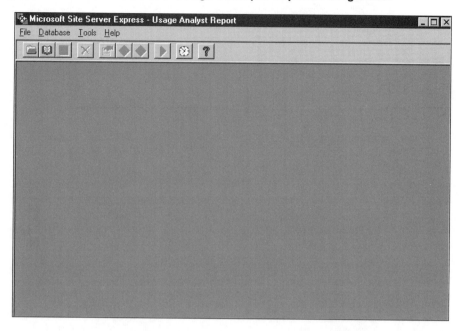

Figure 16.15 Any NT or IIS log file is grist for Usage Analyst's mill.

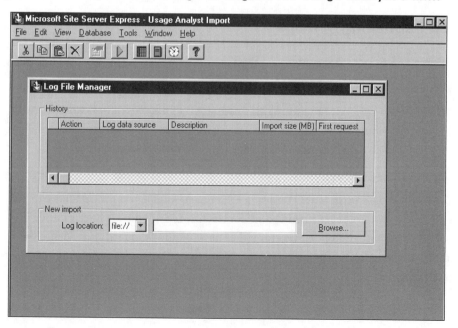

Figure 16.16 UA's reports aren't simple text files, as you can see.

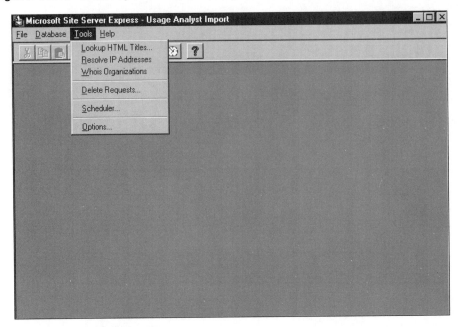

vides JavaScript, since the former is a derivative of and 100-percent compatible with the latter Netscape/Sun Microsystems product.

Web Publishing Wizard

Web Publishing Wizard, once relegated to Microsoft's lesser Internet servers, has moved on up to IIS 4.0. The Wizard leads you by the hand through creating Web pages, as Figure 16.17 demonstrates.

Then, working in conjunction with Posting Acceptor, Web Publishing Wizard helps you distribute those pages by means of an Internet Server Provider, as illustrated in Figure 16.18, or inhouse intranet or Internet servers.

Windows Scripting Host

The **Windows Scripting Host (WSH)** is a language-independent host that can run on all 32-bit Windows platforms, and comes accompanied by VBScript and JavaScript engines. WSH can be run either as a Windows-based host, using the executable WSCRIPT.EXE, or as a command-line-based application, as CSCRIPT.EXE.

Figure 16.17 Your first Web page could start here.

Until the unveiling of Windows Scripting Host, the only native scripting language available in Windows environments was the DOS command language. Although it is fast and small, DOS scripting has its limitations. It's for this reason that WSH

Figure 16.18 Setting up your publishing path is a snap with this Wizard.

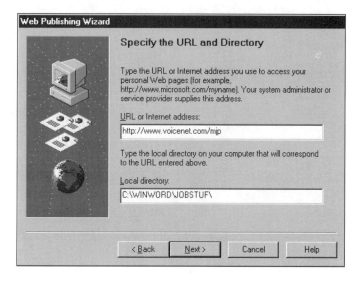

was introduced, allowing users to take advantage of the greater capabilities of languages like VBScript and tools like ActiveX controls.

Windows Scripting Host allows scripts to be executed directly from the desktop or from the command console, without the need to embed those scripts in an HTML document. Just as significant is the fact that WSH places relatively low demands on memory. For these reasons, WSH is an excellent choice for any noninteractive scripting needs, like carrying out such recurring functions as cleanups of a file system, establishing or modifying user profiles, and setting default, login-time environments.

IIS 4.0 Installation and Requirements

Table 16.3 summarizes the hardware demands Internet Information Server 4.0 will make of a computer.

Table 16.3 IIS 4.0 Hardware Requirements

On This Platform	And for This Feature	You'll Need to Provide
Intel x86	CPU	At least a 90MHz 486 DX; we recommend a Pentium 133 as a reasonable minimum.
	RAM	32MB at minimum; at least 48 if you're going to publish any multimedia Web content, or have a busy site.
	free disk	Microsoft says 50MB; we say at least 120, and 200 if possible.
	monitor	SuperVGA, since Microsoft and the Internet and Web in general are leaning more and more toward big, splashy presentations.
Alpha	CPU	At minimum, a 150MHz chip; 200MHz if possible.
	RAM	48MB to crawl, 64MB to run.
	free disk	120–200MB.
	monitor	SuperVGA.

Preinstallation Software Configuration Requirements

Before you can install IIS 4.0, you must first have installed:

- Windows NT Server 4.0

- Service Pack 3 for NT Server 4

- Internet Explorer 3.01 or 3.02

What's more, in order to load IIS or any other system software under NT Server, you must be logged on to the server machine under an account that has Administrator privileges.

Other Preinstallation Concerns

Unlike full-release versions of IIS, alpha and beta versions (in particular, the 4.0 alpha and 4.0 beta 1 versions) cannot be upgraded to the full-blown, official IIS 4.0. So, if you've previously loaded either of these dry runs, you *must* uninstall them before loading the real McCoy.

At the other end of the installation continuum, it's a good idea to finish the installation process rather than canceling, even if you've stutter-stepped somewhere along the way. Bailing out of IIS setup can leave files hidden all over a hard drive that even the most zealous cleanup utility would be hard-pressed to locate, let alone get rid of. So, if you've made mistakes during installation, it's probably better to finish the procedure and then remove the product before starting fresh.

Getting Started with IIS 4.0

As was the case with its earlier incarnations, IIS 4.0's default configuration suffices for most Web publishing scenarios. So, after installing and connecting to the Internet or an intranet, you can immediately begin to publish from your default Web root of

`\Inetpub\wwwroot`

Using the Documentation

Since it has so many new features, both limited and extensive, it behooves you to brush up on using what will surely be your first line of attack in learning those features—IIS online documentation.

To be able to see that documentation at all, the Web service must be running. Assuming that's the case, here are a few points to keep in mind:

- Most navigation will begin from the left frame.

- Single-clicking any heading should allow you to view pages that contain summaries of the material to which that heading pertains.

- Single-clicking the plus and minus symbols will expand and collapse, respectively, the corresponding branches of the contents tree, thereby allowing you to look at or hide topics.

- Use the Search icon at the top of the documentation frame rather than the Search icon in the Internet Explorer or other browser toolbar if you want to carry out a search of the entire body of IIS documentation.

- IIS 4.0 documentation is intended to be displayed in the Verdana font, which can be installed from the path

    System\Font

- IIS 4.0 documentation includes multimedia files. Needless to say (but we'll point it out anyway), if you want to hear the audio portions of the documentation, you need a sound card on your IIS server. Less apparent is the fact that you cannot navigate through the multimedia portions of the IIS 4.0 documentation with the customary quick click of Back or Forward. So enjoy the light show or sound-surround the first time through.

Troubleshooting Ahead of Time

In preparing these final chapters, we worked with the beta 2 release of Internet Information Server 4.0. As is the case with all beta software, bugs and gaps appeared as a result. While most of these will have been resolved by the time you're reading this, not all will be cleaned up. So, we thought it best to review some of the most significant known problems now, as a way of forewarning you, and as a means of providing you with fixes or at least workarounds from the get-go.

Internet Service Manager
We'll use Table 16.4 to acquaint you with ISM's beta blues.

Table 16.4 Working Around Internet Service Manager

For This Problem	Try This Solution
Failure to display or inability to manage WWW or Gopher services	Upgrade all versions of IIS or Personal Web Server anywhere in your site to IIS 4.0. It's earlier releases of either of these applications that most frequently cause this problem for a 4.0 server.
Failure of Tree view to refresh properly	Stop and then restart Internet Service Manager. This problem most frequently is caused by having made changes to Web site or virtual directory paths, without making such changes known to ISM by stopping/restarting.
Inability to manage multiple sites simultaneously	While you can select and view several Web sites at a time with ISM, you cannot stop, start, or set their properties en masse. These tasks must be carried out on a site-by-site, IIS server-by-IIS server basis.

Active Server Pages

Here's one you'll certainly want to keep in mind, since failing to do so could hang your Internet Information Server. Stepping through an **Active Server Pages** (or **.asp**) file in Script Debugger *cannot* be coupled with modifying that file while stepping; if you do, IIS will hang and you'll have to restart your server machine. You can use Script Debugger to make changes to an .asp file; just be sure to do so either before reaching a breakpoint or after the file has run through the Debugger completely.

ISAPI

IIS 4.0, in addition to supporting ISAPI applications, has the ability to run the DLLs that make up such applications either in-process, (in foreground), or out-of-process (in background). But some ISAPI applications and their corresponding DLLs may not perform well, or at all, in out-of-process execution. Among the factors responsible for this lackluster status are exclusive access to files, references to any of IIS's internal data structures, and security loopholes.

When an administrator adds applications to IIS's list of ISAPI applications, such applications, if accessed, will be routed to the default application root in IIS, called **/LM/W3SVC**. And there's the rub; This default application root is defined as in-process only. Therefore, any requests to it will run in-process. And quicker than you could say "Hang My Server," a DLL that expects and needs to run out-of-process, but is requested as in-process, will bring IIS to a halt.

In a somewhat similar scenario, if an ISAPI application DLL has been loaded and is being cached by more than one Web site, clearing the **Cache ISAPI Application** checkbox of the **Application Config** property sheet on the originating server *will not* unload the DLL from memory on any but the originating server. You must clear this checkbox one at a time for all servers involved.

Secure Sockets Layer (SSL)

First, the bad news. IIS 4.0 betas didn't support Proxy Server version 1.0. However, even in beta, IIS 4.0 does support SSL. As a result, it allows you to provide SSL client certificates, if you do the following:

1. In the **Password Authentication Method** section of the **Directory Security** property sheet, click **Edit**.

2. As a result, the next thing you see should be the **Authentication Methods** property sheet. Here, check the **Enable SSL Client Authentication** and **Require SSL Client Authentication** checkboxes.

3. Return to the **Directory Security** property sheet. There, in the **Secure Communications** section, click **Edit**.

4. Having done so, you'll arrive at the **Secure Communications** property sheet, where you must check the **Require Secure Channel** checkbox.

Avoiding TCP Port Conflicts

Any software that distributes Internet services must use TCP/IP to do so. And such port usage follows certain standards. For example, the standard port for the HTTP protocol is TCP port 80, while that for FTP is port 21. So, any Internet-related software already loaded under Windows NT Server might use these or other standard ports, and might, by doing so, make them unavailable to IIS. You'll soon know if this has happened; IIS won't hesitate to tell you. But what may not be as self-evident is what to do next.

If you must change port assignments for IIS *once it is already up and running,* here's what you need to do:

1. Start **Internet Service Manager**.

2. Double-click **IIS**.

3. Double-click the icon that represents the server whose port assignments you must modify.

4. Select the service (e.g., FTP or WWW) you want to change.

5. Pull down the **Action** menu.

6. Click **Properties**.

7. Choose the appropriate property sheet.

8. Change the TCP port number.

9. Click **OK**.

From Here

That concludes our quick cook's tour of Internet Information Server 4.0. In Chapter 17, we'll begin to examine some of the release's most significant features in detail, when we investigate its management tools more closely.

Internet Information
Server 4.0
Management Tools

One of the newest terms to be added to the plethora of Microsoft code names and acronyms is that which characterizes the MS approach to establishing, making available, and making use of a management infrastructure for Windows NT and, in some cases, Windows 95. The folks in Redmond refer to this three-part process as the **Zero Administration Initiative for Windows,** or **ZAW**.

It behooves us to scrutinize this set of components closely for two reasons. First, **Microsoft Management Console (MMC)** is now the presentation method used not only by Internet Service Manager but also by more directly NT-based tools such as Service Manager (see Figure 17.1).

Second, (and this one's the biggie), Microsoft plans to migrate all—repeat, *all*—its Windows NT Server management tools to an MMC form as soon as possible.

So, before we examine IIS 4.0-specific management features, we'll take a quick look at ZAW in general.

Figure 17.1 Service Manager has a new look.

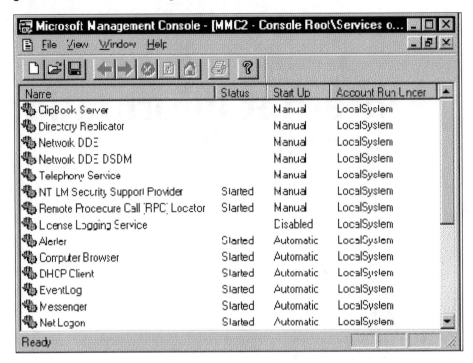

ZAW

In the context of this chapter, the most significant components of the Zero Administration Initiative for Windows are:

- Microsoft Management Console

- Systems Management Server

- Web-Based Enterprise Management

- Windows Management Instrumentation

- Zero Administration Kit

We'll discuss other ZAW components such as the **Windows Scripting Host**, or **WSH**, in later chapters.

Microsoft Management Console (MMC)

Microsoft Management Console (MMC) is not a management tool so much as it is a presentation framework for network administration tools. Any tools that you expect MMC to proffer must be programmed and configured to act as MMC components, called Snap-Ins.

MMC differs from existing management console applications in maintaining no protocol dependencies or object repositories. MMC leaves such details of application architecture to its Snap-Ins. These Snap-Ins can work independently of one another, or in conjunction with related Snap-Ins. The goal of MMC, not yet fully realized at the time this book was being written, is to provide a network or Web administrator with the technology-independent tools needed to create a single point of management of system, network, and user information.

MMC will, in the near future, include Directory Service Administration for the Active Directory Service as a Snap-In. Directory Service Administration will provide managers one means by which common and often time-consuming Net and Web administrative tasks can be carried out (e.g., adding users, managing printers, and monitoring servers). DSA will not only be available as a Snap-In for MMC, but also as a tool that can be used with any frames–capable browser that supports Kerberos authentication.

Systems Management Server 1.2

Systems Management Server is an application for medium and large organizations that have an extensive Windows-based computing environment, and need a management structure to match. Among the tools provided by Systems Management Server are:

- Automated hardware inventory

- Automated software inventory

- Remote network diagnostics

- Software distribution tracking

Unlike some ZAW components, Systems Management Server was available at the time this book was being written.

Web-Based Enterprise Management

Web-Based Enterprise Management, or **WBEM,** is not software per se, but rather a set of standards that seeks to permit the use of Internet technologies as the basis for managing autonomous systems, networks, or the users of either. The WBEM standard is still very much in the development stage. However, parts of it have been ratified by the Desktop Management Task Force, a consortium of industry giants and foot soldiers alike, which includes among its members Compaq, DEC, Dell, Hewlett-Packard, Lexmark, Novell, and other hardware system, peripheral, component, and software manufacturers, under the name **Common Information Model** (CIM).

Windows Management Instrumentation (WMI)

Another significant component of ZAW, and one that is closely related to Web-Based Enterprise Management, is the **Windows Management Instrumentation** (**WMI**) initiative, expected to be implemented with the release of Windows NT Server 5.0. WMI has been designed to provide, from a Windows platform, functionality like that found in older management methodologies such as the **Desktop Management Interface** or DMI.

Zero Administration Kit

The **Zero Administration Kit** (**ZAK**), another ZAW component, uses existing Windows NT Server 4.0 and Systems Management Server tools to set and maintain policies on desktops. The Kit's biggest claim to fame is that it allows administrators to lock down the Windows NT Server 4.0 desktop.

MMC in More Detail

As we mentioned in the section "Microsoft Management Console" earlier in this chapter, MMC is not a management application itself, but rather a framework for

How Old Is Old?

As one of our editors recently said, "A month in computers is like a century anywhere else." DMI illustrates that point. It can only be appropriately termed *older* in the sense that it's been around for more than a year. Related to DMI is another standard called OpenDoc, which addresses the requirements presented by component software that can and must be shared across heterogeneous environments.

management applications. When fully implemented, MMC will run under both Windows NT Server versions 4.0 and later, and current and future versions of Windows 95.

Let's talk further for a moment about Snap-Ins, the logical and physical foundation of MMC. Every Snap-In contains a collection of tools that can be applied individually or in groups. Among these tools are:

- Microsoft Certificate Mapper

- RealAudio ActiveX controls

- Wang Image Edit controls

It is this high degree of tool and tool component modularity that allows network and Web site managers to customize their management tools, and even implement a tool in several levels of complexity, each of which is tailored to the needs and skills of different categories of users.

MMC Architecture

Management Console relies on another *older* technology, the **Multiple Document Interface (MDI)**. Let's put MDI under the microscope for a moment, as a means of gaining a better understanding of MMC.

An MDI application creates windows and frames by means of either the **CreateWindow** or **CreateWindowEx** Win32 functions. First a parent, and then a client window or windows are produced. Such client windows in turn rely on the already-registered, that is, identified to the Registry class called MDICLIENT, using it as the client window's class name. Also required by a client MDI window is the structure **CLIENTCREATESTRUCT**, which must be pointed to by the **lpvParam** parameter of the CreateWindow and CreateWindowEx functions. In fact, **CLIENT-CREATESTRUCT** is at the heart of client window construction under MDI, so let's review it now.

MMC and Internet Service Manager

For our purposes, the most important thing to keep in mind about MMC is that Internet Service Manager in IIS 4.0 has been implemented as part of the MMC framework.

hWindowMenu: The component of **CLIENTCREATESTRUCT** that identifies the Window menu that will control the child window. The titles of child windows are automatically added to the overall Window menu as the children are created, thereby allowing these new windows to be accessed from the overall Window menu.

idFirstChild: The component of **CLIENTCREATESTRUCT** that defines an identifier for the first child window. Any subsequent children are then automatically created with this identifier appropriately incremented.

One example of the use of MDI can be found in Multipad's frame/window procedure, which creates the client window while processing a system message. Figure 17.2 gives an excerpt from the code involved.

Windows created in this way make up the user interface aspect of MMC. This interface, in a manner reminiscent of NT Server's hardware Abstraction Layer, cannot interact directly with Snap-Ins, but rather must do so through another MMC component, the Snap-In Manager. The Snap-In Manager also handles saving frame and window settings into a system file called the **Management Saved Console**, or

Figure 17.2 Take a look at some of the internal C code of an MDI application.

```
case WM_CREATE: { CLIENTCREATESTRUCT ccs;

// Retrieve the handle of the Window menu and assign the first child window

identifier.

ccs.hWindowMenu = GetSubMenu(GetMenu(hwnd), WINDOWMENU);

ccs.idFirstChild = IDM_WINDOWCHILD;

// Create the MDI client window.

hwndMDIClient = CreateWindow( "MDICLIENT", (LPCTSTR) NULL, WS_CHILD |

WS_CLIPCHILDREN | WS_VSCROLL | WS_HSCROLL, 0, 0, 0, 0, hwnd, (HMENU) 0xCAC,

hInst, (LPSTR) &ccs);

  ShowWindow(hwndMDIClient, SW_SHOW); }

break;
```

.msc file. Two components—the .msc file and the user interface—are all that an MMC user will ever see or interact with. The Snap-In Manager and individual Snap-Ins are reserved for designers and programmers.

When a management Console tool such as Event Viewer or Internet Service manager is loaded, any required Snap-Ins are initialized immediately. These Snap-Ins work together to create a namespace; that is, a linear representation of nodes displayed in the tool's tree view that represents what the tool can do. As Figure 17.3 shows, this listing is quite reminiscent of a tree view of files and directories on a hard drive.

Child windows in MMC can be thought of as views of this master namespace.

Snap-Ins

Under Microsoft Management Console, a single Snap-In represents and accomplishes one unit of one type of management behavior. This makes a Snap-In analogous to a quark; it's the smallest unit into which the stuff of console extension can

Figure 17.3 A namespace like this one can include such aspects of a network as users, groups, objects, and tasks.

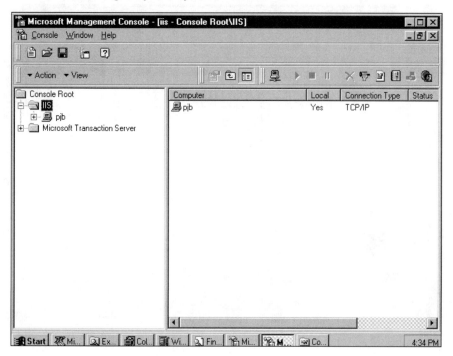

be divided. For the programmers among you, a Snap-In is implemented as an OLE in-proc server that executes in the process context of MMC. What this means to the rest of us is that the DLLs and any supporting controls that make up a Snap-In run as child processes of MMC.

Snap-Ins flesh out MMC in a number of ways, such as adding elements to the viewable namespace, and enhancing a tool by adding features like property pages, toolbars, or Wizards.

Tools and Snap-Ins An administrator can aggregate a number of Snap-Ins, whatever their source, into a single tool that, in many respects, can be dealt with as a document. It is this tool that actually carries out network management tasks. After combining Snap-Ins to create a tool, as we've illustrated in Figure 17.4, an administrator then saves the tool in an MSC file, making it available for reloading at any time.

Packages and Snap-Ins Just as Snap-Ins can be gathered together to form a tool, tools can be aggregated into packages. For instance, a vendor might group:

Figure 17.4 Adding a Snap-In to MMC is—dare we say it—a snap.

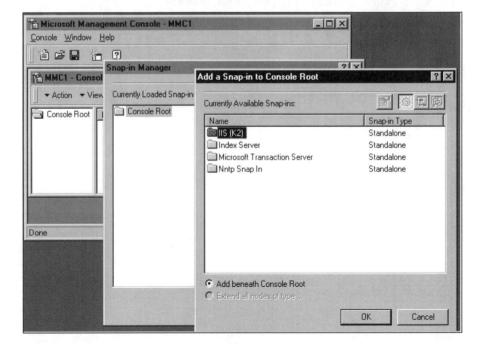

- Several Snap-Ins into a tool which tracks bandwidth usage on a per-service basis

- Several more Snap-Ins into a tool which tracks bandwidth usage on a per-workstation basis

- Still more Snap-Ins into a tool which tracks bandwidth usage on a per-user basis

- All these tools into a single application suite, or package

Types of Snap-Ins Snap-Ins, as we've illustrated in Figure 17.5, can be seen as belonging to one of three categories:

Extension Snap-Ins: Extention Snap-Ins can only be invoked by a parent process that is itself a Snap-In. One example of an extension Snap-In might be a module, perhaps called "View in Cyrillic," which would enable users in Eastern Europe to see a node tree annotated in their native alphabet. Extension Snap-Ins can affect the console, that is, the parent namespace, as well. For instance, an extension Snap-In might enhance and add to information about computers within that namespace.

Standalone Snap-Ins: These are the inverse of extension Snap-Ins. Standalones rely on no other Snap-Ins.

Hybrid Snap-Ins: Hybrid Snap-Ins offer some standalone and some extended functions. One example of a hybrid Snap-In is the NT Server event log, which reads, aggregates, and displays the event logs of individual computers in an NT domain, but which can also operate in a standalone way, by default reporting only on server events.

Extending the Capabilities of a Management Console

Microsoft has defined a number of types of Snap-In functionality; every Snap-In must provide at least one of the following:

Context Menu Extension: To be implemented on a per-node basis, this extension must add items to the context menu of a given node or object.

CREATENEW: To be implemented on a per-node basis, this extension must add items to the **CreateNew** menu-related C structure of the context menu of a given node or object.

Figure 17.5 Here's a yardstick against which you can measure Snap-Ins.

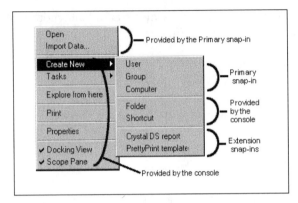

Generalized OLE2 Style: To be implemented to function on a per-result basis, as a window pane, this extension must permit a control or document object in a window's result pane to negotiate for menus to be displayed by means of the standard OLE2 menu-merging interfaces.

Namespace Enumeration: To be implemented on a per-node basis, this extension must list or enumerate the elements in a container, whether it is a dialog box, frame, window, or other. A Namespace Enumeration Snap-In has the option of altering what it produces based on context information passed to it when it is called.

Property Page: To be implemented on a per-node basis, this extension must add one or more property sheets of a fixed size previously defined for the property to a Property page.

TASKS: To be implemented on a per-node basis, this extension must add items to the **Tasks** menu-related C structure of the context menu of a given node or object.

Toolbar and Toolbar Buttons: To be implemented on a per-view basis, such extensions must add an entire toolbar to the window hosting the node being served by the Snap-In.

Wizard Chaining: To be implemented on a per-node basis, this extension must add one or more pages to a Wizard frame or window.

Whichever of these categories it falls into, an individual Snap-In can change its information output based on other information passed to it when it is called. In effect, this means that Snap-Ins are capable of conditional behavior, for example, opening a particular menu only if that menu is appropriate to the workstation requesting it.

Other than the CREATENEW and TASKS extensions, the Snap-In types just outlined deal in some way with the MMC user interface. CREATENEW and TASKS, on the other hand, can be used to group operations to provide integrated command structures. What this means is that under MMC, each node will have a **CreateNew** menu and a **Tasks** menu through which Snap-Ins and tools can be organized and managed. Microsoft, in an effort to allow MMC to reflect the reality of a continuum of skills within organizations, rather than the abstraction of discrete skill levels, has designed MMC in this way in order to provide for the creation of tools with a corresponding spectrum of sophistication.

Enterprise Consoles and MMC Enterprise consoles are defined (on the Microsoft Web site at least) as "the administrative products that support the enterprise, most often in network management." By this definition, such applications can lack robustness when called upon to manage individual clients. It is this shortcoming of enterprise console applications that was one of the motivating forces for the development of MMC.

Because Windows NT Server 4.0 and higher support most popular enterprise console applications, MMC can be integrated with those applications not only to enhance their out-of-the-box functionality, but also to add tools through which Windows clients can be administered. MMC's Snap-Ins-based architecture can easily augment the inventory, device auto-discovery, software distribution, alert collection and suppression, help desk, and similar features that make up most enterprise console applications, as well as provide a single consistent interface for the execution of everything offered by the enterprise console.

Internet Development Tools and MMC The best guess as to the future relationship of Internet development tools like HTML, Java, and so on, can be found in another quote from the Microsoft Web site.

> *"We believe that a reasonable portion of the MMC UI (User Interface) will be Internet technology-based, but there is still a long road ahead before Internet technologies can truly perform some of the more advanced management tasks. Features such as multiselect, advanced window management . . . end-user customization, and advanced drag and drop are impossible, or much more difficult, to implement using [Internet] technologies. . . . Looking to Microsoft's*

own future, . . . *InternetStudio, ActiveServer, NetShow, and many . . . other technologies . . . are, or will soon be, supported."*

All of which is to say that some tools, like Internet Studio, are by their inherent nature good candidates for melding with MMC. But others, such as the Windows Scripting Host mentioned in the *ZAW* section earlier in this chapter, may never make it onto the Microsoft Management Console.

Internet Service Manager as a Snap-In

Since, in the 4.0 release of Internet Information Server, Internet Service Manager has joined the MMC club, we need to walk you through what you must do to use this release's ISM.

To start Internet Service Manager:

1. Click **Start**

2. Point to **Programs**

3. Point to **Microsoft Internet Information Server**

4. Click **Internet Service Manager**

When the MMC main window and one child window are displayed, you'll know that the ISM Snap-In has been loaded and is running.

Usage Analyst

Like MMC and Site Analyst, Usage Analyst can be found not only in IIS 4.0 but also in Microsoft's Site Server suite. Usage Analyst, which includes a report writer offering 50 2D and 3D graph styles and tables, can carry out quite a handful of network analysis tasks, including:

It's Beginning to Look a Lot Like IE4

Microsoft Internet Explorer 4.0, formerly code-named Nashville, clearly resembles MMC. This similarity is intentional, and is intended to shorten the new-tools learning curve. However, MMC and IE4 differ in one very important respect: MMC is an MDI-based application and therefore offers features like the ability to configure tools or add Snap-Ins that Mr. or Ms. Average User are unlikely to need.

- Aggregating data on a variety of servers, including FTP, Gopher, http, and RealAudio servers, from multiple Internet servers and sites.

- Creating usage analysis reports that take advantage of multidimensional data retrieval from any number of row or column dimensions, or calculation parameters.

- Customizing the log database with variables that represent content, time, and user categories.

- Defining and executing complex calculations like:

  - What are the top 10 xxx sorted by number of requests?

  - What are the bottom 20 xxx sorted by number of visits?

  - Show me top files, grouped first by server and then by directory, for all users in New Zealand.

- Handling several standard and extended log file formats from popular Internet servers such as Apache, IIS, Netscape, and O'Reilly.

- Hierarchically configuring log data sources, even those residing on multiple servers, and the association of those sources with any combination of content sites.

Table 17.1 outlines some of the statistics Usage Analyst makes available.

In addition to being a network administrator's most convenient tool since the pocket calculator, Usage Analyst makes a pretty fair detective. It can obtain all of the following information and more for every user who visits your site:

- City and zip or postal code

- Continent of origin

- Country of origin

- Region of origin

- State or province of origin

> **TIP** Microsoft requires you to carry a separate Usage Analyst license for every Web server you intend to monitor.

Table 17.1 Examining Your Network with Usage Analyst

This Parameter	Can Be Obtained for	And Contains Information on
Visit Duration	Single visits or groups of visits, by individuals or groups of users.	The amount of time elapsed between the first and last requests of a visit.
Request Duration	Single pages or groups of pages.	The amount of time elapsed between two consecutive requests within a single visit. In this context, the last request of any visit will always, arbitrarily but understandably, be assigned a Request Duration of 0 by Usage Analyst.
Target Audience(s)	Single or multiple visits by one or more users.	How frequently a user or group of users access specific areas of a site, or the site as a whole.

Where does Usage Analyst get all this input? It extrapolates it from the user's organization or Internet Service Provider Internet domain registration. As if this weren't enough, Usage Analyst, in its Import module, also allows you to carry out a **Whois** inquiry in order to tie down details about previously unencountered Internet domains. Like the data regarding users that it makes available, Usage Analyst includes information on region, state, city, and zip code.

In order to expedite your statistics-gathering, Usage Analyst provides a scheduling utility that operates from a command-line interface and includes a message log. Possibly the only shortcoming of Usage Analyst is that it cannot operate in Windows 3.x environments, since the Analyst is a 32-bit application. However, it interacts just fine with Windows NT Server 4.0 and up, and with Windows 95. Usage Analyst can even produce statistics regarding the performance of a Web server running on either a Macintosh or a UNIX platform, if that server's log files are in a format that Usage Analyst understands.

Usage Analyst System Requirements

It is the Import module of Usage Analyst that interprets log files and builds a database of usage statistics based on those files. We don't want to say it's a resource hog, but let's put it this way: Even Microsoft admits that the Import module is CPU intensive. And Usage Analyst's thirst for server resources doesn't stop there; its Analysis module leans heavily on both CPU and memory.

For these reasons, any server that offers less than the specifications outlined in Table 17.2 is *not* a good candidate for hosting Usage Analyst.

It's more difficult to establish system requirements guidelines for Usage Analyst than it is for many applications. This is because processing time for log files can vary with a number of parameters, such as the size of the log file, the overall server configuration, and even the types of analyses being run, with larger log files or more complex analyses resulting in longer processing time. For instance, on a Pentium 120 with 32MB of RAM, standard analyses, when run against log file databases smaller than 100MB, execute in only a few minutes, but those run against larger databases can take much longer to complete.

Additional Tools Needed

Usage Analyst can do a lot but it can't quite do everything. In order to make the best use of the information Usage Analyst produces, you're probably going to want to acquire the following additional tools:

Microsoft SQL Server, in order to analyze log file databases that add up to more than 75MB each month. You'll have to obtain a separate license for this.

An **Internet connection**, in order to do HTML title lookups, resolve IP addresses, or run Whois inquiries.

Table 17.2 Configuring the Usage Analyst Platform

For This Component	The Absolute Minimum Needed by Usage Analyst Is	Reasonable Performance Can Be Expected from	And Optimal Operation Will Result If You Provide
CPU	120MHz Pentium	133MHz Pentium	166MHz Pentium
Free disk	15MB plus the aggregate size of your log files	30MB plus the aggregate size of your log files	45MB plus the aggregate size of your log files
RAM	16MB (we call this the "dog-slow recommendation")	32MB	64MB

> **TIP** One fairly common Internet operation that can horrendously increase the log processing time required by Usage Analyst is that of reverse DNS lookups. This practice, in which an IP address such as 192.92.22.12 is translated into a hostname such as dccc.edu, may not only cause Usage Analyst to slow to a lope, but also result in its producing inaccurate information. So be careful about carrying out reverse DNS lookups and Usage Analyst imports simultaneously.

Microsoft Excel 7.0 or higher, in order to produce spreadsheet-based reports.

Microsoft Word 7.0 or higher, in order to create reports in Word format.

Usage Analyst does provide some out-of-the-box reporting equipment, including:

- A Microsoft Access runtime

- A precompiled DLL for Microsoft ISAPI

- The source code for server extensions for Netscape NSAPI and Apache

Usage Analyst, Enterprise Edition

As its name suggests, the Enterprise Edition of Usage analyst contains several features that pertain primarily to tweaking the intranet or Internet sites of large organizations for peak efficiency. Among the features that separate Enterprise Edition from Usage Analyst proper are:

- The ability to customize a log file database, for example, by providing cross-referencing of advertisements and user navigation patterns

- The ability to parse query strings in order to carry out the analysis of application parameters such as search queries and results

- The ability to produce detailed reports for advertisers summarizing such parameters as ad views, ad clicks, and ad yield per advertisement

- The ability to support multiple simultaneous analysis sessions

Site Analyst

If any of IIS 4.0's management tools gain the (undeserved) reputation of a toy, it will surely be Site Analyst. This is because of the Analyst's ability to crawl Web sites and create maps of them from the information it picks up along the way.

Site Analyst uses a **spider** to record the links on a page. The Analyst then back- or forward-tracks those links, locating as many new pages and links as it can before producing its WebMap. Each map amounts to a directory or index of all the objects a site contains. So, a WebMap will note image and sound files, HTML pages, Java and PDF files, links, and more. Even more impressive is the fact that a WebMap can record and display all properties associated with such objects.

When creating this visual representation of a site and its contents and resources, you can map all or part of the site. If you map only those portions of the site that are of interest to you, Site Analyst will still be aware of any others, listing them as Unexplored. Conversely, Site Analyst allows you to build maps that depict multiple sites. Finally, whatever type or complexity of map you define, Site Analyst allows you to embed notes that describe the contents of each object in the Web Map, thereby providing not only an additional administrative tool, but one that can be used off line.

Mapping and Security

Firewalls needn't stop Site Analyst. Secure sites or portions thereof can be reviewed by it as long as you provide Site Analyst with any needed user names and passwords. In dealing with Net etiquette rather than Net security, Site Analyst tries to minimize the effects of its activity on the sites it maps. The Site Analyst spider therefore avoids accessing any page more than once, looping, and queries.

What's more, the Site Analyst spider can be paused or aborted by an administrator at any time during the mapping process. Further, the spider's default configuration was designed expressly to preclude overloading Web servers. Finally, the Site Analyst spider identifies itself to Webmasters and gives them the opportunity to prevent it from mapping their site.

Views, Reports, and Customization

Site Analyst offers a number of display formats. Probably the most important and most likely to be used is its Tree View, illustrated in Figure 17.6.

In technical terms, Site Analyst's Tree View displays a site's object hierarchy. Another view available in Site Analyst is called Cyberbolic View, which gives you a look at your site emphasizing the relationships between resources.

Whichever Site Analyst view you're using at any given moment, the object of focus will remain selected, even if you change views, since Tree and Cyberbolic Views are always transparently linked. In addition to hopping back and forth

Figure 17.6 Site Analyst's Tree View is reminiscent of NT Server's Explorer.

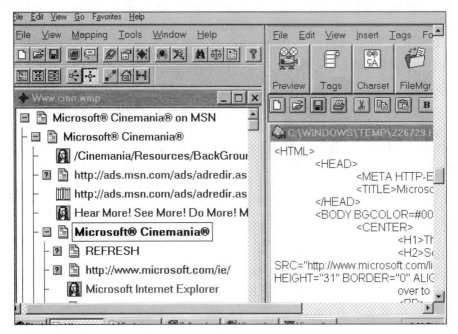

between Tree and Cyberbolic Views, Site Analyst allows you to customize its displays on the fly and in a number of ways, including hiding or showing specific types of links, representing hyperlinks as icons, and viewing or modifying object properties (illustrated in Figure 17.7).

One of Site Analyst's handiest features is that it allows you to verify links at any time, and to define which links it will verify. In fact, Site Analyst allows you to do quite a few link-management tasks, including:

- Choosing link properties to be displayed

- Displaying link reports as an HTML table in a browser

- Exporting link reports to spreadsheets or databases

- Seeing all the links to a page or to any resource

- Sorting on any displayed link property

- Verifying onsite, offsite, all, or previously broken links

Figure 17.7 Site Analyst allows you to view or modify four categories of its properties.

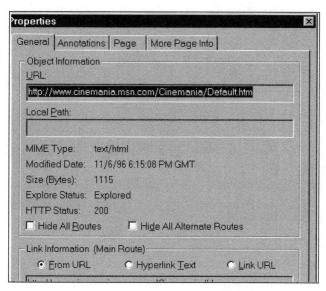

Site Analyst contains more than 20 linked, predefined HTML reports for managing Web content. These include:

- **Comparison Summary**: What's New, and What's Changed Reports, which permit you to compare Web maps with an eye to what the sites they depict, share, what has changed about depicted sites, and what such changes consist of.

- **Error Report**: Presents all unreachable objects on a site, and groups these objects according to the type of error they generated; for instance creating a category for links that generate the ubiquitous 404 Not Found error.

- **Image Report**: Provides a summary of and detailed information regarding all the image files on a site.

- **Link Report**: Makes available information on such site usage parameters as off-site references, incoming links, internal links, and so on.

- **Media Report**: Does for text, audio, and video files what Image Report does for graphics.

Figure 17.8 Site Analyst's main window is deceptive; you can do much more with it than its appearance might suggest.

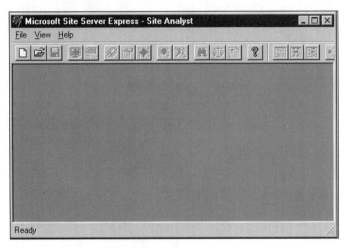

- **Site Integrity Reports:**

  - **Duplicates Report:** Lists duplicate objects by their full URL, and summarizes them with an icon.

  - **Unreferenced Objects Report:** Informs you of resources that no longer have references.

- **Site Summary Report:** A detailed overview of a site that offers map and object statistics, a status summary, and server information.

We'll close our review of Site Analyst with a look at the Analyst's main window, from which all the reports we just walked through can be accessed (see Figure 17.8).

From Here

Having taken a look at IIS 4.0 and its management tools, we can turn to examining what will probably be the area to which you'll most frequently apply those tools. In Chapter 18, we'll talk about the extended Web publishing capabilities of Internet Information Server 4.0.

18

Web Publishing Enhancements
in IIS 4.0

It should come as no surprise that many of the most enticing features of IIS 4.0 are its Web publishing tools. In this chapter, we'll review the most significant ones.

Web Publishing Wizard

Web Publishing Wizard supports a number of WebPost Service Providers, such as CompuServe, Sprynet, and **Global Network Navigator (GNN)**. It includes its own WebPost Service Provider through which the Wizard can post pages to such popular Web servers as HTTPD from the National Center for Supercomputing Applications or NCSA; APACHE, the public domain Web server so widely used on UNIX platforms and indicated by many sources as the Web server with the largest installed base world-wide; and, of course, IIS. In a nutshell, the Web Publishing Wizard posts pages by connecting to an **Internet Service Provider (ISP)** or to an intranet, figuring out the appropriate protocol to use, and then uploading those files to a directory on the target machine.

Web Publishing Wizard Requirements

While the point we're about to make may seem self-evident, it's worth making anyway, since without this task, you may be unable to use Web Publishing Wizard.

Configure your Web browser appropriate to the type of remote host, and means of connecting, which will be presented when you upload pages. For example, if you're going to be publishing to a corporate intranet, set up the browser accordingly. Or, if uploading your pages means talking to an ISP, set up your browser to take that into account. Then test connectivity from the browser. If it can connect to the host to which you'll be publishing, Web Publishing Wizard will also be able to do so.

Starting Web Publishing Wizard

You can run Web Publishing Wizard in a couple of ways, but the more reliable is this:

1. Click **Start**

2. Click **Programs**

3. Click **Accessories**

4. Click **Internet Tools**

5. Double-click **Web Publishing Wizard**

Or, you can start the Wizard from NT Server, Workstation, or Windows 95 Explorer in this way:

1. Start **Explorer**

2. Pull down the **Tools** menu

3. Choose **Find**

4. Choose **Files or Folders**

5. Enter the string ***wpwiz*** in the text box search area

6. Click the application **Wpwiz** (see Figure 18.1)

Posting Idiosyncracies

Web Publishing Wizard can post files or directories to any ISP, as long as that provider is running a standards-based Web server that offers the FTP protocol. Even if the ISP through whom you wish to publish doesn't use a standard server, you can still post there, *if* the ISP maintains a posting information file named postinfo.html at the root URL of its Web server.

Figure 18.1 It's a bit roundabout, but this path still leads to Web Publishing Wizard.

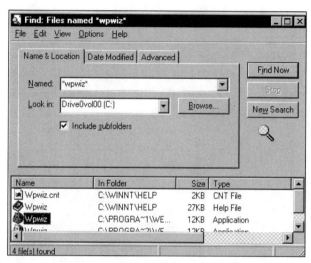

Web Publishing Wizard can even post through a proxy server. If your browser of choice is Internet Explorer 3.0 or later, make sure its proxy information is correctly configured by taking the following steps whose endpoint we show in Figure 18.2:

1. Right-Click the desktop's **Internet Explorer** icon

2. Click **Properties**

3. Click **Connections**

4. Click **Change proxy settings,** and make any needed corrections in the resulting display

If you're not using Internet Explorer, you must edit NT's registry by running **regedit.exe** and updating the key **HKEY_LOCAL_MACHINE\System\ CurrentControlSet\Services\WebPost\Providers** to include values like those shown in Figure 18.3.

Posting Acceptor

Posting Acceptor can be considered an analog and a successor to Web Publishing Wizard. Posting Acceptor is an add-on to IIS that allows you to use the **HTTP Post** protocol as part of providing a server-based Web publishing host to users who'd like to post Web content to your machine.

Figure 18.2 This page must be accessed if you're to post around a proxy server.

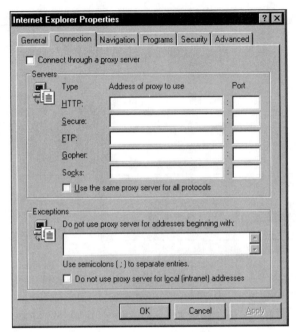

What Posting Acceptor Does

Posting Acceptor, which works not only with IIS 4.0 but also with Peer Web Services and Personal Web Server, accepts content from Web Publishing Wizard and from Netscape Navigator 2.02 or later; if that content comes to the Acceptor through a standard HTTP connection. In other words, Posting Acceptor acts as a surrogate recipient for IIS, taking in files from clients using either of the publishing tools just mentioned. Posting Acceptor can also work with a cluster of servers, as long as it is teamed up with Microsoft's **Content Replication Service**, or **CRS**.

When you install Posting Acceptor, you also install two sample pages, one of which acts as a template for content originating with Netscape Navigator, and the other that plays the same role for Internet Explorer. Then, when a client attempts an upload, an Active Server Pages file called **upload.asp** determines the type of browser that initiated the upload attempt, and directs that browser to the appropriate sample page. Table 18.1 summarizes this process as well as others through which Posting Acceptor does its work.

Figure 18.3 Here's an example of what the Registry wants to know before it will allow you to post around a proxy server.

```
"internetaccesstype"=hex:03,00,00,00

"ProxyServer"="http://proxyservername; ftp=ftp://ftpgateway"

"ProxyOverride"="<local>"
```

Table 18.1 Posting Acceptor's Components and Their Use

The Component	That Consists of	Does This
Active Server Pages file **upload.asp**	A file that determines the type of client browser and refers it to the appropriate content-uploading form.	Automatically refers the browser to **uploadX.asp** if the browser is ActiveX capable, or to **uploadN.asp** if it is not.
ActiveX Upload control **flupl.cab**	A control that can post content files, when the control is embedded in a Web page.	Allows users to drag and drop files and folders in order to upload them.
ASP PostInfo file **postinfo.asp**	A file used by Posting Acceptor to configure client browsers for posting content.	Holds the PostingURL and TargetURL that Posting Acceptor requires.
CRS Mapping Module **crsmapr.dll**	Content Replication Service module that maps target URLs to physical locations on a server's hard drive.	Gets URLs, and compares them with the target. If a match is found, the corresponding physical location on the server's hard drive is reported back to Posting Acceptor.
File System Mapping Module **cpshost.dll**	Another module that maps target URLs to physical locations on a hard drive.	Establishes a mapping between the target URL and the hard drive as a result of talking to IIS, Personal Web Server, or Peer Web Services.
Postinfo.eg	A file at the Web root of a server.	Acts as an example of a line that needs to be added to default.htm, that is, to a client's homepage, so that it can act as a PostInfo file.

Continued

Table 18.1 *Continued*

The Component	That Consists of	Does This
Posting Acceptor ISAPI **cpshost.dll**	An ISAPI module that is the keystone of Posting Acceptor.	Receives posted files and saves them to the indicated server target URL.
Sample page for clients using HTTP **uploadN.asp**	ASP file containing a form with HTTP Post fields.	Allows browsers based on the HTTP Post protocol to upload to a server running Posting Acceptor.
Sample page for clients using ActiveX to upload **uploadX.asp**	ASP file that holds the ActiveX Upload control flupl.cab.	Allows browsers that support ActiveX to talk to Posting Acceptor.

Background Functions

Posting Acceptor does a number of jobs in the background that are nonetheless important if not critical to Web page uploads. We'll review two of these behind-the-scenes tasks now.

Authenticating Publishers

Posting Acceptor will allow client publishing software to authenticate against your Web server through any of the authentication mechanisms supported by IIS or the two PWSs. What's more, if you've installed a Security Certificate on your Web server, content publishers can upload securely, because they, like your server, can make use of the **HyperText Transfer Protocol Secure**, or **HTTPS**. One caution here, though: In order to be able to upload via HTTPS, the client must itself be able to support the **Secure Sockets Layer**, or SSL, protocol family.

Processing After Receiving Posts

Posting Acceptor will allow you to perform backend or after-upload processing to content if you've configured it to make such processing available. That setup requires no more than editing the PostInfo file to define a post-processing URL. Posting Acceptor then accesses this secondary URL, which contains all upload-related information *except* the contents of Web page files sent by a client. The Posting Acceptor's stand-in module substitutes a list of locations and sizes of the content files that were just handed to your server. If no PostInfo file exists, you can still specify a post-receipt URL by adding it to the uploadN.asp sample page, after the PUBLISH keyword.

As part of any post-receipt processing, Posting Acceptor appends to any form-related data a request to post already contains, information on the locations to which each uploaded file was saved. For each such file, Posting Acceptor's back end is therefore aware of:

- **FileName**, in the form of the name of the original HTML page

- **FileExtension**, most frequently given as .htm

- **FilePath**, consisting of a value such as c:\testload\testfils

- **FileSize**, specified as an integer number of kilobytes, such as 32

Setting Up Posting Acceptor

Before installing Posting Acceptor, check Table 18.2. It outlines bare-bones minimums the Acceptor will need.

Table 18.2 Minimum Requirements for Posting Acceptor

In This Area	Installing Posting Acceptor Under Windows NT Server Requires	Installing Posting Acceptor Under Windows NT Workstation Requires	Installing Posting Acceptor Under Windows 95 Requires
CPU	486/33 or higher Intel processor, or Alpha RISC processor	486/33 or higher Intel processor or Alpha RISC processor compatible with Windows NT	386DX or higher Intel processor (486/33 or higher recommended)
RAM	16MB required, 64 recommended (by Microsoft, not us)	16MB required, 64 recommended	8MB required, 24 recommended (once again by Microsoft, not us)
Free Disk	10MB for Posting Acceptor itself, plus a reasonable amount for uploaded content	10MB for Posting Acceptor itself, plus a reasonable amount for uploaded content	10MB for Posting Acceptor itself, plus a reasonable amount for uploaded content

Continued

Table 18.2 *Continued*

In This Area	Installing Posting Acceptor Under Windows NT Server Requires	Installing Posting Acceptor Under Windows NT Workstation Requires	Installing Posting Acceptor Under Windows 95 Requires
Web Server	IIS 3.0 or later	Peer Web Services 3.0 or later	Personal Web Server 1.0a or later
Visual Controls	Active Server pages	Active Server pages	Active Server pages
Content Replication	Content Replication System recommended but not required by Microsoft	No content replication supported	No content replication supported

Once you've confirmed that your server meets these needs, you can, as you install and set up Posting Acceptor, fine-tune it to:

- Accept its default component directory locations, or allow you to specify your own

- Select the Target URL and Posting URL to which users will post

- Work with CRS

- Track outstanding posts, that is, posting requests for which the Acceptor still awaits receipt of content

Next, we'll talk about two of these tasks.

Choosing Target URLs and Posting URLs

Choosing these URLs is simple. For browsers, like Internet Explorer, that rely on the WebPost API, all you need do is modify the file **postinfo.asp** to accurately reflect the URLs you have in mind. And setting up these references for browsers like Netscape Navigator isn't any more difficult. In this case, just modify the file **uploadN.asp** file instead.

Table 18.3 A Quick Look at Posting Acceptor's Upload Controls

To Control This Posting Acceptor Parameter	You Must Set the Variable	Whose Default Value Is
The maximum number of outstanding posts the Acceptor will be allowed to have pile up	MaximumOpenTransactions	200 posts
The maximum amount of time a post request will be allowed to wool-gather, or to take to post its content	OpenTransactionsTimeout	600 seconds

Tracking Outstanding Posts

The folks who designed Posting Acceptor know a thing or two. They built in limitations on two of its parameters, which are intended to help keep a large number, or a few very large, outstanding posts from devouring your Web server. Table 18.3 sketches these parameters, each of which can be edited in the Registry, and presents their default values.

To tweak either of these parameters, open, and edit as appropriate to your environment, the registry key **HKLM\Software\Microsoft\WebPost\Acceptors\CPSHost.**

Performance Monitor Counters

Posting Acceptor passes only one object to NT Server's Performance Monitor. This single object, however, holds several counters. We've outlined these, and the information they can give on Posting Acceptor performance, in Table 18.4.

Table 18.4 Performance Monitor Counters Originating in Posting Acceptor

This Counter	Represents
Bytes Received/Sec	Number of bytes received by Posting Acceptor per second
Current Posts	Number of posts currently being processed by Posting Acceptor
Failed Posts/Sec	Percentage per second of posting requests that do not complete successfully

Continued

Table 18.4 *Continued*

This Counter	Represents
Files Received/Sec	Number per second of successfully received content files
Maximum Posts	Maximum number of posts during the entire time Posting Acceptor has been active
Posts Received/Sec	Average number of posts received per second
Re-posts/Sec	Average number of re-posts per second
Successful Posts/Sec	Average number of successful posts per second
Total Bytes Received	Total number of bytes received since Posting Acceptor has been active
Total Failed Posts	Total number of failed posts since Posting Acceptor has been active
Total Files Received	Total number of content files received since Posting Acceptor has been active
Total Posts Received	Total number of posting requests since Posting Acceptor has been active
Total Re-posts Done	Total number of re-posts since Posting Acceptor has been active
Total Successful Posts	Total number of successful initial posts since Posting Acceptor has been active
Unresolved Posts	Total number of posts awaiting commitment by the client since Posting Acceptor has been active

Posting Acceptor and Event Viewer

Posting Acceptor isn't as chatty with NT Server's Event Viewer as it is with Performance Monitor. Logs created by Event Viewer record only:

- What error or warning the posting attempt generated, if any

- What URL was given as the target for the posting attempt

- Which client and user attempted to post

Script Debugger

IIS 4.0's Script Debugger, whose main window we've depicted in Figure 18.4, lets you locate and correct script errors by allowing you to change the values of script variables and properties, control script execution, and discover and deal with script errors in several ways.

In the remainder of this section, we'll examine each of these capabilities more closely. We'll pay particular attention to how Script Debugger carries out tried-and-true debugging techniques like working with breakpoints, stepping through source code, and more.

Changing Values

Script Debugger works with scripts that are executing, not merely with static source code. For this reason, any script parameters that you change while the Debugger is running will be immediately reflected in a real-world way; that is, in how the script performs as it continues to execute.

Figure 18.4 Nothing's running at the moment, but Script Debugger is still on the alert.

Only one window is involved in either viewing, or viewing and modifying, values in a running script. Script Debugger's Command window is all you'll need to do either job.

Controlling Program Execution

The most common way of controlling program execution within any debugger is to set breakpoints, or points in the script's execution at which the debugging tool will automatically step in. IIS's Script Debugger is no exception. When you set breakpoints within a script that the Debugger is sifting through, the line of code that holds that breakpoint appears in red in the editing window.

At every breakpoint you define in this way, Script Debugger will pause execution of the script and ask you if, and in what way, you'd like to execute the individual lines that make up the remainder of your script. Most frequently, programmers walk through code modules line by line when running a debugger; Script Debugger makes this technique available. And as you step through the lines of your script that follow the breakpoint, Script Debugger displays the results of the execution of each line.

Discovering and Dealing with Errors

Not all scripting languages will react in the same way to the same parameter or condition. For example, VBScript strongly dislikes attempts to divide by zero, and produces an error if you try to do so. JScript, on the other hand, will overlook such illogic. The way in which Scripting Debugger is enabled can affect its results, too. For instance, if a server script in whatever language contains a runtime error, and debugging has not been enabled for that application, any error messages generated will be sent to the client browser. While it is possible to identify or, in the parlance of programming, trap errors by means of statements embedded within scripts, it's easier to do so through Script Debugger.

Script Debugger, like all such tools and for fairly obvious reasons, is most effective at nosing out *logic errors*. Let's go back to Programming 101 for a moment and review just what we mean by that phrase.

A logic error is what's happened when a script has run to completion but has produced nonsense, or at least results that you know cannot be accurate. For instance, any script that is supposed to check user input against the series of prime numbers (numbers that can be evenly divided only by themselves or by 1) and refuse to accept user entries outside this set of integers, but allows a user to key in, and accepts as valid a value like 4, most likely has a logic error in it. Such scripts are prime candidates for Script Debugger. The Debugger will, however, use differing methods to point out the errors it finds. If it locates an error in a server script, Script Debugger will display the line number in the error message it generates. This line number corresponds to the line in the ASP page that contains the error. Errors in the ASP files of client scripts, on the other hand, cause Script Debugger not to point out line numbers from that ASP file, but rather to indicate a line number in the HTML output of the ASP page. So, before you can completely corner client-side errors, you'll have to use the client browser to look at the HTML source for the page in question.

Even Script Debugger can't catch everything. For instance, some functions and objects, like VBScript's record set object, can return values that are inaccurate because they have been affected by some related process, such as a database server. SQL Server is one example; it sometimes does not return useful values when used in conjunction with certain properties of the record set object. So, despite our blanket endorsement of Script Debugger at the beginning of this section, any script that manipulates this object might be more easily debugged by embedding code such as that shown in Figure 18.5.

Choosing a Script to Debug

Among the many useful aspects of Script Debugger is its ability to comb through scripts for any document currently being displayed by Internet Explorer, or any other ActiveX debugging host. But Script Debugger can't read your mind; you'll have to tell it which script you want it to examine. Here's how to do so:

Figure 18.5 This is actually pseudocode, but we think you'll understand its intent.

```
Do While Not RecordSet.EOF

' As long as the end of the record set hasn't been reached   ...

' Do whatever error trapping you have in mind.

RecordSet.MoveNext

' Then move on to the next record in the set.

Loop

' Finally, repeat the whole sequence until you reach the end of the set.
```

1. Pull down Internet Explorer's **View** menu.

2. Click **Running Documents** to see a list of applications currently running.

3. Click the name of the application you want to debug from the drop-down list.

4. Click the **plus sign** next to the application name if you need to see a list of open documents for that application.

5. Double-click a document name to open it and begin debugging.

Setting Breakpoints and Stepping through a Script

We discussed the value of breakpoints in the section *Controlling Program Execution* earlier in this chapter. Now let's talk about what you must do to set those points.

1. If the document you need to debug contains a client script, you must first display the document in Internet Explorer, and then choose **Source** from Explorer's **View** menu.

2. If the document you want to clean up holds a server script, you must start Script Debugger as a standalone application before carrying out the step just outlined.

3. In either case, once you're running Script Debugger, put your insertion point *within* the line that you want to specify as a breakpoint.

4. Pull down Script Debugger's **Debug** menu.

5. Click **Toggle Breakpoint**.

The next thing you should see is the line you just indicated displayed in red. Now, to use this breakpoint, you can either:

1. Do something like click a button in Internet Explorer in order to restart the script you're debugging, if you're dealing with a client script.

2. Refresh the document in the browser, if it's a server script you are working with.

Once you've taken whichever of these steps is appropriate, Script Debugger will allow execution of the script to proceed, but will pause at the first breakpoint found, thereby letting you walk through the remainder of the script one line at a time.

To step through a script, choose one of the commands shown in Table 18.5 from that same **Debug** menu.

Table 18.5 Debugger "Walk-Through" Commands

This Command	Causes Script Debugger to
Step Into	Move to the next line of the script, including those contained in any module called by that next line
Step Out	Stop stepping through a procedure before reaching its end
Step Over	Skip procedures indicated (these are still executed, however)

Clearing Breakpoints

While all breakpoints in a script are cleared automatically when you reload that script, be it client or server, to Internet Explorer, you may on occasion want to clear just one breakpoint. Here's how to go about it:

1. Place the insertion point in the line (make sure it's displayed in red) that you wish to remove from breakpoint status.

2. Pull down Debugger's **Debug** menu.

3. Click **Toggle Breakpoint**.

   You should now see the line in question in the normal color for its font.

   Clearing all breakpoints manually is even easier. Just pull down the **Debug** menu and click **Clear All Breakpoints**.

Viewing the Call Stack

Viewing the call stack, that is, looking at the list that Script Debugger maintains of all procedures, functions, and other code modules that are executing at any given point during the running of a script, can help you trace what happens as that script wends its way through a series of nested procedures. You can also use the call stack to navigate within a script to a specific procedure, in order to take a shortcut to setting breakpoints there, changing variable values there, and so on.

   Here are the steps to take to view the call stack:

1. Pull down Internet Explorer's **View** menu.

2. Click **Call Stack**.

   Once the call stack is displayed, you need only to double-click the name of the procedure to which you want to jump.

> **TIP** Be aware that using the call stack to navigate to another procedure has no effect on the line from which you jumped off. Even setting a breakpoint or variable value in the procedure to which you jump may not affect the script's overall execution, since that execution, once you restart it after setting the breakpoint or value, will pick up from the line you leaped from, rather than the line you jumped to. In similar fashion and for much the same reason, the context of a script may remain unchanged if you hop back and forth between modules, regardless of what you set between hops.

From Here

In Chapter 19, we'll proceed from examining the Web publishing tools presented by IIS 4.0 to investigating its schemes for keeping what you publish secure, when we look into Internet Authentication Server.

Internet
Authentication Server

The more successful your network and Internet or intranet site are at serving the needs of your users, the more users you will have, and the greater your concern for security will become. Particularly in situations in which a large number of users access your site by a dial-up connection, you'll want to do everything you can not only to ensure that connections are secure, but that users don't employ then as springboards to areas of your site in which they don't belong. Internet Information Server 4.0 provides you with tools that allow you to closely monitor dial-up connections and the nature of sessions conducted across them. These tools are bundled under the label **Internet Authentication Server (IAS)**.

Know immediately, though, that IAS requires that any ISP with which it interacts supports the **Remote Access Dial-In User Services** protocol, or **RADIUS**. Indeed, IAS itself relies on RADIUS to carry out the authentication, access authorization, and accounting of users who connect to an organization's intranet through a remote dial-in.

RADIUS rests on two concepts:

Network Access Servers (**NAS devices**), which are server platforms whose responsibility it is to communicate with end users attempting dial-in access. NAS devices are also clients of Internet Authorization Server.

Point to Point Tunneling Protocol, or **PPTP**, running on the RAS, which takes in a user's initial authentication request, restructures it into a packet RADIUS will understand, and then forwards it to Internet Authentication Server.

IAS, as we've shown in Figure 19.1, compares user identification information forwarded to it by a NAS device against its own database to verify a user password. If the password is correct, IAS sends a message back to the NAS, called an ACCESS-ACCEPT packet, telling the NAS to allow the user onto the network. If the password is incorrect, an ACCESS-REJECT packet is sent instead, and the user is disconnected automatically and immediately.

An ACCESS-ACCEPT packet does more than just allow a user in the front door. It also tells a NAS device what access privileges are to be allotted to the user in question. IAS can authorize users for specific protocols, specific services such as host logon facilities, or specific network addresses. NAS devices then handle the nuts and bolts of restricting users to those protocols, services, and addresses.

Figure 19.1 Only those user access attempts that have been verified by IAS cause it to tell a NAS device to allow the user on board.

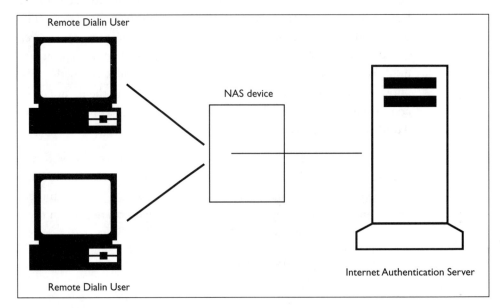

Remote Dialin User

NAS device

Internet Authentication Server

Remote Dialin User

NAS devices and IAS have one other type of conversation. At the beginning and end of each dial-up session, a NAS will send accounting information to IAS, which, while it can vary depending upon who manufactured the NAS device, will include such information as:

- IP address assigned to the user

- Number of characters or packets the user transferred, in either direction

- Username

- User session time

Private Networking

Authentication, authorization, and accounting of users are nowhere more important than within an organization's private network. Housing critical and sensitive information as it does, such a network must be provided extensive abilities in these areas. For this reason, IAS was designed to act as an organization's security back end to Internet-based, end-to-end access. Because IAS, like all of Internet Information Server, is so closely interwoven with Windows NT, and in particular with NT's security features, it can protect an organization's data very effectively. What's more, IAS can be configured to interact with other members of Microsoft's security suite, known as the **Internet Remote Access System**, or **IRAS**, to tighten security even further.

For example, it is through interaction with Windows NT Server's own user authentication schemes that IAS decides who to welcome in and who to turn away; information in the Domain controller tips this balance one way or the other. Or, in a slightly different scenario, an organization's ISP can, through its own RADIUS implementation, tailor user access. For example, IAS can permit User A to dial in to an environment, but not to dial out, or to dial out only at specified times or to specific sites, thereby preventing recreational Web surfing.

IAS's use of PPTP adds yet another layer of security to dial-in access. PPTP also authenticates a user against the NT Domain controller, and can be configured to encrypt traffic between the remote client from which the user logs on, and IAS/NT.

TIP IAS can be set up to capture such information into a log.

Such encryption can even prevent the ISP through which a user accesses your network from knowing anything about such sessions. IAS can interact with ISPs in one more interesting and useful way. It can capture accounting information from the ISP and use that information to track network usage.

How IAS Works: The Request/Authentication Sequence

Let's provide a little more detail about how IAS does its job. When a user connects to a NAS, the user of course will provide it an ID such as *petrovsk@voicenet.net*. This ID-bearing access request travels through the NAS at the ISP to IAS or another RADIUS server at the ISP, which:

- Reads the user ID

- Verifies that it is valid in environment X

- Forwards the access attempt to IAS at environment X, which then checks the request against its user database, in our example's NT Server's domain database

At the NT Domain Controller stage of this process, username and password must match *exactly* against a record in NT's user database. For instance, if a username should match, but not the password entered with it, IAS won't think twice. It will send an ACCESS-REJECT message to the requesting NAS device, and then simply throw away the access request.

Internet Remote Access System

IAS, whose console we've illustrated in Figure 19.2, is, as mentioned earlier, a member of a larger category of Internet security software known as the **Internet Remote Access System** (**IRAS**). In addition to IAS, IRAS includes:

> **Connection Point Services**, or **CPS**, which is made up of **Connection Point Server** and **Connection Point Administration**. Connection Point Server automates the updating of remote users' access IDs and of the types of network services they may use. Connection Point Administration manages such information.

> **Connection Manager Administration Kit**, or **CMAK**, includes a dialer utility, and a wizard through which customized versions of Connection Manager can be created for clients' NT Workstation 4.0 or Windows 95.

Figure 19.2 This unassuming console screen is IAS's window on your network.

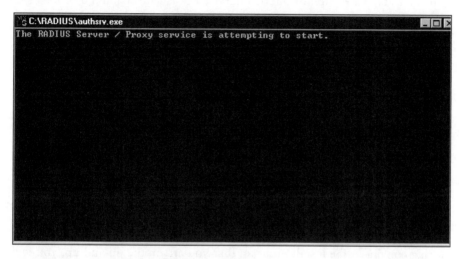

Site Setup and Its Effect on IAS

While it's very good at what it does and very thorough, IAS, like all software, can be circumvented or even hacked. Therefore, some common-sense precautions are in order for your IAS implementation.

In order to prevent its being hacked into, IAS should be installed on a machine completely dedicated to acting as a RADIUS server. Further, this machine should be physically isolated from all but its administrators. Finally, the ability to lock the IAS server, both through software and physical means (such as a plain old key on the keyboard or power switch), will also help to ensure that the server is secure.

Internet Authorization Server System Requirements, Installation, and Configuration

IAS has installation requirements quite similar to those of IIS 4.0's other significant features. It needs:

- At least 14MB free space on a hard drive for installation files only

- At least 10MB on that drive for its runtime use

- Windows NT Server version 4.0 or higher

- Service Pack 3 or later

- The non-HTML version of Internet Service Manager, version 3.0 or later

At least with the beta 2 release of IIS 4.0, installing Internet Authorization Server is not included as part of the overall setup utility and Wizard. You must load IAS separately. Here's what's involved.

Double-click the appropriate, that is, the ix86 or \alpha, version of the link Internet Authorization Server setup in the Install screen of the release CD. Figure 19.3 shows this display.

The next thing you'll see is a cautioning message, reminding you that you're dealing with sensitive data, as Figure 19.4 illustrates.

After clicking OK on this screen, you are presented with another request for confirmation of your wish to copy IAS's files (see Figure 19.5).

Having convinced the install program that you are on the up-and-up, you will briefly see an introductory screen like that shown in Figure 19.6.

Figure 19.3 Perhaps because of its own need for security, IAS installation is segregated from that of IIS 4.0 at large.

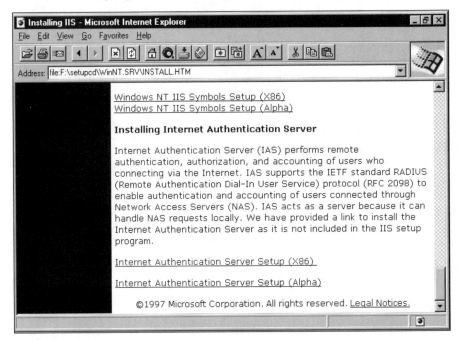

Figure 19.4 Apparently even CDs can't be assumed to be bug- or virus-free.

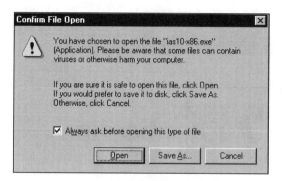

Next, you'll see another Welcome screen, but one with a twist. As Figure 19.7 shows, this screen cautions you to exit all applications before proceeding with the installation of IAS; we assume because that installation references existing network setup information, and might therefore disrupt any applications drawing on that information.

We've illustrated in Figure 19.8 the last significant bit of information you have to supply to IAS's installation procedure: your name and affiliation. After feeding this information to the program, it should run smoothly and quickly to completion, even asking if you want to start the server's administrative arm immediately.

The IAS run time includes not only the IAS server that communicates with NAS devices, but also the administrative tool just mentioned, called **Internet Authentication Service Properties (IASP)**, by means of which IAS must be configured and can be administered. IASP is a visually based tool that allows you to define a number of the server's characteristics, such as:

- Client settings, that is, the RADIUS and NAS devices to which IAS will connect

- Logging settings, which enable or disable IAS accounting, define the intervals at which IAS will generate a log, and specify where that log will be stored

Figure 19.5 IAS's installation routine wants to be sure.

Figure 19.6 NT, your computer (our's is a Pentium), and the IAS installation routine are all quick enough to keep this screen on your monitor for only about three seconds.

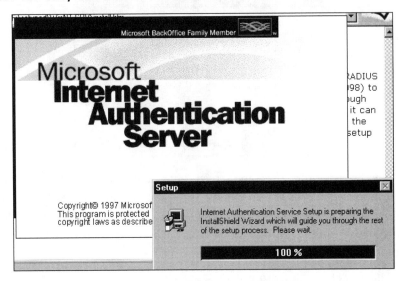

Figure 19.7 Note the caution in the center of this display.

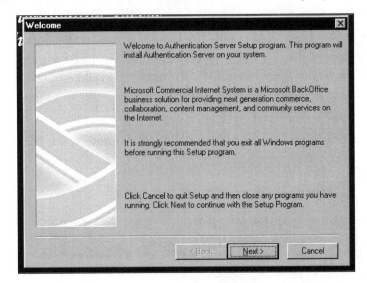

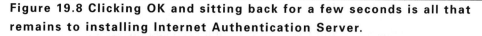

Figure 19.8 Clicking OK and sitting back for a few seconds is all that remains to installing Internet Authentication Server.

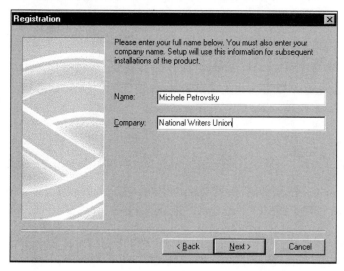

- Profiles, the sets of user characteristics that include authorization and access parameters

- Service settings, a more down-on-the-metal set of guidelines that lay out the maximum number of threads IAS will support, the RADIUS port numbers it will use, and the specific events it will pass to the NT Event Log

After you install IAS, you must set up its console (illustrated in Figure 19.2) to take in authentication requests from clients (that is, from NAS devices) and either forward them to a RADIUS or IAS server at an ISP, or authenticate them locally. This configuration doesn't take place at the console itself; it must be done through the Internet Authentication Service Properties dialog. Here's an overview of what's involved in this setup:

1. Open Internet Authentication Service Properties.

2. Set authentication service properties.

3. Register NAS clients of IAS.

4. Create RADIUS profiles for those clients.

5. Set up the logging service.

6. After you're satisfied with IAS's configuration, stop and then restart the server in order to lock in its characteristics.

In order to carry out these tasks, you'll need to have a good deal of information at the ready, including:

• The IP address or DNS name, and password, of all NAS devices and ISP RADIUS servers to which IAS will connect

• Whether or not such ISPs can transfer accounting information to IAS

• Whether or not such ISPs use the default RADIUS UDP port numbers

• Whether or not these ISPs have the ability to strip prefixes and suffixes from usernames before forwarding those names to IAS

• Whether or not these ISPs require that specific RADIUS attributes be assigned to dial-in users accessing your IAS through their RADIUS service

• Whether or not your IAS server has appropriate privileges within the NT domain of which it is a member to allow it to authenticate dial-in users against the NT user database for that domain

Now, let's flesh out our sketch of what is needed to configure IAS:

1. Open Internet Authentication Service Properties.

2. Set authentication service properties to include the RADIUS UDP port numbers supplied by ISPs.

3. Register the ISP's RADIUS servers as NAS devices, that is, as clients of IAS.

4. Ensure that RADIUS profiles for those clients include any details of operation that IAS requires, such as stripping prefixes from usernames.

5. Set up the logging service to include those events you wish Event Viewer and its logs to capture and reflect.

6. After you're satisfied with IAS's configuration, stop and then restart the server in order to lock in its characteristics.

IAS Service Properties

The Service page of IAS Properties displays and allows you to change the basic parameters outlined in Table 19.1.

Registering NAS Clients with IAS

The Clients page of IAS Properties displays and allows you to change the characteristics outlined in Table 19.2.

RADIUS Profiles and IAS Logs

IAS's Properties Profiles tab lets you view or change profiles for individuals or groups of users, and to define those profiles as sets of RADIUS attributes. IAS provides sample profiles as a means of acquainting you with the RADIUS characteris-

---

> **TIP** At the time this book was being written, the most recently defined RADIUS defaults were given in RFC 1812 for authentication, and RFC1813 for accounting.

Table 19.1 IAS Service Properties and Their Values

This Property	Should Be Set to
Maximum Threads	The maximum number of concurrent authentication requests that you want IAS to handle; must be a value between 10 and 63.
Authentication	The port number to be used by your RADIUS authentication services, if different from the default.
Accounting	The port number to be used by your RADIUS accounting services, if different from the default.
Capture to NT Event Log	Have packet traffic that you wish to be informed of through Event Viewer checked; these include: • Malformed (incorrectly structured) packets • Authentication packets, made up of authentication requests, access approvals, and access denials • Accounting packets, made up of requests for and approval or denial of the forwarding of accounting information

Table 19.2 IAS Client Properties and Their Values

This Property	Should Be Set to
IP Address	That of the NAS device that you're identifying to IAS
DNS Name	That of the NAS device that you're identifying to IAS
Password	That of the NAS device that you're identifying to IAS

> **TIP** The passwords mentioned in Table 19.2 are often referred to in IAS documentation as *shared secrets*.

tics of common network configurations. Modifying these or your own home-grown profiles is simple; you need only click the **Profiles** tab, choose **PPP**, and click **Edit**.

IAS's Logging Service is also simple to set up. All you need to do is click the **Logging** tab, check or uncheck **Enable accounting log** as appropriate, and if you care to, define the size at which an existing log file will be closed and a new one created, as well as the file subsystem in which IAS logs will live. In other words, you set up IAS logging as you do all NT logging. We've set up Table 19.3 to sketch part of the structure of IAS logs.

The remaining fields in an IAS log record like that shown in Figure 19.9 represent parameters like packet counts for the various packet categories we presented in Table 19.3.

Table 19.3 IAS Log Parameters

A Value like	Which Can Occur in These Log Fields	Represents
207.67.131.21	1st or 7th	The IP address of a NAS device client
10/06/97	2nd	The date the record was written to the log
05:25:41	3rd	The time (in military time) the record was written to the log
AuthSrv	4th	The type of RADIUS server running; most probably will always equal AuthSrv, NT's shorthand for *Internet Authentication Server*
RADIUS	5th	The type of authentication proxy running

Figure 19.9 IAS packs a lot of information into each record in its log.

```
207.67.131.61,03/13/1997,07:37:03,AuthSrv,RADIUS,4,207.68.137.62,5,10,61,0,1,40,2
,45,1,6,7,44,00000001,46,30,41,0
```

Starting and Stopping Internet Authentication Server

You can start or stop IAS from either Internet Service Manager or from Windows NT Server Manager. These steps, the first two of which we've illustrated in Figure 19.10, will stop IAS from NT:

1. Click **Start.**
2. Click **Programs.**
3. Choose **Administrative Tools (Common).**
4. Double-click **Server Manager.**
5. Select the NT server with which IAS is affiliated.
6. Pull down the Manager's **Computer** menu.
7. Click **Services.**
8. Choose **RADIUS Server/Proxy.**
9. Click **Stop.**

In similar fashion, you can use NT Server tools to configure Internet Authentication Server to start automatically. Just follow these steps:

1. Click **Start.**
2. Choose **Programs,** then **Administrative Tools.**
3. Double-click **Server Manager.**
4. Pull down the **Computer** menu and choose **Select Domain.**
5. Identify the domain with which IAS is affiliated.
6. Choose the computer on which IAS is installed.
7. Once again on the **Computer** menu, click **Services.**
8. Select **RADIUS Server/Proxy** and click **Startup.**

Figure 19.10 You can stop or start IAS from these windows.

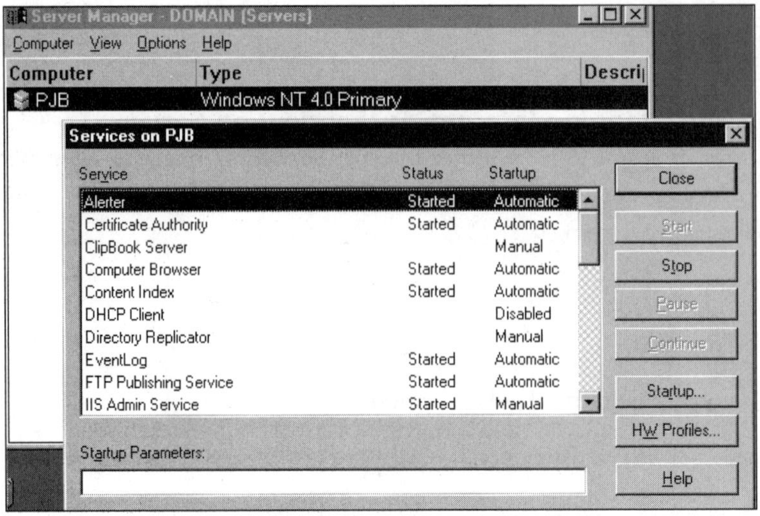

9. For **Startup Type,** check **Automatic.**

10. For **Log On As,** check **System Account** and **Allow Service to Interact with Desktop.**

That's all there is to it.

Common Communication Problems

Communications between IAS and its RADIUS or NAS clients can fail. If they do, it's often because of inconsistencies in how the two parties to the electronic conversation handle shared passwords, or username prefixes and suffixes. In this section, we'll review examples of such problems, and offer solutions to them.

Shared Passwords

Every pair of RADIUS clients and servers share a password, also sometimes called a *shared secret*, which must be identical on both the client and the server. If such passwords don't match, neither authentication nor accounting packets will be accepted by either member of the client/server pair. Therefore, you must take great care in setting up such passwords. In this context, it's especially important to remember that they are case sensitive.

```
User1@large.org

new.user1@large.org
```

Prefixes and Suffixes

Communication between RADIUS clients and a RADIUS server like IAS will fail if the client does not remove, or does not properly represent, prefixes or suffixes from usernames. The RADIUS server uses these names to authenticate the user. Therefore, as was the case with shared passwords, missing, unnecessary, or incorrect username prefixes and suffixes, like those in Figure 19.11, can cause a user to be denied access without an obvious reason.

Event Viewer Error Messages

Table 19.4 summarizes two of the most common Event Viewer IAS-related error messages, and suggests solutions to the problems they represent.

IAS Error Messages

Table 19.5 outlines IAS error messages and what you can do about them.

Table 19.4 Common IAS Errors as Seen by Event Viewer

The Message	Indicates	And Can Be Dealt with By
An error occurred while processing file USERS. The system cannot find the file specified.	The USERS file, which must be present if IAS is to run at all, and which is contained in the file Adminui.mdb, cannot be found	Checking and if need be correcting IAS configuration information, and then stopping and restarting IAS
An error occurred while processing line *n* of file CLIENTS: Address Expected.	A client with an incorrect DNS name in the Clients IAS Properties page	Either correcting the DNS name or specifying the client's IP address

Table 19.5 Common IAS-Generated Error Messages

The Message	Indicates	And Can Be Dealt with By
Service property changes have been applied and will take effect next time the authentication service is started.	Configuration changes to the IAS database have been saved, but the files that the server reads have not been updated	Stopping and restarting IAS
The log file directory is invalid. Please enter a valid log file directory.	You've asked IAS to place its logs in a directory that doesn't exist (it won't create directories)	Resubmitting the request for log file storage, using an existing directory
A current password is required. Please enter a current password.	A mismatch between RADIUS server and client passwords or *shared secrets*	Correcting the passwords, and then stopping and restarting IAS
An IP address must contain numbers between 0 and 255.	An IP address supplied to IAS has a component outside this range in one of its four octets	Pinging the machine you're trying to reach to determine if the IP address is correct

From Here

In the next (and last) chapter, we'll take a look at Transaction Server, Internet Information Server 4.0's application distribution arm.

20

Transaction Server

Transaction Server, the IIS 4.0 tool responsible for developing, deploying, and managing server applications, includes a number of components:

- Application programming interface

- Explorer-based user interface

- Resource dispensers

- Runtime environment

We'll review all these features in this last chapter.

Transaction Server's Architecture

Transaction Server is built upon a highly modular paradigm. In this section, we'll take a look at the Server's most important feature categories.

Application Components

Microsoft has designed Transaction Server application components to be **Common Object Module,** or **COM,** in-process server modules implemented as **Dynamic Linked Libraries (DLLs).**

> **TIP** For *in-process*, substitute *running in relationship to some other module.*

What's the bottom line? Basically, since Transaction Server components are managed by the Server, which automatically takes care of such factors as concurrent execution, context discovery and tracking, resource distribution and sharing, and security, you're free to develop your application as if it had your Web server platform entirely to itself. Because Transaction Server converses and interacts with other related servers such as those dishing out databases and system or network resources, the Server can guarantee that any transactions your application puts out will, without regard to any others that are running concurrently:

- Be handled as atomic transactions, that is, be isolated from other executing requests

- Be handled consistently, that is, according to defined parameters such as priority of execution

- Be committed in such a way as to produce durable changes, or changes in, for example, a database, which are executed and locked in at the moment of submitting a transaction

Transaction Server Executive

Transaction Server's Executive is another DLL, one that supplies runtime services to Server and application components. Since we're dealing with a Server that in effect nit-picks the details of execution of an application, the Executive's tasks heavily emphasize memory and other server resource management; for example including handling all aspects of the thread and object context requirements of transaction-based applications. Just as easy to understand, if you give it a moment's thought, is the fact that Transaction Server's Executive runs in the background.

> **TIP** As a mnemonic, think of *durable changes* as not only placing a key in a lock, but turning the key as well. In transaction-based application programming and database terms, a durable change is one that is carried out immediately and fully, rather than, for instance, waiting until a database table is closed to update it with values that have, until that point, been cached or buffered.

Server Processes

A Transaction Server *server process* in some way contributes to the execution of one or more application components. Such processes, for example, the verification of database access rights, can simultaneously sustain dozens or hundreds of clients, in this case meaning requests from application components. Transaction Server allows you to set up multiple server processes on a single Transaction Server platform, with each such process representing unique sets of privileges, error management parameters, and so on. This ability of Transaction Server, not only to walk and chew gum, but also to hum a tune and listen to music at the same time, means that your applications need not concern themselves with any common ground or lack thereof in server resource distribution or application performance requirements. Transaction Server takes care of such factors by allowing you to load its processes or components into other applications such as SQL Server, into client processes, or simply to run them autonomously.

Resource Dispensers and Resource Managers

Transaction Server resource dispensers are services that manage nondurable shared state of the application components within a process. In English, this means that resource dispensers distribute and track the usage of and need for such temporary circumstances of an application's execution as the value currently present in a text entry box of a Web page. Transaction Server makes two resource dispensers available: the ODBC resource dispenser and the Shared Property Manager.

The ODBC resource dispenser is actually the ODBC 3.0 Driver Manager. Whatever you want to call it, this resource dispenser, automatically loaded when Transaction Server is installed, manages database connections for Transaction Server components that talk to ODBC databases. This dispenser does its job by keeping pools of database connections available, so as to be able to supply those connections to application objects as quickly and efficiently as possible. The ODBC resource dispenser automatically associates connections with an object and its transactions, and just as automatically reclaims and redistributes those connections when a given process no longer needs them.

Transaction Server's Shared Property Manager, rather than providing and tracking the allocation of transitory use of server resources, instead offers synchronized access to application-defined, but process-wide, variables. So, one example of what Shared Property Manager does is the maintenance of a Web browser's visits history.

Unlike its resource dispensers, Transaction Server's resource managers are services that distribute and monitor durable data, that is, data that at one point or another has spent or will spend time on a hard drive rather than only in memory. Examples of such data might, in a community college's case, include:

- A record of all courses in which a given student has enrolled, either during the current semester or in past ones

- A record of all courses that a given student has completed, either during the current semester or in past ones

- A record of all grades in all courses that a given student has received in past semesters

Transaction Server's resource managers don't work alone, however, but rather operate in conjunction with Distributed Transaction Coordinator to provide an application with atomic, isolated transactions. Transaction Server can also work with external resource managers such as SQL Server version 6.5, or any resource manager that uses the OLE Transactions protocol.

Distributed Transaction Coordinator

While not, in the strictest sense, a part of Transaction Server, the **Distributed Transaction Coordinator**, or **DTC**, is important to it. DTC, which was initially released as part of SQL Server, coordinates transactions, allowing them to be executed as atomic; that is, as unique and autonomous, even if they draw upon multiple resources, resource managers, or even server platforms. DTC uses a two-phase commit protocol, in effect checking first before finally executing a transaction, and thereby ensuring that the result of the transaction will, when made available to resource managers, be correct and consistent regardless of which manager is looking at that result. If, for example, a particular transaction is, for whatever reason, aborted, all resource managers, rather than only those directly involved in the unsuccessful attempt, will immediately be aware not only of the failure but also of the parameters presented by the transaction after that failure.

Hardware and Software Requirements

To run Microsoft Transaction Server, you must, according to Microsoft, meet certain hardware and software requirements, which include:

- A CD-ROM drive

- A minimum of 30MB free space on the hard drive, to cover full installation of Transaction Server

- A Windows NT-compatible computer

- Any display supported by Windows NT version 4.0

- At least 32MB of memory

- SQL Server, version 6.5 or later, or another ODBC-compatible database and database driver

- Visual Basic, Enterprise Edition, version 4.0 or later; or Visual C++, version 4.1 or later with the **Active Template Libraries** (**ATL**) version 1.1 or later, as well as the Win32 SDK; or the Java Virtual Machine installed with Microsoft Internet Explorer 3.01 or later, as well as Visual J++ 1.0 or later

- Windows NT version 4.0 or higher

That's what the folks in Redmond say you'll need to be successful in loading and using Transaction Server. Now, here are our more real-world recommendations. (Any item that appears in the previous list but not in the following list has passed muster with us.)

- At least an 8-speed CD-ROM drive

- A minimum of 50MB free space on the hard drive to cover full installation of Transaction Server and to avoid working too close to the edge, so to speak

- A Windows NT-compatible computer that is at least a 133MHz Pentium

- Any display supported by Windows NT version 4.0

- At least 48MB RAM (remember what it is your server platform will be doing with Transaction Server)

TIP If you want to make Transaction Server available to Windows 95 clients, you'll also need to load DCOM for Windows 95 on those clients.

> **TIP** Be aware that, in order to validate your installation of Transaction Server, you must, during that installation, load the files referred to by Setup as pertaining to Transaction Server Development. Also be aware that, if you're just taking Transaction Server out for a spin, uninstalling it will automatically also unload *all* user-defined packages the Server has created and managed.

Runtime Environment

Transaction Server's run time addresses not only application development and deployment, but also the management of distributed applications. The runtime offers services like:

- Automatic management of processes and threads

- Control of distributed transactions (defined as units of work that are atomic, that is, that either succeed or fail as a whole)

- Distributed security for the control of the invocation and use of objects

- Graphical user interface

- Object and object instance management

Transaction Server asks only one thing in return for all these tools: It must be associated with an application capable of producing and using ActiveX **Dynamic-Link Libraries,** or **DLLs.** What this means is that you've got Visual Basic, Visual C++, Visual J++, and more available to you as development tools. In similar fashion, Transaction Server can interact with many relational database systems, file systems, and document storage paradigms, thereby making it possible to include, for instance, Oracle and Access databases, as well as FAT and NTFS files, in the same application.

Transaction Server Explorer

Like all 32-bit Windows Explorers, that belonging to Transaction Server allows you to view tree-based listings of, and even manipulate, all files under Transaction Server's control. In other words, if a file exists anywhere in Transaction Server's runtime environment, the Server's Explorer will lead you to it and allow you to manage it.

Once again, like its fellow Explorers, Transaction Server's file manager displays its collection of files in its left pane. The Explorer's Status window can simultaneously present you with usage information for any component in any application you've implemented and distributed. Finally, you can use the Transaction Statistics window to obtain summary statistics about recently executed transactions.

Transaction Server APIs

While it is intended to develop and deploy server-based applications, Transaction Server can still, to some extent, handle those applications built and run on a client. Such applications must, however, access Transaction Server objects in an out-of-the-ordinary way.

Client applications that will run outside Transaction Server's runtime environment must use standard COM APIs, such as CoCreateInstance in Visual C++, to call upon Transaction Server objects. In addition, client applications can use the Server's TransactionContext interface to combine one or more Transaction Server objects into an atomic transaction, commit an atomic transaction, and abort an atomic transaction.

As you might expect, developing server-based components, which to Transaction Server means modules that will be registered and will run from the Transaction Server runtime environment, gives you many more coding, execution, and management options, including:

- **ObjectContext,** which allows you to prevent a transaction from being committed or declare that it has completed; to instantiate other Transaction Server objects or to include those objects within the current object's transaction; and even to ascertain if, and which, security measures have been enabled.

- **ObjectControl,** which allows you to specify whether Transaction Server should recycle objects rather than successively constructing and then destroying them.

- **SecurityProperty,** which allows you to determine which other module has called, or created, the current object.

Let's talk a little further about these alternatives for server-based applications.

ObjectContext

Every object that runs in Transaction Server's environment has an associated **ObjectContext**. Every such object can access its context with the function **GetObjectContext**.

GetObjectContext is in effect a pointer to the ObjectContext of the Transaction Server object currently in use. The function relies on a runtime (as opposed to user-level) interface called the ObjectContext interface. It is this interface, which amounts to a form of interprocess communication, that ultimately obtains the current object's context. The ObjectContext interface is in turn made up of several code modules or methods, including:

- **CreateInstance**, which creates a new instance of a Transaction Server object by using the current object's context.

- **SetAbort**, which causes the transaction within which the current object is executing to cease running, and sends an interprocess signal that says that the object has completed its task and will be deactivated when the flow of program execution is returned to the module that called the current object and transaction.

- **SetComplete**, somewhat similar to SetAbort except that it does not cause the current method to stop executing prematurely, but rather simply sends a signal saying that the module's work is done.

- **DisableCommit**, which prevents updates based upon the current object's status from taking place because of some inaccuracy or incompleteness in that status.

- **EnableCommit**, the mirror image of DisableCommit, which permits updates based upon the current object's status, *whether the work of the object and its corollary code modules is completed or not.*

- **IsInTransaction**, which simply signals whether or not the current object is executing within a transaction.

- **IsCallerInRole**, which sends a signal that indicates whether or not the code outside the server process that called the current object (for example, a client application or browser) is in some specific role, such as requesting database access.

- **IsSecurityEnabled**, which sends a signal that says whether or not secure transmission has been associated with the current object. By default, security is always enabled for server-based processes and is only disabled for client-based processes.

- **SafeRef,** a function that an object uses to derive a pointer to itself. This pointer can then be passed to objects or methods outside the current object's executing environment.

- **SharedProperty,** which sets or gets a shared property's current value by means of the method **Value,** which is what really does the work.

- **SharedPropertyGroup,** which creates and grants access to shared properties, and employs these methods:
  - **CreateProperty,** which sets up a shared property and assigns it a name, represented by a character string, through which the property can be uniquely identified within the group.
  - **CreatePropertyByPosition,** similar to CreateProperty but identifies the shared properties it creates by a numeric index rather than a name.
  - **Property,** which gives you a pointer to a shared property when you give it a property name.
  - **PropertyByPosition,** the index-based clone of Property.

- **SharedProperty Manager,** which keeps all parts of a server process informed about the state or value of global parameters; that is, those that affect all such components. The SharedProperty Manager in turn relies upon the **SharedPropertyGroup Manager,** which can create shared property groups and access existing ones. The SharedPropertyGroup Manager makes several programming methods available, including:
  - **CreatePropertyGroup,** which creates a new shared property group and returns a pointer to it.
  - **Group,** which simply returns a pointer to an existing shared property group.
  - **get_NewEnum,** which returns a pointer to an enumerator that can then be used to walk through, in order, the shared property groups in a process.

Transaction Server Sample Applications

As a means of acquainting you with what it can do, Transaction Server provides two sample applications: a banking program and a hockey multiuser game. Let's take a look at the first of these as a means of further investigating Transaction Server's capabilities and tools.

Banking

This simple transactional database application, whose main window we've illustrated in Figure 20.1, can help teach you how to use Transaction Server's application programming interfaces. In order to do so, you must configure both Transaction Server and the sample application by following specific steps. We'll walk you through those steps next.

Setting Up the Sample Bank Application

In overview, being able to use Transaction Server's Sample Bank application means:

- Having SQL Server Enterprise Edition 6.5 available

- Installing Transaction Server, to produce an interface like that shown in Figure 20.2

- Installing the Sample Bank package

- Setting up an ODBC data source

- Telling Transaction Server's Explorer to track the Sample Bank package

- Running the Bank Client

Figure 20.1 This Visual Basic-based banking application can carry out all essential banking functions.

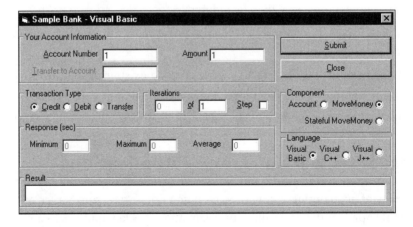

Figure 20.2 Like most of IIS 4.0, Transaction Server has an MMC look.

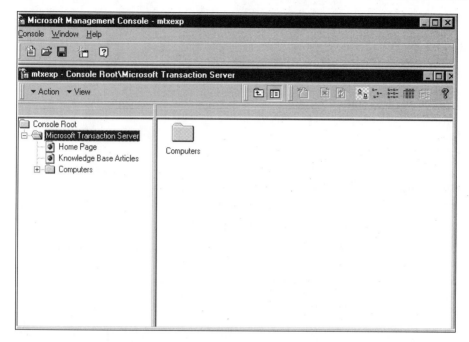

Let's break down this list into manageable chunks. To install the sample Banking application, follow these steps:

1. Click **Start**.

2. Click **Programs**.

3. Select **Microsoft Transaction Server**.

4. Double-click **Transaction Server Explorer**.

5. In the Explorer's right pane, double-click **My Computer**.

6. Still in the right pane, double-click **Packages Installed**.

7. Pull down the **File** menu.

8. Click **New**.

9. Click **Install pre-built packages**.

10. Click **Add**.

11. Choose **Sample Bank.pak** from the list that is displayed.

12. Click **Open**.

13. Click **Next**.

14. When the **Set Package Identity** dialog is displayed, choose **Interactive user**.

15. When the **Installation Options** dialog is presented, define an installation directory.

16. Click **Finish**.

Monitoring the Sample Bank Application

To tell Transaction Server's Explorer how you expect it to monitor the Sample Bank application, you need to do the following:

1. In the right pane of Transaction Server's Explorer, double-click **Sample Bank**.

2. Now double-click **Components**.

3. Pull down the **View** menu.

4. Click **Status** to see usage information for the Sample Bank application's components.

5. Click **New Window** on the View menu in order to neaten up Explorer's display; its windows have a tendency to overlap.

6. Click **Transaction Statistics** in the new window's left pane and you'll get information on the execution of, rather than components related to, processes. (Back at the View menu, clicking **Hierarchy** allows you to hide the left pane of the new window, thereby focusing on transactions statistics, which are automatically refreshed as components run.

Connecting a Database with the Sample Bank Application

Configuring an ODBC data source for the Sample Bank application carries a slightly shorter To Do list.

1. Open **Control Panel**.

2. Double-click the **ODBC** icon.

3. Open the **Data Sources** dialog.

4. Click **Add**.

5. Choose **SQL Server**.

6. Enter **MTxSamples** in response to the request for a datasource name.

7. Enter **local** in response to the prompt for a server.

8. Click **Options**.

9. Enter an appropriate default database name in response to the request for an Account table. For instance, you might want to use the ubiquitous SQL database pubs.

10. Open **SQL Server Enterprise Manager**.

11. Pull down the **Server** menu.

12. Choose **SQL Server**.

13. Click **Start**. If, as a result, you see a green stoplight icon, you'll be assured that SQL Server is running and you've properly configured the ODBC datasource for the Sample Bank application.

Running the Sample Bank Application

Finally, here's what you must do to run the Sample Bank application's client.

1. First, ensure that Distributed Transaction Coordinator is running. To do that:

   a. In Transaction Server Explorer's left pane, point to **My Computer**.

   b. Pull down the Explorer's **Tools** menu.

   c. Choose **MS DTC** from the **Tools** menu.

   d. Click **Start**.

2. Next, in that same **Start** menu, click **Programs**.

3. Point to **Microsoft Transaction Server**, then to **Samples**.

4. Now click **Bank Client**, if need be using the New Window trick we discussed earlier.

5. Finally, just sit back and watch Explorer's displays as they're automatically updated.

> **TIP** One thing that'll surely catch your eye is that the Sample Bank application's first transaction takes longer to complete than any of the others. Since this first transaction creates and loads the sample bank database tables, this plodding is understandable.

IExpress

While not a part of Transaction Server proper, the IIS 4.0 feature known as **IExpress** bears mentioning in this chapter. IExpress is in strictest terms a part of the **System Developer's Kit (SDK)** for Internet Explorer 4.0, but IExpress shares in Transaction Server's mission of developing and deploying distributed applications.

IExpress is to that mission what Web Publishing Wizard is to Web page creation and distribution. Completely Wizard-driven, IExpress automates every aspect of application deployment. It begins with a greeting, as shown in Figure 20.3.

Then IExpress asks a number of questions, like:

- The purpose of the package you're about to deploy (Figure 20.4)

- The title you wish your application to present to users (Figure 20.5)

Figure 20.3 IExpress says hello.

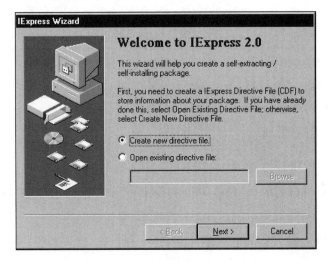

Figure 20.4 IExpress wants to know what your application will handle.

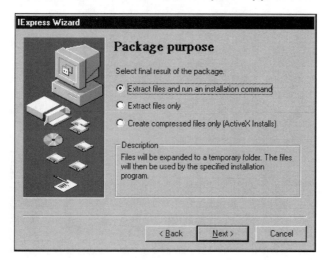

- Confirmation prompts you wish to present to users accessing your application across a network (Figure 20.6)

- License agreements, if any, associated with your application

Figure 20.5 Name your application something more original than we did.

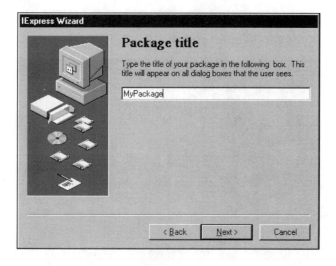

Figure 20.6 This is application deployment in detail.

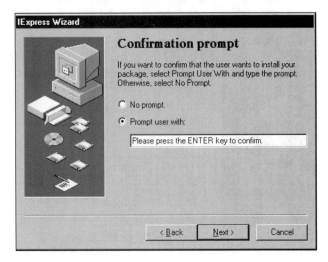

- The path to the files on your server that make up the application

- Any command needed to access the application

and much more. When you've answered these and a dozen or so more requests from IExpress, you'll find yourself with a display like that shown in Figure 20.7, a confirmation of the configuration and deployment of your distributed application.

Figure 20.7 IExpress lets you save application configuration information for reuse at a later time.

Part Five

Appendices

Windows NT Server
4.0 Quick Reference

This appendix is a quick reference to Windows NT Server 4.0 commands, dialogs, menus, and menu items, and is in the form of a table with its entries alphabetized.

However, it does present the point of access associated with each item. We've included only commands in NT Server proper and in a very few cases, in its add-ons. For an IIS Quick Reference, turn to Appendix B.

Tool:
Access through Share Permissions

Category:
Dialog

Reached Through:
My Computer ---> (select the desired file or directory) ---> File menu ---> Shares ---> Permissions

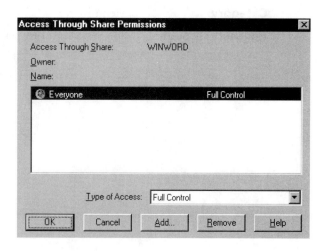

Tool:
Account Policy

Category:
Dialog

**Reached
Through:**
Account Item,
Policies Menu,
User Manager
for Domains

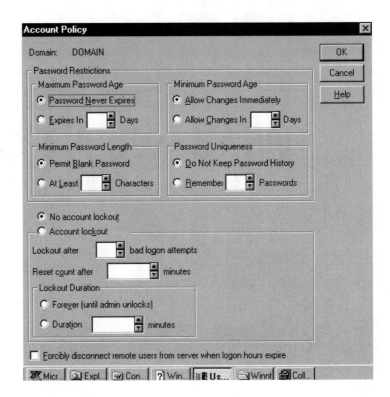

Tool:	Account
Category:	Menu Item
Reached Through:	Policies Menu of User Manager for Domains

Tool:
Account
Information

Category:
Dialog

**Reached
Through:**
Properties
Item, Users
Menu, User
Manager for
Domains

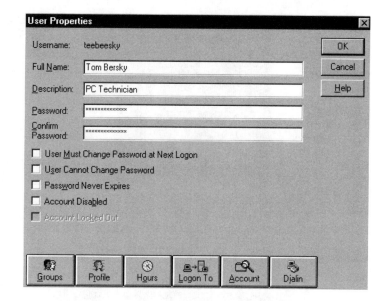

User Properties			×

Username: teebeesky

Full Name: Tom Bersky

Description: PC Technician

Password: ***************

Confirm
Password: ***************

☐ User Must Change Password at Next Logon
☐ User Cannot Change Password
☐ Password Never Expires
☐ Account Disabled
☐ Account Locked Out

OK   Cancel   Help

Groups   Profile   Hours   Logon To   Account   Dialin

Tool: Add Computer to Domain

Category: Menu Item

Reached Through: Computer Menu, Server Manager

Tool: Add Printer

Category: Wizard

Reached Through: Start ---> Programs ---> Administrative Tools --->
                       Administrative Wizards

Tool:
Add Share
Permissions

Category:
Dialog

**Reached
Through:**
My Computer
---> right-click
to display
menus --->
click Sharing

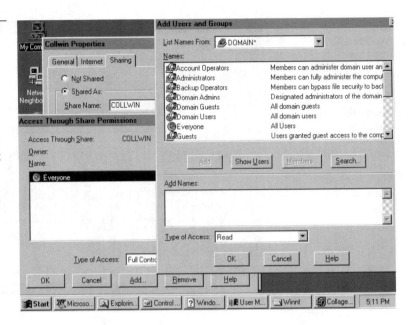

Tool:
Add to Alert

Category:
Dialog

**Reached
Through:**
Edit Menu,
Performance
Monitor

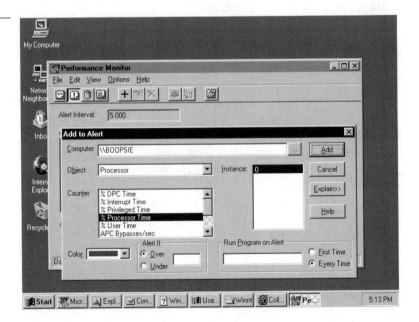

Tool:	Add to Chart
Category:	Menu Item
Reached Through:	Edit Menu, Performance Monitor

Tool: Add to Chart	
Category: Dialog	
Reached Through: Edit Menu, Performance Monitor	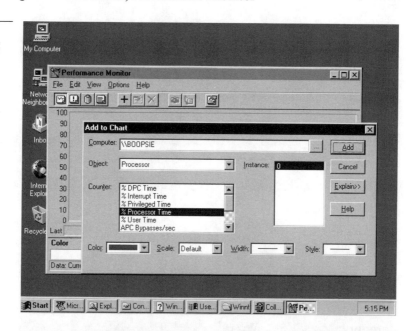

Tool: Add to Log	
Category: Dialog	
Reached Through: Edit Menu, Performance Monitor	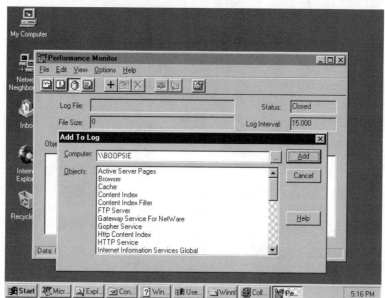

Tool:	Add to Log
Category:	Menu Item
Reached Through:	Edit Menu, Performance Monitor

Tool: Add Trusting Domain	
Category: Dialog	
Reached Through: User Manager for Domains ---> Policies Menu ---> Trust Relationships Menu Item	

Add Trusting Domain

Trusting Domain:

Initial Password:

Confirm Password:

OK

Cancel

Help

Tool:	Add User Account
Category:	Wizard
Reached Through:	Start ---> Programs ---> Administrative Tools ---> Administrative Wizards

Tool:	Addresses
Category:	Menu Item
Reached Through:	Capture Menu

Tool:	Administrative Tools
Category:	Menu
Reached Through:	Start

Tool:
Administrative
Wizards

Category:
Dialog

**Reached
Through:**
Programs
Menu

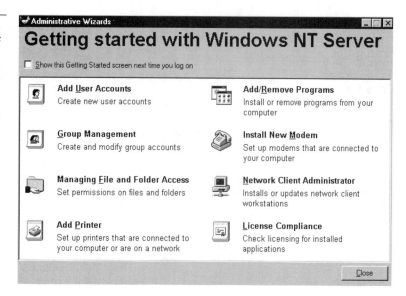

Tool:
Advanced IP
Addressing

Category:
Dialog

**Reached
Through:**
Control Panel
---> Network
---> Protocols
---> (select the
protocol you
desire) --->
Properties

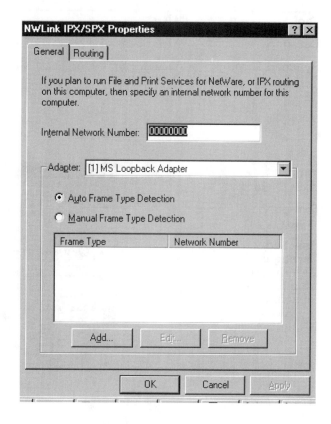

Tool:
Advanced
Settings for
COM

Category:
Dialog

**Reached
Through:**
Printer Wizard
---> (select a
serial port) --->
Configure --->
Ports --->
Settings --->
Advanced
Settings

Tool: Alert

Category: Menu Item

Reached Through: View Menu, Performance Monitor

Tool:
Alert Options

Category:
Dialog

**Reached
Through:**
Performance
Monitor --->
Options menu
---> Alerts
Menu Item

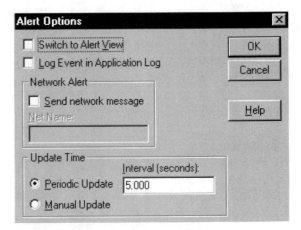

Tool:	Auto Refresh
Category:	Menu Item
Reached Through:	Option menu, Registry editor

Tools:	Backup
Category:	Menu Item
Reached Through:	Administrative Tools Menu

Tool:	Backup
Category:	Window
Reached Through:	Programs

Tool:
Backup
Information

Category:
Dialog

**Reached
Through:**
Start --->
Programs --->
Administrative
Tools --->
Backup

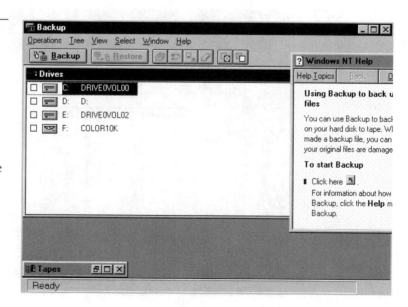

Tool:	Capture
Category:	Menu
Reached Through:	Network Monitor

Tool:	Change System Settings
Category:	Menu Item
Reached Through:	Option menu, Registry editor

Tool:	Chart
Category:	Menu Item
Reached Through:	View Menu, Performance Monitor

Tool:
Chart Options

Category:
Dialog

Reached Through:
Performance Monitor ---> View Menu ---> Chart Menu Item

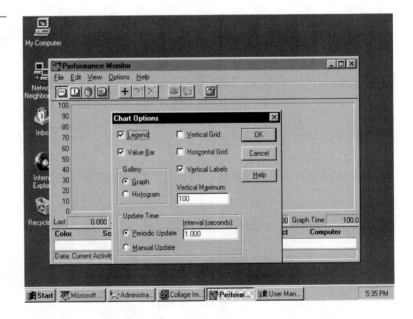

Tool:	Commit Changes Now
Category:	Menu Item
Reached Through:	Partition Menu of Disk Administrator

Tool:	Computer
Category:	Menu
Reached Through:	Server Manager

Tool:
Configure LPT
Port

Category:
Dialog

**Reached
Through:**
Start --->
Programs --->
Administrative
Tools --->
Administrative
Wizards --->
Add Printer

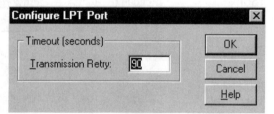

Tool:
Configure Port
Usage

Category:
Dialog

**Reached
Through:**
Control Panel
---> Modem
---> Install
New Modem
---> Remote
Access Setup

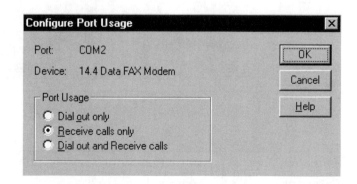

Tool:	Confirm on Delete
Category:	Menu Item
Reached Through:	Option menu, Registry editor

Tool:	Connect Server
Category:	Dialog
Reached Through:	SQL Server

Tool:
Connect to
Printer

Category:
Dialog

**Reached
Through:**
My Computer
---> Printers
---> Add
Printer --->
(check
*Network
Printer server*)

OR

Start --->
Programs --->
Administrative
Tools --->
Administrative
Wizards --->
Add Printer
---> (check
*Network
Printer server*)

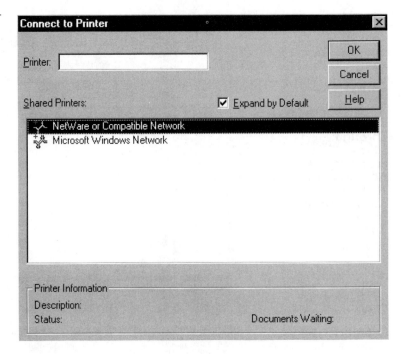

Tool:	convlog (to convert log file formats)
Category:	command
Reached Through:	Start ---> Run

Tool:	Copy
Category:	Menu Item
Reached Through:	User Menu, User Manager for Domains

Tool:
Copy of [user account]

Category:
Dialog

Reached Through:
User Manager for Domains
---> User Menu
---> Copy
Menu Item

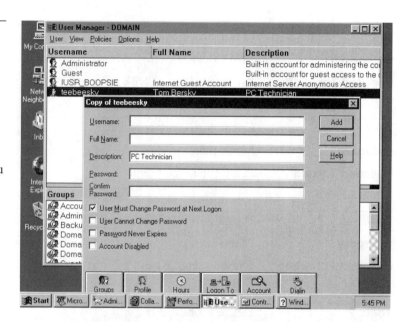

Tool:
Create Logical Drive

Category:
Dialog

Reached Through:
Disk Administrator
---> Partition Menu --->
Create Menu Item

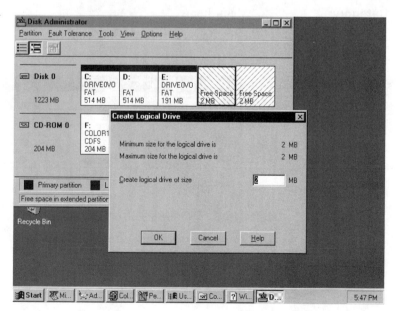

Tool:	Create Partition
Category:	Menu Item
Reached Through:	Partition Menu of Disk Administrator

Tool:	Create Stripe Set
Category:	Menu Item
Reached Through:	Partition Menu of Disk Administrator

Tool:	Create Stripe Set With Parity
Category:	Menu Item
Reached Through:	Fault Tolerance Menu

Tool:	Data From
Category:	Menu Item
Reached Through:	Option menu, Registry editor

Tool:	Delete From Chart
Category:	Menu Item
Reached Through:	Edit Menu, Performance Monitor

Tool:
Dialin
Information

Category:
Dialog

**Reached
Through:**
Dialin Button
of New User or
Copy User
Dialogs, in
User Manager
for Domains

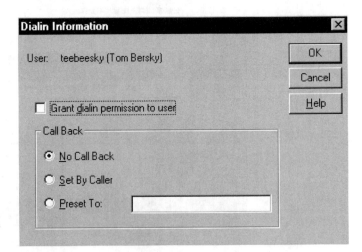

Tool:
Directory
Permissions

Category:
Dialog

**Reached
Through:**
Windows NT
Explorer
--->right-click
to display
Properties
Menu

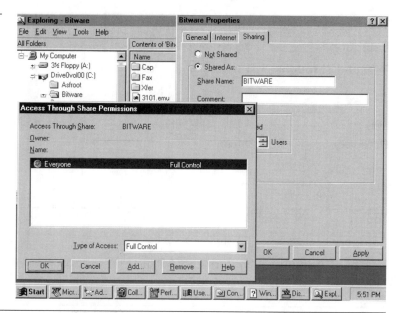

Tool:	Disk Administrator
Category:	Menu Item
Reached Through:	Administrative Tools Menu

Tool:	Display
Category:	Menu
Reached Through:	Capture Summary Window of Network Monitor

Tool:	Display Filter
Category:	Dialog
Reached Through:	CaptureSummary Window, Display Menu, Network Monitor

Tool:	Edit
Category:	Menu
Reached Through:	Performance Monitor

Tool:	Edit Chart Line
Category:	Menu Item
Reached Through:	Edit Menu, Performance Monitor

Tool:	Establish Mirror
Category:	Menu Item
Reached Through:	Fault Tolerance Menu

Tool:	Fault Tolerance
Category:	Menu

Tool:	File
Category:	Menu
Reached Through:	Performance Monitor

Tool:	File and Print Servers for NetWare
Category:	Dialog
Reached Through:	Control Panel ---> File and Print Services for NetWare

Tool:	
File Sharing	
Category:	
Dialog	
Reached Through:	
My Computer ---> (select the desired file or directory) ---> File menu ---> Shares ---> Permissions	

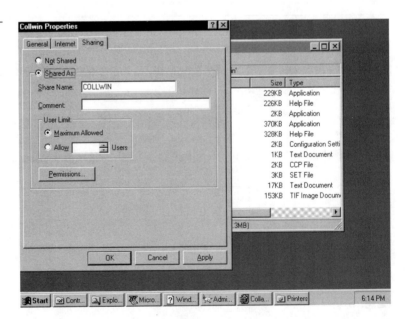

Tool:	Font
Category:	Menu Item
Reached Through:	Option menu, Registry editor

Tool:
Format Drive

Category:
Dialog

Reached Through:
Disk Administrator ---> Tools ---> Format

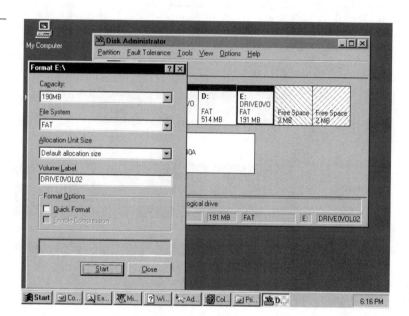

Tool:	fsconvert (to convert a FAT file system to an NTFS one)
Category:	command
Reached Through:	Start ---> Run

Tool:
Group
Memberships

Category:
Dialog

**Reached
Through:**
User Manager
for Domains
---> User Menu
---> Groups
Button

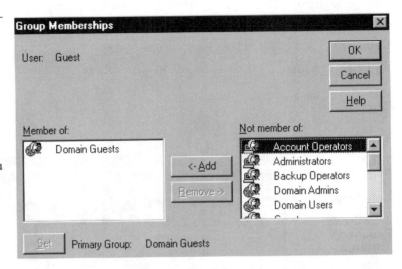

Tool:
Hardware
Setup

Category:
Dialog

**Reached
Through:**
Backup --->
Operations
Menu --->
Hardware
Setup Menu
Item

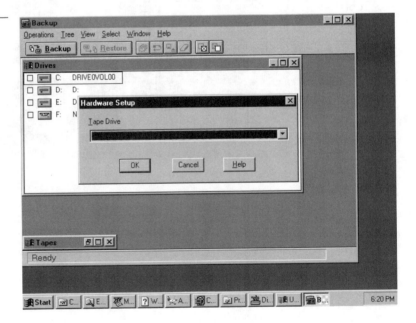

Tool:	hostname (returns the name of the DNS host)
Category:	command
Reached Through:	Start ---> Run

Tool:
Identification
Changes

Category:
Dialog

**Reached
Through:**
Server
Manager --->
Computer
Menu --->
Synchronize
Entire Domain
Menu Item

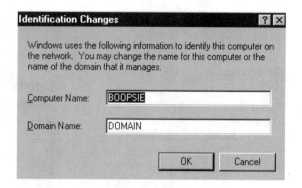

Tool: Input Log File Timeframe

Category: Dialog

Reached Through: Performance Monitor ---> Edit Menu ---> TimeLine

---

Tool:
Install Driver

Category:
Dialog

**Reached
Through:**
Control Panel
---> Tape
Devices --->
Drivers

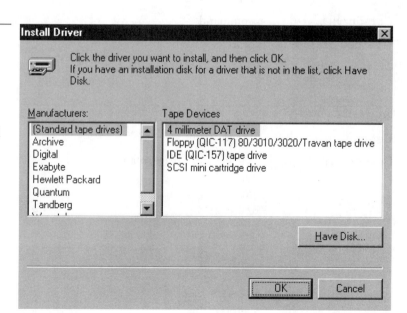

Tool:
Install New
Modem

Category:
Dialog

**Reached
Through:**
Control Panel
---> Modem

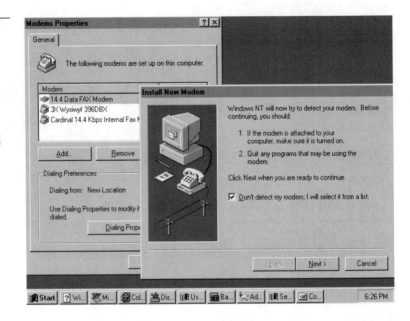

Tool:	ipconfig (returns all TCP/IP, WINS, and DNS configuration information)
Category:	command
Reached Through:	Start ---> Run

Tool:	Log
Category:	Menu Item
Reached Through:	View Menu, Performance Monitor

Tool:
Logon Hours

Category:
Dialog

**Reached
Through:**
User Manager
for Domains
---> User Menu
---> New User
OR Copy --->
Hours Button

Tool:
Logon
Workstation

Category:
Dialog

**Reached
Through:**
User Manager
for Domains
---> User Menu
---> New User
OR Copy --->
Account
Button

OR

User Manager
for Domains
---> User Menu
---> Properties

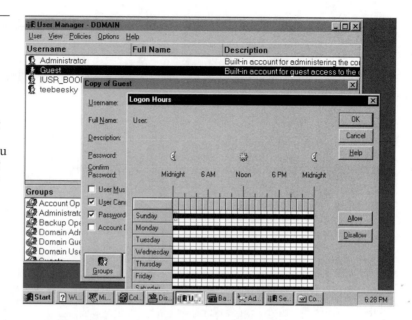

Tool:
Manage
Exported
Directories

Category:
Dialog

**Reached
Through:**
Control Panel
---> Server --->
Replication
---> Directory
Replication
---> Export
Directories --->
Manage

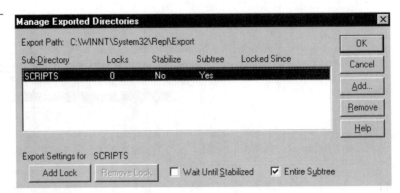

Tool:
Map Network
Drives

Category:
Dialog

**Reached
Through:**
Windows NT
Explorer --->
Tools Menu
---> Map
Network
Drives Menu
Item

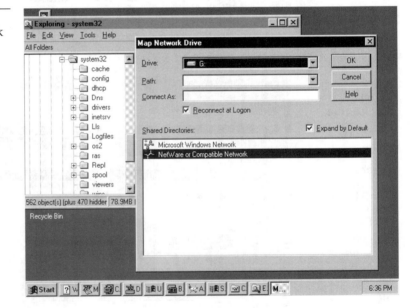

Tool:	nbtstat (returns information about NetBios names and addresses)
Category:	command
Reached Through:	Start ---> Run

Tool:	netstat (returns information on TCP/IP and UDP connections)
Category:	command
Reached Through:	Start ---> Run

Tool: Network Client Administrator	
Category: Dialog	
Reached Through: Programs ---> Administrative Tools ---> Network Client Administrator	

Tool:	Networks
Category:	Menu Item
Reached Through:	Capture Menu

Tool:	New Chart
Category:	Menu Item
Reached Through:	File Menu, Performance Monitor

Tool:
New Global
Group

Category:
Dialog

**Reached
Through:**
User Manager
for Domains
---> Users
Menu ---> New
Global Group
Menu Item

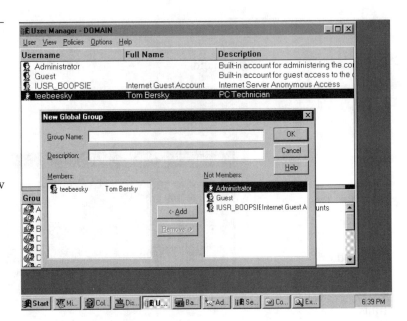

Tool: New Global Group

Category: Menu Item

Reached Through: User Menu, User Manager for Domains

Tool:
New Local
Group

Category:
Dialog

**Reached
Through:**
User Manager
for Domains
---> Users
Menu ---> New
Local Group
Menu Item

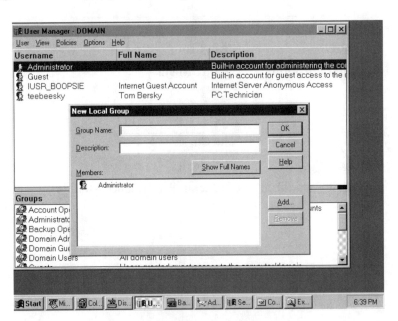

Tool:	New Local Group
Category:	Menu Item
Reached Through:	User Menu, User Manager for Domains

Tool:	New Log Settings
Category:	Menu Item
Reached Through:	File Menu, Performance Monitor

Tool:
New Share

Category:
Dialog

**Reached
Through:**
Control Panel
---> Gateway
Service for
NetWare --->
Configure
Gateway --->
Add

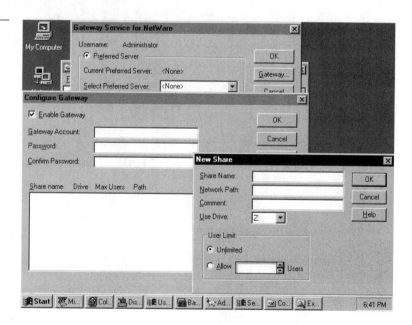

Tool:
New User

Category:
Dialog

Reached Through:
User Manager for Domains ---> Users Menu ---> New User Menu Item

New User   ⊠

Username:	[ ]	Add
Full Name:	[ ]	Cancel
Description:	[ ]	Help
Password:	[ ]	
Confirm Password:	[ ]	

☑ User Must Change Password at Next Logon
☐ User Cannot Change Password
☐ Password Never Expires
☐ Account Disabled

| Groups | Profile | Hours | Logon To | Account | Dialin |

Tool:	New User
Category:	Menu Item
Reached Through:	User Menu, User Manager for Domains

Tool:	Operations
Category:	Menu
Reached Through:	Backup

Tool:	Options
Category:	Menu
Reached Through:	Registry Editor

Tool:
Owner

Category:
Dialog

**Reached
Through:**
My Computer
---> Printers
---> (select a
printer) --->
Properties --->
Security

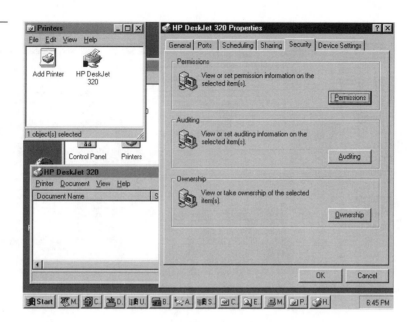

Tool: Partition

Category: Menu

Reached Through: Disk Administrator

Tool:
Per Seat
Licensing

Category:
Dialog

**Reached
Through:**
Start --->
Programs --->
Administrative
Tools --->
License
Manager --->
(select *Clients*
[*per seat*])

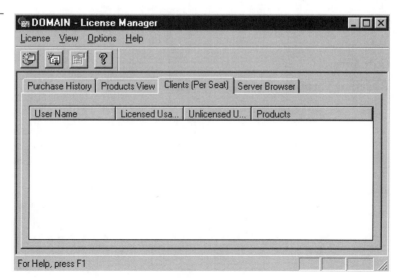

Tool:
Per Server
Licensing

Category:
Dialog

**Reached
Through:**
Start --->
Programs --->
Administrative
Tools --->
License
Manager --->
Server Browser

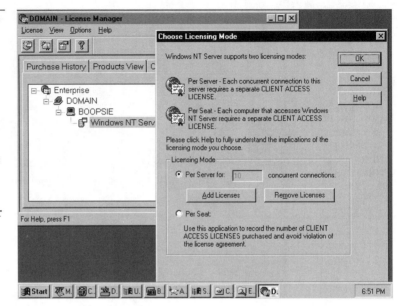

Tool:	ping (tests the ability to connect to an IP address)
Category:	command
Reached Through:	Start ---> Run

Tool:	Policies
Category:	Menu
Reached Through:	User Manager for Domains

Tool:
Printer
Auditing

Category:
Dialog

**Reached
Through:**
Control Panel
---> Printers
---> Properties
---> Security

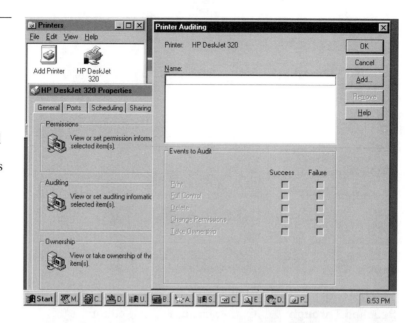

Tool:
Printer
Permissions

Category:
Dialog

**Reached
Through:**
Control Panel
---> Printers
---> Properties
---> Security

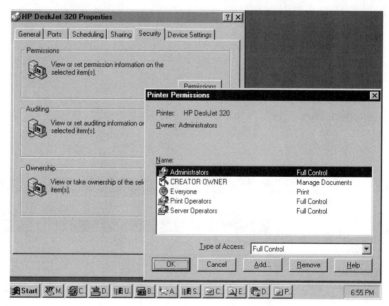

Tool:	Programs
Category:	Menu
Reached Through:	Start

Tool:	Promote to Primary domain controller
Category:	Menu Item
Reached Through:	Computer Menu, Server Manager

Tool:	Properties
Category:	Menu Item
Reached Through:	User Menu, User Manager for Domains

Tool:	Read Only mode
Category:	Menu Item
Reached Through:	Option menu, Registry editor

Tool:	regedt32
Category:	command
Reached Through:	Start ---> Run

Tool:
Remote Access Setup

Category:
Dialog

Reached Through:
Control Panel ---> Modem ---> Install new Modem ---> Properties

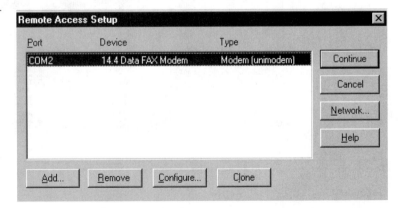

Tool:
Repair Disk
Utility

Category:
Dialog

**Reached
Through:**
Start ---> Run
---> rdisk
(typed into the
Open text box)

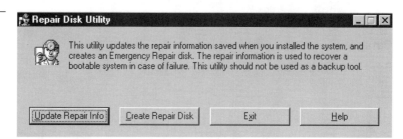

Update Repair Info	Create Repair Disk	Exit	Help

This utility updates the repair information saved when you installed the system, and creates an Emergency Repair disk. The repair information is used to recover a bootable system in case of failure. This utility should not be used as a backup tool.

Tool:	Restore
Category:	Menu Item
Reached Through:	Partition Menu of Disk Administrator

Tool:	route (displays a server's TCP/IP routing table)
Category:	command
Reached Through:	Start ---> Run

Tool:
Run

Category:
Dialog

**Reached
Through:**
Start

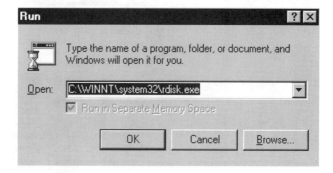

Run

Type the name of a program, folder, or document, and Windows will open it for you.

Open: C:\WINNT\system32\rdisk.exe

☑ Run in Separate Memory Space

OK   Cancel   Browse...

Tool:	Save
Category:	Menu Item
Reached Through:	Partition Menu of Disk Administrator

Tool:	Save Settings on Exit
Category:	Menu Item
Reached Through:	Option menu, Registry editor

Tool:	Select
Category:	Menu
Reached Through:	Backup

Tool:
Select
Components

Category:
Dialog

**Reached
Through:**
Windows NT
Setup

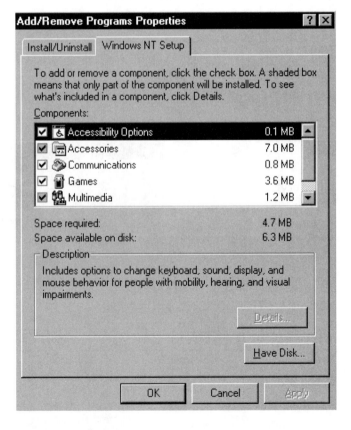

Tool:
Select
Computer

Category:
Dialog

**Reached
Through:**
Performance
monitor --->
View Menu
---> Chart
Menu Item;
AND Edit
Menu ---> Add
to Chart Menu
Item

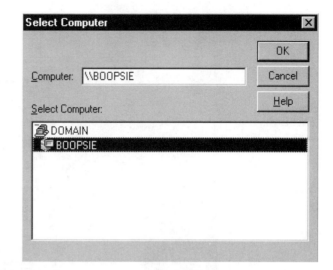

Tool:
Select Domain

Category:
Dialog

**Reached
Through:**
User Manager
for Domains
---> User Menu
---> Select
Domain Menu
Item

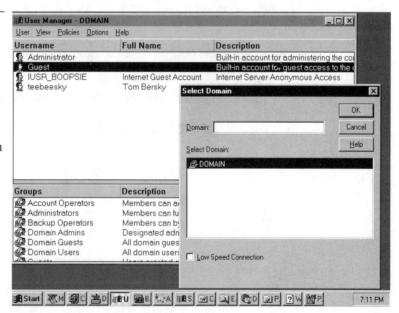

Tool:	Select Domain
Category:	Menu Item
Reached Through:	User Menu, User Manager for Domains

572

Part Five • Appendix A

Tool:
Select Network
Adapters

Category:
Dialog

**Reached
Through:**
Control Panel
---> Network
---> Properties
---> Add --->
Adapter

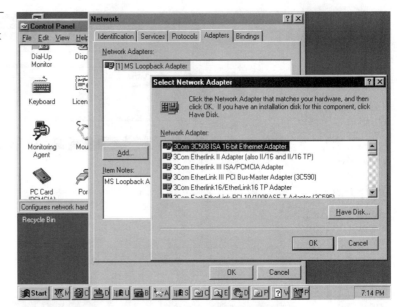

Tool:
Select Users

Category:
Dialog

**Reached
Through:**
User Manager
for Domains
---> User Menu
---> Select User
Menu Item

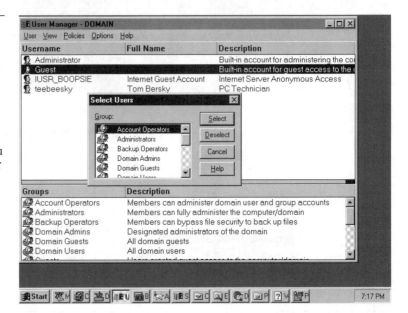

Tool:	Select Users
Category:	Menu Item
Reached Through:	User Menu, User Manager for Domains

Tool:	Send Message
Category:	Menu Item
Reached Through:	Computer Menu, Server Manager

Tool:
Settings for
COM

Category:
Dialog

**Reached
Through:**
Start --->
Programs --->
Administrative
Tools --->
Administrative
Wizards --->
Add Printer
Wizard

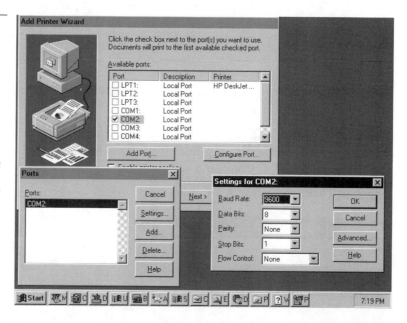

Tool:
Special
Directory
Access

Category:
Dialog

**Reached
Through:**
Windows NT
Explorer --->
right-click --->
Properties --->
Security --->
Permissions

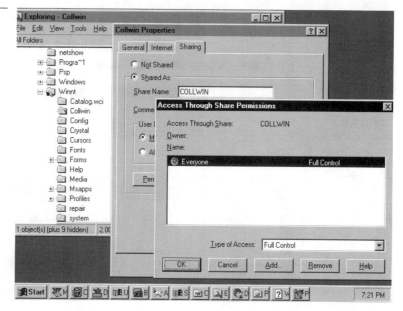

Tool:	Special File Access
Category:	Dialog
Reached Through:	Windows NT Explorer ---> right-click ---> Properties ---> Security ---> Permissions

Tool:	Synchronize an Entire Domain
Category:	Menu Item
Reached Through:	Computer Menu, Server Manager

Tool:	tracert (traces the path to a destination IP address)
Category:	command
Reached Through:	Start ---> Run

Tool:	Tree
Category:	Menu
Reached Through:	Backup

Tool: Trust Relationships	
Category: Dialog	
Reached Through: User Manager for Domains ---> Policies Menu ---> Trust Relationships Menu Item	

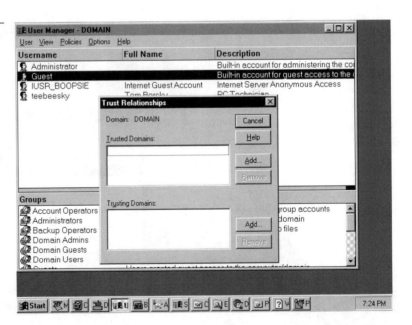

Tool:	Trust Relationships
Category:	Menu Item
Reached Through:	Policies Menu of User Manager for Domains

Tool:	User
Category:	Menu
Reached Through:	User Manager for Domains

Tool:
User
Environment
Profile

Category:
Dialog

**Reached
Through:**
User Manager
for Domains
---> User Menu
---> Select User
Menu Item --->
Profile Button

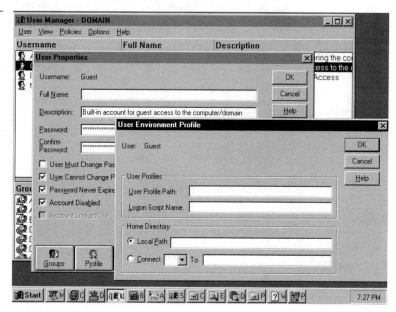

Tool:
User Rights
Policy

Category:
Dialog

**Reached
Through:**
User Manager
for Domains
---> Policy
Menu ---> User
Menu Item

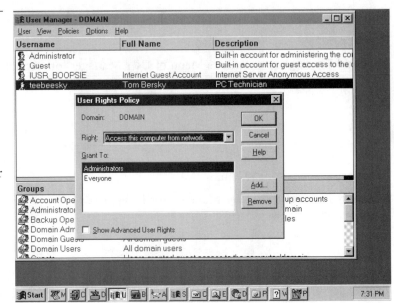

Tool:	View
Category:	Menu
Reached Through:	Performance Monitor

Tool:	View
Category:	Menu
Reached Through:	Backup

Tool:
Virtual
Memory

Category:
Dialog

**Reached
Through:**
Control Panel
---> System --->
Properties --->
Performance

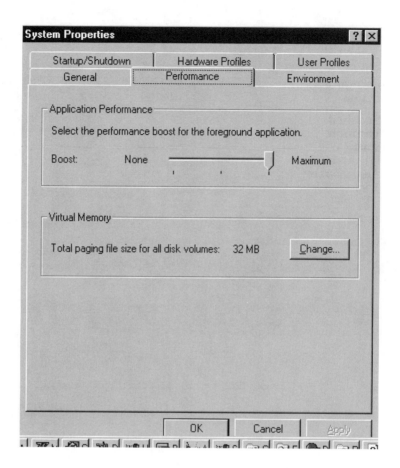

Tool:	Window
Category:	Menu
Reached Through:	Backup

Tool:
Windows NT
Diagnostics

Category:
Dialog

**Reached
Through:**
Start --->
Programs --->
Administrative
Tools

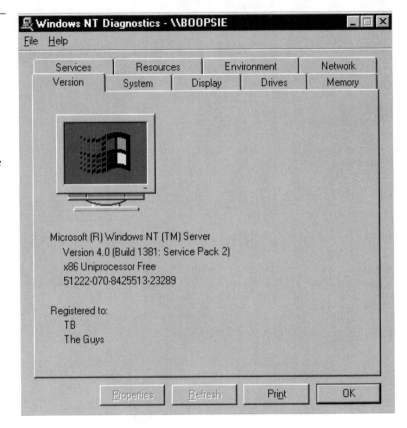

B

Internet Information Server
Quick Reference

T his appendix, as you might expect, is much more brief than the one on
NT Server. Appendix B covers only two topics: Internet Service Manager and
Key Manager.

Tool:
Internet Service
Manager's
default view

Accessed by:
Start --->
Programs --->
Microsoft
Internet
Information
Server --->
Internet Service
Manager

Tool:
Connect to
Server dialog

Accessed by:
Internet Service
Manager --->
Properties
(menu) --->
Connect to
Server (menu
item)

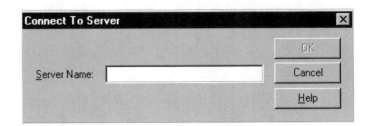

Tool:
Finding All
Servers dialog

Accessed by:
Internet Service
Manager --->
Properties
(menu) --->
Find All
Servers (menu
item)

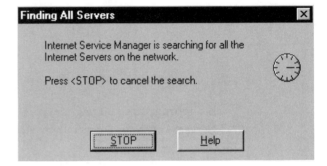

Tool:
Internet Service
Manager's
Server view
(with FTP ser-
vice selected)

Accessed by:
Internet Service
Manager --->
View (menu)
---> Servers
(menu item)

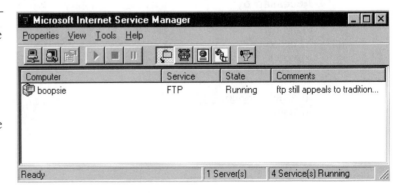

Tool:
Internet Service
Manager's
Server view
(with gopher
service
selected)

Accessed by:
Internet Service
Manager --->
View (menu)
---> Servers
(menu item)

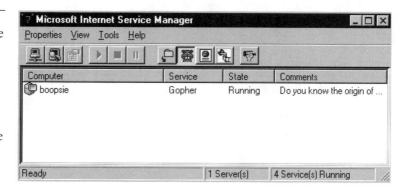

Tool:
Internet Service
Manager's
Server view
(with WWW
service
selected)

Accessed by:
Internet Service
Manager --->
View (menu)
---> Servers
(menu item)

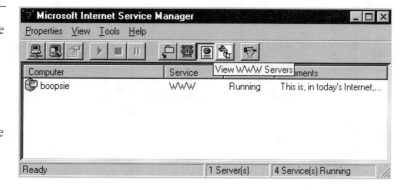

Tool:
Internet Service
Manager's
Server view
(with NetShow
service
selected)

Accessed by:
Internet Service
Manager --->
View (menu)
---> Servers
(menu item)

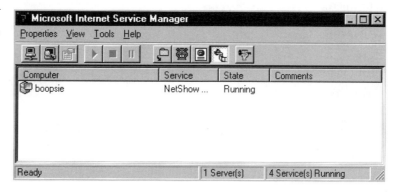

Tool:
Internet Service
Manager's
Server view
(with all ser-
vices selected,
and sorted by
service)

Accessed by:
Internet Service
Manager --->
View (menu)
---> Servers
(menu item)

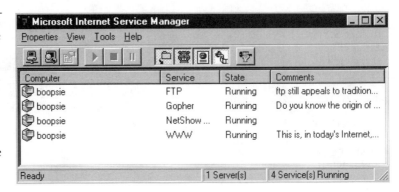

Tool:
Internet Service
Manager's
Server view
(with all ser-
vices selected,
and sorted by
comment)

Accessed by:
Internet Service
Manager --->
View (menu)
---> Servers
(menu
item)Internet
Service
Manager --->
View (menu)
---> Servers
(menu item)

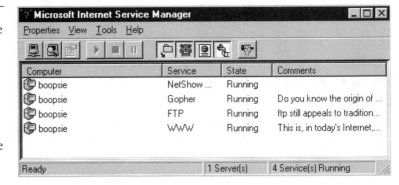

Tool:
Internet Service
Manager's
Service view
(with all ser-
vices selected)

Accessed by:
Internet Service
Manager --->
View (menu)
---> Services
(menu item)

Tool:
FTP Service's
Properties
Sheets

Accessed by:
Internet Service
Manager --->
View (menu)
---> Services
(menu item),

and

Internet Service
Manager --->
Properties
(menu)

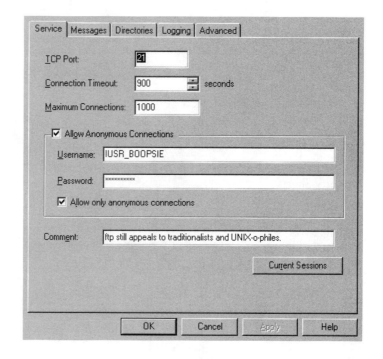

Tool:
Gopher
Service's
Property Sheets

Accessed by:
Internet Service
Manager --->
View (menu)
---> Services
(menu item),

and

Internet Service
Manager --->
Properties
(menu)

| Service | Directories | Logging | Advanced |

TCP Port: `70`

Connection Timeout: `900` seconds

Maximum Connections: `1000`

Service Administrator

Name: `Administrator`

Email: `Admin@corp.com`

Anonymous Logon

Username: `IUSR_BOOPSIE`

Password: `**********`

Comment: `Do you know the origin of the term gopher?`

OK   Cancel   Apply   Help

Tool:
NetShow On-
Demand
Service's
Property Sheets

Accessed by:
Internet Service
Manager --->
View (menu)
---> Services
(menu item),

and

Internet Service
Manager --->
Properties
(menu)

| Service | Directories | Logging |

Limits

Maximum Clients: `500`

Max. Aggregate Bandwidth (bits/sec): `5000000`

Maximum File Bitrate (bits/sec): `2000000`

Note: All changes will only affect newly connected clients

Security

☐ Enable File Level Access Checking

Comment:

OK   Cancel   Apply   Help

Tool:
WWW
Service's
Property Sheets

Accessed by:
Internet Service
Manager --->
View (menu)
---> Services
(menu item),

and

Internet Service
Manager --->
Properties
(menu)

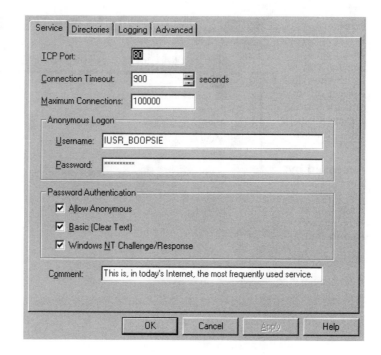

Tool:
Internet Service
Manager's
Service view
(with the All
option
selected)

Accessed by:
Internet Service
Manager --->
View (menu)
---> Services
(menu item),

and

Internet Service
Manager --->
Properties
(menu)

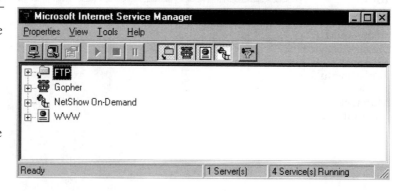

Tool:
Internet Service
Manager's
Service view
(with the All
option selected
and after dou-
ble-clicking the
indicated ser-
vice)

Accessed by:
Internet Service
Manager --->
View (menu)
---> Services
(menu item),

and

Internet Service
Manager --->
Properties
(menu)

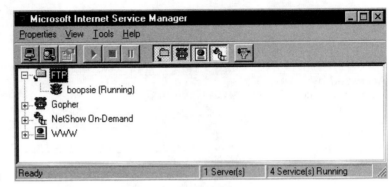

Tool:
Key Manager

Accessed by:
Internet Service
Manager --->
Tools (menu)
---> Key
Manager
(menu item)

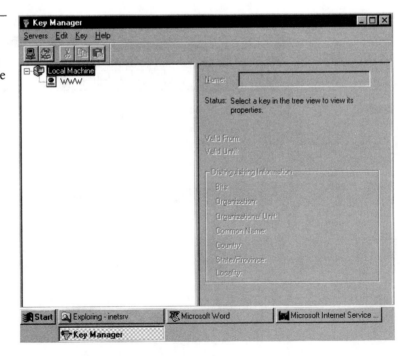

References

The items in this appendix are both print and electronic sources of information on networking in general, the Internet in particular, Windows NT, and Internet Information Server.

General Networking

Computer Science Division, University of California at Berkeley (http://www.cs.berkely.edu) Everything you wanted to know about networking but didn't think you could find

Data Communications Networking Devices, 3rd Edition (Gilbert Held; Wiley, 1992)

DOS UNIX Networking and Internetworking (Michael J. Burgard and Kenneth D. Phillips; Wiley, 1993)

Issues of TCP/IP Networking (http://www.pvc.maricopa.edu/~preston/nag/node23.html)

Mastering ISDN (Mike Sapien and Greg Piedmo; Sybex, 1995)

Mastering Serial Communication (Peter W. Gofton; Sybex, 1994)

Networking (http://andes.ip.ucsb.edu:80/manny/links.html)

Networking Interfaces (http://www.pvc.maricopa.edu/~preston/nag/node24.html)

PC Week Intranet and Internet Firewall Strategies (Ed Amoroso and Ronald Sharp; ZD Press, 1996)

TCP/IP Networking Information (http://www.forest.net/advanced/tcpip.html)

Understanding Data Communications, Fifth Edition (Gilbert Held; SAMS, 1996)

The Internet

Connect Your LAN to the Internet: Cost-Effective Access for Small Businesses and Other Organizations (Thomas W. Madron; Wiley, 1996)

Getting Started with the Internet (Joan Brady Lumpkin and Susan B. Durnbaugh; Wiley, 1995)

The Internet (http://home.microsoft.com/using/using.asp) A hefty grab bag of links to areas of the Microsoft Web site that contain information on MS Internet-related products

The Internet Dictionary (Christian Crumlish; Sybex, 1995)

Microsoft Developers Network (http://www.microsoft.com/msdn) Links to software and technical articles

Microsoft Site Builders Network (http://www.microsoft.com/intranet/contents.asp) Entry point to the area of the MS Web site that deals with intranet technologies

Microsoft Systems Journal (http://www.msj.com) Online version of the magazine about programming for Windows and the Internet; includes scads of source code listings available for download

MIND (Microsoft Interactive Developer) The magazine of Internet and Web technologies; on your newsstand or online at http://www.microsoft.com/mind

Windows NT

Fast Track to NT Server 4 (Robert Cowart and Boyd Waters; Sybex, 1996)

Hacking Microsoft (http://www.c2.org/hackmsoft)

Mastering Windows NT Server 4 (Mark Minasi; Sybex, 1996)

Networking Windows NT (John D. Ruley, David Dix, David W. Methvin, Martin Heller, Arthur H. Germain, James E. Powell, Jeffrey Sloman, Eric Hall; Wiley, 1994)

Ugly Details about Windows NT Internals (http://www.ntinternals.com)

Windows NT (ftp://ftp.microsoft.com/bussys/winnt/kb/index.txt; An index of hundreds of WINNT articles available for download)

Windows NT (ftp://ftp.microsoft.com/bussys/winnt)

Windows NT Administration FAQ (http://www.iftech.com:80/oltc/admin/admin.stm)

Windows NT Server 4 Security, Troubleshooting, and Optimization (New Riders Press, 1996)

Internet Information Server

Internet Information Server (http://www.microsoft.com/iis/default.asp)

Internet Information Server (http://www.microsoft.com/infoserv)

Internet Information Server (ftp://ftp.microsoft.com/IIS/KB)

Mastering Microsoft Internet Information Server (Peter Dyson; Sybex, 1996)

Understanding the Internet and Internet Information Server (http://www.metplx.com/infoserv/docs/OVER.HTM)

Unlocking Microsoft Internet Information Server (New Riders Publishing, 1996)

D

TCP/IP Networking
Summary

This appendix discusses what we feel to be the TCP/IP concepts you *must* know and understand if you're to be at all comfortable with networking in general, Windows NT Server, and Internet Information Server.

Appendix D looks at:

- The OSI model
- Protocols
- Transmission media types
- Topologies
- Connectivity devices
- Addressing and routing
- TCP/IP-related utilities

The OSI Model, Protocols, and Media

Of the factors that molded the Internet of today, probably the most important is the **Open Systems Interconnection Reference (OSI)** model for networks.

OSI was developed by **ISO**, the **International Organization for Standardization**. The model's reason for being is to act as a pattern against which network software should be written. Therefore, adherence to the OSI model does not of itself guarantee interconnectivity, but such adherence does make it easier for networks to talk to one another.

Adherence means that any software that results will share the same general structure. That structure is mandated by the seven layers of the OSI model; Table D.1 examines those layers.

Table D.1 The OSI Model Demystified

The Layer Called	Is Numbered	And Handles
Physical	1 (the lowest OSI layer)	The connection between the network node, whatever the nature of that node, and the data transmission medium, whatever the nature of that medium.
		Note that data transmission media include not only cable of a number of sorts but also microwave and satellite devices. *Any* piece of hardware that is involved in connecting a node to a transmission medium is governed by the specifications set out in the Physical Layer of the OSI model. So, this layer governs not only network interface cards (NICs) and cabling, but also the above-mentioned microwave and satellite transmitters, as well as other connectivity components like **repeaters** (boxes that boost a weakening signal so that it can go further along the path it was sent, rather than fading out).
		Physical-layer hardware performs only one function: It passes along the zeroes and ones of a binary data stream to whatever other Physical-Layer device or devices are its next-door neighbors.
		Standards like **10BaseT** (for data cable made up of an unshielded twisted pair of copper wires, such as telephone wire) and specifications like **IEEE 802.3** (known to most of us simply as Ethernet) draw upon the OSI model's Layer 1.
Data Link	2	Error detection and correction; portioning of the data stream into packets; access to the transmission medium.

Table D.1 *Continued*

The Layer Called	Is Numbered	And Handles

It is at the Data Link Layer that the nature of the activities conducted by the layer goes from being accomplished by hardware to being carried out by software. Layer 2 of the OSI model uses a number of protocols and software methods to carry out its various responsibilities. Among these are:

- *FDDI.* The protocol that accomplishes access to a network built on optical fiber cable. The FDDI protocol relies on a method called *token-passing*, in which a token, signifying the right to transmit, is passed from node to node but can, along with that right, be used by only one station at a time.

- *Ethernet.* Not only a colloquialism for a type of cable, but also a protocol that controls access to networks transmitting across such cable. Both cable and protocol were first defined in the standard, published by the Institute of Electrical and Electronic Engineers (IEEE), and numbered **802.3**. Ethernet uses an access method indicated by what is surely one of data processing's longest acronyms—**CSMA/CD**.

  This stands for **Carrier Sense Multiple Access with Collision Detection**, which means that any network employing Ethernet as its Data Link protocol consists of a number of nodes (multiple access), all listening to the transmission medium until it becomes quiet—that is, available (carrier sense)—all scrambling to be the next to transmit, but kept from shouting all at once (collision detection).

Network	3	Routing.

Layer 3 uses two general categories of protocols to accomplish its job of selecting the most efficient route possible for a packet to travel between its source and

Continued

Table D.1 *Continued*

The Layer Called	Is Numbered	And Handles
		destination, based on the condition of the network at any given moment. These categories are:

* Connection-oriented protocols, which reserve the path between source and destination—that is, create and guard the connection, before transmitting data packets. Few of today's Internet's Layer 3 protocols belong to this category.

* Connectionless protocols, which do not seek to clear the path between data source and data destination before sending packets on their way. The IP portion of TCP/IP and the IPX member of Novell's IPX/SPX protocol suite are examples of connectionless protocols.

The Layer Called	Is Numbered	And Handles
Transport	4	Routing services beyond those offered by the Network Layer.

Among these additional routing-related services are:

* Error detection

* Error correction

* Multiplexing (the combination of several low-speed data streams into a single, wider-bandwidth but higher-speed stream)

Because the functions of the Network and Transport Layers are so closely related, it should come as no surprise that two of the most widely used Layer 4 protocols are the other halves of the two Network Layer examples just given—that is, TCP and SPX.

The Layer Called	Is Numbered	And Handles
Session	5	Establishes and maintains the nature of the conversations between two systems.

The Session Layer does this by making two types of chats available to the connected systems. The type is

Table D.1 *Continued*

The Layer Called	Is Numbered	And Handles
		established when the end-to-end connection is made, and it cannot be changed for the duration of the colloquy. Only breaking the link and reconnecting offers the opportunity to move from one to the other of conversations delimited in the Session layer.
Session	5	Two types of conversation: • *Two-way alternate* conversation, in which, although the dialogue does travel in either direction, only the sender or receiver, *not both*, may transmit at any point in time. • *Two-way simultaneous* conversation, in which both parties "talk" at once.
Presentation	6	Translates application-generated requests for services into terms that the lower levels of the OSI model, or even other applications on other computers running across the network, can understand. For *application*, substitute *WordPerfect* or *Excel*. Read *services* as anything provided by Layers 2 through 5.
Application	7	Provides access to applications on remote systems. Application Layer protocols are grouped as one of the following: • *Application Service Elements*, which are standalone software modules. That is, they talk to or rely on no other pieces of code while doing their jobs. • *Application Service Objects*, which are groupings of program modules that function as if they were a single routine.

It bears repeating that the OSI model is just that: a conceptual framework *only*, against whose specifications actual software is created. Therefore, it is certain that two separate, unique Transport Layer protocols such as SPX and TCP will share at least most of the functions they perform, but none of the ways in which they perform them.

Topologies, Protocols, and Connectivity Devices

The evolution of **Local Area Networks** (**LANs**) had nearly as much impact on the character of the modern Internet as did the OSI model.

Before there were computer networks—which is to say prior to the 1960s—there were, of course, only computers. These machines were usually refrigerator-sized or larger. Communicating with them took place on their terms, by means of specialized *job control* or *command language* sequences entered at monochrome, text-based monitor/keyboard combinations, or even print (hard copy) terminals. The phrase *computer network*, if it was used at all in this era, referred to such a collection of terminals, physically attached to a mainframe or minicomputer.

A LAN is simply a data communications network that is confined to a limited physical expanse, such as a single office suite or college lab. LAN's corollary WAN (Wide Area Network), on the other hand, extends over very large physical or geographical spaces.

How did we get from the primitive networks of the 1960s to LAN and network being, in most people's minds, just a nano-breadth short of synonymous? LANs achieved this status simply by employing, in ways appropriate to their limited scope, all the Internet technologies we've discussed to this point, and more.

LANs apply those technologies through their *topologies*, which are the physical layouts, the blueprint, or the visual outline of the network. Four topologies make up the great majority of LAN layouts:

- Bus (also frequently called backbone)
- Mesh
- Ring
- Star

Like the terms LAN and WAN, these names are quite descriptive. The sections below examine each of these LAN outlines in more detail.

As you can see from Figure D.1, the bus LAN topology is nothing more than a single, uninterrupted length of cable that makes up the backbone of the network and from which nodes are dropped. Because neither end of the backbone is attached to anything, both must be terminated. That is, they must be plugged up, not so much to prevent signal leakage as to preclude a signal that has reached the end of the cable from echoing back in the direction it just traveled and thereby corrupting other signals.

Connecting two or more bus-based LANs to each other or to the Internet could require any or all of the hardware and software tools described in Table D.2.

Table D.2 Bus-Based LAN Shopping List

Type of Component	Component	Needed Because
Software	TCP/IP protocol suite	Bus topologies are almost always built on Ethernet cable.
	Routing software such as OSPF	You want to connect your bus LAN to another or to a LAN that uses a different topology.
Hardware	Repeaters	If your backbone extends beyond the hundred or so feet, a signal traveling along Ethernet cable begins to lose coherence. Note we didn't say lose volume or lose strength. If only volume were at stake, simpler devices such as amplifiers would suffice. However, it's as much the character of the signal as its strength that degenerates during such trips. In addition, amplifiers would bring to the table their own complications, such as boosting the strength of interference as well as of signal. So, repeaters it must be.
	Bridges	You want to connect your backbone to another, which, luckily, is running the same protocol suite and therefore needs no protocol translation.
	Routers	You want to connect your backbone to one that uses a different protocol suite. Or you want to optimize such network characteristics as load levels once the two LANs are joined.

Continued

Table D.2 *Continued*

Type of Component	Component	Needed Because
	Gateways	You want to connect your bus-based LAN to a completely dissimilar environment such as a mainframe-based network. Or you want to connect your LAN to an Internet service provider (ISP) through which you plan to communicate with a number of environments that have nothing in common with your LAN.

Mesh topologies like the example shown in Figure D.2 were designed to circumvent one of the thorniest problems faced by networks following the OSI model: how to prevent, rather than simply detect, signal collisions on a shared transmission medium.

A mesh does so by refusing to share that medium. All nodes in a pure mesh topology are directly connected to all other nodes. As you might imagine, this can very quickly become both bulky and costly. To build a mesh LAN, you must have n^2 NICs and n^2 cable lengths, where n is the number of nodes. We've summarized this flaw of mesh topologies in Table D.3. The last column of this table assumes NICs priced at $125 each and cable runs of 10 feet, at $5 each.

Obviously, a fully mesh topology is seldom found in the real world.

Figure D.1 A typical bus topology.

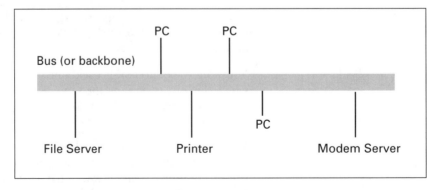

TCP/IP Networking Summary

Figure D.2 A mesh would appear like this from a bird's-eye view.

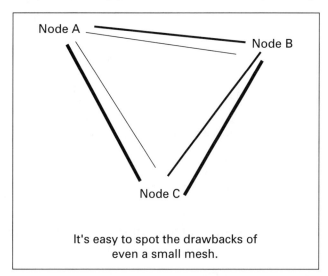

It's easy to spot the drawbacks of
even a small mesh.

Ring topologies are somewhat like meshes in being more the province of theory than of fact. However, unlike with meshes, it is possible to find at least some working examples of rings. These examples, however, may differ from the physical ideal in Figure D.3.

This difference is one of physical structure only, however. Functionally, all ring networks, whatever their appearance, act as if they truly were arranged in a perfect circle. That is, the signals they transmit follow a path that begins and ends at the

Table D.3 One Not-So-Little Drawback of Mesh Topologies

A Mesh LAN of This Many Nodes	Will Need This Many NICs	And This Many Cable Runs	Thereby Costing About This Much More Than Any Other LAN Topology with the Same Number of Nodes
3	9	9	$780 (the cost of the six extra NICs and the 60 extra feet of cable)
7	49	49	$5460 (a whopping $5250 for the 42 extra NICs and an appreciable $210 for the 42 extra cable lengths)
12	144	144	$17,680, $17,000 of which is for NICs alone

Figure D.3 Token-passing networks use this topology.

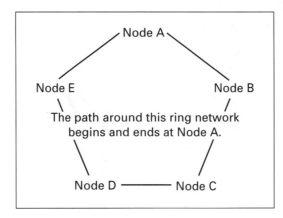

same node. Such a path is dictated by the token-passing access scheme that ring-based LANs employ.

The star topology was devised in an effort to overcome one of the most serious problems encountered by bus-based LANs (Figure D.4).

Such environments frequently experience downtime of several or most of their nodes when only a single fault exists in the LAN's transmission medium. For instance, one cable short or one terminator that has stopped terminating can isolate

Figure D.4 The star is the most popular LAN blueprint.

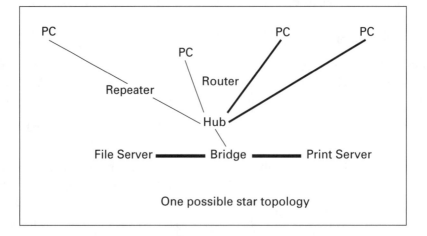

every network node that precedes it on the backbone from the rest of the network. In fact, everything physically preceding the fault is no longer on the network once the fault occurs.

Needless to say, such circumstances cannot be tolerated in a busy or even in an inactive LAN. Reworking the topology was only part of the solution, however. As a direct result of that reorganization, star-based LANs that consist of more than a handful of nodes require additional hardware to function efficiently. That hardware includes hubs as well as other devices discussed in the section "A Summary of Connectivity Devices."

A Summary of Connectivity Devices

This section explains some common terms in connectivity:

- *Hubs.* A hub is no more than a piece of network hardware that acts as a gathering point for wiring. Hubs are needed by buslike or starlike ring topologies to provide a common connectivity point the physical layout fails to offer.

- *Repeaters.* Repeaters may be needed to boost the signal on LANs whose *total overall* length of cable exceeds 100 feet.

- *Bridges.* Bridges connect networks or portions of networks that run the same data link layer protocols.

- *Routers.* If you need to connect a segment or an entire network to another that uses a different protocol suite, or if you need to optimize network characteristics like route selection once the two entities are joined, you'll need a router.

- *Gateways.* Connecting network environments that are dissimilar at every OSI level will require a gateway.

Addressing and Routing

A node on a network or on the Internet can lay claim to several types of addresses, but probably the most important one is the address that's referred to variously as the *Internet address*, the *TCP/IP address*, or simply the *IP address*. Whichever of these names appeals to you (they appear here in ascending buzzword-value order), they mean the same thing. Each indicates the address, composed of four integers separated by periods, that uniquely defines *any node* on *any network anywhere in the world*. No small claim, but it's true!

Transport Control Protocol/Internet Protocol (TCP/IP) is actually a dynamic duo of data communications software. TCP handles the creation and reassembly of packets, which is the dissection of a message into packets at the transmitting end and the corollary rejoining of those packets into the original message at the receiving end. IP, for its part, takes care of addressing the packets TCP has created. In addition, there can be, depending upon the complexity of the network across which messages must be dispersed, other members in the TCP/IP *suite*.

In strict technical terms, the IP address is a sequence of 48 bits and is composed of **octets**, an octet being eight bits. For ease of reading, a period separates the octets, as in the address 207.103.113.153.

This definition differs from the one a couple of paragraphs back because, to a programmer, the word *integer* implies that the value at hand is signed—that is, preceded implicitly or explicitly by either a plus (+) or minus (-)— and that the value in question is either 16 or 32 bits long.

It is this system of addresses upon which TCP/IP routing relies. In 1974, the protocol known as **Network Control Protocol (NCP)**, upon which ARPANet, the granddaddy of the Internet, had relied for packet and routing management, was superseded by TCP/IP, the Transport Control Protocol/Internet Protocol group of programs. TCP/IP was and is a more sophisticated means of accomplishing routing than was NCP. Indeed, TCP/IP has become the de facto standard for data communications which must take place across a variety of network operating systems.

There is an entire subgroup of Transport Layer protocols known as **routing protocols**. Adding to the tangle is that not all routing protocols are created equal. In reality, they're about as uneven as possible, in both the services they offer and the ways they accomplish them.

For example, the TCP/IP protocol suite can work with all the following routing protocols:

- Border Gateway Protocol (BGP)

- Exterior Gateway Protocol (EGP)

- Interior Gateway Routing Protocol (IGRP)

- Intermediate System-to-Intermediate System Protocol (IS-IS)

- Open Shortest Path First Protocol (OSPF)

- Routing Information Protocol (RIP)

However, neither IPX/SPX nor **AppleTalk**, the Apple-proprietary protocol suite, can use any of the entries in this list. What's more, none of these TCP/IP-based routing protocols are the same as any other member of the group; each has its quirks. For instance:

- BGP deals not with the idea of hosts or even networks, but rather with that of **autonomous systems**, which it defines as any set of devices connecting networks or network segments.

- EGP is used solely to connect large networks, such as NSFNET, to one another.

- IGRP will work as well on routes between segments of a network as between networks. It enjoys the additional flexibility of having several configurable characteristics, among them such routing-critical parameters as load levels and bandwidth.

- OSPF was designed specifically to be used in TCP/IP environments. Given the pervasiveness of this protocol suite, it should come as no surprise that OSPF is similarly ubiquitous. But it does have its drawbacks, such as being deaf to non-TCP/IP suites such as AppleTalk.

The evolution of the Internet is illustrated in Figure D.5.

TCP/IP-Related Utilities

The first two or three years of this decade saw the Internet go from a text-based, cryptic-command-controlled, largely programmer- and engineer-used environment to the colorful, graphics-laden, it's-as-easy-as-powering-up-your-PC Net we've become familiar with. Although most of the tools we still use were created by those

Figure D.5 An Internet Timeline.

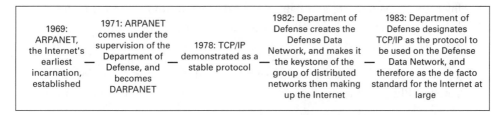

programmers and engineers, we've become so accustomed to their much less techie modern form that we might not recognize their original incarnations. The following is a list of those initial forms.

- *telnet.* The **telnet** (telecommunications network) and **ftp** (file transfer protocol) commands, in their original form, carry a very strong flavor of the UNIX operating system from which they sprung. To this day, you could enter the following at any UNIX command line: **telnet 179.34.59.12.** Doing so (assuming you have a live modem, a correct IP address, and an account on the system represented by that address) would allow you to log in to the remote host in question.

- *ftp.* FTP, or in correct UNIX notation, **ftp**, isn't as friendly as telnet. To use it from the same command line, you could establish the connection by means of a telnet like the one above and then change your working directory to the one housing the files you wished to obtain or to the one where you wished to place files. Carry out a **get** or **put** subcommand respectively to do those operations. Or you could somewhat streamline your task by using ftp to establish the connection as well as to carry out data transfer. Whichever method you chose, you'd also have to be aware that ftp has its own command prompt, different from that of UNIX proper. Also, your ability to transfer data is limited by UNIX's scheme of file and directory permissions, meaning, for instance, that if the system administrator of the remote host has set those permissions up in such a way as to deny the ability to write to a given directory to your login account, you won't be able to place files in that directory, no matter which of the above two ftp wrinkles you choose.

- *gopher.* **Gopher**, although developed under UNIX, had, from its introduction in 1991, a strictly **graphical user interface** (**GUI**). Through this interface, a gopher will seek out and retrieve text-based information (UNIX still had something to say about the matter!) at any site on the Internet that is identified as a gopher site.

  Why the name gopher? This trail-blazing software was developed at the University of Minnesota and named after that institution's mascot. Its name is also a play on words, as in, "What do I do at work? I go get things for everyone; I'm a go-fer."

- *SLIP and PPP.* The **Serial Line Internet Protocol** (**SLIP**) and the **Point-to-Point Protocol** (**PPP**) both allow a computer, whatever its nature, to connect to the

Internet by means of a serial channel such as a telephone line. PPP is more sophisticated than SLIP in providing error detection and data compression; SLIP, on the other hand, is included in most versions of UNIX, still the predominant operating system among large Internet hosts.

What prompted the invention of these new protocols? The phrase *serial channel* is the answer. TCP/IP, the protocol suite used almost exclusively between large Internet hosts, ordinarily runs on Ethernet or coaxial cable, the most common example of which is that piece of black-plastic-coated wire through which your TV or VCR grabs cable television programs. Such cable, nicknamed **coax**, consists of a number of bundles of copper wire arranged circularly within a protective sheath. The cable as a whole shares a single common axis, hence the name. Coax cable has a much wider bandwidth—which means it can carry a greater range of frequencies of electronic signal—than does serial telephone wire, which was designed to carry only that range of frequencies of which the human voice is capable.

- *The World Wide Web.* The British researcher Tim Berners-Lee, working at CERN, the European Laboratory for Particle Physics, developed the software that underlies the World Wide Web to allow physicists the world over, whatever their native language, easy access to data related to their studies. At the core of this and all Web software is the concept of hypertext.

Hypertext does not consist of highly emotionally charged words, but is a scheme for relating blocks of information, regardless of the computer on which that information resides. To do so, it relies on Internet concepts like IP addresses. But hypertext, or hypertext links, follow the lead set by gopher in allowing the user to move from one item in the relational chain to the next by strictly visually driven means. Clicking on a highlighted or underlined word or phrase will display the information indicated by that word or phrase.

This method is far preferable to command-line-driven access to information, as with telnet and ftp. This high degree of friendliness and the release around the world in 1992 by CERN of its WWW software were the most recent bits of fuel on the fire of today's Internet frenzy. The Web is almost solely responsible for that obsession. In 1994 alone, use of the Web grew by more than *350,000* percent. It remains by far the most frequently used means of access to Internet-offered information.

E

Bug Fixes and FAQs: Excerpts from the Microsoft Web Site

This section includes almost-verbatim excerpts from the area of the MS Web site that posts bugs uncovered by users and fixes for those bugs suggested by users or by Microsoft itself. We include, from the hundreds available, sample bug reports that we think reflect a wide range of environments.

The items in this appendix have been edited only to bring their format into agreement with that of the book as a whole. Otherwise, you're reading them as they would appear at the NT Server section of the Microsoft Web site.

Bug Fixes and FAQs

These bug reports and fixes date from February and March of 1997. It is possible that additional information regarding the problems they describe has been posted to the Microsoft Web site since then. If your NT or IIS server is experiencing any of these glitches, check the MS web for updates.

Upgrade to Windows NT 4.0 May Not Keep All Registry Settings

When you upgrade from Windows NT 3.51 to Windows NT 4.0, entries under the following registry key are not maintained:

HKEY_LCAL_MACHINE\SYSTEM\CurrentControlSet\Control\ServiceGroupOrder\
List.

Cause

This key is overwritten during the Windows NT 4.0 Setup process, and old settings
are not maintained.

Resolution

Reinstall the program or driver to create the new class entry in Windows NT version 4.0.

Microsoft has confirmed this to be a problem in Microsoft Windows NT version
4.0. We are researching this problem and will post new information in the
Microsoft Knowledge Base as it becomes available.

Play Button Unavailable When CD Is Reinserted in CD-ROM Drive

When you are playing an audio CD, if you eject the CD using the button in CD
Player or the eject button on the CD-ROM drive and then reinsert the CD, the **Play**
button may remain unavailable.

If you stop playing the CD in CD Player, eject it with the button on the CD-
ROM drive and then reinsert the same CD, the **Play** button works normally.
However, if you do this and insert a different CD, the **Play** button is available, but
does nothing when you click it.

Cause

The Autorun feature in Windows NT 4.0 has been disabled.

Resolution

Stopping and restarting the CD Player program makes the **Play** button work correctly
again. If the Autorun feature has been disabled, enabling it also resolves the issue.

> **N O T E** When any CD is reinserted, CD Player may seem to read the CD
> (the light may blink on the CD-ROM drive), but the behavior described
> above still occurs.

Delay When a Word 7.0 File Is Being Saved to Windows NT 4.0 Server

In Microsoft Word version 7.0, there is a delay when you save a modified document to a network drive that is located on a Windows NT 4.0 server.

> **WARNING** Using Registry Editor incorrectly can cause serious, systemwide problems that may require you to reinstall Windows NT to correct them. Microsoft cannot guarantee that any problems resulting from the use of Registry Editor can be solved. Use this tool at your own risk.

Cause

The Windows NT client was ignoring the oplock (opportunistic lock) break request from the server.

Workaround

To work around this problem, you can disable an optimization called oplock on the remote Windows NT server or you can apply the hotfix following these steps:

1. Start the Registry Editor (Regedt32.exe).

2. Find the following key:
   \HKEY_LOCAL_MACHINE\SYSTEM\CurrentControlSet\Services\
   LanmanServer\Parameters.

3. Add the following entry, if it is not already present:

   Value Name: EnableOplocks

   Data Type: REG_DWORD

   Data: 0

   If the entry already exists, set the data to 0.

4. Exit the registry.

5. Shut down and restart Windows NT.

For additional information about oplocks, please see the following article in the Microsoft Knowledge Base: ARTICLE-ID: Q129202.

Opportunistic Locking on Windows NT

Disabling oplocks might cause a slight decrease in performance, but should not be noticeable.

Status

Microsoft has confirmed oplocks to be a problem in Windows NT version 4.0. A supported fix is now available, but has not been fully regression-tested and should be applied only to systems experiencing this specific problem. Unless you are severely impacted by this specific problem, Microsoft recommends that you wait for the next Service Pack that contains this fix.

Printing from Windows NT 4.0 to NetWare 3.12 Seems Slow

(The information in this article applies to Microsoft Windows NT Workstation version 4.0.)

Connectivity between Client Services for NetWare (CSNW) and Novell NetWare 3.12 print queues may be slow in Windows NT Workstation 4.0. Programs that use printers connected to NetWare 3.12 print queues may seem to start slowly.

Status

Microsoft is researching this problem of slow printing and will post new information in the Microsoft Knowledge Base as it becomes available.

Sony Spressa SCSI CD-ROM Drive May Not Be Detected

Windows NT Setup may not detect the Sony Spressa CDU-920S SCSI CD-ROM drive.

Cause

The Sony Spressa CDU-920S is shipped with the Parity, ID1, ID2, and Prevent/Allow settings preset to On. Note that the Parity jumper is also known as the Device Type jumper.

Resolution

Remove the Parity/Device Type jumper. Note also that the firmware version must be 2.0B. For information about removing jumpers or determining the firmware version, contact Sony Corporation.

NTBackup Does Not Properly Eject Tapes on DLT Tape Devices

Under Windows NT 4.0, from GUI or command-line mode of Ntbackup.exe, the eject command does not unload the tape on DLT style tape drives. The tape will rewind but doesn't unload. One can complete the unload process by pressing the **Unload** button on the DLT tape device.

Under Windows NT 3.51 (GUI only), the tape rewinds. When you hear a click, which means the tape is unloaded, you can lift the handle to remove the tape.

Workaround

Use the **Unload** button to complete the operation preparing the tape for removal from the device. Also, Adaptec EZ-SCSI 4.0 supports the proper unloading of the tape.

Microsoft has confirmed this to be a problem in Windows NT 4.0. We are researching this problem and will post new information in the Microsoft Knowledge Base as it becomes available.

Change of Printer IP Address Not Recognized by Spooler

If you create an LPR printer in Print Manager and specify the printer's host name instead of an IP address, then change the printer's IP address on the DNS server or in the hosts file, the Spooler service does not recognize the new IP address and will log an Event ID 2004 error.

The Spooler service resolves the host name to an IP address only once, when Spooler service starts up.

Workaround

When the IP address of a printer is changed, stop and restart the Spooler service.

Status

Microsoft has confirmed this to be a problem in Windows NT version 3.51 and 4.0. A supported fix is now available, but has not been fully regression-tested and should be applied only to systems experiencing this specific problem. Unless you are severely impacted by this specific problem, Microsoft recommends that you wait for the next Service Pack that contains this fix.

Troubleshooting Printing Problems in Windows NT 4.0
This article describes how to troubleshoot printing problems in Windows NT 4.0.

Printing to a Local Device
To troubleshoot a problem printing to a local drive, verify that you can print from a command prompt.

From a non-PostScript printer, type "**dir > lpt1**" (without quotation marks) at a command prompt.

If you are using a PostScript Printer, refer to Microsoft Knowledge Base ARTI-CLE-ID: Q64859.

Testing the Connection to a PostScript Printer Plotter
See the following Web site: http://hpcc997.external.hp.com/cposupport/plotters/support_doc/BPP01244.html.

This tests to determine if the parallel port driver and the hardware are working correctly. If you do not receive any output, get garbled output, or receive an "Unable to write to port" message, check the following hardware issues:

- Check the cable to see if it meets the IEEE 1284 specification. If it does, it is marked on the cable itself.

- Remove any switch boxes.

- Perform a self-test on the printer. If it prints correctly, the issue is with Windows NT or the program.

  Note: Printing from a command prompt does not work if the printer is a PostScript Printer.

Printing from Wordpad or Notepad
Printing from a Wordpad or Notepad tests the printer driver. If it prints correctly, the problem lies with the program. However, this does not mean that Windows NT is not involved. Windows NT may not be running a particular printing command that the program requires. (See the "Program" section of this article.) If it does not print correctly, the problem may be in the printer driver. Try the following:

- If it is a PostScript printer, load the Apple LaserWriter NT driver. This is a very basic PostScript driver, and using it will determine whether the problem is related to the particular PPD file for the printer.

- If the printer is non-PostScript, load the Generic/Text Only printer driver. This is a very basic driver, and using it will determine whether the basic printing stack is working properly.

- If it is a plotter, load the Hewlett-Packard HP-GL/2 Plotter driver. If the device does not print with the basic drivers, see the "Printing Stac" section of this article. If it does print, see the "Program" section.

Printing to a Network Device

If you're printing to a network device, try the following:

- Verify basic network connectivity.

- Check user rights, protocols, share names, and so on to determine if you can see the server. Copy files to a share on the print server using File Manager in Windows NT 3.x or Windows NT Explorer in Windows NT 4.0. If you cannot access the server, you may not be able to access the printer.

- Create a local printer and redirect the port to the network server. Create a local printer and in the Ports section, create a new port. Click **Local**, and type the server and printer name for the printer (use the \\servername\printername syntax). Use this port for the local printer. This determines whether there is a problem with the copying of files from the server to the workstation that occurs when you use a Connect To setup or click **Network Printer** in the Add Printer Wizard.

Printing from an MS-DOS-Based Program

If you are printing from MS-DOS, try the following:

- Make sure that the **NET USE** command has been run to map the LPT port to the network share. If it has, delete it and remap the port. If it then works, there may be an issue with ghosted connections. A command may need to be run in the login script to remap the port each time you log on.

- If it is still not printing, try typing "**dir > LPT<x>**" (without quotation marks) where <x> is the number of the port being mapped. If it still does not print, double-check the networking.

> **N O T E** Printing from MS-DOS-based programs does not work if the printer is a PostScript Printer.

Using LPR or Printing to a JetDirect Card Using the TCP/IP Protocol

If your printing problem involves LPR or a JetDirect Card, use one of these methods:

- Ping the IP address. If it fails, check the network connectivity and verify IP addresses.

- Create an LPR port to the printer and then create a local printer connected to that port. This is the recommended way to connect to a JetDirect printer. Sharing this printer on the network allows the computer to act as a print queue for the JetDirect printer.

For additional information, see ARTICLE-ID: Q124735 in the Microsoft Knowledge Base.

Err Msg: There Are No Print Processors... Creating a Printer

Remove the printers, delete all the files from the Winnt\System32\Spool\Drivers\ W32x86 folder, and reinstall the printers. This refreshes all the printer files.

For additional information, please see ARTICLE-ID: Q135406 in the Microsoft Knowledge Base.

AutoCAD 13

A White Paper on Autodesk's World Wide Web site describes how to configure AutoCAD 13 to print correctly in Windows NT. See the following site:http://www.autodesk.com/support /techdocs/acadpp/ td130759.htm.

IIS Execution File Text Can Be Viewed in Client

(The information in this article applies to Microsoft Internet Information Server, versions 2.0 and 3.0.)

On February 23, 1997, Microsoft was alerted to a posting regarding an Internet Information Server (IIS) security exposure. This bug permits the publication of IIS executable files via a complicated string of commands sent from a Web browser to an IIS server. Because of this security exposure, Internet users can view Active Server Pages (ASP), Internet Server API applications (ISAPI), Internet Database

Connector (IDC) applications, or Common Gateway Interface (CGI) applications within an IIS publication installation.

Resolution
Get the hotfix mentioned below, which has been posted to the following Internet location. from the service Internet (anonymous FTP) to ftp ftp.microsoft.com, you can download any of these self-extracting files:

- Change to the bussys/winnt/winnt-public/fixes/usa/nt40/hotfixes-postSP2/iis-fix/ folder.

- Get Readme.1st (for instructions on downloading and installing the hotfix).

  Or use the following full URL on your client browser: FTP://ftp.microsoft.com/bussys/winnt/winnt-public/fixes/usa/nt40/hotfixes-postSP2/iis-fix/readme.1st.

Status
Microsoft has confirmed this bug to be a problem in Microsoft Internet Information Server versions 2.0 and 3.0. A supported fix is now available, but has not been fully regression-tested and should be applied only to systems experiencing this specific problem. Unless you are severely impacted by this problem, Microsoft recommends that you wait for the next Service Pack that contains this fix.

Remove Old Device Drivers before Installing Windows NT 4.0
When you upgrade to Windows NT 4.0 from an earlier version of Windows NT, disable all nonessential services and devices before beginning the upgrade.

In order to ensure a clean, stable upgrade from Windows NT 3.x, disable or remove third-party services and devices. If you do not, these devices or services may try to start during the reboot between the character-based and GUI-based portions of setup. This situation may cause the computer to display a debug screen (for example, "STOP 0x0000050" or "STOP 0x0000001E") and halt, or to become so unstable that setup cannot finish.

If a driver or service is not required for system operation, disable it before upgrading to Windows NT 4.0. If a driver or service is required for system operation (such as a SCSI controller or network card), obtain a driver for Windows NT 4.0 from the third-party provider and have the driver available on a floppy disk for use during the upgrade process.

To disable a driver, follow these steps:

1. In Control Panel, double-click **Devices**.

2. Click the third-party driver you want to disable, and then click **Startup**.

3. In the Device dialog box, click **Disabled**, and then restart the computer.

4. In Control Panel, double-click **Devices** and verify that the device did not start.

To disable a service, use the following steps:

1. In Control Panel, double-click **Services**.

2. Click the third-party service you want to disable, and then click **Startup**.

3. In the Service dialog box, click **Disabled**, and then restart the computer.

4. In Control Panel, double-click **Services**, and then verify that the service did not start.

Troubleshooting Internet Service Provider Login Problems

This article describes how to troubleshoot problems when you can connect to your Internet service provider (ISP) but you cannot log in or be authenticated.

Problems logging into an ISP can be related to configuration problems with Dial-Up Networking (DUN) in Windows NT or problems with your ISP. This article discusses only login problems, not modem or dialing problems. For additional information, please see ARTICLE-ID: Q161516 (Troubleshooting Modem Problems Under Windows NT 4.0) in the Microsoft Knowledge Base.

Accept Any Authentication Including Clear Text

If you are having trouble logging into your (ISP), the first troubleshooting step is to configure DUN to accept any authentication, including clear text. To do so, follow these steps:

1. In Dial-Up Networking, select the phone book entry for your ISP.

2. Click **More**, click **Edit Entry**, and then click **Modem Properties**.

3. Click the Security tab.

4. Click "**Accept any authentication including clear text.**"

5. Try to connect to your ISP.

Open a Terminal Window

If you are using clear text and you continue to have problems logging in to your ISP, you may need to use a terminal window if the ISP is expecting additional information (other than your user name and password). To open a terminal window after you connect, follow these steps:

1. In Dial-Up Networking, select the phone book entry for your ISP.

2. Click **More**, click **Edit Entry**, and then click **Modem Properties**.

3. Click the Script tab.

4. Click **Pop Up A Terminal Window**. This forces the use of clear text (PAP) authentication.

5. Try connecting to your ISP again.

6. If the PPP/SLIP account requires you to log in using a terminal window, do so, and then type **SLIP** or **PPP** at a terminal prompt to actually start the session.

   When you log in to some ISPs, you may need to prefix your user name with characters such as *S* or *P* or *PPP* and so on. Contact your ISP to see if your user name needs any special prefix.

Using a Script

If you must enter information other than your user name and password, you may need to contact your ISP for assistance in creating a script file to use with Dial-Up Networking.

Windows NT includes several basic script files including Ppp.scp, Slip.scp, and Cis.scp. When you use the CompuServe Information Service (CIS) script, you must use your CIS ID for your user name. For example, <XXXXX,XXXX>. See the Script.doc file in the Winnt\System32\Ras\Script folder for information about using these files. If you have problems creating a script file to automate your login, contact your ISP.

If you have a SLIP account, you must use a terminal window or a script file to connect. When you are using a SLIP account, most ISPs display your IP address for the session in the terminal window. Most providers inform you of the IP address with a message similar to one of these: "Your IP address is <###.###.###.###>" or "SLIP session from <###.###.###.###> to <###.###.###.###>." In this case, the second number is usually your IP address. You need to enter this in the IP Address box. If the address is the same every time you connect, you can change it in the phone book entry in TCP/IP settings.

LCP Extensions and the Multilinking Protocol

You may also have trouble connecting if your ISP's Point-to-Point protocol (PPP) server does not support LCP extensions or the Multilinking protocol (MP). For example, to use MSN, the Microsoft Network, as your ISP in Windows NT 4.0, you must disable MP.

If you do not have Service Pack 2 or later installed, you can disable MP by disabling LCP extensions using the following steps:

1. In Dial-Up Networking, select the phone book entry for your ISP.

2. Click **More**, click **Edit Entry**, and then click **Modem Properties**.

3. Click the Server tab, and then clear the Enable PPP LCP Extensions check box.

4. Try connecting to your ISP again.

For additional information about the effects of disabling LCP extensions, use the right mouse button to click **Enable PPP LCP Extensions** on the Server tab, and then click **What's This?** on the menu that appears.

If you have Service Pack 2 installed, use the resolution described in ARTICLE-ID: Q161368 (Service Pack 2 May Cause Loss of Connectivity in Remote Access) in the Microsoft Knowledge Base.

Internet Information Server 4.0
Quick Reference

This appendix is an effort to encapsulate the most significant features and concepts of the newest IIS release. It contains a few-dozen-plus IIS 4.0 concepts, and links them to not only the IIS component to which they relate, but also to the networking territory to which they pertain.

Concept	Relates to	Pertains To
ACCESS ACCEPT	Authentication Server	Message sent after correct entry by user of logon name and password, which allows user access to the network.
ACCESS REJECT	Authentication Server	Message sent after incorrect entry by user of logon name and password, which denies user access to the network.

Continued

Concept	Relates to	Pertains to
Active Directory Service Interfaces	Web Publishing, Transaction Server	Users' ability to access directory systems that rely on differing paradigms, through a single interface.
Active Server Pages File **upload.asp**	Posting Acceptor	Automatically refers the browser to **uploadX.asp** if the browser is ActiveX-capable, or to **uploadN.asp** if it is not.
Active Templates Library (ATL)	Transaction Server	A Visual Basic component required for applications to be deployed under Transaction Server.
ActiveX Upload Control **flupl.cab**	Posting Acceptor	Allows users to drag and drop files and folders in order to upload them.
ASP PostInfo File **postinfo.asp**	Posting Acceptor	Holds the PostingURL and TargetURL that Posting Acceptor requires.
Atomic Transactions	Transaction Server	Program segments or instructions that rely on no other such segments or instructions.
Authentication Server	All Areas of IIS	The ability of a server to authenticate remote users who access the network via dial-up.
Certificate Mapper	MMC	An MMC feature that tracks the distribution of authentication certificates across a network.
CRS Mapping Module **crsmapr.dll**	Posting Acceptor	Gets URLs, and compares them with the target. If a match is found, the corresponding physical location on the server's hard drive is reported back to Posting Acceptor.

Concept	Relates to	Pertains to
Distributed Transaction Coordinator	Transaction Server	Coordinates the execution of transactions with a two-phase commit protocol.
Durable Changes	Transaction Server	Changes that affect data stored on disk, rather than data temporarily residing in memory during an application's processing.
File System Mapping Module **cpshost.dll**	Posting Acceptor	Establishes a mapping between the target URL and the hard drive as a result of talking to IIS, Personal Web Server, or Peer Web Services.
HKEY_LOCAL_ MACHINE\System\ CurrentControlSet \Services\WebPost\ Providers	Web Publishing Wizard	The Registry key that must be edited to permit the use of browsers other than Internet Explorer 3.x and up.
In-Process	Transaction Server	Modules that execute as part of another module or process.
Internet Remote Access System (IRAS)	Authentication Server, as Well as IIS as a Whole	IRAS has several components in addition to Authentication Server:
		• Connection Point Services, comprised of the Connection Point Server and Connection Point Administration tool. Connection Point Services automate the process of updating subscribers' computers with new access numbers and service types.
		• Connection Manager Administration Kit (CMAK). CMAK includes a dialer and

Continued

Concept	Relates to	Pertains to
		provides a wizard for creating customized versions of Connection Manager for clients using Windows NT 4.0 and Windows 95.
Mail Server	Such Existing IIS Features as NetMeeting	Users' ability to exchange mail and other data across servers operating differing mail, conferencing, and Web servers.
Microsoft Management Console	All Areas of IIS	Supplies a standardized interface to all IIS (and NT) administrative tools.
Multiple Document Interface	All Areas of IIS	The means by which the MMC-driven IIS 4.0 administrative interface can create display frames and windows on the fly, as appropriate to the needs of the tool of the moment.
Network Access Servers (NAS)	Authentication Server	Servers, seen as devices by Authentication Server, that feed it user access attempts to be allowed or denied.
News Server	Such Existing IIS Features as NetMeeting	Users' ability to post to newsgroups across servers running differing mail, news, and Web servers.
ObjectContext	Transaction Server	Allows you to prevent a transaction from being committed or declare that it has completed; to instantiate other Transaction Server objects or to include those objects within the current object's transaction; and even to ascertain if, and which, security measures have been enabled.

Concept	Relates to	Pertains to
ObjectControl	Transaction Server	Allows you to specify whether Transaction Server should recycle objects rather than successively constructing and then destroying them.
Point to Point Tunneling Protocol (PPTP)	Authentication Server	Protocol that creates and maintains secure connections within an intranet, by preventing user access to areas of that intranet not specifically authorized to him or her.
Postinfo.eg	Posting Acceptor	Acts as an example of a line that needs to be added to default.htm, that is, to a client's homepage, so that it can act as a PostInfo file.
Posting Acceptor	Web Publishing	A Web server's ability to, and facility in, accepting content for publication.
Posting Acceptor ISAPI **cpshost.dll**	Posting Acceptor	Receives posted files and saves them to the indicated server target URL.
RADIUS	Authentication Server	Remote Access Dial-In User Service, the protocol that is the basis for Authentication Server.
Request Duration	Usage Analyst	The amount of time elapsed between two consecutive requests within a single visit.
Resource Dispensers	Transaction Server	Components that provide data or other resources to distributed applications.
Resource Managers	Transaction Server	Components that data and other resources among the modules of an application, and among applications.

Continued

Concept	Relates to	Pertains to
Sample Page for Clients Using ActiveX to Upload **uploadX.asp**	Posting Acceptor	Allows browsers that support ActiveX to talk to Posting Acceptor.
Sample Page for Clients Using HTTP **uploadN.asp**	Posting Acceptor	Allows browsers based on the HTTP Post protocol to upload to a server running Posting Acceptor.
Script Debugger	Web Publishing	Developers' efforts to quickly and efficiently create and implement scripts, both server- and client-based, which control Web pages and access to them.
SecurityProperty	Transaction Server	Allows you to determine what other module has called, or created, the current object.
Shared Property Group	Transaction Server	A set of characteristics shared across modules within an application.
Shared Property Manager	Transaction Server	Provides synchronized access to application-wide variables.
Site Analyst	Web Publishing, MMC	Visually based Web site administrative tool.
Snap-Ins	MMC, and Indirectly, All Areas of IIS	The basis of the scheme under which applications making up tools or features add-ons can be identified to MMC in general, and to Internet Services Manager in particular; ISM is itself considered an MMC Snap-In.
Spider	Site Analyst	Tool that crawls Web sites as the basis for creating maps of them.

Concept	Relates to	Pertains to
Target Audience(s)	Usage Analyst	How frequently a user or group of users access specific areas of a site, or the site as a whole.
Tools	MMC, and Indirectly, All Areas of IIS	Aggregates of Snap-Ins that have been configured to carry out a specific function, and have been identified to MMC as such an aggregate.
Transaction Server	Web Publishing	Provides a high degree of control over the deployment and management of distributed applications, particularly those, like many Web pages, that interact with databases.
Usage Analyst	Internet Services Manager	Provides statistics on site usage above and beyond those offered by ISM.
VBScript and JScript	Web Publishing	Allow developers a high degree of control over how client browsers will present Web content, and what users can do to interact with that content.
Visit Duration	Usage Analyst	The amount of time elapsed between the first and last requests of a visit.
Web Publishing Wizard	Web Publishing	Can be viewed as a Wizard-driven version of FrontPage.
Web-Based Enterprise Management	All Areas of IIS	A standard, still very much under development, for the use of Internet technologies in the management of intranets and their users.

Continued

Concept	Relates to	Pertains to
WebMap	Site Analyst	A visual representation of the structure of, and relationships within, a Web site.
Windows Management Instrumentation	All Areas of IIS	A set of methods and technologies for network management, still under development, which can be viewed as Microsoft's answer to such schemes as DMI, originated by IBM, Novell, and others.
Windows Scripting Host	MMC, Web Publishing	As much related to creating batch files to automate system and network administration as to scripting in the Web Publishing sense.
Zero Administration Initiative for Windows	All Areas of IIS	An effort to create a standardized administrative architecture and interface for Windows NT and its components.

Glossary

We've included every significant IIS, NT, and networking term in this glossary. Its contents are not categorized, however, so you'll find the terms mixed throughout.

10Base2 is thin Ethernet or coax.

10Base5 is thick Ethernet; an older form of the cable.

10BaseT is unshielded twisted pair (phone) cable.

An **abstract** is a summary of a document or HTML page created by Index Server; also referred to as a characterization.

Access Control List (ACL) is a set of Windows NT permissions that allow some users to access a file or directory while denying access to others.

An **account policy**, under Windows NT Server 4.0, is a set of ranges of values for the parameters of user accounts.

ActiveX, announced by Microsoft in March 1996, is a group of technologies that allows you to use OLE controls on the Web. ActiveX components can be written in C, C++, or Java.

To **aggregate** is to gather the results of some process; in an IIS context, most frequently used in discussing Index server.

Amplitude is the height of the wave that makes up one cycle of an electromagnetic signal; in sound, it is analogous to volume.

Analog signals are electromagnetic signals that can exist in a wide range of states; the type of signal transmitted by telephone lines.

An **applet** is a Java term for an executable application module.

AppleTalk isApple's proprietary protocol suite; it includes individual protocols at a number of OSI levels.

Application Program Interface (API) consists of software modules by means of which existing applications may be customized; for example, ISAPI (Internet Server Application Program Interface).

Application Service Element is a standalone software module that acts as an OSI level 7 protocol.

Application Service Object is a software module that, with other members of the group to which it belongs, acts as a protocol for OSI's Application Layer.

Archive is a synonym for **backup**; also, the type of file created by a backup.

Arithmeticals are actions or operators that are made up of simple arithmetic; in programming, most frequently includes the actions addition, subtraction, multiplication, division, and exponentiation.

Authentication is the process by which security-related information is verified; usually used in the context of passwords.

To **autodetect** means to find by itself; usually used in the context of installation software determining the hardware and applications already present on the system to which additional software is being loaded.

A **backup** is a copy of data and/or software created as insurance against the possibility of loss or corruption and corollary system or network downtime.

Bandwidth is a range of frequencies in electromagnetic signals.

Banyan is a LAN vendor; producer of the network operating system called Vines.

Base memory address is the bottom of a range of memory addresses that may be used by certain hardware or software components; for example, video drivers will have a base address that is different from that of printer drivers.

Baud is an older term applied to rates of data transmission; roughly equivalent to Kbps, but not exactly the same.

Binary is a numbering system that has only two types of units: 1 and 0.

Binding is the association of a protocol with a network adapter.

A **bit** is a binary digit; that is, the 0 or 1, the only two "letters" in a computer's alphabet.

Bitmap is a process whereby the placement of individual bits on a display is specified programatically. Bitmapping allows a high degree of definition in displays.

BMP is a file name extension used to indicate Windows bitmap format files.

Boolean is both a type of logic and a set of operators that represent aspects of that logic. Boolean operators can produce only two results: true and false. AND, OR, and NOT are common Boolean operators, used by many programming languages and environments.

Breaker, word is a utility in Index Server that identifies words in a document and where they are located within a sentence.

A **bridge** is a hardware component that can connect segments of a network that require no protocol translation. Many bridges have some processing capabilities, allowing them to ensure that the segment-specific traffic they monitor remains within the segment. In addition, bridges have the ability to act as repeaters, so when a bridge is in use, a repeater is seldom if ever needed.

Browsing is data processing jargon for skimming through data in order to find a desired value.

Bus or **bussing** is the circuitry that handles the exchange of signals between the components on or attached to a PC's motherboard.

A **byte** is a computer's representation of what would be to us a single readable or printable character; a byte can be made up of anywhere from five to eight bits.

Cache is an area of memory or disk that has been reserved for and is used solely by frequently executed program instructions or frequently accessed data.

Case-sensitive distinguishes between upper- and lowercase letters.

Catalog, under Index Server, is the directory in which its data is stored.

Catapult is the code name under which Microsoft Proxy Server was known during its development, and the nickname by which it is still called.

Certificate, in Windows NT and IIS, refers to the verification of SSL keys.

Certificate request is the process that creates key pairs and requests their verification.

CGI, Common Gateway Interface, is a standard for a Web-related scripting language that accomplishes communications between external programs and an HTTP server.

Changer is a type of CD-ROM device that houses many CDs but plays only one at a time.

Child process is an executing computer program that was started by another such program; in an IIS context, most frequently used in discussions of Index Server.

Class, in C++ terms, is analogous to typedefs in Pascal or structures and unions in other programming languages; in effect, a grouping of variables, variables and data, or even variables, data, and software modules.

A **client** is any Customer or customer group that has an identifying set of attributes in Internet Authentication Server unique to that account.

Clients and servers refer to a station on a LAN that requests, rather than houses and distributes, services such as applications, print services, and so on. Clients have local disk, processing, and memory, but are seldom as powerful as servers.

Coax, short for coaxial cable, is most commonly applied to thin Ethernet.

Column is another term for a database field.

Compression Control Protocol (CCP) is an encryption protocol used with Point-to-Point Tunneling Protocol (PPTP).

Concentrator is a form of smart or active hub. A concentrator not only can act as a nexus for individual connections, but also can strengthen a signal in the same way a repeater does.

Connectionless refers to a protocol that does not try to reserve a path between sender and receiver before transmitting.

Connection-oriented, in reference to a protocol, is one that seeks to establish and guard the connection between sender and receiver of data before transmitting that data.

Convlog is a utility provided by Windows NT Server 4.0 to convert log files from one format to another.

Corpus, under Index Server, is the collection of documents and HTML pages it indexes.

Counters, under Windows NT Server 4.0, form a very large collection of performance parameters that may be monitored; counters exist not only for NT itself, but for all its adjuncts, including Internet Information Server.

CSMA/CD, Carrier Sense Multiple Access with Collision Detection, is the method of access to the network transmission medium most frequently found in Ethernet LANs.

Cursor, under Index Server, is a pointer into a context index.

DDE, dynamic data exchange, is another term for interprocess communication.

Default is a value or set of values presented by software for some of its parameters, which will be used unless you specify otherwise.

A **delimiter** is a special kind of operator that indicates the beginning or end of a value or expression.

DHCP, Dynamic Host Configuration Protocol, is a protocol that in effect assigns Internet addresses on the fly as they become available from a pool.

Digital signals are electromagnetic signals that can exist in only one of two states; the type of signal generated within computers.

Discrete signal is another name for digital signal.

Disk duplexing is a RAID technique that fully duplicates drive contents, but assigns an individual controller to each drive so duplicated.

Disk mirroring is a RAID technique that completely duplicates all information on a hard drive to another drive, but uses only one controller to access both drives.

DLL, Dynamic Link Library, a library of software modules that can be accessed and executed by other programs.

DMZ network is a network, often virtual, that sits between, can be accessed from, but filters the exchanges between, networks.

DNS, Domain Name Server, is an application that tracks remote hosts and the Internet domain names under which they operate.

Domain, on the Internet, is a portion of an address that indicates the broad category an entity belongs to; under Windows NT Server, the logical (as opposed to physical) grouping of network resources to which a user connects.

Domain controller, under Windows NT, is the computer that houses user, security, and file system management data; may be either a primary or backup domain controller.

A **driver** is a software module that carries out a specific but usually narrowly defined and low-level task; one example is a modem driver.

Dynamic refers to data or applications that may change regularly and spontaneously.

EIDE, extended integrated drive enhancement, is a souped-up IDE.

EISA, extended industry standard architecture, is a souped-up ISA.

E-mail or e-mail address refers to electronic mail. Addresses for this type of mail are most commonly of the form somebody@somewhere.xxx. What precedes the @ is the user's mail name on his or her home system. What follows that sign is what's called the domain name. Domain names include an identifier not only of the organization in which the message originated, but also of the type of organization it is. Some e-mail addresses, however, are of the form 12345.67890@ someplace.xxx. The period-separated portion of such an address is the equivalent of the somebody part of the more common type. Probably best known among this second category of e-mail addresses are those of CompuServe. In fact, addresses following this format are often called CompuServe addresses.

EMWAC, European Microsoft Windows Academic Centre, is a format for log files, among other things.

Engine is data processing jargon for a software module or group of modules that carry out a specific but relatively complex task; one example is a search engine.

Ethernet can apply to either networking hardware (as in thin Ethernet) or software (as in Ethernet protocols, often used as a colloquialism for TCP/IP).

Even parity looks for an even number of 1s in a byte.

Event is a data processing term for an action such as pressing a key or clicking the mouse, or for software-related occurrences such as exceeding of limits defined for the value of a particular parameter.

Extensions, in an ISAPI context, are code modules that have a relatively broad applicability, as opposed to filters, whose functions are more narrowly defined.

FAT, file allocation table, is the means of file management created for and made familiar by DOS.

FDDI, Fiber Distributed Data Interface, is commonly known as fiber optic cable. It is very fast, running at a minimum of 100Mbps, and very clean; that is, subject to little or no distortion or attenuation of signal.

A **field** is a single element of information within a database; for example, last name or zip code might be fields in an employee database.

Filter, content, is an Index Server component that reads a document from disk and extracts its contents.

Filter DLL is a DLL made up of filter modules.

Filtering, in data communications, is usually used in terms of packet filtering, a process whereby specified types of protocols may be denied access to a network.

A **firewall** is essentially a software module that sits between a network and those trying to access the network, preventing certain categories of activity from getting through.

Folder is the term used under Windows NT and Windows95 for *directory*.

Free-text query, under Index Server, is a type of query in which a user supplies words, phrases, or complete sentences as the basis for the query.

Frequency is the interval required for the completion of one cycle of an electromagnetic signal; in sound, it is analogous to pitch.

Front end is an application or hardware component that carries on initial processing for another application or hardware component, thereby freeing the latter for tasks more germane to it.

FSCONVERT is the utility provided with Windows NT Server 4.0 that will convert a FAT to an NTFS file system.

Fuzzy Query refers to queries that search for and retrieve not only specified terms but terms resembling those specified.

FTP, File Transfer Protocol, is used to place or retrieve files from remote UNIX systems. It is still widely used on today's Internet, albeit with GUI front ends.

Gateway consists of hardware devices that connect environments in need of protocol translation at every level of the OSI model.

GET is an HTML command meaning, in effect, retrieve the data specified.

GIF is the extension portion of a filename that indicates the Graphics Interchange Format.

A **gigabyte** is a bit over a billion bytes, or $1024 \times 1024 \times 1024$.

Global pertains to all computers on a network; under Windows NT Server, the term has the additional connotation of spanning domains.

Gopher is file location and retrieval software. It is the earliest example of the GUI-driven applications we've become so used to on the Internet.

Hardware Abstraction Layers (HALs) are software packages that allow an operating system to ignore hardware-level services such as interrupts.

Hardware Compatability List (HCL) is Microsoft's extensive list of Windows NT Server 4.0-compatible components.

Hexadecimal is a numbering system that works in units of 16 and uses as symbols not only the digits 0 through 9, but also the letters A through F.

Hiding is data processing jargon for preventing users from being aware of the existence of a computer or network resource.

Home directory is the directory in which a user or application begins work.

HTML, hypertext markup language, is a system of annotation to accomplish text formatting; used in World Wide Web files.

Hypertext is text that is linked to related information, allowing that information to be immediately accessed, regardless of where it is stored.

IDC, Internet Data Connector, is in effect, an HTML front end to ODBC.

IDE, integrated drive enhancement, is a type of hard drive controller that places much of the disk management circuitry on the controller card rather than on the drive proper.

IEEE, the Institute of Electrical and Electronic Engineers, is responsible for developing many of today's Internet technologies.

Inetpub is the name of the directory under which Windows NT Server places its Internet Information Server services and data.

Internet means internetworks; a global network of computer networks.

InterNIC, Internet Network Information Center, is the closest thing to a governing body for the Internet. It is responsible for such things as assigning IP addresses.

An **intranet** is a localized network that employs Internet technologies.

IP address, in TCP/IP-based networks, is that address of four portions, separated by periods, that uniquely identifies the device to which it is assigned.

IPX/SPX is Novell's answer to TCP/IP; that is, the native NetWare transport/ network level protocol suite.

IRQ is an interrupt request; in effect, the signal sent by software to a CPU to tell the CPU that it has a need for processing of some sort.

ISA, industry standard architecture, is a standard for the construction of PC buses.

ISDN, Integrated Services Digital Network, refers to high-speed data communications lines.

ISP, Internet service provider, is a service company that provides a direct TCP/IP connection to the Internet.

JAVA is Sun Microsystems' object-oriented programming language. It bears a strong resemblance to C and C++ and is one of the most widely used tools for Web development.

JPEG in a filename extension indicates a file of the format devised by the Joint Photographer's Expert Group.

JScript is Microsoft's answer to Java from Sun Microsystems and to JavaScript from Netscape.

Jukebox is another name for a CD changer.

Kbps, Kilobits (not bytes) per second, is a measurement of data transmission.

Key is analogous to a user password, but in the context of a workstation and its access to a network running SSL.

A **kilobyte** is a little over 1000 bytes; to be precise, 1024.

LAN, Local Area Network, is a data communications network that occupies a limited physical spread.

Local pertains to a particular computer; under windows NT Server, it has the further connotation of within a domain.

Locale, under Index Server, indicates language.

Logical is another term for Boolean (operators or values).

Master index is a persistent index that contains the indexed data for a large number of documents.

Mbps stands for megabits (not bytes) per second.

A **megabyte** is a little over 1 million bytes; to be exact, 1024×1024 or 1,048,576 bytes.

Metadata, under Index Server, is data that describes other data such as that in the content index.

MIME, Multi-purpose Internet Mail Extension, is a system of nomencalture for files intended to be transferred across the Internet.

MMC, Microsoft Management Console, is a new administartive software approach adopted by Microsoft for Internet Information Server 4.0, and is also to be employed in Windows NT Server 5.0.

Modem stands for modulate/demodulate, the process by which the digital signal generated by computers is translated to analog so that it can be sent across phone lines and then retranslated to digital at the receiving computer's end.

Modulation consists of three significant methods: frequency modulation, amplitude modulation, phase modulation.

MPEG is a filename extension indicating that the file in question is in the format devised by the Motion Picture Experts Group.

Multi-adapter is frequently used in the context of providing multiple ISDN connections through a single PC slot.

Multicast, in data communications, is a form of TCP/IP transmission that simultaneously transmits the same data to multiple users.

Multikernel architecture is a method of software architecture, used by Windows NT and other operating systems, that isolates various levels of services from one another for the purpose of protecting them.

Multiplexing is the process of combining several relatively low-bandwidth (i.e., of limited frequency range) data streams into a single, wider-bandwidth stream.

A **multiplexor** is a hardware device that accomplishes multiplexing.

Multiport is usually used in the context of add-on cards that provide several serial ports to a single PC slot.

National Language Support (NLS) helps applications developed for the Win32 application programming interface (API) adapt to the language- and locale-specific needs of users around the world.

NCSA, National Center for Supercomputing, is the creator of, among other things, the log file format called Common Log File Format.

NetBEUI, NetBIOS Extended User Interface, is an early PC transport-level protocol.

NetBIOS, Network basic input and output services, is the API through which DOS originally talked to networks.

NetMeeting, at the time this book was written, was a still-in-beta Microsoft product that accomplishes Internet-based conferencing.

NetShow is one of the five features that distinguish IIS 3.0 from IIS 2.0; it consists of both live and on-demand components for the Internet distribution of multimedia presentations.

NIC, Network Interface Card, is the adapter needed to connect any device to a network's transmission medium.

A **node** is any end-point device on a network. Most frequently the device is a computer of some sort, but it may also be a printer, communications device, or other component.

Noise words is Index Server's term for words that are not significant to a search; like *a* or *the* in English.

Normalizer is an Index Server component that converts words to a standard representation before placing them in an index.

Normandy is a code name or nickname for a grab bag of Microsoft products like an Internet locator service and a content replicator. At the time this book was written, they were still in beta.

NSFNET is the wide-area network established by the National Science foundation. It became the core of the U. S. Internet.

NT stands for new technology (literally).

NTFS, the NT file system, is one of two file management systems available for use with Windows NT Server 4.0; the other is FAT.

NWLink is the IPX/SPX protocol bundled with Windows NT Server 4.0.

Object, in the parlance of C++, Java, and other similar languages, refers to program or data modules. So, an object could be the cursor, an icon, or the data you enter into a field in a dialog.

Object Linking and Embedding (OLE) is a technique involving the management of software modules in such a way as to allow data in one application to be accessible to others.

Octal is a numbering system that works in units of 8 rather than 10, as does our decimal system.

Octet is a group of eight bits, usually used in the context of a single portion of an IP address.

Odd parity looks for an odd number of 1s in a byte.

Open Database connectivity (ODBC) is Microsoft's model for remote database management systems. ODBC databases include Access and SQL Server.

Open Graphics Interface (Open GI) is a set of standards against which graphical user interfaces (GUIs) may be programmed to ensure a common structure and components and portability across applications.

Operand is the unit upon which an action will be performed; for example, in the expression 3 + 4, 3 and 4 are operands.

Operator is a symbol that represents an action to be performed; for example, the arithmetical operator +, which indicates addition.

OSI model is the conceptual model developed by ISO to serve as a standard against which network software could be developed and networks thereby interconnected.

Overhead disk is the amount of space required to store the index information.

Packet refers to one of the portions into which data communications messages are divided before being transmitted.

Packet switching is the practice by which the various packets making up a single message travel different paths to their destination and are reassembled only after arriving.

Parallel data streams are made up of bytes whose component bits are transmitted simultaneously.

A **parity bit** is a bit used for error detection.

PCMCIA is a standard for laptop computer components.

Perl stands for **Practical Extraction and Report Language**. Perl is interpreted, as opposed to compiled, and resembles the UNIX mini-language in that it can scan text files, extract information from them, and report on that information. At the time this book was written, versions 4 and 5 of Perl were available.

Permissions are usually synonymous with rights. Under Windows NT Server, they are distinguished from rights as follows: rights pertain to something a user can do, such as carry out a backup; permissions pertain to access to data and applications.

Persistent index is an Index Server term for an index whose data is stored on a disk.

A **pointer**, in programming, is a data type that stores the address of a variable, rather than data.

POST is an HTML command meaning, in effect: Write the data specified.

POTS means **plain old telephone system**; the classic analog, dial-up phone.

PPP, point-to-point protocol, is widely used in PC connections to the Internet.

A **profile** is a template for software or user capabilities.

Promoting/demoting is the practice, under Windows NT Server 4.0, of giving or taking away from a backup domain controller the status of primary domain controller.

Property is a file characteristic such as author or size.

Property value is the value of a file property, such as the value for the author property of "James Burke."

PROPID, in Index Server, is an integer that uniquely identifies a document property; it can be decimal or hexadecimal.

Protocol is software that establishes the rules according to which computers exchange data.

Proxy is a type of firewall that acts on behalf of a computer in establishing a network connection; that is, the firewall pretends to be a computer seeking network access.

Proxy server is an application that distributes and manages proxies.

QBE, Query by Example, is a means of inquiring of a database, used in many Microsoft and other products, in which a specific value is supplied to a database, with the understanding that it should find matches to that value.

Query is the process of searching for specific data in a set of files and returning links to the files containing that data.

RAID, redundant arrays of inexpensive disks, is seldom truly inexpensive.

A **record** is the collection of all fields that make up a single complete unit of information within a database; in an employee database, for instance, a record would consist of all data pertaining to a single employee.

Regex is an acronym for **regular expression.**

Regular expression is a term used primarily in UNIX environments to indicate a range of values; for example, *?abc* indicates any string ending in the letters *abc* and beginning with any other single character.

Relationals are operators that indicate the relationship between quantities or entities. In programming, it most frequently includes the relationships greater than, greater than or equal to, less than, less than or equal to, equal to, and not equal to.

Repeater is a hardware device that regenerates signals. It is used on network segments of a length or nature sufficient to cause those signals to deteriorate.

Replicating, under Windows NT Server 4.0, refers to creating a complete and exact copy of a file system or some portion of a file system.

A **resource** is any tool—whether software, hardware, or data—made available by a computer or computer network.

Restriction, under Index Server, is a query term that narrows the scope of a query.

Result set is information returned by a process. In an IIS context, it is most frequently used in terms of Index Server.

Rights are the ability to do something to or with computer-stored data, as in the right to execute a program.

RIP, Routing Information Protocol, is a TCP/IP-related protocol that helps determine the best route for a packet.

RISC, Reduced Instruction Set Computing, is in effect, chips that have been streamlined to provide more efficient processing.

A **router** is a hardware device that functions at OSI level 4. It routes packets, chooses optimum paths for those routes, and translates between protocol suites.

Routing is the process by which the packets making up a message are sent to their destinations.

Row is another term for a database record.

RPC, remote procedure call, is the execution of a software module that is stored not locally, but on a remote computer.

SAP, service addressing protocol, is used under NetWare to make clients aware of network services that are available.

Scan is the action of checking all files and directories for modifications among the virtual roots selected for indexing. When Index Server is first activated it must scan all directories and files to find the documents that may have changed since Index Server was shut down. Scanning is a background operation that allows queries to be executed. Once scanning is complete, Index Server can usually use change notifications to keep its indexes up to date.

Schema, also known as data dictionary, is a blueprint that defines the nature and structure of the data housed in a database.

Scope, under Index Server, defines the set of documents that will be searched; scopes can be directory paths, volumes, etc.

SCSI, small computer systems interface, is a type of controller, one of whose greatest strengths is the ability to daisy-chain devices; that is, to connect several peripherals to a computer by means of a single port.

Serial refers to data streams in which the bits that make up a byte travel one at a time.

Shadow index is the persistent index created by merging word lists and sometimes other shadow indexes into a single index.

Sleep is a data processing term for temporarily pausing the execution of a program, usually for a predefined interval; sleep cycles are most commonly defined in fractions of seconds.

SLIP, Serial Line Interface Protocol, with PPP, is the protocol used in PC-to-Internet connections.

Smart tower is a CD tower with its own CPU and memory, which can therefore exist as an autonomous network node.

SMTP, Simple Mail Transfer Protocol, is used to transfer mail within the Internet; similar to FTP.

Snap-In is a collection of tools that can be applied individually to services within Internet Information Server 4.0. One example of a Snap-In is Microsoft Certificate Mapper.

SNA, Simple Network Architecture, is an IBM-created network model.

SNMP, Simple Network Management Protocol, generates status messages regarding network and components.

Sockets, in effect, mean a virtual port. In technical terms, a socket is actually a combination of two numbers: the IP address of the device, and a port number specific to the device. Note that the port number refers not to a physical port, but to a logical port, which in TCP/IP terms gives an indication of the type of packets being transferred.

Spooling is the process by which temporary print files are created; derives from the days when tape was the only computer storage medium.

SQL, Structured Query Language, is a standard for database manipulation and the retrieval of data from databases based upon questions or queries.

SSI, Server side includes, are IIS Web server commands that allow the HTTP service to be customized. Some SSIs are:

- *Include.* Add the contents of a specified file to the HTML output.
- *Echo.* Add the contents of the specified environment variable to the HTML output.
- *Fsize.* Add the size in bytes of the specified file to the HTML output.
- *Flastmod.* Add the date the specified file was last modified to the HTML output.
- *Exec.* Execute a shell command.
- *Config.* Modify the formatting of date or time output.

SSL, Secure Sockets Layer, is a protocol that functions at the presentation level of the OSI model to carry out tasks such as encryption.

SSL2 and **SSL3** are specific releases of the Secure Sockets Layer protocols.

Standalone server, under Windows NT, is a computer that houses no network-management information like that found on controllers, but simply distributes resources, applications, or data.

Start bit, in serial transmissions, indicates the beginning of a message unit.

Static refers to data or applications that undergo little or no change.

Status code/return code is a code, usually a low-value integer, that indicates the status of a completed process; for example, under UNIX, a return code of 0 tells you that the process, perhaps a directory listing, that generated the code completed successfully.

Stop bit, in serial transmissions, indicates the end of a message unit.

Stream, in an IIS context, most frequently used in terms of NetShow, refers to a multicast or broadcast stream of data.

Structure, in many programming languages, among them C, C++, Java, and so on, is a compound variable whose component individual variable may be of different data types.

Subnet or **subnetwork** is a portion of a LAN or other network that can contain up to 254 unique IP addresses.

Subnet mask is a variety of Internet address that references the subnet to which a device belongs.

Synchronization, under Windows NT Server 4.0, is the process of ensuring that network resource data on backup and primary domain controllers is the same; that is, it has been updated at the same intervals.

Table is a single occurrence, iteration, or instance of a database's data file.

TCP/IP, Transport Control Protocol/Internet Protocol, one of the most widely used protocol suites, is found in Ethernet networks.

Telnet, telecommunications network, is a TCP/IP-related utility that accomplishes remote access via dial-up.

TIF is a filename extension that indicates that the file in question is formatted according to the **Tagged Image format.**

Time slice is a specific amount of time dedicated to computational task.

Timeout occurs when something ceases to function.

Token-passing is a system of network access in which a token indicating the right to transmit circulates constantly among nodes.

Topology is a blueprint or outline of the pattern of physical layout of a network.

Tower is a type of CD-ROM device that houses several CD drives in a single cabinet.

Translating BIOS is a PC BIOS capable of resolving hard disk addresses; that is, of translating into lower-megabyte representations disk addresses that in reality denote areas of a drive beyond 540 megabytes.

Transmission medium is most frequently cable, but can also include satellite and microwave.

Trust, under windows NT Server 4.0, is a relationship between domains that allows the users authorized by one to access resources on the other.

UART, Universal Asynchronous Receiver/Transmitter, is a chip on a PC mother-board that controls serial transmissions both within and external to the PC.

Unicast refers to TCP/IP transmissions, that, although they may send the same information to a number of individuals, must make an individual copy of that information for each user involved.

Unshielded twisted pair is telephone wire used for network connections.

UPS means **uninterruptible power supply.**

URL, Uniform Resource Locator, is the format for World Wide Web addresses.

Vanilla is data processing slang for common, ordinary, or usual.

VBScript is an analog to Perl, Javascript, and other Web-related script languages; it exists as a subset of Visual Basic, which can act as an extension to HTML.

Virtual is a data processing term applied to any resource whose logical or conceptual nature differs from its physical, as in virtual addresses, or addresses that do not represent specific physical locations but mimic those locations.

VM is most frequently—and as used by Microsoft—a **virtual machine**; in effect, a synonym for engine.

WAIS is a set of protocols used by WANs.

WAN, Wide Area Network, is a network spanning a very large geographical area.

Win32 is a 32-bit Windows applications.

WINS, Windows Internet Naming Service, is an earlier Windows form of domain name service.

WinSock, or Windows Sockets, is a networking API that accomplishes such TCP/IP-related tasks as ftp and telnet in Windows environments. WinSock 2.0, the most recent WinSock version, is supported by windows NT 4.0, and in turn supports AppleTalk and IPX/SPX as well as TCP/IP.

Wizard is a GUI based tool frequently found in Microsoft applications, which leads a user by the hand through some processes such as creating a document or configuring a component.

XBase/BroadY is a designations of the form used to describe the type of Ethernet cable to which they are applied. Interpret them as follows: For X, whatever its value, read maximum number of megabits per second that the cable can transmit. For Base, if that is the second parameter, read Baseband, or limited frequency, transmission. For Broad, if that is the second parameter, read Broadband, or wide frequency range, transmission. For Y, substitute the number of cable lengths of 100 meters to which a segment using this type of cable is limited. So, 10Base2, or thin Ethernet cable, runs at 10Mbps, is baseband, and can have a single segment no longer than 200 meters.

Index